55095

Bring

Bringing Back the Parties

David E. Price
Duke University

A division of
Congressional Quarterly Inc.
1414 22nd Street, N.W., Washington, D.C. 20037

Copyright © 1984, Congressional Quarterly Inc.

All rights reserved. No part of this publication may be repro-
duced or transmitted in any form or by any means, electronic
or mechanical, including a photocopy, recording, or any information storage and retrieval system, without permission
in writing from the publisher.

Second Printing
Printed in the United States of America

Library of Congress Cataloging in Publication Data

Price, David Eugene.
    Bringing back the parties.

    Includes index.
    1. Political parties—United States. 2. United States—Politics and govern-
ment—1945- . I. Title.
JK2261.P74 1984   324.273   83-26151
ISBN 0-87187-304-4

For Lisa

Preface

In this book I attempt to present an overview of the American party system for college and university students of politics, party leaders, and general readers interested in the subject. More than most texts, the book is organized around a theme: the *health* of the parties, their decline and renewal. The book also devotes considerable attention to public and party *policy*—the effects of legislative enactments, court decisions, and party rules on party health, and the changes that might contribute to "bringing the parties back."

This is not a *non*partisan book: it offers an unapologetic brief for strengthened parties. It is, however, *bi*partisan in the sense that it surveys the recent history of the Democratic and Republican parties and welcomes renewal on both sides of the aisle. The book draws on my academic work as a political scientist and my experience as executive director and chairman of a state party and as staff director of the Democratic National Committee's Commission on Presidential Nomination.

I am deeply indebted to many friends and colleagues for their help. Albert Beveridge, James Ceaser, William Keech, Mac McCorkle, and Robert Peabody reviewed the manuscript or parts of it and offered valuable suggestions. Advance copies of works in progress were made available to me by Herbert Alexander, William Crotty, James Davis, Michael Malbin, Nelson Polsby, Michael Preston, Byron Shafer, and James Sundquist.

Numerous current or former staff members of the national party committees have been especially generous in granting interviews and responding to my requests for information: Bernard Aronson, Michael Baroody, Mark Braden, Marta David, Gene Eidenberg, Joseph Gaylord, Phil Kawior, John Stewart, and Scott Wolf. I am similarly indebted to Ted Van Dyk of the Center for National Policy, Paul Jensen of the National Policy Exchange, Alvin From of the House Democratic Caucus, and Robert Liberatore and Charles Cook of the Senate Democratic Policy Committee.

I cannot begin to acknowledge all those who have helped me track down bits and pieces of data, but I must offer special thanks to Sharon Snyder of the Federal Election Commission; Kay Lawson and Jerome Mileur of the Committee for Party Renewal; Martin Plissner and Ward Sloane of CBS News; George Frampton, Jr., of the John Anderson campaign; Wayne Walker of Congressional Quarterly; my academic colleagues Thad Beyle, John Bibby, Walter Dellinger, Malcolm Jewell, and

David Olson; DNC Committeeman James Roosevelt, Jr.; and Ann Fishman, Louise Lindblom, Robert Perkins, Sandra Perlmutter, Janice Rodgers, Philip Smith, and Judy Van Rest of the national party committees.

I have continued to draw on the careful work Herbert Hedden did as research director of the Commission on Presidential Nomination. At Duke, I have had the benefit of Jon Ham's and John Bauer's services as research assistants. I am also grateful to the Duke University Research Council for underwriting trips to Philadelphia and Washington in connection with this project.

For conscientiously typing and retyping the manuscript and keeping her sense of humor throughout, I thank Mary Umstead. Thanks also go to other members of the Duke political science staff who helped: Susan Cash, Caryn Richards, Louise Walker, and Wanda Taylor.

One of this project's greatest pleasures has been working with the highly competent and supportive editorial staff at Congressional Quarterly. I am especially indebted to the successive directors of CQ Press, Jean Woy and Joanne Daniels, for their interest in the project, and to Barbara de Boinville for her superb editorial work.

Finally, for tolerating my preoccupations with party and my weekends and evenings in the study, and for much, much more, I thank Lisa, Karen, and Michael.

David E. Price

Chapel Hill, North Carolina
December 1983

Contents

Tables and Figures

Figures

Bringing Back the Parties

Introduction

Since the late 1960s, controversy has surrounded the American party system. Few aspects of American politics have displayed a comparable amount of change, some inadvertent, some deliberately induced. As a result, many standard generalizations about the parties have been undermined, and doubts have arisen concerning their capacity to continue to perform their historic functions.

Jefferson-Jackson banquet speakers, to be sure, still like to herald the Democratic party as the "oldest party organization in the world." (Only the British Conservatives and Liberals, depending on how one reads the historical continuities, might pose rival claims; Labour dates only from 1905.) The Republicans, dating from 1854, have only slightly less to boast about. The American two-party structure has been, by most measures, an extraordinarily stable one. Nor will every government text need to be rewritten tomorrow. Many of the characteristics of the American party system that they generally catalogue continue to hold true: our parties are relatively nonideological in appeal, projecting an image of moderation; they are broadly based, drawing from a range of socioeconomic groups; they lack well-defined criteria of membership and are organizationally decentralized; and they possess comparatively modest resources for enforcing loyalty or discipline among their adherents and officeholders.

But if such a list points up the persistence of the system's basic traits, it also identifies areas of recent movement and change. Trends in participation and alterations in procedure have made it more likely that activists in both parties will stake out extreme positions, deemphasizing the politics of moderation and compromise. National party organizations have assumed roles that qualify the picture of organizational diffusion—in promoting and enforcing internal reform for the Democrats, in financial and campaign leadership for the GOP. Congressional Republicans demonstrated remarkable discipline in 1981 in enacting President Ronald Reagan's economic program. Thus even the broadest textbook generalizations are showing some signs of strain. And, of course, so is the party system itself. Analyses of party "decline" have begun to appear with some regularity. But here, too, all the evidence does not point in one direction: while recent years have seen an upsurge in split-ticket voting and in the professed independence of party allegiance, they also have witnessed

1

substantial institutional development among state and national party organizations. And now polls suggest that partisan identification may even be making a modest comeback within the electorate.

Despite conflicting evidence, there is ample reason to be concerned about the parties' health and viability. This book will survey the current state of the parties and argue that "bringing the party back" is a worthwhile goal in light of the functions parties have played and can play in a democratic political order. Policy can make a difference in this endeavor. While much that has befallen the parties can be attributed to social and technological changes that are unlikely to be reversed, public policy and party rules have had and can have an independent and critically important impact. Accordingly, the bulk of the book will examine policy areas relevant to the health of the parties and to the kinds of changes that are called for if the parties' role is to be enhanced.

Chapters 1-3 will discuss the extent of reliance upon and loyalty to the parties within the electorate; the roles and resources of local, state, and national party organizations; and the place of the parties in government. In Chapter 4 we ask why such matters should concern us, tracing the historic role of the parties and arguing that forces currently threatening to displace them do not portend well for our politics.

Chapter 5 is the first of several chapters examining in more detail the impact of public law and party rules and procedures on the strength of the parties. We look first at state election law and the determinations of the federal judiciary, then at presidential nomination and delegate selection procedures (Chapters 6 and 7), campaign finance statutes (Chapter 8), and party machinery for formulating and influencing policy (Chapter 9). This survey will be accompanied by a closer study of the most recent Democratic party commission on presidential nomination, a body that set party renewal as an explicit goal, and at recent national party councils and conferences aimed at policy formulation. These case histories illumine the political context in which the parties may attempt to help themselves—the significant, sometimes intractable, constraints on change, but also the manifold possibilities that exist for carving out a creative and assertive party role. Then, in a brief concluding chapter, we speculate about what "renewed" parties might look like—parties that do not attempt to recreate a bygone era but are adapted to the needs and circumstances of the present.

Parties and the Public 1

In surveying the current state of American parties, we will look first at their popular bases, where the evidence of their "decline" seems strongest. To analyze the role of the parties as shapers and organizers of electoral choice requires a focus on two questions: Are the parties becoming "realigned," shifting in an enduring way either in their electoral strength or in their appeals to different segments of the population? To what extent are the parties losing their hold on their electorate and their role in the structuring of electoral choice? While it is the second question that primarily will concern us, it is necessary initially to consider the first.

Party Realignments

During most of the nation's history, the parties have been forces of stability and moderation, seeking to build broad electoral coalitions and to deflect emerging political conflict. As will be noted in Chapter 4, there is a historical irony in this: the parties, feared by the founders as instruments of "faction," became, by virtue of their breadth and inclusiveness, insulators of the system against sharp breaks and turns in policy. They performed a stabilizing function far more effectively than did the founders' preferred constitutional checks and balances. But the parties also could become instruments of change—not simply the incremental change required to accommodate vocal groups in the party coalition, but the greater changes demanded by large segments of the population at times of historical crisis.

Historical Watersheds

During three periods—the 1850s, 1890s, and 1930s—societal upheavals destabilized the existing partisan balance, led one or both parties to stake out new positions and to accentuate their differences, and induced many individuals to deviate from their family's or group's long-term

3

party allegiance.[1] The pre-Civil War realignment left the new Republican party, as the party of national union, ascendant in most northern states and the Democrats dominant in the South. The second realignment, stemming from the agrarian revolt and the capture of the Democratic party by prosilver forces in the 1890s, greatly strengthened the Republican party in the cities and industrialized areas of the North and left the GOP dominant nationally until the Great Depression. The third alignment, precipitated by the economic collapse of the 1930s and the parties' contrasting approaches to recovery, left the Democratic party ascendant nationally and with a new claim on the loyalties of urban, working-class, black, and ethnic voters.

Such realignments do not wipe the political slate clean. Patterns dating from previous periods of upheaval may persist. For example, the Democrats in 1896 and 1900 largely failed to attract the midwestern Republicans who might have been expected to support them on economic grounds: "If they believed in silver, they believed still more deeply in the party of Abraham Lincoln, the Union, and the Homestead Act." [2] An even more striking example of the persistence of Civil War patterns is the endurance of Democratic voting in the South (and Republican voting in antisecession southern Appalachian counties) through two major and numerous lesser periods of political upheaval.

The likelihood that realignments will not be complete is increased by the organizational and ideological looseness both parties display; even during times of polarization and conflict, disaffected partisans often can find enough slack and diversity within their party to let them retain their allegiance. Their psychological attachment to the party, moreover, and other rewards of continued loyalty may represent a substantial barrier against defection. Still, the realignment phenomenon demonstrates that issue positions have been an important component of party identification. When issues have been felt keenly and widely, the parties have become critical instruments of political adjustment and change.

Realignments generally do not occur precipitously. Only after a period of time can one determine whether a dramatic election result represents a short-term deviation from established partisan behavior or a more enduring shift in allegiance. The realignment portended by the 1932 election, for example, was not fully evident until it was confirmed by the election outcomes of 1934 and 1936. Reverberations at the state and local levels continued for many years as Populist and Progressive organizations that had existed as third parties or as factions within the Republican party gradually made their way into the Democratic fold. From this perspective the Dixiecrat revolt of 1948 and the continuing defection of southern conservative Democrats to Republican and independent ranks represent less the beginnings of a new alignment than a continuation of the shifts of the 1930s.

The protracted character of party realignment bears witness to the durability of party ties. While realignment periods find substantial numbers of people becoming detached from inherited allegiances or even "converting" from one party to the other, such individual changes are generally less important than the impact of the new generations entering the electorate. Even during the New Deal, increases in Democratic strength seem to have come more from the mobilization of new groups of voters than from the conversion of longtime Republicans. It thus took a number of years for the full extent of the realignment to manifest itself. And it could have taken considerably longer—or been far less sweeping— had there not been large numbers of nonparticipating, uncommitted citizens who had "accumulated" in the population during the quiescent 1920s:

> The young (in particular the children of immigrants), newly naturalized citizens, and women all contributed to the pool of nonimmunized citizens which the Democratic party was able to mobilize in the space of several elections. The Smith candidacy in 1928, the depression, and Roosevelt's New Deal policies gave the Democrats an appeal among these groups which was translated into votes and into a persisting Democratic majority. It was this mobilization of new populations, rather than the conversion of Republicans, which constituted the substance of the realignment.[3]

Realignment Overdue?

Is a realignment comparable to those of the 1890s and 1930s currently in the making? If so, what might be the new lines of cleavage? During the past 20 years there has been much speculation on this question. The fact that past upheavals have tended to occur in 36- to 40-year cycles has led some to regard a new alignment as overdue. Patterns of disaffection and disengagement from the parties have appeared, particularly among the young, that are somewhat reminiscent of the prerealignment decade of the 1920s. Voting patterns have displayed a volatility that far surpasses the fluctuations normally seen in a postrealignment period, and many of the issues that have come to the fore have cut across rather than reinforced the electoral divisions characteristic of the New Deal era.

Much of the initial scholarly interest in realignment centered on Gen. Dwight D. Eisenhower's substantial victories in the presidential elections of 1952 and 1956. But the persistence of most people's party identifications during this period and the return in 1960 of voting that more closely followed party lines suggested that Eisenhower's personal popularity had little long-term significance for the Republican party. Similarly, Lyndon B. Johnson's landslide victory of 1964 and Richard Nixon's overwhelming defeat of George McGovern in 1972 did not produce lasting shifts in party identification. For a time it appeared that Ronald Reagan's 1980 victory, while less impressive than those of Nixon and Eisenhower (Reagan's share of the vote was 50.7 percent, compared with 57.4 percent for Eisenhower in 1956 and 60.7 percent for Nixon in 1972), might portend more significant long-term movements in the electorate than had those earlier landslides. Two respected journalists, examining mid-1981 poll results that showed a one-year increase of four percentage points in the share of the electorate claiming a Republican identification and a drop of eight percentage points for Democratic identifiers, suspected that they were looking at "the most important

political development in half a century: the Republican realignment." [4]
But by the time of the 1982 midterm elections, leading national polls
showed (and the election results confirmed) a return to the partisan
balance recorded in mid-1980. [5]

This is not to say that patterns of party identification have remained
static during the postwar years. Norman Nie and his associates summa-
rize the most important demographic changes:

> The Democratic party has become more black, less southern, and has
> developed a larger "silk-stocking" component [i.e., more high-status
> northern WASPs]. The Republican party, in contrast, has become more
> southern, less black ... and relatively less of a silk-stocking and Protes-
> tant party compared to the fifties. [6]

Many of these shifts have made sense in terms of the party positions
staked out during the New Deal years. The presence of many elements in
the New Deal coalition (for example, the "solid South" and Catholics)
owed less to the ideological and policy conflicts that shaped that era than
to preexisting patterns of identification. As James Sundquist explains,
"Over the years, the ethnic and geographic lines have eroded as the New
Deal party system settled into place and activists, from whatever region
or family background, gravitated to the Democratic party and conservatives, from whatever demographic group, found their natural home in the
Republican party." [7] Such shifts have been encouraged by attitude
changes within these groups—increased conservatism among southern
whites and Catholics, for example, and increased liberalism among blacks
and upper status Protestants. [8]

Not all of the issues that have arisen have neatly fit the liberal-
conservative framework, however. Some of them have divided the electorate in ways that have crosscut rather than reinforced the New Deal's
ideological divisions and thus have seemed to have a serious realignment
potential. But despite the presence of such issues and an electorate
seemingly ripe for realignment, the predicted large-scale shifts have not
occurred.

Sundquist has examined four issues potent enough to unsettle the
electorate but not strong enough to place politics on a new footing. [9] The
issue of *communism*, carried to hysterical lengths by Sen. Joseph McCarthy during the 1950s, first raised the possibility of realignment. But
President Eisenhower and the Republican leadership eventually repudiated McCarthy's tactics and, because both parties were avowedly anti-
communist, the issue was largely reduced to a debate about means. The
issue prompted a few voters to stray from their Democratic allegiance and
still finds echoes in the rhetoric of conservative Republicans, but it did
not split the parties or polarize the electorate. A lasting realignment did
not result.

The second issue, *race*, has had more lasting effects on party allegiance, although its impact has been concentrated in the South, and it
has mainly unsettled patterns of Democratic loyalty that antedated the
1930s. The New Deal upheaval turned American blacks from their inherited allegiance to the party of Lincoln to an almost monolithic Demo-

cratic identification. Although Franklin D. Roosevelt was at pains to deemphasize civil rights issues, postwar presidents and party leaders could hardly ignore this glaring omission from the New Deal agenda or fail to respond to their black and liberal constituencies. The Dixiecrat revolt of 1948 and George Wallace's presidential candidacies from 1968 to 1976 were the most tangible indications of the polarizing effect of race on the Democratic coalition. The moderate stance the Republican party generally maintained on the issue, however, limited its potential to prompt full-scale partisan conversions.[10]

A third issue, *Vietnam*, badly split the Democratic party in the 1960s and contributed to Nixon's 1968 and 1972 presidential victories. But far from taking opposite positions, the two parties at about the same time yielded to public sentiment that American policy be reversed. Although the Vietnam issue had important electoral effects—increasing disaffection from the parties and politics in general, and stimulating considerable "issue voting"—it did not prompt a partisan realignment. However, another set of issues that arose during these years was widely recognized to have realignment potential. Dubbed the *social issue* by Richard Scammon and Ben Wattenberg—"public attitudes concerning the more personally frightening aspects of disruptive social change" [11]—it incorporated fears of racial agitation and reactions to anti-Vietnam protest. It also included other elements: ghetto and campus riots, rising crime, drug use and cultural revolt among young people, a loosening of moral codes, and a perceived breakdown of law and discipline. The rising salience of these issues led Walter Dean Burnham to predict the increasing importance of new "fracture lines" in the American electorate:

> ... black against white, peripheral regions against the center, "parochials" against "cosmopolitans," blue-collar whites against both blacks and affluent liberals, the American "great middle," with its strong attachment to the values of the traditional American political formula, against urban cosmopolitans, intellectuals, and students who have largely left that old credo behind.[12]

The initial ambivalence of a number of Democratic leaders on this cluster of issues encouraged politicians such as Wallace and Nixon to exploit them and prompted observers such as Scammon and Wattenberg to warn that if Democrats were to avoid an unfavorable realignment they must separate the race issue from the social issue ("That being 'liberal' should equate with being soft on mugging or soft on disruption is absurd")[13] and come down hard on law and order. To some extent, that is what happened. The social issue retained enough potency to allow the Republicans to pin their "three As" slogan (acid, amnesty, and abortion) on McGovern, much to his detriment in 1972. But the winding down of the Vietnam war, the efforts of the Democrats to regain the initiative on questions of law and order, and the Watergate episode reduced the salience of the social issue and its potential for inducing shifts in party allegiance.

Implications of 1980 Election

The 1980 election raised the possibility that the eclipse of the social issue had been only temporary and that those who had predicted the emergence of a new Republican majority had not been wrong so much as premature.[14] Reagan's ascendancy within the Republican party represented a triumph for those who wished to graft onto traditional Republican economic conservatism the social conservatism of the New Right on issues such as abortion, busing, and school prayer, and a hard line in international affairs. The victory of Reagan and of 16 new Republican senators (most of them ultraconservatives) suggested that a "majority" composed of self-styled conservatives "could indeed be mobilized, if candidates appealed to all the conservatives—not just those who were conservative on the old issues of domestic economic policy but those whose conservatism was aroused by the 'giveaway' of the Panama Canal or the Sandinista takeover in Nicaragua or the cluster of moral and social issues." [15]

An analysis of the 1980 vote confirms that the Democrats and independents voting for Reagan were disproportionately drawn from those holding conservative views on the domestic role of government, on national defense, and on issues such as busing and the Equal Rights Amendment. This more broadly based conservatism had considerable appeal across income lines, thus further unraveling the class voting characteristic of the New Deal realignment.[16] But whether the 1980 pattern pointed toward a longer term shift in the parties' ideological appeal and bases of support was difficult to tell. Certain features of Reagan's electoral coalition suggested that 1980 bore a closer resemblance to 1952, when an amiable Republican candidate reaped the benefit of a short-term anti-Truman, anti-Democratic protest, than to the realigning election of 1932.

First, many voters seem to have voted for Reagan in spite of, rather than because of, his extreme conservatism. In fact, Reagan made a conscious effort to moderate his image in the course of the campaign, most conspicuously in his televised final-week debate with President Jimmy Carter. Only a small minority of the voters in 1980 placed social issues at the top of their priority list (7 percent, down from 34 percent in 1972), and on these and most other issues, even those who voted for Reagan perceived his position to be more conservative than their own. Many of those who rejected the label "liberal" nonetheless favored the liberal position on specific policy issues. In one 1978 poll, 82 percent of self-styled "conservatives" favored "government help with medical costs"; 71 percent of conservatives favored "government guaranteed jobs for all"; and 55 percent supported "government restrictions on handgun sales." Surveys throughout 1980 showed most voters to be opposed to sizable cuts in spending for health, education, and related services. While Reagan enjoyed substantial support for his first round of budget reductions, viewed by many as an attack on waste and inefficiency, by mid-1981 almost half of the electorate thought the cuts had gone too far, and only 19 percent thought they should go farther.[17]

Second, even those who hold consistent conservative positions often are not conservative across the entire domestic programs/foreign policy/social issues spectrum. Many traditional economic conservatives are ill at ease with New Right zealotry on issues such as abortion and school prayer, while many of the "populist" conservatives attracted by the New Right's moral stands still favor governmental assistance to small business and farmers and are frightened at the prospect of weakened Medicare or Social Security programs. It is not clear, then, that those attracted by some aspects of Reagan's across-the-board conservatism would consistently favor a Republican party staked out in that position, particularly if the Democratic party avoided the liberal "extremes." Those that the Republicans would have to attract to forge a new conservative majority would represent a rather unstable amalgam, and many of its elements would continue to be attracted by one aspect or another of Democratic "moderation."

Finally, Reagan himself has not made the social issues a priority of his administration. Much to the disappointment of his erstwhile allies of the New Right, his primary focus during and since the 1980 campaign has been on the economy and the role of government. The president's emphasis, far from displacing the lines of debate and conflict characteristic of the New Deal, has tended to reinforce them. And this may be as promising a path to Republican resurgence as an attempt to shift the ideological fault lines would be.

The evidence on this latter point is mixed. Democratic politicians and publicists have long assumed that to focus the electorate's attention on "bread and butter" economic issues, and away from the New Right's social and foreign policy agendas, would automatically work in their favor. As we have noted, most Americans remain "operational liberals," favoring a range of activist governmental programs and policies, even when they regard themselves as conservatives. But Reagan certainly has demonstrated that economic issues can be approached effectively from the conservative side, with a focus on inflation and taxes displacing the traditional Democratic emphasis on economic and personal security. Reagan's successes in building public support suggest that large numbers of people, who in less prosperous times or prior to the adoption of basic welfare-state measures might have favored a stronger governmental role, now often perceive their economic interest to lie in the opposite direction. Basic economic security has given many people the luxury of indulging in attacks on government as the source of whatever ails or annoys them—a time-honored American practice. Middle-income groups are increasingly perceiving themselves less as the beneficiaries of domestic programs and more as the contributors.[18] This makes it more likely that the ascendance of economic issues, far from reinforcing the "positive" view of government associated with the Democrats, could have the contrary effect. As Sundquist notes:

> FDR had convinced enough working class and middle-class voters that their interests were antithetical to the interests of the rich to form a dominant coalition of the lower and middle groups against the upper.

Reagan, as had George Wallace, managed just the opposite: he persuaded millions of voters in the great middle—including many well
below the income median—to look not to the top but to the bottom for
their class enemy. The political adversary of the hard-working, tax-
paying, God-fearing typical American family would no longer be the
corporate tycoon or the plutocrat of Wall Street but the "welfare
queen," whose exploits Reagan endlessly related in campaign speeches.
Middle-class envy of the rich would be turned into middle-class resentment of welfare cheats and loafers, a resentment inevitably intensified by whatever degree of racial antipathy any individual voter might
feel.[19]

In other words, the unraveling of the class voting patterns characteristic
of the New Deal probably owed as much to shifts in voters' perceived
economic and class interests as to the displacement of these concerns by
noneconomic issues.

The Republicans may or may not be able to reassemble the elements
of the Reagan coalition in 1984 and succeeding elections. But neither the
voting patterns of 1980 nor subsequent election and poll results portend a
major, enduring partisan realignment. Racial and social issues continue to
draw disaffected conservative Democrats to the Republican banner, but
the GOP still has substantial incentives for moderation in these areas,
lest it drive away others who identify or vote Republican. And economic
issues continue to dominate the policy agenda. This leads Sundquist to
argue that a *reinforcement* of the New Deal system, whereby the parties
accentuate their differences on the role of government and domestic
economic policy, and voters relate to them on these terms, is more likely
than any prospective realignment. Obviously, this does not gainsay the
possibility of substantial Republican (or, for that matter, Democratic)
gains, but these would take place mainly along the system's existing fault
lines.[20]

There is, however, another possibility, which the realignment debate
addresses only obliquely. A number of analysts, in trying to make sense of
the fits and starts toward realignment during the past 30 years, have not
found developing patterns so much as volatility and disarray. Probing for
the bases of shifts in party allegiance, they have found party allegiance *as
such* to be in a drastically weakened state. Hence, the possibility arises
that party realignment might become a moot question, giving way to
"dealignment" as people's political allegiances are displaced from the
party system altogether. Perhaps the party structure can no longer bear
the weight it has borne historically in structuring political conflict and
serving as an instrument of policy change. That is the possibility raised
by Walter Dean Burnham and others who have discerned "the onward
march of party decomposition."[21]

The Decline of Party Allegiance

"Party affiliation, once the central thread connecting the citizen and
the political process, is a thread that has certainly been frayed," conclude
Norman H. Nie and his associates. "Citizens are less likely to identify

Table 1-1   Partisan Identification Nationwide by Decade, 1952-1980

	1950s	1960s	1970s	1980
Strong Democrat	22%	22%	17%	18%
Weak Democrat	24	25	24	23
Independent Democrat	8	9	12	11
Independent	7	9	14	13
Independent Republican	6	7	10	10
Weak Republican	14	14	14	14
Strong Republican	13	12	9	9

NOTE: Figures do not total 100 percent because of rounding and the presence of "don't know"/"no answer" responses. Survey began in 1952.

SOURCE: Center for Political Studies, University of Michigan. Adapted in part from data presented in *American Parties in Decline* by William J. Crotty and Gary C. Jacobson (Boston: Little, Brown & Co., 1980), 27-28.

with a party, to feel positively about a party, or to be guided in their voting behavior by partisan cues." [22] We will consider in turn each of these indicators of the electorate's attachment to the parties.

Party Identification

Party identification data suggest that interparty shifts may be less significant than the general trend away from allegiance to *either* party. Table 1-1 shows that the percentage of citizens identifying themselves as "strong" partisans has declined nationwide from 35 to 27 since the 1950s, with substantial losses occurring in both Republican and Democratic ranks. At the same time those declaring themselves "independent" have increased from 21 to 34 percent of the electorate. Since the crosscutting issues of the early 1970s have declined in salience, this trend toward independence has leveled off and even given some signs of receding slightly. But no substantial reversal of the pattern, which has affected all population groups and has been especially pronounced among southerners, Catholics, and high-status northern Protestants, is likely.[23]

The trend toward independence, like the smaller shifts between the parties, has been concentrated among younger voters. Some 45 percent of potential voters under 30 now claim independent status, compared with 27 percent of those over 50. Only 16 percent of those age 18 to 30 say they are "strong" partisans, while 37 percent of those over 50 so describe themselves. This pattern is not entirely new: throughout the postwar period younger voters have been less inclined than their elders to declare a party allegiance. Typically, however, higher levels of identification have developed as young voters have gained exposure to the parties through years of political participation. Party identification, once established, has not been easy to dislodge. Current surveys show that the generation whose political loyalties were already established by the early 1950s has largely resisted taking on an independent identification. But those who came to maturity in succeeding years have not proven equally steadfast;

their socialization experiences, rather than turning them toward the parties, have led even those who claimed a party tie to question and sometimes to abandon that allegiance. Meanwhile, the number of new voters professing partisan independence from the start has almost doubled—from 26 percent in 1952 to 49 percent of those first voting in 1980.[24]

Generational replacement is thus critically important—far more important than defections among formerly committed individuals—in explaining the decay of party identification in the electorate.[25] Recent surveys suggest that fewer of the young voters who are identified with one of the parties are now inclined to abandon that identification than was the case in the 1960s and 1970s. But there are far fewer young identifiers than there used to be, and there is no evidence to suggest that those who enter the electorate as independents are once again moving toward partisan attachment. The Twenty-sixth Amendment, ratified in 1971, increased the electoral weight of young voters. Thus the prevalence and persistence of "independence" among the young is the major reason for the national dealignment trend (and the first line of attack for anyone who wants to do something about it).

Trends in the South, the region most affected by postwar political changes, represent an exaggerated version of what has been going on in the nation as a whole.[26] Realignment has been more in evidence in the South than elsewhere, but there, too, such trends have been overshadowed by massive dealignment—with the notable exception of the black community. Southern blacks, confronted by state and local Democratic organizations that were often hostile to their interests, lagged behind their northern counterparts in abandoning the Republican party; they were about 25 percent Republican and 10 percent independent in identification through the 1950s. But the move of the Republican party rightward in 1964 and thereafter, and the increasing moderation of local Democratic appeals and practices, resulted in substantial shifts in

Table 1-2   Partisan Identification Among White Southerners by Decade, 1952-1980

	1950s	1960s	1970s	1980
Strong Democrat	34%	26%	15%	17%
Weak Democrat	37	29	32	25
Independent Democrat	6	7	9	10
Independent	4	11	16	14
Independent Republican	5	7	9	9
Weak Republican	8	9	11	15
Strong Republican	5	8	7	7

NOTE: Figures do not total 100 percent because of rounding and the presence of "don't know"/"no answer" responses. Survey began in 1952.

SOURCE: Compiled by Jon Ham from Center for Political Studies, University of Michigan, data.

the Democrats' favor. By 1980 southern blacks were 71 percent Democratic in identification (compared with 72 percent nationwide), with only 6 percent (compared with 5 percent nationwide) identifying with the GOP.

Trends in identification among white southerners are shown in Table 1-2. Democratic identification has fallen from 71 to 42 percent since the 1950s, and the percentage of "strong" Democrats (17 percent) is less than it is in the nation as a whole. Republicans have benefited from this shift: Republican identifiers in 1980 comprised 22 percent of the southern white electorate, compared with 13 percent in the 1950s. But the more significant movement has been toward increased independence of party. Some 33 percent of southern whites in 1980 professed their independence, a figure close to the national one and more than twice what it was in the 1950s.

What explains these changes in southern partisanship? The decrease in the proportion of Democrats in the electorate is partly attributable to patterns of migration: northerners bringing their Republican and independent proclivities with them (more than one-third of Republican identifiers in the South grew up outside the region) and Democratic-identifying blacks and whites from rural areas leaving the South. But realignment and dealignment trends are only slightly less pronounced among native southerners than within the white electorate as a whole. Paul Beck attributes a "significant share" of this change to "racial conservatives' desertions of the Democratic party because of its racial policies," but he and other analysts find racial issues to have declined in salience and in their relevance to partisan shifts.[27] Class attitudes also appear to have played some role: the abandonment of Democratic identification has been most common among higher status voters. But the main forces at work seem little different from those that have weakened partisan attachments in the nation as a whole. Within 25 years they have brought the distribution of partisan and independent identifications in the South into congruence with the national pattern, with the new generations of voters, in the South as elsewhere, leading the way.

One aspect of the data on party identification in the South raises broader questions about the relationship between dealignment and realignment. Is a dealigned electorate ripe for realignment? While noting certain parallels between the present and the prealignment situation of the 1920s, Nie and his associates regard a new alignment as less likely than the continuation of "the current system of individualistic voting choice between ad hoc electoral organizations mediated by television."[28] But Raymond Wolfinger and Robert Arseneau, examining the voting behavior of "dealigned" southerners, find patterns that suggest the possibility of renewed partisan attachments. They differentiate between "pure" independents and those who acknowledge leaning toward a party (see Table 1-2), noting that the latter vote for the presidential candidate of their preferred party no less frequently than those acknowledging a "weak" identification with the party. Southern Republican-leaning independents, for example, have voted for Republican presidential nominees at an average rate of 90 percent since 1952, a rate identical to that of "weak" Republicans. Wolfinger and Arseneau conclude, "In short, partisan Independents are really closet Democrats and Republicans, not people without attachments to a party." If one includes these independent partisans with other partisans in analyzing southern patterns of change, the trend toward dealignment, while still pronounced, appears less overwhelming: "the more substantial and significant development is the continued increase in the number of white Southerners who identify with the Republican party and whose loyalty to Republican presidential candidates belies the claim that party ties have dissolved in the South." [29] It remains to be seen, however, whether such "leanings" will crystallize into loyalties sufficiently firm to guide voting consistently at the congressional and local levels.

Parties and Voting

Electoral data show the erosion of party ties in the electorate to be even further advanced than the trends toward independent identification suggest. Even those expressing a partisan identity are increasingly defecting from party in their voting. This is most obvious at the presidential level. Democrats in 1952 and 1956 defected to vote for Eisenhower at what seemed then to be extraordinarily high levels (about 27 percent). Yet as Table 1-3 shows, the overall defection rates from both parties for the 1976 election have been matched in every election since then but one (1960). The high point was reached in 1972 when 42 percent of Democratic identifiers voted for Nixon. Even the 1976 election, widely viewed as a return to conventional party voting, saw 17 percent of partisan identifiers in the electorate crossing over in their presidential vote. The trend was even more pronounced in 1980, when 22 percent of Democratic voters voted for Reagan, 5 percent of Republicans voted for Carter, and 5 percent of the Democrats and 6 percent of the Republicans voted for John Anderson.

Year-to-year variations in the number of identifiers defecting from one party or the other are clearly related to the popularity of individual presidential nominees. Defectors have often felt little constraint to vote for congressional, state, and local candidates of the same party as their presidential choice. Here, too, 1972 represents an extreme case: of the 377 congressional districts that gave a majority of their vote to Nixon, more than half (189) sent a Democrat to the House of Representatives. [30] In general, voting at the congressional and state levels has adhered more closely to party lines. But the figures on congressional and state and local elections in Table 1-3 leave no doubt that the trend away from party voting has penetrated far below the presidential level and has steadily increased in magnitude. Surveys since 1972 have found more than half of the electorate splitting their vote at the state or local level.

The trend toward ticket splitting and other defections from party in voting, unlike the movements toward independent identification, are not concentrated among young or first-time voters. The decline of straight-ticket voting has occurred at about the same rate in all generations. As Nie and his associates point out, "the commitment to political parties that kept the older cohorts constant in their strong identification does

Table 1-3 Defections from Party in Presidential, House, and State and Local Elections, 1956-1980

	Presidential Elections			House Elections	State and Lo-cal Elections
	Percent of Democrats for Repub-lican Party or Other	*Percent of Republi-cans for Democratic Party or Other*	*Percent of all Identifiers Defecting*	*Percent of Identifiers Voting for Other Party*	*Percent of Identifiers Splitting Ticket*
1956	27	4	17	9	28
1958				10	26
1960	19	7	14	12	29
1962				10	38
1964	10	28	17	15	40
1966				15	44
1968	29	12	23	18	46
1970				15	46
1972	42	7	27	18	55
1974				18	56
1976	19	15	17	19	n.a.
1978				21	n.a.
1980	27	11	21	23	51

SOURCE: Center for Political Studies, University of Michigan. Adapted in part from data presented in *The Changing American Voter* by Norman H. Nie, Sidney Verba, and John R. Petrocik (Cambridge: Harvard University Press, 1979), 51.

not impede them from following the general tendency toward split ticket voting." [31] Voting behavior thus suggests a loosening of the hold of party on the electorate that goes considerably beyond what people's reports of their subjective party ties would suggest.

What is likely to guide and inform voting in the absence of the party cue? One trend, toward increased "issue voting," has attracted particular attention because of its possible implications for party realignment.[32] The coherence and consistency of voters' policy views have increased since the 1950s, a trend seemingly related both to increasing levels of education and to the more ideologically distinctive appeals parties and candidates have made since the Eisenhower years. Voters also have begun to use issues more frequently as a standard of candidate evaluation and to rely more heavily on this evaluation in casting their vote. And they have developed a clearer view of the ideological and policy differences between the parties. As we have noted, the past 30 years have seen a "settling" of the New Deal alignment as those favoring an active governmental role have made their way into the Democratic fold and conservatives have joined the Republican ranks. It is difficult to tell precisely what contribution the increases in issue awareness and in attitude consistency have made to this process, but the 1960s in particular saw an increase in the congruence of voters' policy and party preferences.

Despite the greater relevance of issue and ideology to party allegiance, the overall impact of issue voting has been to lessen reliance on party cues. The multiplicity of issues and the fact that they often divide the electorate in crosscutting rather than mutually reinforcing ways have made it difficult to mold them into a coherent partisan appeal. Moreover, issues fluctuate in their salience from election to election and between electoral levels in the same election, partly because of the promotional efforts of candidates and single-issue organizations. Issue appeals come to the voters piecemeal, often unmediated by the parties. Voting on the basis of issues thus is more likely to prompt deviations from party than to undergird renewed party fidelity. As Gerald Pomper observes:

> Voters are not ignorant about the Democratic and Republican appeals, but disdainful. While they show more awareness of issues, and of party stands on issues, they do not consistently adjust their loyalties accordingly.... The American electorate today seems clear about where it stands and where the parties stand, and apparently separates these perceptions increasingly when it votes.... Seen as not relevant, parties are bypassed, with the voters making their choices on the basis of their own issue preferences and those of the candidates.[33]

Pomper, Sundquist, and other analysts are intrigued by the possibility that increasingly "clearheaded" and ideologically consistent parties could turn this heightened issue awareness to their own account, invigorating their bases of support and revitalizing their electoral role. But as long as the issues crosscut the electorate in contradictory ways and no one cluster of issues clearly dominates the others, the parties will have strong incentives to seek the middle ground, and the likely effect of strong issue appeals will be to prompt partisan defections in voting.

Attitudes Toward the Parties

Public images of and attitudes toward the parties have become considerably less positive in the last 30 years. This helps explain the dealignment trends just described and gives a further indication of popular disengagement from the parties. Numerous surveys have documented a similar loss of public confidence in a broad range of public and private institutions. Most indicators of political cynicism and mistrust rose steadily throughout the 1960s and 1970s, reflecting public reactions to racial unrest, the Vietnam war, and the Watergate revelations.[34] But the parties were a particularly likely object for this increasing alienation, for as Chapter 4 will show, strong currents of antiparty sentiment have always existed in American political culture. Public opinion polls in the postwar period suggest that this traditional ambivalence has increased: the public's regard for and confidence in the party system have suffered a significant further decline.

The Center for Political Studies in its election-year surveys has asked respondents what they like and dislike about the Democratic and Republican parties. During the 1950s more than 60 percent of the electorate responded with a positive evaluation of their own party and negative words about the opposition. But since 1972, a majority of respondents—compared with some 30 percent in the fifties—have responded with a negative evaluation of *both* parties. Similarly, questions concerning the attentiveness of parties to people's opinions and their role in helping "make the government pay attention to what the people think" have drawn a steadily declining number of affirmative responses.[35]

Jack Dennis's examination of attitudes in Wisconsin points up additional aspects of the electorate's antiparty disposition. While Wisconsin has an unusually strong nonpartisan tradition, the parallels Dennis is able to draw to national surveys suggest that it is not an atypical case. By 1976 only 37 percent of the respondents agreed that party labels should be kept on the ballot, compared with 67 percent in 1964. Some 80 percent of the Wisconsin electorate agreed that the parties created unnecessary conflict and confused issues. (Between 45 and 55 percent of the national electorate has persistently said that there are no important differences between the parties.) Some 89 percent of the Wisconsin respondents in 1976, up from an already high 82 percent in 1964, endorsed the idea of voting for "the best candidate, regardless of party label"; Gallup's national sample endorsed voting for "the man" rather than the party by 84 percent in 1968, up from 75 percent in 1956. Whereas 23 percent of Wisconsin respondents agreed in 1964 that a legislator should "follow his party leaders, even if he doesn't want to," only 10 percent agreed 10 years later.[36]

Such survey questions, blunt instruments at best, are subject to varying interpretations. Martin Wattenberg suggests that the survey data reveal an increase not so much in negative attitudes toward the parties as in a kind of neutrality and indifference. He concludes that the barriers to party revitalization may not be as formidable as some have assumed. But even his picture is not very hopeful. Wattenberg finds that strong positive feelings about the parties are declining sharply, and fewer voters regard party differences as relevant to the issues they care about.[37] Figure 1-1 points up the coincidence of these patterns with the trend noted above: voters' reduced reliance on party as a standard to evaluate candidates. The overall picture is one of an electorate increasingly detached from (if not hostile toward) the parties and inclined to disregard the party cue.

Students of voting behavior disagree about the long-term significance of the trends toward independent identification, split-ticket voting, and negative or indifferent attitudes toward the parties. Some minimize the trends themselves, stressing that party is still the best predictor of most people's vote; they mainly attribute massive defections to the "idiosyncracies of particular elections."[38] Others suggest that the trends may be more cyclical than linear, creating conditions for the revitalization of the parties as realigning issues develop or the New Deal divisions are reinforced.

Clearly, parties continue to play a critical role in giving shape and continuity to electoral choice. Current trends by no means point to their inexorable decline. But there has been an unmistakable erosion of the ties binding the electorate to the parties, and continued decline and electoral

Figure 1-1   Party as a Point of Reference for Voters, 1952-1980

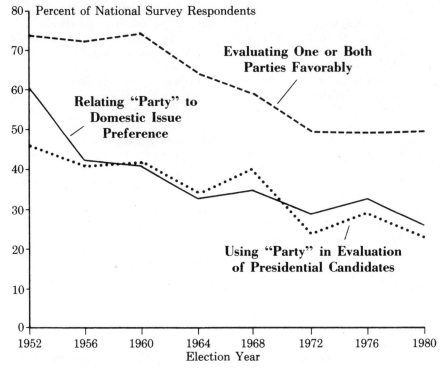

80 ┐ Percent of National Survey Respondents

Evaluating One or Both
Parties Favorably

Relating "Party" to
Domestic Issue
Preference

Using "Party" in Evaluation
of Presidential Candidates

Election Year

SOURCE: Compiled from Center for Political Studies data presented in *The Changing American Voter* by Norman H. Nie, Sidney Verba, and John R. Petrocik (Cambridge: Harvard University Press, 1979), 56-58; M. P. Wattenberg, "The Decline of Political Partisanship in America: Negativity or Neutrality?" *American Political Science Review* 75 (December 1981): 946-948; and S. J. Eldersveld, *Political Parties in American Society* (New York: Basic Books, 1982), 84.

volatility seem as likely as any reconstitution on the model of the 1930s. As Chapter 4 will elaborate, the factors that might replace parties as shapers of electoral choice seem unlikely to produce a net gain either in the rationality of voters' decisions or in the accountability of government. Quite the contrary. The signs of the decline of party-in-the-electorate are pronounced, worthy of sustained attention and concern.

NOTES

1. The following account draws on Angus Campbell, "A Classification of the Presidential Elections," in *Elections and the Political Order*, Campbell et al. (New York: John Wiley & Sons, 1967); Walter Dean Burnham, *Critical Elections and the Mainsprings of American Politics* (New York: W. W. Norton & Co., 1970); James Sundquist, *Dynamics of the Party System*, rev. ed. (Washington: The Brookings Institution, 1983); and Norman H. Nie, Sidney Verba, and John R. Petrocik, *The Changing American Voter* (Cambridge: Harvard University Press, 1979), chap. 5, 13.

2. Sundquist, *Dynamics*, 165-166.
3. Kristi Andersen, "Generation, Partisan Shift and Realignment: A Glance Back to the New Deal," in *Changing American Voter*, 77; see also Warren E. Miller and Teresa E. Levitin, *Leadership and Change: The New Politics and the American Electorate* (Cambridge, Mass.: Winthrop Publishers, 1976), 253-256. For an argument that Andersen underestimates the incidence of cross-party conversions, see Sundquist, *Dynamics*, 229-239.
4. Adam Clymer and Kathleen Frankovic, "The Realities of Realignment," *Public Opinion* (June-July 1981): 42.
5. *Gallup Poll*, release dated March 10, 1983.
6. Nie, Verba, and Petrocik, *Changing American Voter*, 241. See also Everett Carll Ladd, Jr., with Charles D. Hadley, *Transformations of the American Party System* (New York: W. W. Norton & Co., 1975), chap. 5.
7. Sundquist, *Dynamics*, 448.
8. See Nie, Verba, and Petrocik, *Changing American Voter*, chap. 14. The index of "liberalism" used (p. 246) includes responses on race and communism as well as the standard New Deal questions on economic welfare programs and the role of government.
9. Sundquist, *Dynamics*, chaps. 15-17.
10. For an argument that racial attitudes have had a determinative effect since 1964 on the party choices of new identifiers—and that such gradual "evolution" may be as important a mechanism of partisan change as more dramatic realignments—see Edward F. Carmines and James A. Stimson, "Issue Evolution, Population Replacement, and Normal Partisan Change," *American Political Science Review* 75 (March 1981): 107-118.
11. Richard M. Scammon and Ben J. Wattenberg, *The Real Majority* (New York: Coward, McCann & Geoghegan, 1970), 43.
12. Burnham, *Critical Elections*, 169.
13. Scammon and Wattenberg, *Real Majority*, 287.
14. See Kevin P. Phillips, *The Emerging Republican Majority* (Garden City, N.Y.: Anchor Books, 1970).
15. Sundquist, *Dynamics*, 421.
16. Ibid., 424. See also Paul Abramson, John Aldrich, and David Rohde, *Change and Continuity in the 1980 Elections*, rev. ed. (Washington, D.C.: CQ Press, 1983), chap. 5.
17. See Sundquist, *Dynamics*, 433-436; Abramson, Aldrich, and Rohde, *Change and Continuity*, chap. 6; and Robert M. Entman and David L. Paletz, "Media and the Conservative Myth," *Journal of Communications* 30 (Autumn 1980): 154-165.
18. This view is given some credence by the fact that during the past two decades the percentage of the income of median-income families claimed by taxes has doubled (to about 23 percent) while the rate for those in the upper brackets has climbed much more slowly. See Everett Carll Ladd, Jr., *Where Have All the Voters Gone? The Fracturing of America's Political Parties* (New York: W. W. Norton & Co., 1978), 47.
19. Sundquist, *Dynamics*, 424.
20. Ibid., 437-449.
21. See Burnham, *Critical Elections*, chap. 5; and idem, "American Politics in the 1970s: Beyond Party?" in *The American Party Systems: Stages of Political Development*, 2d ed., edited by W. N. Chambers and W. D. Burnham (New York: Oxford University Press, 1975), chap. 11.
22. Nie, Verba, and Petrocik, *Changing American Voter*, 57, 73.
23. The same polls that led to speculation that a Republican realignment might be under way in 1981 also revealed a substantial decrease in the percentage of professed independents. By 1983, however, this figure had climbed back to its 1980 level. *Gallup Poll*, release dated March 10, 1983.
24. Data from Center for Political Studies, the University of Michigan.
25. See Nie, Verba, and Petrocik, *Changing American Voter*, 59-73; Miller and Levitin, *Leadership and Change*, 192-199; and Helmut Norpoth and Jerrold G. Rusk, "Partisan Dealignment in the American Electorate: Itemizing the Deductions since 1964," *American Political Science Review* 76 (September 1982): 522-537.
26. This discussion draws on Paul A. Beck, "Partisan Dealignment in the Postwar South," *American Political Science Review* 71 (June 1977): 477-496; Bruce A. Campbell, "Patterns of Change in the Partisan Loyalties of Native Southerners: 1952-1972," *Journal of Politics* 39 (August 1977): 730-761; Nie, Verba, and Petrocik, *Changing American Voter*, 217-229; and Raymond Wolfinger and Robert B. Arseneau, "Partisan Change in the South, 1952-1976," in *Political Parties: Development and Decay*, ed. Louis Maisel and Joseph Cooper (Beverly Hills: Sage Publications, 1978), chap. 6.
27. See Beck, "Partisan Dealignment," 489-494; Wolfinger and Arseneau, "Partisan Change," 199-203; Sundquist, *Dynamics*, 403-408.
28. Nie, Verba, and Petrocik, *Changing American Voter*, 354.
29. Wolfinger and Arseneau, "Partisan Change," 189-206. For comparable observations on the partisan "leanings" of independents nationwide, see Bruce Keith et al., "Further Evidence on the Partisan Affinities of Independent 'Leaners' " (Paper delivered at the annual meeting of the American Political Science Association, Chicago, Ill., 1983).
30. Burnham observed: "Had the electoral conditions of the 1920 Harding landslide [i.e., straight-ticket voting] prevailed in the 1972 Nixon landslide, the Republicans would have elected about 350

representatives. Instead, they won only 191, far short of a party majority." "Politics in the 1970s," 321.

31. Nie, Verba, and Petrocik, *Changing American Voter*, 68.
32. This account draws on ibid., chaps. 7-10, 12; and Gerald Pomper, *Voters' Choice* (New York: Dodd, Mead & Co., 1975), chap. 8.
33. Pomper, *Voters' Choice*, 183. See also Nie, Verba, and Petrocik, *Changing American Voter*, 167. They find voter evaluations of candidates in terms of party ties to have been decreasing while evaluations in terms of issue positions was increasing during the period from 1952 to 1972.
34. See Jack Citrin, "The Changing American Electorate," and Everett Carll Ladd, Jr., "Political Parties and Governance in the 1980s," in *Politics and the Oval Office*, ed. Arnold J. Meltsner (San Francisco: Institute for Contemporary Studies, 1981), 47-57, 65-69. On the relationship of policy dissatisfaction to political alienation, see Arthur H. Miller, "Political Issues and Trust in Government: 1964-1970" and Miller's subsequent exchange with Jack Citrin, *American Political Science Review* 68 (September 1974): 951-1001.
35. Nie, Verba, and Petrocik, *Changing American Voter*, 57-58; Jack Dennis, "Changing Public Support for the American Party System," in *Paths to Political Reform*, ed. William J. Crotty (Lexington, Mass.: Lexington Books, 1980), 42-44.
36. Dennis, "Changing Public Support," 38-39, 54-56.
37. Martin P. Wattenberg, "The Decline of Political Partisanship in the United States: Negativity or Neutrality?" *American Political Science Review* 75 (December 1981): 941-950. On the failure of increasing numbers of voters to perceive important differences between the parties, see Ladd, "Political Parties and Governance," 67-68.
38. See Richard G. Niemi and Herbert F. Weisberg, eds., *Controversies in American Voting Behavior* (San Francisco: W. H. Freeman & Co., 1976), 413-420.

Party Organizations 2

Our assessment of the current state of the American parties thus far has concentrated on the levels of identification, approval, and electoral cue taking within the parties' popular bases. We now consider the parties in their more institutionalized forms—as multilayered local, state, and national organizations and (in Chapter 3) as networks of coordination and control within and among units of government.[1] The condition of the parties at one level often has a discernible impact at another. For example, the decline of party allegiance in the electorate has encouraged candidates to bypass or preempt state and local party organizations when organizing their campaigns. Any adequate assessment of the state of the parties, however, must look at each of these facets of party life independently. Examining the parties as institutions will provide evidence of party decline, but evidence of a more mixed and ambiguous sort than that provided by electoral data.

Party at the Grass Roots

Local Organizations

The best-known and most tightly structured party organizations in the United States have been the local "machines," generally located in large eastern and midwestern cities. These organizations flourished after the Civil War and dominated political life in many cities well into the twentieth century. They were usually hierarchical in structure: the line of command from the "boss" and his lieutenants to ward and precinct leaders was well-established, standards of loyalty and effective performance were well-defined, and the organization's control of jobs and patronage provided a potent arsenal of rewards and sanctions. The party relied financially on assessments of its elected and appointed officeholders and also on contributions from those doing business with the city or county. Captains or committeemen at the ward and precinct levels were the key middlemen in the system: their positions in the organization, and the jobs they often held in city or county government, were dependent on their ability to deliver the vote on election day. They maintained close ties with their constituencies, providing aid to families in need, help in obtaining jobs or governmental services, and a measure of recognition and status to those who became involved in the organization. Milton Rakove aptly summarizes how machine politics work: "An effective political party needs five things: offices, jobs, money, workers, and votes. Offices beget jobs and money; jobs and money beget workers; workers beget votes; and votes beget offices." [2]

Political reformers since the late nineteenth century have attacked party machines' endemic favoritism and corruption, internal autocracy, inefficiency and waste, and status quo bias with regard to existing policies and power relationships. Less often appreciated have been the machines' positive accomplishments in an era of rapid urban growth and change. They helped overcome division and deadlock among fragmented governmental structures, sometimes on behalf of projects as far-reaching as the New York subway system or New Haven redevelopment. They provided channels of political participation and upward mobility for immigrant groups and the economically disadvantaged. And they constituted an unofficial welfare system; "What tells in holdin' your grip on your district," George Washington Plunkitt, the best-known boss of New York's Tammany Hall, explained, "is to go right down among the poor families and help them in the different ways they need help." [3] Fred Greenstein offers a balanced assessment:

> Even from the limited standpoint of the nineteenth-century city resident's desire for physical security, machines had their deficiencies. Party benevolences, after all, were not the citizen's as a matter of legal right. They might always be withdrawn. Furthermore, the party's favors to the voter's employer might negate its services to him—for example, by permitting the continuation of hazardous working conditions in a factory. In time, however, the immigrant or his children were able to use the party as an effective vehicle for increasing their own leverage in the political system. Since in the final analysis the parties were dependent on winning elections, they found it necessary to accommodate to the changing desires of voters. After the early demands for minimal material security came stirrings for group recognition. Therefore, each wave of new immigrants gradually worked its way—and was recruited—into the ranks of party leadership. [4]

The resilience of the machines bears witness to the "fit" between the functions they performed and the circumstances of urban life. Their eventual decline resulted less from reformers' zeal than from changes in those conditions that gave them a distinctive social role to play. [5]

Reform measures have reduced the resources that fueled the party machines and have placed limits on "boss" control. The growth of the national civil service has curbed the number of patronage positions that local organizations can distribute. Comparable reforms at the state and local levels have removed many positions from party control, a trend that recently has been reinforced by court decisions limiting the use of patronage (see Chapter 5). Labor agreements sometimes have had similar effects, protecting workers from dismissal on political grounds. Competitive bidding and required audits have placed constraints on the exchange relationships between party leaders and officeholders and their preferred contractors and suppliers. Key city and county offices have been made the objects of nonpartisan election in many jurisdictions, and responsibility for nomination to those offices that have remained partisan has almost universally been transferred from party caucuses to direct primaries.

The social conditions that gave rise to the machines also have changed. In some ways the machines can be regarded as the victims of their own success: the children of those immigrants, whose mobility the machine (sometimes) served, in time became less dependent on the sorts of jobs, favors, and recognition the party had to offer and less inclined to submit to the organization's demands. The local party's role as public benefactor has been largely displaced by unemployment insurance, workmen's compensation, Social Security, and other social welfare programs. As urban populations have become better educated and more acculturated to middle-class values, they have taken on more of the country's traditional antiparty attitudes. And the new campaign technology—especially television and direct mail—has reduced the dependence of candidates and voters alike on local party organizations.

Thus the urban machine in its classic form has almost become an extinct species. The Chicago organization, tightly controlled for two decades by Mayor Richard Daley (1955-1976), was often described as the last of the big-city machines. In a 1980 study Thomas Guterbock estimated that some 20,000 jobs in Chicago remained under party control.[6] The organization suffered a setback in 1979 when Daley's designated successor was defeated by Jane Byrne in the mayoral primary, but Byrne moved quickly to repair her ties with party regulars. The machine seems less likely to recover from its most recent defeat, however. Harold Washington, a black U.S. representative, defeated Byrne (and Daley's son, State's Attorney Richard M. Daley) in a 1983 mayoral primary campaign aimed explicitly at the Democratic organization. Terming the machine "a mortally wounded animal," Washington has kept party regulars at arms length since assuming office. Ironically, his ability to reward his own followers has been limited by antipatronage court decisions that, in effect, have secured many machine appointees against dismissal. But those decisions also represent a significant obstacle to any future return to a party-based patronage system.[7]

In most cities one or both parties still have a network of precinct leaders, a reasonably well-defined organizational structure. But these organizations often display considerable "slack"—performing "at a minimal level of efficiency, without too much system, in a rather hit-and-miss mode of operation." [8] Studies of party precinct leaders in Detroit in 1956 and 1980, for example, conclude that organization is inadequate in one or both parties in over one-half of the county's precincts; less than one-third of the precinct leaders in either party perform the three basic tasks of voter registration, door-to-door canvassing, and election-day roundup.[9]

It is too simple, however, to find in these historical trends an unmitigated process of party decline. First, machine politics on the Chicago model has never been the norm in most American cities and towns, much less in the country's rural areas. In most places, most of the time, party organizations have displayed more "slack" than the machine metaphor would suggest and have relied much less exclusively on patronage and other economic incentives. Second, the evidence of the decline of the machines themselves is mixed. As Raymond Wolfinger suggests, it is misleading to judge the historical trend simply by looking for "united and hierarchical party organizations"; machine politics may persist even though jobs and favors are dispersed by multiple factions or organizations within the party.[10] In fact, the contemporary migration of dependent populations to the cities and the creation of government jobs through proliferating social programs would seem to create new possibilities for patronage politics.

Wolfinger acknowledges that party organizations in many places have not taken advantage of these apparent possibilities; this may have more to do with regional variations in political culture and style, he suggests, than with any sociological trends that doom machine politics to extinction.[11] He perhaps overestimates the potential of the machines to make a comeback even on their own home ground.[12] Many of the new governmental positions carry technical or professional qualifications that patronage appointees find difficult to meet. Moreover, in filling jobs public officials must confront the claims of racial, neighborhood, or other groups now inclined to seek direct representation, unmediated by the party. Public and media attitudes still inhibit the politicizing of governmental programs and functions. In fact, they tempt officeholders to declare their independence of party in making appointments and other decisions. Still, machine politics is far from dead in many places. According to a recent national survey, one-fourth of the county chairs in both parties rated as a "very important" aspect of their job the recommending or clearing of patronage appointees.[13] Making political appointments, rewarding faithful workers, and assisting voters in their dealings with government remain critical components of the parties' organizational strength.

Finally, it is important to recognize that movement away from the machine model presents the parties with new organizational possibilities. The passing of the machine has by no means always left an organizational vacuum. In many cities, regular party organizations have been challenged or displaced by partisan clubs, often organized around "good government" or policy concerns. In other places the central party organizations either have been taken over or have adapted to the interests and values of activists who find the machine model repugnant or irrelevant to their goals. These new-style party organizations seldom display the discipline and hierarchical control that characterized the classic machines; indeed, a desire for internal party democracy often has been a major reason for their formation. But modern party reformers have tended to differ from their Progressive Era counterparts in a crucial respect: "their strategy is to work within and take control of the parties, rather than to reject the legitimacy of parties." [14] Thus have the new-model parties continued to perform many of the functions traditionally associated with the urban machines, albeit in a different style and utilizing a different mix of resources.

An intriguing bit of evidence comes from national polls measuring the incidence of personal contact of voters by campaign workers. Although television and other modern campaign tools have reduced candidates' reliance on local party organizations, personal-contact campaigning—whereby voters are contacted in person or by phone and "favorable" respondents are recontacted and turned out on election day—still has a significant effect. [15] Such activity, long a staple of urban party organizations, actually seems to have increased in recent presidential campaigns. Center for Political Studies surveys show that between 24 and 32 percent of the adult population has been personally contacted in recent presidential campaigns, about twice as many as reported such contacts in the 1950s. Precise information is not available as to whether the canvassers were working for party, candidate, or other organizations, but it seems likely that a good portion of this activity has been carried on by the parties. Most personal-contact campaigning, moreover, still occurs in metropolitan areas. [16] While this does not suggest that political machines are on the way back, it does indicate that extensive voter-contact activities are being carried out by new-style as well as more traditional party organizations.

National surveys of party organizations in counties reinforce this conclusion. In neither the Democratic nor Republican party are the county organizations highly institutionalized. Only about 13 percent have permanent headquarters, and 8 percent have any paid staff. This "lack of structure does not necessarily imply a low level of programmatic activity," however. Some 50 percent of these organizations now carry out voter-registration and/or get-out-the-vote drives, more than half operate headquarters during the campaign season, and some two-thirds organize fund raising or other campaign events. In both parties, campaign activities at this level have stepped up appreciably since the mid-1960s. Although candidates are tending to handle their own media campaigns, local-party involvement in campaign coordination, voter contact, and fund raising has increased substantially. [17]

Thus the decline of the urban machine cannot be regarded as the decline of the party per se. This is fortunate because to equate the two would be to conclude that party renewal was unlikely indeed. The conditions that allowed the machines to flourish have changed irreversibly. But the task of assessing the parties' prospects remains. This requires a closer look at the new-model party organizations—at the attitudes and goals of their adherents, the roles they have assumed, and their place in the larger political system.

Styles of Partisan Participation

Contemporary students of American parties have focused considerable attention on how members' attitudes and motivations influence the character and the strength of the parties. The weakening of party organizations has been linked to changes in the orientations activists have brought to their party roles.

James Q. Wilson's influential study, *The Amateur Democrat,* examines Democratic club politics as it developed in New York, Chicago, and Los Angeles during the 1950s. Wilson distinguishes the "new" politicians not by their ideology—the Democrats tend to be liberal, the Republicans strongly conservative—but by the *style* of politics they practice. These "amateurs," as Wilson calls them, see politics as the realm of ideas and principles. This contrasts with the priority given electoral victory and the maintenance of the organization by the conventional machine politicians ("professionals") whom the amateurs are displacing and challenging. The clear articulation of principles and policies, which amateurs see as central to the party's role, are viewed by the professionals as secondary to the primary goal of "gaining power and place for one's self and one's party." [18]

Wilson and others have perceived these issue-oriented amateurs as a threat to the stability and moderation of the party system. Believing that political parties ought to be "programmatic, internally democratic, and largely or entirely free of reliance on material incentives such as patronage," [19] amateurs seem likely to move them in doctrinaire and self-defeating directions. Party organizations catering to amateurs, critics claim, will have a narrower appeal than traditional organizations and will be less able to prompt sustained involvement. Amateurs, attracted to the party by what Wilson calls "purposive" incentives, may well fall away if their issue declines in salience or if the organization fails to champion their concerns.

Traditionally, party activists have been attracted by the "material" incentives of jobs and patronage, supplemented (and in the twentieth century increasingly supplanted) by "solidary" incentives such as social recognition and status, group membership and identification, conviviality and excitement.[20] Organizations fueled by these incentives have every reason to adopt moderate and inclusive issue appeals to maximize their electoral return; at the same time they have the wherewithal to enforce conformity to whatever stances the party takes and to avoid defections on the part of those whose favored candidates or positions do not prevail within party councils. While an amateur-dominated party would display a sharpened issue stance, it might lose the capacity to rally the broad electorate and to keep its own troops in line.

Such hypotheses about the rise of political amateurism and its threat to the viability of the parties raise three subsidiary questions: (1) Is amateurism a coherent concept, reflective of a single pattern of political participation? (2) How prevalent is the amateur syndrome? (3) Is this brand of participation as corrosive of party strength as its critics have charged?

(1) The notion of amateurism developed by Wilson and translated into survey questions by subsequent researchers includes several components: (a) responsiveness to purposive, as opposed to material or solidary, incentives; (b) a "purist" devotion to principle, as opposed to a pragmatic willingness to compromise; (c) an emphasis on clarity and correctness on

issues more than electoral victory or organizational maintenance; (d) a commitment to intraparty democracy and to the open debate of issues and procedures within the organization; and (e) a tendency to make commitment to or work for the party conditional on the presence of a favored candidate or issue.

While such attitudes and motivations may complement and reinforce one another, they do not refer necessarily to a single political style or orientation.[21] They may be present in different actors in varying combinations and degrees of intensity. Persons placing great value on the adoption of correct policy stands, for example, may vary considerably in their willingness, having received only "half a loaf" in such deliberations, to work on behalf of the party and its candidates.

(2) The different shadings that researchers have given to the concepts of amateurism and professionalism make it difficult to generalize about the prevalence of these styles in a variety of party settings. Nevertheless, significant trends can be discerned. Samuel Eldersveld's extensive study of the Democratic and Republican parties of Detroit and Wayne County, Michigan, explores precinct leaders' reasons for first becoming active. Eldersveld finds "impersonal" goals (a desire to influence policy or fulfill community obligations—roughly comparable to Wilson's purposive incentives) to be most important. But in many cases solidary goals and incentives (a strong identification with the party, a sense that politics is part of one's "way of life," social contacts and friendships, fun and excitement) also play a role. In discussing the rewards they derive from politics, these precinct leaders rank "social contacts" far above moral or issue-related satisfactions. Many of those who initially were motivated by policy concerns or a sense of community obligation soon became "acclimated and socialized to expect personal satisfactions and to stay in party work because of them." For party leaders above the precinct level, personal motivations still can take quite tangible form—business contacts, for example, or political preferment. For precinct leaders such patronage is rarely available, but the less tangible solidary benefits of sociability and recognition often serve as an effective substitute. Detroit's parties, Eldersveld concludes, attract people with a "rich variety of motivations, drives, and needs" and draw less on ideological motivations than "those with reformist visions might have hoped." [22]

In updating portions of the Detroit study in 1980, Eldersveld finds little reason to alter his earlier conclusions. Policy and community-service motivations rank even higher; 59 percent of the precinct leaders give these as their reasons for initial party involvement (compared with 42 percent in 1956). But a majority of these respondents point to social and personal rewards and satisfactions in explaining their continuing involvement.[23]

Another aspect of the amateurism syndrome is touched upon in Eldersveld's examination of the "power orientations" of party leaders. Here, too, conventional politics has hardly been displaced. A majority of Democratic and Republican leaders at the district and precinct levels give preeminence to electoral victory as a party goal and are willing to sacrifice their preferred issue positions to that end. But such dilemmas prompt considerable confusion and ambivalence; Eldersveld discerns a "diminution in 'power-winning' perspectives as one descends the hierarchy ... especially for the Republicans." [24]

In general, the scattered studies that have built on Wilson's and Eldersveld's work suggest that the attitudes associated with amateurism have become more common but that the "rich variety" of purposes and roles within and among party organizations remains. Studies of party leaders in locales as diverse as Manhattan, the suburbs of New York and Washington, rural Illinois, and selected Massachusetts and North Carolina communities have found purposive and/or impersonal concerns to rank high in attracting people to politics and inducing them to seek leadership positions. But solidary commitments and rewards continue to play a critical role in tying activists to party organizations, and party leaders generally still give primacy to local organizational and constituent-service tasks.[25]

The orientations of state party chairmen, like those of district and precinct party leaders, display a blend of old politics and new.[26] Half of the chairmen in both parties describe a desire to influence policy as their single most important reason for becoming active in party work, and almost an equal number describe developing the party's policy positions as an important part of their job. But for many, hammering out a platform is primarily a brokerage role rather than an opportunity to initiate proposals. And most chairmen seem to give traditional organizational tasks—the nurturing of local structures, campaign coordination, candidate recruitment, fund raising, and the dispensing of patronage—higher priority than the pursuit of specific policy goals.

Studies of the local and state leaders representing their organizations at national conventions provide further evidence of the rise of "amateur" orientations in both parties. Here the choice of Barry Goldwater as the Republicans' presidential nominee in 1964 represents a landmark event. The Goldwater phenomenon, Aaron Wildavsky confessed, was a "great mystery" to observers of American politics, whose "expectations concerning the behavior of parties and politicians [were] violated."

> Ordinarily, we expect both major parties to choose popular candidates with a good chance of winning. The death wish is not supposed to be dominant among politicians. Party leaders are expected to conciliate groups of voters in order to get at least part of their vote.... And the major parties often accommodate themselves to the most popular part of the opposition's policies in order to enhance their prospects of victory. Yet none of these things happened—at least on the Republican side—in 1964. Why? [27]

Wildavsky's primary answer was the prevalence of "purism" among those making the party's choice. To be sure, there were special conditions (such as the unlikelihood of victory in any case and the absence of a viable moderate candidate) that weakened the hand and the resolve of the party's more pragmatic leaders. But among party activists at the convention, Wildavsky saw evidence of a more general trend away from the politics of accommodation.

Concentrating on that aspect of the amateur syndrome that eschews compromise and is willing to forego electoral advantage for the sake of ideological correctness, Wildavsky found a correspondence in style between the Goldwater conservatives and the liberal reformers described by Wilson. The Goldwater purists, in fact, "went even further in their willingness to cast aside whole groups of voters who did not agree with them." Some 80 percent of the Goldwater delegates displayed a purist orientation, typified by the reflections of a rural Pennsylvania delegate attending his first convention:

> Now, for the first time in my life, we have a candidate who acts as he believes. He doesn't change his position when it is expedient. . . . I don't believe I should compromise one inch from what I believe deep down inside.[28]

The tumultuous 1968 Democratic convention in Chicago persuaded Wildavsky that the purist style "was beginning to emerge on the left as it previously had with the Goldwaterites on the right. . . . McCarthy's great attraction was his political style . . . as the antithesis of the unscrupulous politician who changes his views on public policy in order to curry favor with the electorate."[29] Using a broader definition of amateurism and more systematic survey techniques, John Soule and his associates examined the incidence and the effects of this style among the 1968 and 1972 Democratic delegates. They estimated that some 23 percent of the 1968 delegates could be classified as amateurs and a considerably larger number (61 percent) could be thought of as "semiprofessionals"—holding a number of attitudes characteristic of the amateur orientation. The 1972 Democratic convention saw some increase (from 16 to 27 percent) in the number of consistent "professional" responses, but the far greater movement was toward amateurism: those displaying this style now numbered 51 percent of the delegates. Amateurism was strongly related to support for Eugene McCarthy in 1968 and to support for George McGovern, George Wallace, or Shirley Chisholm in 1972.[30]

Although the trend toward delegate amateurism at Democratic conventions has receded slightly since 1972, it has by no means been decisively reversed. One research team, using the delegates' ranking of the goals of party unity versus forthright issue articulation as their means of distinguishing amateurs and professionals, found professionalism (which according to their measure could claim only 36 percent of the 1972 delegates) to be moving toward a 50-50 balance in both the 1974 midterm conference and the 1976 convention.[31]

To some extent, increases in national convention "amateurism" reflect the changing bases of local party recruitment noted earlier. It also seems likely that presidential politics selects out those local activists with strong policy interests. Beyond this, a number of analysts have suggested that changes in the rules governing delegate selection, particularly in the Democratic party, have given substantial advantages and incentives to issue and candidate enthusiasts. We will examine the impact of rules changes on convention participation in more detail in Chapter 7. Certainly the increased number of amateurs at the "reformed" Democratic convention of 1972 suggests that rules changes were a factor of some importance. But it is difficult to separate the impact of the rules from the effects of McGovern's successful insurgency on the composition of the convention, and the continuing strength of "purist" impulses at Republican conventions (where rules changes have been far less extensive) suggests that party reform is only one of the many factors at work.

Thomas Roback estimated that some 42 percent of the 1972 Republican delegates would qualify as amateurs. The party had an incumbent president, however, and the national party leadership had shifted "from Barry Goldwater purism to Nixon pragmatism over the last decade." The ideological and stylistic inclinations of many of the delegates therefore "had to be blurred and muted to fit the prearranged 1972 'game-plan.' " [32] Such constraints fell away at the post-Watergate 1976 convention: "The purist ideological fervor that had been aroused by Goldwater in 1964, and had been temporarily extinguished in Miami Beach [in 1972] flared anew." [33] While the number of delegates qualifying as amateurs probably was not much greater than in 1972 (comparable figures are not available), their impact on the nomination contest and the platform was profound. The 1976 Republican purists were overwhelmingly supportive of Ronald Reagan's insurgent candidacy and of an ideologically "correct" conservative platform. They often regarded the convention proceedings and the party apparatus as illegitimately "stacked" against them, and many of them subsequently declined to work for the Gerald Ford-Robert Dole ticket.[34]

(3) Clearly, styles of political participation at all levels have moved, albeit irregularly, in the directions noted by the students of amateurism in large-city party organizations 20 years ago. In certain respects this threatens the parties' organizational strength. Obviously, an organization's resources are diminished if the support of its active members becomes conditional on the presence of a favored issue or candidate or if its adherents become less concerned about the organization's unity and maintenance. The decreased interest in electoral victory, the willingness to precipitate and perpetuate internal divisions and to write off ideological opponents, and the growing impatience with conciliation and compromise are potentially destructive trends, given the broad-gauged character of American parties and the kinds of identifications and incentives that have bound them together.

Several caveats, however, are again in order. Many of the laments for the passing of professionalism have a nostalgic and unrealistic air about them, underestimating both the eclecticism of the old style and the impediments to its reinstatement. As we have seen, the role of patronage in fueling party organizations has been declining for many years; the precise character and mix of the material and solidary incentives to party involvement have varied widely. Solidary incentives have become an effective replacement for patronage and preferment in some instances but not always. For example, Robert Salisbury's analysis of St. Louis politics in the 1960s found ward committee participation to be largely "habitual," "rooted in family socialization." Such participation, he concluded, was "less enthusiastic, less regular, and less effectual than more purposive involvement" and had much to do with the parties' moribund state.[35]

It is no longer feasible for the parties in most locales to rely solely on the traditional mix of tangible and intangible personal inducements. Given the availability of such material and social benefits from other sources, and the interests that a better educated and more middle-class clientele brings to politics, party organizations must offer purposive incentives if they are to survive. Therefore, the attitudes and values of the amateur must be seen not simply as a threat but also as a resource for organizational renewal—an enduring feature of the political landscape to which the parties must adapt and for which they must provide an outlet.

Both professionalism and amateurism represent tendencies rather than unidimensional styles; the mixed forms in which they can appear in real life complicate any assessment of their implications for party strength. Recent conventions suggest, for example, that professionals might not be as committed to uniting behind a winning nominee as has sometimes been supposed. The evidence is somewhat mixed: Republican regulars, led by Gov. Nelson Rockefeller, refused to unite behind Goldwater in 1964, and one study found the followers of Hubert Humphrey and Henry Jackson adopting an increasingly purist style in 1972 as McGovern gained the nomination.[36] But another study of the 1972 convention found party officeholders (presumably strong in professional orientation) considerably more likely than other delegates to step up their campaign activity after the convention and apparently much less influenced in that decision by whether they had been on the winning side.[37] As for the McGovern delegates, surveys found them modifying their negative views of the organized party very little, even as they solidified their victory. But many of them behaved more like professionals as they tempered platform provisions for the sake of their electoral appeal.[38] It is not accurate to conclude, as have some critics of the Wilson and Wildavsky typologies, that the "style" one adopts mainly depends on whether one is winning or losing at the moment. Clearly, however, stylistic emphases and combinations can vary considerably with political circumstances.

As amateurs move into positions of party leadership they may adopt attitudes and practices more conducive to long-term organization building. Wilson found that "many of the amateurs with long experience and personal stakes in politics acquired the habits and motives of the professional," although the views of their followers required them to maintain their "amateur standing" carefully and otherwise limited the acceptable techniques of organizational maintenance.[39] Several studies have suggested that purposive incentives have a greater potential for sustaining party involvement than Wilson and others supposed.[40] But for most amateurs whose involvement has continued, personal and/or solidary incentives seem to have become intermingled with those policy interests that first drew them into politics.[41]

"Pure" amateurism can be and often is combined with attitudes and motivations more conducive to the sustaining of party organizations. Observers at the 1982 Democratic Midterm Conference, for example, suggested that most delegates were neither traditional "hacks" nor ideo-

logical "purists" but, as Rep. Michael Barnes put it, "newer, sophisticated, issue-oriented regulars." In both parties, many of yesterday's
amateurs and reformers have become today's regulars. But they seem to
have become more pragmatic in the process and in many cases to have
made an enduring commitment to the party as an organization.[42]

Reform groups in politics, Tammany's Boss Plunkitt observed, "were
mornin' glories—looked lovely in the mornin' and withered up in a short
time, while the regular machines went on flourishin' forever, like fine old
oaks." [43] Political reality is now somewhat more complicated. Ideology
and policy interests are still deficient as a sole foundation for enduring,
adaptive party organizations, but the material incentives on which the
machines were built have long since faded in their relevance. The question is not whether one pure orientation or another will prevail, but
whether the policy and candidate interests that increasingly motivate
party activists will prompt lasting commitments to the parties as institutions. If they do, the new styles of participation can give the parties new
vitality and a greater capacity for addressing society's needs.

State and National Organizations

State Parties

The current condition of state party organizations, like that of local
organizations, does not support easy generalizations about party decline.
There has been a long-term diminution of the state parties' control of the
nomination process, of their role in campaigns, and of patronage and
other resources with which to attract and reward party workers. These
trends are much further advanced in some places than in others. Thousands of state jobs in Pennsylvania, Indiana, and other states are still
awarded on a patronage basis, for example, and some 11 percent of state
party chairs in the early 1970s reported that they still had "complete
control" over the dispensing of patronage (although a much larger number—53 percent—reported that the governor now controlled such matters).[44] And some additional signs of party resiliency have appeared since
the 1960s: many state parties have undergone considerable financial and
organizational development and have adapted with some success to the
changing campaign environment.

It was the direct primary—first adopted on a statewide basis in
Wisconsin in 1903 and used in all but a handful of states within 14
years—that most decisively reduced the influence of state party organizations over nominations. "Through the history of American nominating
practices," V. O. Key observed, "runs a persistent attempt to make
feasible popular participation in nominations and thereby to limit or to
destroy the power of party oligarchies." [45] Authority to make nominations
for state offices was originally placed with party members of the state
legislatures. But attacks on such practices as "a dark and foul *aristocracy*
in disguise," together with the discrediting of "King Caucus" at the
national level by the followers of Andrew Jackson, led to the spread of
state nominating conventions. The conventions also eventually came to

be regarded as instruments of leadership control, and Progressive reformers regarded their displacement by direct primaries as one of their most
significant achievements. "No longer," proclaimed Robert LaFollette, the
most prominent early champion of the reform, "will there stand between
the voter and the official a political machine with a complicated system of
caucuses and conventions, by the easy manipulation of which it thwarts
the will of the voter and rules official conduct.... Each citizen shall
exercise his choice by direct vote, without the intervention or interference
of any political agency." [46]

The adoption of the direct primary did not fatally weaken most state
organizations. [47] But it did remove direct responsibility for the parties'
most important decisions from party caucuses and conventions; it encouraged divisions and reduced the incentives for compromise among
party leaders by enabling them to take their differences to the broader
electorate; and it lessened the dependence of candidates and officeholders on the organized party, tempting some to pursue an "outside" strategy. State party organizations were not equally cohesive or influential
before reform, and the adoption of the direct primary did not affect them
all to the same degree. As we will see in Chapter 5, a factor of considerable importance continues to be the diverse laws that govern the nomination process in the states. Some states, for example, have retained a role
for party conventions either in making nominations for certain offices or
in endorsing primary candidates, and there has even been a slight trend
toward restoring such party prerogatives in recent years. [48] Working in the
opposite direction, however, have been alterations in the nomination
process at the presidential level. The 26 presidential primaries established during the Progressive Era did not prove as durable as primaries at
other levels and their number eventually receded to 15. Since 1968,
however, presidential primaries again have proliferated, and other
changes in presidential nomination procedures have further reduced the
role of state party organizations (see Chapter 7). The overall pattern
seems clear: if one's criterion of organizational strength is the control that
parties have over the nomination function, most state organizations have
long been in a period of declining health.

A look at campaign functions also provides considerable evidence of
party displacement. Campaigns have become more candidate-centered,
and candidate organizations now rely less on the party for raising money,
advertising, and mobilizing the vote. The movement of party nominations
to the primary arena and the general weakening of party organizations
have encouraged these trends. The parties are no longer in control, they
have less to offer, and candidates increasingly feel that they are on their
own. But new modes of campaigning have made an independent contribution to party displacement, particularly during the last 30 years.

A key development has been the rise of television as the dominant
campaign medium for most federal and statewide races. The presence of
this new, powerful stimulus has often made the "image" of the individual
candidate a more important electoral cue than his party label; it has
become less necessary and probably less effective for candidates to communicate with voters through party channels. Direct-mail solicitation and

political action committees now dominate the fund-raising scene. New polling, data-analysis, and marketing techniques encourage a "scientific" approach to campaigning. A new breed of political professionals has arisen—campaign management consultants and firms specializing in polling, media, direct-mail, and organizational techniques. These experts, as Larry Saboto argues, can perform a number of key campaign functions more effectively than most party organizations:

> Their polls reveal the public's wishes more precisely than ward leaders ever could; their television advertising substitutes for party workers as the middlemen between candidates and voters; and their direct mail and organizational devices provide money, support, and troops with a greater loyalty to the individual candidate than to a conglomerate, coalition party.[49]

While some of these professionals work with and through party structures, many of them no doubt would agree with the assessment of campaign consultant Joseph Napolitan: "The new technologies make parties, if not obsolete, certainly obsolescent." Having little confidence in or loyalty to the parties, they often encourage candidates to organize their campaigns outside of the party apparatus and to run "apart from, or even against, their party label." [50]

In the midst of these unmistakable party-weakening trends, however, a number of state parties have experienced significant growth and development as organizations. A research team based at the University of Wisconsin-Milwaukee studied the phenomenon extensively and found, paradoxically, that the "disaggregation" of the parties in the electorate, the reduction of the party role in managing campaigns and in the nomination process, and the "institutionalization" of state party organizations seem to have occurred simultaneously. Using measures of institutionalization that take account of the stability and continuity of headquarters operations, the size and specialization of staff, and the extent of party building and campaign activity, these analysts concluded that state parties since the early 1960s have "developed into relatively strong and durable organizations." [51]

One indicator of organizational development is the size and permanence of operations at party headquarters. A survey of state parties in 1957 revealed that only 45 state parties hired *any* full-time professional staff; of these, only 17 hired more than one full-time professional.[52] In 1960, fewer than half of the state parties had permanent headquarters. By 1982, all but five of the 100 state parties maintained headquarters, and 90 or more of them employed a salaried executive director and/or a full-time, paid chairman. The average state party now has a staff of seven, and one-fourth of them have staffs of 10 or more.[53] These staffs are generally too small to permit a high degree of specialization, and there is still some fluctuation in staff size between campaigns and other periods. But the overall picture reveals substantial professionalization and growth.

Budget figures tell a similar story. Table 2-1 permits a comparison of the financial resources available to a sample of two-thirds of the state parties in 1961 and 1979. With the definition of "marginality" adjusted

Table 2-1 Comparison of State Party Budgets, 1961 and 1979

Percent of Organizations in Each Category			
1961			*1979*
Marginal (0-$50,000)	69%	(0-$100,000)	31%
Medium ($50,001-$150,000)	19%	($100,001-$300,000)	43%
High (more than $150,000)	12%	(more than $300,000)	26%
Sample size	67		68
Mean	$64,924		$292,038
Median	$37,950		$193,803

SOURCE: Cornelius P. Cotter et al., "State Party Organizations and the Thesis of Party Decline" (Paper delivered at the annual meeting of the American Political Science Association, Washington, D.C., 1980). Revised and updated figures furnished courtesy of the authors.

for inflation, the number of organizations falling into that category has declined by more than half. In 1979, a nonelection year for most states, the budgets of 26 percent of the state parties exceeded $300,000—still a modest figure when compared with soaring campaign budgets but one that nonetheless reflects improved fund-raising capacities and expanded headquarters operations. Sixteen states, moreover, have adopted some form of public financing of campaigns, and in eight of these some or all of the funds go to the parties (see Chapter 8).

The extent and the pace of state party institutionalization have displayed significant regional and interparty variation. Southern state parties tend to be less developed organizationally than nonsouthern parties, and the Democratic state parties are generally less institutionalized than those of the GOP. Southern Democratic parties had an average of four staff members in 1980, for example, compared with 12 aides for the average northern Republican organization. In nonsouthern states, the average Republican party budget was 2½ times as large as the average Democratic budget. Since 1960, Republican parties, North and South, have shown marked increases on most indices of organizational strength; southern Democratic parties, many of them experiencing serious Republican competition for the first time, also have registered gains—pulling almost even with the nonsouthern Democratic parties, which have shown a slight decline. Despite such variations, it is still possible to generalize: "Both parties were organizationally stronger at the state level in 1980 than they were in the 1960s." [54]

An important component of institutionalization for most state parties has been an increase in campaign capabilities. More than two-thirds of the state organizations operate ongoing voter registration and/or get-out-the-vote programs (compared with 39 percent 20 years ago). Over half report conducting (or contracting for) public opinion polls. Eighty percent publish a newsletter with some regularity. Over 50 percent are heavily involved in platform and campaign issue development. Nearly all

(89 percent) conduct workshops for candidates and/or party workers. Most still contribute money to candidates, but this kind of activity seems to be on the decline, as does the state parties' role in recruiting candidates.[55]

Long-term shifts may be under way in the *kind* of campaign roles state parties play. The control of these organizations over nominations and candidate recruitment has declined, and candidates are increasingly looking outside the parties for direct financial support and professional services, especially as they plan their media campaigns. But the parties seem to be carving out an important ancillary campaign role for themselves. They provide a forum for issue enthusiasts and are sometimes able to engage these and other activists in contacting voters and performing other tasks that benefit the party ticket. They often assume responsibility for the "human side" of campaigns, organizing the dinners and rallies, coordinating local-party activity, and providing the opportunities and the structures for grass-roots involvement. While candidates may be reluctant to relinquish control of their financial and media campaigns, it is often in their interest to have the party provide services and organize activities from which they and other candidates on the ticket can benefit in common—and which they would find it inefficient and costly to organize on their own.

For example, polling and precinct targeting are expensive and complex operations that candidates, most of the time, feel no need to keep under their personal control. Nor does it normally make sense for each candidate to gear up separate voter registration or get-out-the-vote efforts. It is in areas such as these, many of them reminiscent of traditional party activities but others utilizing sophisticated new equipment and techniques, that modern state parties have begun to find their niche. Candidates vary, of course, in their support of the party and in their willingness to see money and manpower channeled toward party organizations. But there is some evidence that they are beginning to appreciate the advantages of revitalized parties to themselves as campaigners and as officeholders. A division of labor between party and candidate organizations is emerging that gives state parties a prominent and stable campaign role.

National Party Organizations

Although the nation's first party system developed sporadically and with a great deal of local variation, it was highly centralized in the performance of its most important function: the nomination of presidential candidates in congressional party caucuses. With the passing of this system after the Jacksonian revolution, the nation lost whatever chance it might have had for something resembling a parliamentary system, with the party caucus bridging the constitutionally divided branches of government. Nor was any other group of national party leaders in a position to replace the congressional caucus; once national conventions were instituted in the 1830s, control over presidential nominations shifted decisively to local and state leaders. Convention rules placed almost no restrictions on how the states chose their delegates or how a delegate's votes were tabulated and cast.

The new system, however, did create a need for a continuing national body to call and make arrangements for the national conventions; this, in addition to a desire for better coordination of presidential campaigns, led to the formation of the Democratic National Committee (DNC) in 1848. The new Republican party followed this precedent at its first national convention, establishing the Republican National Committee (RNC) in 1856.[56]

These committees hardly served as instruments of party centralization. They were constituted in a way that stressed their federal character, with each state electing a single member (two members after committeewomen were provided for in the 1920s). Each state had complete control over the qualifications and methods of selection of its representative. At an early point, moreover, party members in Congress formed their own national committees. The National Republican Congressional Committee was formed in 1866, at a time when Republicans in Congress feared that President Andrew Johnson might use the national party machinery to their detriment. House and Senate Democrats formed a campaign committee at the same time. Both parties organized separate Senate campaign committees after the Seventeenth Amendment provided for the popular election of senators in 1913. While the congressional committees often worked cooperatively with the RNC and DNC, they continued to represent a decentralizing force within the national parties. Hugh Bone noted in 1958 that the Capitol Hill committees remained "jealous of their independence and quick to resist 'encroachment' by the national committees." [57]

As corporate bodies, the national committees had a rather ephemeral existence; they were fittingly described as "umbilical cords between national conventions." Some national chairmen, such as Mark Hanna (Republican, 1898-1904) and William Barnum (Democrat, 1877-1889), exercised strong influence over presidential nominations, campaign operations, and/or executive appointments. But such influence was highly variable and generally was based on a brokerage capacity vis-à-vis powerful state and local chieftains. Attempts on the part of presidents or party chairmen to influence state and local nominations for congressional candidates were rare—and when attempted, rarely successful. For example, James Farley, Democratic national chairman under Franklin D. Roosevelt, wrote that the president had violated a "cardinal political creed" in attempting to purge 13 anti-New Deal Democrats in the 1938 primaries. Farley's reaction (which was a factor in his later break with the president) has led Austin Ranney to observe:

> When a powerful national party chairman describes his president's efforts to prevent the renomination of congressmen working against the national party program as "the unwarranted invasion of outsiders" and as "interference in purely local affairs," we can well understand the judgment of most political scientists that the net result of party development from 1824 to the 1950s was to make American parties the least centralized in the world.[58]

A major function of the national committees from their inception in the mid-nineteenth century was the organization of presidential campaigns. It was not until after World War I, however, that the parties set up permanent headquarters and began to hire professional staff members to serve between elections. This transition began for the Republicans under Chairman Will Hays (1918-1921) and for the Democrats after the unsuccessful 1928 campaign. John Hamilton became the Republicans' first full-time paid chairman in 1936, Robert Hannegan the DNC's in 1944. By the 1950s, the RNC staff averaged more than 300 in presidential election years and almost 100 otherwise; the DNC staff was somewhat smaller. Both committees operated with budgets just short of $3 million in presidential years and around $1 million in other years. But staff turnover, from the chairman on down, was high, the finances of the national committees uncertain, and their roles subject to considerable fluctuation. In the early 1960s two respected analysts suggested that the "homelessness" of the two committees—"renters in [a series of] obscure buildings amid the splendid structures which house the lobbying activities of labor and industry"—aptly symbolized their lack of "permanence, stability, or institutional importance." [59]

Modern trends in national party organization must be assessed against this background of extensive decentralization and limited institutional development. Whatever decline the national parties have suffered has not been from a pinnacle of strength. Nonetheless, they have been weakened and displaced in ways that parallel what has happened to party organizations at other levels. Modern national chairmen have far less patronage at their disposal than did their counterparts in the time of Roosevelt or even during the Truman and Eisenhower administrations. National party leaders have largely been displaced in the management of presidential campaigns and in their liaision role vis-à-vis Congress, the executive branch, and outside groups. The new system of presidential nomination reduces the power and discretion of the national convention and, with it, the brokering role of the national party leadership. Taken together, these developments provide ample reason to speak of national party decline.

And yet the national parties, even more than the state parties, have reasserted themselves in important ways, adjusting their role to changing circumstances. A number of commentators have discerned a process of party "nationalization" or intraparty "integration' since the 1950s.[60] The national parties have become more active in relation to their state and local organizations—both in *regulating* their operations (especially in the Democratic party) and in *promoting* and *financing* their activities (particularly in the GOP).

Party "Nationalization"

Pressures to modify the almost total deference accorded state organizations arose first and most strongly in the Democratic party. The 1948 Democratic national convention, faced with a Deep South "Dixiecrat" revolt, nonetheless seated several state delegations that were pledged, in effect, to withhold support from the national ticket. But the DNC subsequently unseated six "disloyal" committee members from Alabama, Louisiana, Mississippi, and South Carolina, and the next two national conventions featured heated battles over what sort of pledge of loyalty could be required of a state's delegates. The matter was resolved when the 1956 convention passed a resolution requiring state Democratic parties selecting national convention delegates to "undertake to assure" that the convention's nominee would be listed under the Democratic label on that state's ballot. (In 1948, Dixiecrat nominee Strom Thurmond had been listed as the "Democratic" nominee in the four states listed above.) As important as the resolution's content was the precedent it established: national party agencies could place conditions on the selection of delegates by the states.[61]

This authority was taken several steps further in the 1960s. The challenge in 1964 to the all-white Mississippi regular delegation by the Freedom Democratic party resulted in the appointment of a Special Equal Rights Committee and the adoption of its proposed rules for the 1968 convention: delegates were to be selected in a nondiscriminatory fashion and in open and publicized party meetings. Then, after the tumultuous Chicago convention of 1968, the McGovern-Fraser Commission promulgated extensive and detailed guidelines to govern delegate selection in the states (see Chapter 6). This represented an unprecedented exercise of national party control:

> The commission was mandated by a national convention, appointed and encouraged by a national chairman, and given real clout by a national committee. The guidelines required the state parties to make radical changes in many of their accustomed ways of doing things, and the state parties all got into line. The national agencies' only sanction was their power to refuse convention seats to delegates from non-complying state parties; but it proved quite powerful enough.[62]

A further step in the Democratic party's "procedural nationalization" was taken in 1974 with the adoption for the first time of a party constitution.[63] The new charter by no means abandoned the party's decentralized, federal structure; attempts to institute card-carrying party membership were resisted, for example, as were devices designed to tie candidates more closely to national platforms. But the charter reinforced national commission reforms for the selection of convention delegates. Equal state representation on the DNC was replaced with a system giving greater weight to population and the size of the Democratic vote, thus strengthening the DNC's credentials as a representative national body. And the charter promoted the national committee's further institutionalization, establishing specialized structures for the review of disputes and challenges, financial development, and the provision of education and training services.[64]

The Republican party has likewise undergone procedural nationalization, although to a lesser extent than the Democrats. While the GOP has no formal party charter, it has long had a detailed, codified set of rules covering RNC and national convention procedures. The rules governing the RNC were expanded and modified considerably in 1975 on the recommendation of the party's "Rule 29 Committee," but the intent seems to have been less to institutionalize the party per se than to constrain the powers of the national chairman and to lessen the potential for White House control.[65] The GOP also has placed some additional constraints on state delegate selection procedures, but it has consistently declared its intent to forego the Democratic path to reform and to respect the independence of state parties. Still, the case for party nationalization is far stronger for the Republicans than for the Democrats. The alternative path to national party renewal pursued by the GOP—financial and organizational development—is more unambiguously productive of party strength than is procedural reform, and the Republicans have pursued this course with remarkable success.

The modern foundations were laid by Chairman Ray Bliss (1965-1969), who took office after Barry Goldwater's crushing loss, when the RNC, as he put it, was little more than "a second-rate answering service."[66] Bliss expanded the party's fledgling direct-mail fund-raising program, developed training programs and research services for local candidates and organizations, and organized the Republican Coordinating Committee to develop and publicize policy positions. Funds were raised and plans laid for a national headquarters building (dedicated in January 1971), the first owned by either national party. Bliss's dismissal by Richard Nixon was only one of the misfortunes visited by that president upon his party. But Bliss's groundwork proved essential for the party-building efforts of Bill Brock, who became national chairman after the Democrats recaptured the presidency in 1976.

"As old-style party machines have waned," Michael Malbin reported in the midst of the 1980 campaign, "a new Republican organization has emerged—a multimillion-dollar bureaucracy in Washington that employs 350 and plays an increasingly important role in all aspects of Republican campaigning and party policy."[67] Brock's six-year tenure as national chairman was marked by an emphasis on rebuilding the party's state and local base, extraordinarily successful direct-mail fund raising, and the projection of an image of the GOP as "the party of ideas." National party activities included the following:

- *State party development.* Some 15 regional political directors and four regional finance directors were appointed to work with state party organizations. The political directors coordinated the work in the states of the RNC, the National Republican Congressional Committee (NRCC), and the National Republican Senatorial Committee (NRSC), and they were instrumental in identifying marginal races and allocating national funds. The RNC in 1977 and 1978 also paid the salary of an organizational director in each state party headquarters. (This program was dropped in 1979).
- *Recruitment and training.* The RNC involved itself to an unprecedented extent in state legislative and other local races. The NRCC chairman was credited with helping persuade 100 congressional candidates to run in 1980. A new RNC unit, the Local Elections Campaign Division, worked with state parties to target "winable" districts, recruit candidates, and provide training for candidates and their managers. In 1980 an LECD staff of 31, including 14 field coordinators, worked with some 4,000 legislative candidates.

- *Technical services.* The RNC in 1980 processed some 130 surveys for candidates in addition to five national polls. It processed voter-registration lists for drives in a number of states and provided Republican candidates with precinct-targeting data. The "Repnet" program gave state parties access to the RNC's data-processing capabilities. The national party also had sizable legal, research, media production, and editorial-layout staffs available for consultation and assistance. About 70 congressional candidates were aided by the RNC and NRCC in the production of their TV spots.

- *Financial assistance to candidates.* The RNC estimated the value of its cash and in-kind support for Republican candidates in the 1980 elections at $6.2 million, plus $4.6 million, the maximum allowable, for the presidential campaign. This included contributions totaling $1.7 million for 775 targeted state legislative races. To the $1.7 million given by the RNC to congressional candidates, the NRCC added $3.2 million and the NRSC $5.4 million.[68]

- *Institutional advertising.* The GOP sponsored a $9.4 million television advertising campaign that ran throughout 1980. Unlike most political advertising campaigns, this one focused on the parties, both in its indictments of "Democratic failures" and in its central message: "Vote Republican. For a Change."

- *Issue development.* Five Advisory Councils were formed in 1977, with substantial participation by members of Congress and former Republican administration officials. These groups met over a three-year period, producing an extensive series of attractively packaged pamphlets (for example, "Carter Defense Policy: A Republican Critique"; "A National Effort to Stop Inflation") and laying groundwork for the 1980 platform.

- *Communications.* The RNC developed an extensive publication program that included *Commonsense,* a semi-academic quarterly; *First Monday,* the monthly party magazine; and numerous items disseminating "opposition research," such as "The Carter Record" and "Democratic Watch '80." Themes and materials developed by the RNC were an important component of the national campaign and benefited Republican campaigns across the country.

Brock left the RNC in 1981, and many staff members took positions within the new administration. With a Republican in the White House, the RNC necessarily lost much of its independence. "The President is the leader of our party," Chairman Richard Richards emphasized, "and we take our cues from him." [69] Although policy development, communications, and other operations were greatly scaled down and/or changed in focus, the attrition was in no way comparable to what happened to Ray Bliss's RNC after Nixon's election. The national party's organizational and financial base was more secure and the value of its campaign role more widely recognized—both by the many candidates who had received help and by an administration that saw how the party could make its task of political mobilization easier. Thus as the midterm elections approached, national party operations exceeded in some respects the levels they had reached in 1980.

The RNC raised more in 1981-1982 (some $83 million were contributed to its federal accounts, with a donor base of 1,600,000) than it had before the presidential election, and both the NRCC and NRSC raised more than twice as much as they had in 1979-1980. With the reapportionment of congressional districts largely completed, the RNC in 1982 placed less emphasis on state legislative races than in 1980, but the committee still gave $600,000 to state legislative candidates and placed 10 LECD coordinators in the field. The RNC again carried out an institutional advertising campaign, this time to the tune of $15 million. Throughout 1982 it hammered home successive themes: "Republicans are beginning to make things better," "Give the guy [Reagan] a chance," and finally "Stay the course." The congressional campaign committees increased their services, offering state-of-the-art polling and media-production assistance to their candidates.

The high level of national party activity and support substantially affected the midterm results. The GOP suffered a net loss of 26 House seats and none in the Senate—losses much smaller than the state of the economy and the president's standing in the polls would have led one to predict. Without the activities of the national GOP committees, encouraging attractive contenders to run and providing generous support and essential services once they were in the race, the party's midterm losses would have been substantially greater.[70]

This new national-level activism has centralized Republican party operations. Republican leaders in recent years frequently have chided their Democratic counterparts for restricting the independence of state and local organizations. The revitalization of the national GOP committees, however, has exerted centripetal forces as strong or stronger than those created by the Democrats' procedural reforms—albeit in a way that offers the state parties more in return. Leon Epstein aptly compares Republican activity with the federal government's grants-in-aid system:

> Like categorical grants allocated to states and cities that agree to carry out federal programs in accord with federal standards, the RNC funds and other assistance went to parties and candidates willing and able to maintain organizations or conduct campaigns serving general Republican purposes.[71]

National GOP committees have not given their aid indiscriminately; they have targeted their efforts for maximum effect, often making their aid conditional on the willingness of the candidate or the local organization "to utilize the kind of professionally managed campaign which the RNC and NRCC have found to be most successful." [72] Fund-raising assistance to the state parties, particularly any sharing of contributor lists, has been on the RNC's own terms.

Not surprisingly, this has provoked occasional resistance, when national fund raising has competed with local efforts or when the national party has worked outside of state and local organizations in recruiting and supporting candidates. The 1980 national convention passed a rule (26f) requiring the RNC to obtain the approval of a state's national committee members before contributing to a candidate in that state's Republican primary. But most state organizations most of the time apparently have regarded national party programs as beneficial to their own efforts. The fact that the RNC has not extensively pursued *procedural* nationalization has no doubt contributed to that perception.

Of course, there are often good political reasons for deferring to state and local judgments and for spreading campaign funds around with something less than scientific precision. The campaigns of congressional incumbents offer particularly powerful lessons in the limits of central control: the NRCC and NRSC have been hesitant to withhold funds or to threaten to do so from even the most independent-minded members. Still, the net effect of the financial and organizational successes of the national Republican party has been to strengthen its position vis-à-vis the party's candidates and its state and local organizations. Such shifts are not necessarily zero-sum in character; the national party's growing strength obviously has made resources and roles available to its state and local affiliates that they scarcely could have claimed otherwise.[73] But important shifts in the direction of party nationalization have taken place.

In recent years the national Democratic party has been far less successful organizationally and financially than the GOP. The presidential losses of 1968 and 1972 jolted the party, leading to intense conflicts over internal reform. But the pressures to develop aggressive political and financial strategies were not as strong. The Democratic party still controlled Congress; its members retained access to extensive staff resources and often to reliable financial support from labor and/or from PACs inclined to ingratiate themselves with incumbents. The need that Republican members felt for assistance from their party and for concerted party efforts to capture marginal seats was much less intense on the Democratic side. Nor did the national Democratic party organization enter the 1970s from a position of strength. President Lyndon B. Johnson had allowed the DNC to languish, and the committee agreed to assume $9.3 million in primary and general election debts from Hubert Humphrey's and Robert Kennedy's 1968 presidential campaigns. This hamstrung the party at precisely the time it should have been investing its receipts in the development of a direct-mail operation. Apart from an experiment with telethons in the mid-1970s, the party was slow to adapt to the new fund-raising environment created by the campaign finance laws and direct-mail technology. "We have lost ten to twelve years," DNC Chairman John White said in 1980. "We are now where we should have been in 1969." [74]

Jimmy Carter and his White House staff did little to strengthen the national committee. Its limited 1980 campaign role was almost totally directed at the president's reelection. Wholly subordinate to the Carter-Mondale committee, the DNC, as one staff member acknowledged, became "a place to put the C-team." [75] The DNC and the two Democratic congressional campaign committees raised $18.8 million in 1979-1980, less than one-sixth of the Republican total. The DNC provided some computer and consultation services for voter registration and/or get-out-the-vote drives in 24 targeted states, held a few candidate training sessions, and produced and disseminated radio "actualities," but its campaign operations were at best a pale reflection of the RNC's.[76] In the areas of institutional advertising, field operations, and funding for legislative and other local races, the DNC was not able to make even a minimal effort.

The loss of the presidency and of the Senate in 1980 devastated the Democratic party and pointed up the contribution party organization and finance had made to the GOP's comeback. Charles Manatt, elected DNC chairman in early 1981, described his goal as "trying to do the kind of job that Bill Brock did." [77] Subsequent years have seen some progress. The party leadership has given high priority to direct-mail fund raising. Between 1980 and 1982 the DNC more than tripled its donor base, although its 220,000 contributors still paled in comparison with the RNC's 1,600,000. The DNC produced some "institutional" ads of its own in 1982 (for example, a Republican elephant blundering through a china shop, smashing pieces labeled "social security" and "jobs"), although it had less than $1 million available to air them nationwide.[78] From a special nonfederal account, the DNC contributed some $350,000 to 1982 gubernatorial races (compared with the RNC's $1.1 million). The party's program of campaign workshops and candidate services improved markedly, although in 1982 the budgets for the DNC's political and campaign services (including regional training academies, issue seminars for candidates, and a development program for state parties) still totaled less than $0.5 million. The total operating budget for the DNC in 1982 was only $8 million, compared with $38 million for the RNC.

Some new life also has been evident in the Democratic campaign committees. Both the Democratic Senatorial Campaign Committee (DSCC) and the Democratic Congressional Campaign Committee (DCCC) raised three times as much money in 1981-1982 as in 1979-1980, and they were able to give substantially more support to their candidates ($3.2 million, up from $1.7 million). The DCCC, in particular, contributed in a more concentrated and targeted fashion and plowed substantial sums back into the development of its direct-mail operation. Tables 2-2 and 2-3 permit a further comparison of national committee operations. Extreme Democratic-Republican disparities of scale are evident, and the rates of financial growth between the 1980 and 1982 campaign seasons suggest the gap is not likely to narrow appreciably in the short run. But it can no longer be said that the Democratic party's "nationalization" is solely a matter of procedural reform as opposed to organizational development. Roles pioneered by the RNC and its coordinate congressional committees are being assumed by the Democratic party as well. As columnist David Broder observed in early 1983:

> Since 1980 the Democrats have been doing what the Republicans did under Brock: raising money and pumping it back into party-building projects at the state and local level, while cementing relationships with mayors, governors, state legislators, and members of Congress. The Democrats' progress has been less dramatic, so far, but it is sufficient to make the Republicans nervous about their financial-organizational edge. . . . Having written at considerable length on the weaknesses of the parties, I am delighted to see that the invalids are sitting up and taking nourishment.[79]

Table 2-2 Receipts and Contributions by National Party Committees (Federal Accounts Only), 1979-1982 (in millions of dollars)

	1979-1980			1981-1982		
	Net Receipts*	Number of Contributors	Contributed to (or Spent for) Candidates	Net Receipts*	Number of Contributors	Contributed to (or Spent for) Candidates
Democratic National Committee	$ 15.1	60,000	$ 4.0	$ 16.2	220,000	$ 0.2
Democratic Congressional Campaign Committee	2.1	15,000	0.6	6.5	72,000	0.8
Democratic Senatorial Campaign Committee	1.7	3,000	1.1	5.6	39,000	2.4
Total Democratic Committees	$ 18.8		$ 5.7	$ 28.4		$ 3.4
Republican National Committee	76.2	870,000	6.2	83.5	1,600,000	1.9
National Republican Congressional Committee	28.6	700,000	3.2	58.0	1,200,000	7.5
National Republican Senatorial Committee	23.3	175,000	5.4	48.9	270,000	9.3
Total Republican Committees	$128.1		$14.9	$190.5		$18.6

* Figures are for receipts minus transfers. Refunds, however, are included in FEC receipt totals. RNC data suggest this may result in an overstatement of Republican committee receipts by as much as 2 percent.

SOURCE: For committee receipts and contributions, Federal Election Commission reports. For donor base, estimates by committee staffs and by *National Journal*, May 23, 1981, 923.

Table 2-3 Precampaign Staffing Levels, National Party Committees

	Republican	*Democratic*
National committee		
Administrative	99	37
Finance	105	23
Political	100	39
Communications and research	57	7
Total	361	106
House campaign committee	95	31
Senate campaign committee	85	21

NOTE: Data represent number of staff members as of September 1983. Furnished by committee sources.

The national parties, as we have seen, have become less important in handling executive appointments, distributing patronage positions, and managing presidential campaigns over the past three decades. Yet, in the altered political environment of the 1980s, national party organizations have found new roles—roles that hold out some hope, although surely no guarantee, of longer run party revitalization and renewal.

NOTES

1. The tripartite distinction of parties in the electorate, parties in government, and parties as organizations is taken from V. O. Key's classic text, *Politics, Parties, and Pressure Groups*, 5th ed. (New York: Thomas Y. Crowell Co., 1964), 163-165.
2. Milton Rakove, *Don't Make No Waves, Don't Back No Losers* (Bloomington: Indiana University Press, 1975), 164.
3. William Z. Riordon, *Plunkitt of Tammany Hall* (New York: E. P. Dutton, 1963), 27.
4. Fred I. Greenstein, *The American Party System and the American People*, 2d ed. (Englewood Cliffs, N.J.: Prentice-Hall, 1970), 60; see also Gerald M. Pomper, Rodney Forth, and Maureen Moakley, "Another Machine Withers Away: For Better? For Worse?" *American Politics and Public Policy*, ed. Allan P. Sindler (Washington, D.C.: CQ Press, 1982), 157-159, 183-184.
5. See Robert Merton, *Social Theory and Social Structure*, rev. ed. (Glencoe, Ill.: The Free Press, 1957), 71-82, 193-194; and Fred I. Greenstein, "The Changing Pattern of Urban Party Politics," *Annals of the American Academy of Political and Social Science* 353 (May 1964): 1-13.
6. Thomas M. Guterbock, *Machine Politics in Transition: Party and Community in Chicago* (Chicago: University of Chicago Press, 1980), 15, 27, 34. While Guterbock found Chicago's party organization to have retained its hierarchical structure and its critical reliance on patronage, he detected changes in other areas, particularly in the sort of electoral appeals the organization was constrained to make. The dispensing of favors or recognition no longer sufficed to mobilize voters; party leaders had to make symbolic appeals and identify with broader sorts of community improvement if they were to keep their electoral base intact. Ibid., chaps. 7-10.
7. See the judgments issued by U.S. District Court Judge N. J. Bua, Northern District of Illinois, Eastern Division, April 4 and June 21, 1983, pursuant to *Michael L. Shakman* v. *Democratic Organization of Cook County*, 508 F. Supp. 1059 (1981) and 481 F. Supp. 1315 (1979). On Washington's election see Michael Preston, "The Election of Harold Washington," *PS* 16 (Summer 1983): 486-488.
8. Samuel J. Eldersveld, *Political Parties in American Society* (New York: Basic Books, 1982), 145. See also Frank Sorauf, *Party Politics in America*, 4th ed. (Boston: Little, Brown & Co., 1980), 67-72.
9. The data do not, however, suggest a decline in organizational activity in Detroit over the 24-year period; among Democrats, the level of activity actually has shown a slight increase. See Samuel J.

Eldersveld, *Political Parties: A Behavioral Analysis* (Chicago: Rand McNally & Co., 1964), chap. 13, and idem, *Parties in American Society*, 146-148. A study of Pittsburgh precinct committeemen reveals comparable levels of activity/inactivity, but with some signs of decline during the 1970s— more positions unfilled, a failure to recruit younger leaders, fewer signs of ongoing activity. See Lee S. Weinberg, Michael Margolis, and David Ranck, "Local Party Organization: From Disaggregation to Disintegration" (Paper delivered at the annual meeting of the American Political Science Association, Washington, D.C., 1980).

10. Raymond Wolfinger, "Why Political Machines Have Not Withered Away and Other Revisionist Thoughts," *Journal of Politics* 34 (May 1972): 374-377. In a more recent study Michael Johnston also concludes that patronage politics "has not withered away" in New Haven. But in examining how 675 Comprehensive Employment and Training Act (CETA) jobs were disposed of there in 1974, he finds that conventionally assumed patterns of organizational maintenance did not hold; ethnic particularism apparently overshadowed considerations of vote maximization and the rewarding and recruitment of workers. See Johnston, "Patrons and Clients, Jobs and Machines: A Case Study of the Uses of Patronage," *American Political Science Review* 73 (June 1979): 385-398.

11. Wolfinger, "Political Machines," 383-398. The author is particularly intrigued by the case of California, which although it has "a cosmopolitan population and an urban, industrial economy, also displays virtually no signs of machine politics." (398)

12. On the variety of factors contributing to the recent decline of the Democratic machine in a northeastern metropolitan county, see Pomper, Forth, and Moakley, "Another Machine Withers Away," 162-173. For an account of the pitfalls Mayor Kevin White confronted when he attempted to recreate a machine in Boston in the late 1970s, see Fox Butterfield, "Troubles of Boston's Mayor are Tied to Political Machine," *New York Times*, December 26, 1982, 1, 20.

13. James L. Gibson et al., "Whither the Local Parties?" (Paper delivered at the annual meeting of the Western Political Science Association, San Diego, California, 1982), 18 and Table 6.

14. Greenstein, "Changing Pattern," 11.

15. In the highly publicized and well-advertised Gore-Brock Senate campaign in Tennessee in 1970, Democratic voter contact still had a measurable effect, increasing turnout by some 4 percent in minority precincts and decreasing the defection rate among Democratic identifiers in low-income white precincts. See David E. Price and Michael Lupfer, "Volunteers for Gore: The Impact of a Precinct-Level Canvass in Three Tennessee Cities," *Journal of Politics* 35 (May 1973): 410-438.

16. Michael M. Wolfe, "Personal-Contact Campaigning in Presidential Elections" (Paper delivered at the annual meeting of the Midwest Political Science Association, Chicago, Ill., 1979), 9-15.

17. Gibson et al., "Whither the Local Parties?" 16, 25, 27 (Tables 3, 9, 10). See also Paul A. Beck, "Environment and Party: The Impact of Political and Demographic County Characteristics on Party Behavior," *American Political Science Review* 68 (September 1974): 1229-1244; and James L. Gibson et al., "Assessing Institutional Party Strength" (Paper delivered at the annual meeting of the Midwest Political Science Association, Chicago, Ill., 1981), 37-42.

18. James Q. Wilson, *The Amateur Democrat: Club Politics in Three Cities* (Chicago: University of Chicago Press, 1962), 4.

19. Ibid., 340.

20. Peter B. Clark and James Q. Wilson, "Incentive Systems: A Theory of Organization," *Administrative Science Quarterly* 6 (September 1961): 129-166.

21. See E. Gene DeFelice, "Separating Professionalism from Pragmatism: A Research Note on the Study of Political Parties," *American Journal of Political Science* 25 (November 1981): 801-802, 806; and C. Richard Hofstetter, "The Amateur Politician: A Problem in Construct Validation," *Midwest Journal of Political Science* 15 (February 1971): 31-56.

22. Eldersveld, *Political Parties: A Behavioral Analysis*, 132, 278, 287, 303.

23. Eldersveld, *Parties in American Society*, 177-179. Precise comparisons with studies that have used Wilson's typology are complicated by the fact that some of the incentives Eldersveld regards as "impersonal" (politics as a "way of life," strong subjective attachment to the party) seem, in Wilson's terms, to be more "solidary" than "purposive."

24. Eldersveld, *Political Parties: A Behavioral Analysis*, 226-227.

25. Robert S. Hirschfield, Bert E. Swanson, and Blanche D. Blank, "A Profile of Political Activists in Manhattan," *Western Political Quarterly* 15 (September 1962): 489-506; Dennis S. Ippolito and Lewis Bowman, "Goals and Activities of Party Officials in a Suburban Community," *Western Political Quarterly* 22 (September 1969): 572-580; Ippolito, "Motivational Reorientation and Changes among Party Activists," *Journal of Politics* 31 (November 1969): 1098-1101; Bowman, Ippolito, and William Donaldson, "Incentives for the Maintenance of Grassroots Political Activism," *Midwest Journal of Political Science* 13 (February 1969): 126-139; Bowman and G. R. Boynton, "Recruitment Patterns among Local Party Officials: A Model and Some Preliminary Findings in Selected Locales," *American Political Science Review* 60 (September 1966): 667-676; M. Margaret Conway and Frank B. Feigert, "Motivation, Incentive Systems, and the Political Party Organization," *American Political Science Review* 62 (December 1968): 1159-1173.

26. The generalizations that follow draw on Charles W. Wiggins and William L. Turk, "State Party Chairmen: A Profile," *Western Political Quarterly* 23 (June 1970): 330-331; and Robert J.

48   *Bringing Back the Parties*

Huckshorn, *Party Leadership in the States* (Amherst: University of Massachusetts Press, 1976), chap. 5.

27. Aaron Wildavsky, "The Goldwater Phenomenon: Purists, Politicians, and the Two-Party System," in *The Revolt Against the Masses* (New York: Basic Books, 1971), 246-247.

28. Ibid., 253, 255-256.

29. Wildavsky, "The Meaning of 'Youth' in the Struggle for Control of the Democratic Party," in *The Revolt Against the Masses*, 270, 282.

30. John W. Soule and James W. Clarke, "Amateurs and Professionals: A Study of Delegates to the 1968 Democratic National Convention," *American Political Science Review* 64 (September 1970): 888-998; Soule and Wilma E. McGrath, "A Comparative Study of Presidential Nomination Conventions: The Democrats 1968 and 1972," *American Journal of Political Science* 19 (August 1975), 501-517. Interview questions tapped the delegates' commitment to intraparty democracy and to programmatic parties, the primacy they gave to electoral victory, their willingness to compromise, and whether their work for the party depended on the presence of favored candidates or issues. While recognizing that the various components of amateurism did not always cohere, the authors nonetheless treated their responses interchangeably as indicators of a single orientation. See also Jeane Kirkpatrick, *The New Presidential Elite* (New York: Russell Sage Foundation, 1976). Using questions designed to determine whether delegates placed a high value on party service and took the party's organizational well-being into account in making their decisions, Kirkpatrick found that 44 percent of the 1972 Democratic delegates were "unconcerned with or opposed to giving weight to organizational maintenance." (138) On the relation of this "organizational support index" to amateur/professional indices, see 136, 157, 570.

31. Denis G. Sullivan et al., "Candidates, Caucuses, and Issues: The Democratic Convention, 1976," in *The Impact of the Electoral Process*, ed. Louis Maisel and Joseph Cooper (Beverly Hills: Sage Publications, 1977), 116-117. A greater similarity between 1972 and 1976 delegates was found by John S. Jackson, III, Jesse C. Brown, and Barbara L. Brown, "Recruitment, Representation, and Political Values: The 1976 Democratic National Convention Delegates," *American Politics Quarterly* 6 (April 1978): 206-207 (replicating questions asked of 1972 delegates by Kirkpatrick, *New Presidential Elite*, 126).

32. Thomas H. Roback, "Amateurs and Professionals: Delegates to the 1972 Republican National Convention," *Journal of Politics* 37 (May 1975): 441, 444, 462. Kirkpatrick finds a more "professional" orientation toward the convention's goals and a higher ranking on the organizational support index for 1972 Republican delegates than Roback's data would lead one to expect. Kirkpatrick, *New Presidential Elite*, 126, 139.

33. Thomas H. Roback, "Motivation for Activism among Republican National Convention Delegates: Continuity and Change 1972-1976," *Journal of Politics* 42 (February 1980): 184.

34. Denis G. Sullivan, "Party Unity: Appearance and Reality," *Political Science Quarterly* 92 (Winter 1977-1978): 640-643.

35. Robert Salisbury, "The Urban Party Organization Member," *Public Opinion Quarterly* 24 (Winter 1965-1966): 563. See also Weinberg et al., "Local Party Organization," who find that an increasing number of Pittsburgh committeemen display the characteristics of the "jaded professional," doing only the "minimum necessary to maintain his political job or . . . to stay in the party leaders' good graces." (8, 24)

36. See Denis G. Sullivan et al., *The Politics of Representation: The Democratic Convention 1972* (New York: St. Martin's Press, 1974), chap. 5.

37. John J. Havick, "Amateurs and Professionals at the 1972 Democratic Convention," *Polity* 10 (Spring 1978): 448-457.

38. Sullivan et al., *Politics of Representation*, chaps. 4-5; Jeffrey L. Pressman and Denis G. Sullivan, "Convention Reform and Conventional Wisdom: An Empirical Assessment of Democratic Party Reforms," *Political Science Quarterly* 89 (Fall 1974): 546-558.

39. Wilson, *Amateur Democrat*, 5.

40. Roback, "Motivation for Activism," 195-200; Ippolito, "Motivational Reorientation," 1098-1101.

41. Bowman, Ippolito, and Donaldson, "Incentives for the Maintenance of Activism," 132-137; Eldersveld, *Political Parties: A Behavioral Analysis*, 287; Conway and Feigert, "Motivation, Incentive Systems, and the Party Organization," 1169.

42. See Rhodes Cook, "Democrats Develop Tactics; Laying Groundwork for 1984," *Congressional Quarterly Weekly Report*, July 3, 1982, 1591. An extensive study of delegates to state party conventions in 1980 found high levels of *both* purposive motivation and party loyalty, and a positive correlation between the two; see Alan Abramowitz, John McGlennon, and Ronald Rapoport, "If The Party's Over, Who are All Those People Wearing Funny Hats?" (Paper delivered at the annual meeting of the American Political Science Association, Denver, Colo., 1982).

43. Riordon, *Plunkitt*, 17.

44. Huckshorn, *Party Leadership in the States*, 111-113.

45. Key, *Politics, Parties, and Pressure Groups*, 371. See also Austin Ranney, *Curing the Mischiefs of Faction: Party Reform in America* (Berkeley: University of California Press, 1976), 62-69, 115-134.

46. Quotes from Ranney, *Curing the Mischiefs of Faction*, 124-125; and James S. Chase, *Emergence of the Presidential Nominating Convention, 1789-1832* (Urbana: University of Illinois Press, 1973), 64.

47. For a wide variety of assessments by state chairmen and political scientists at a time when considerable disillusion with the Progressive reforms was setting in, see the special issue of the *Annals of the American Academy of Political and Social Science* 106 (March 1923): 45-54, 103, 122, 138, 153, 175-176.

48. On recent efforts to reintroduce preprimary party endorsements in Massachusetts and California, see Kay Lawson,"California: The Uncertainties of Reform," and Jerome Mileur, "Massachusetts: The Democratic Party Charter Movement," in *Party Renewal in America*, ed. Gerald M. Pomper (New York: Praeger Publishers, 1980), 129, 132, 163-164.

49. Larry Sabato, "Gubernatorial Politics and the New Campaign Technology," *State Government* 53 (Summer 1980): 151. See also Robert Agranoff, ed., *The New Style in Election Campaigns*, 2d ed. (Boston: Holbrook Press, 1976).

50. Larry Sabato, *The Rise of Political Consultants* (New York: Basic Books, 1981), 286, 289.

51. Cornelius P. Cotter et al., "State Party Organizations and the Thesis of Party Decline" (Paper delivered at the annual meeting of the American Political Science Association, Washington, D.C., 1980), 36. See also Huckshorn and Bibby, "State Parties in an Era of Political Change," in *The Future of American Political Parties*, ed. Joel L. Fleishman (Englewood Cliffs, N.J.: Prentice-Hall, 1982), 93-98; Gibson et al., "Assessing Party Organizational Strength," *American Journal of Political Science* 27 (May 1983): 193-222; and John Bibby et al., "Parties in State Politics," in *Politics in the American States*, 4th ed., edited by Virginia Gray, Herbert Jacob, and Kenneth Vines (Boston: Little, Brown & Co., 1983), 76-85.

52. Alexander Heard, *The Costs of Democracy* (Garden City, N.Y.: Anchor Books, 1962), 364.

53. Huckshorn, *Party Leadership in the States*, 254-255; Huckshorn and Bibby, "State Parties in an Era of Change," 94, 96.

54. Bibby et al., "Parties in State Politics," 83. See also Gibson et al., "Assessing Party Organizational Strength," 211-215; and Cotter et al., "State Organizations and Thesis of Party Decline," 8 and Figures 2-3.

55. Gibson et al., "Assessing Party Organizational Strength," 201-205. See also Bibby et al., "Parties in State Politics," 81. They note that "the extent of recruitment is inversely related to the desirability of the office and the party's electoral prospects"—i.e, the party's role is likely to be greatest in legislative or other low-visibility contests, and/or where the prospects for victory are poor.

56. See the accounts in Cornelius Cotter and Bernard Hennessy, *Politics Without Power: The National Party Committees* (New York: Atherton Press, 1964), 13-16, 20-22; and Ranney, *Curing the Mischiefs of Faction*, 171-180.

57. Hugh A. Bone, *Party Committees and National Politics* (Seattle: University of Washington Press, 1958), 150.

58. Ranney, *Curing the Mischiefs of Faction*, 179.

59. Cotter and Hennessey, *Politics Without Power*, 7-8. See also Cornelius Cotter and John F. Bibby, "Institutional Development of Parties and the Thesis of Party Decline," *Political Science Quarterly* 95 (Spring 1980): 2-12.

60. General treatments include Charles Longley, "Party Nationalization in America," in *Paths to Political Reform*, ed. William Crotty (Lexington, Mass.: Lexington Books, 1980), chap. 5; Longley, "National Party Renewal," in *Party Renewal in America*, chap. 5; John F. Bibby, "Party Renewal in the National Republican Party," in *Party Renewal in America*, chap. 7; and Cotter and Bibby, "Institutional Development of Parties."

61. This account draws on Cotter and Bibby, "Institutional Development," 13-17; and Ranney, *Curing the Mischiefs of Faction*, 180-187.

62. Ranney, *Curing the Mischiefs of Faction*, 185.

63. See Longley, "Party Nationalization in America," 172-175.

64. On the politics of the 1974 midterm conference that adopted the charter, see Sullivan, Pressman, and Arterton, *Explorations in Convention Decision Making*, chap. 3. Some charter proponents sought a strengthening of the national party as an end in itself, taking a position similar to that of the "responsible-party" advocates described in Chapter 4 of this book. But others, many of whom were "perceived as weakly enough identified with the party to make a walkout threat credible," (63) seemed to regard the charter as a means for promoting demographic representation and the influence of their groups within the party. This led many "regulars" to conclude that the party's organizational strength would be best served by continued decentralization.

65. Bibby, "Party Renewal in the Republican Party," 105. The RNC chair was given a fixed term of two years, for example, and his discretion in appointing the Executive Committee was curtailed. Bibby attributes these actions to resentment at the way President Nixon's party chairmen had been named and at their tendency "to act as presidential agents rather than as RNC spokesmen."

66. David Broder, "Bliss Remembered," *Washington Post*, August 12, 1981, A25. On the programs initiated by Bliss, see John F. Bibby and Robert J. Huckshorn, "Out-Party Strategy: Republican National Committee Rebuilding Politics, 1964-66," in *Republican Politics*, ed. Bernard Cosman and Robert J. Huckshorn (New York: Praeger Publishers, 1968), 212-231.

67. Michael J. Malbin, "The Republican Revival," *Fortune*, August 25, 1980, 85. The account of Republican campaign efforts that follows also draws on Bibby, "Party Renewal in the Republican Party"; M. Margaret Conway, "Political Party Nationalization, Campaign Activities, and Local Party

Development" (Paper delivered at the annual meeting of the Midwest Political Science Association, Cincinnati, Ohio, 1981); Thomas E. Mann and Norman J. Ornstein, "The Republican Surge in Congress," in *The American Elections of 1980,* ed. Austin Ranney (Washington, D.C.: American Enterprise Institute for Public Policy Research, 1981), chap. 8; and David Adamany, "Political Parties in the 1980s," in *Money and Politics in the United States: Financing Elections in the 1980s,* ed. Michael J. Malbin (Chatham, N.J.: American Enterprise Institute for Public Policy Research/Chatham House, 1984), chap. 3.

68. Republican National Committee, *1981 Chairman's Report,* 12, 22-24; Federal Election Commission release, February 21, 1982.

69. Dom Bonafede, "Can the DNC Adjust to Being a Minority? Can the RNC Reverse 50 Years of History?" *National Journal,* September 5, 1981, 1583.

70. Gary C. Jacobson, "Reagan, Reaganomics, and Strategic Politics in 1982: A Test of Alternative Theories of Midterm Congressional Elections" (Paper delivered at the annual meeting of the American Political Science Association, Chicago, Ill., 1983). For an overview of national party activity in the 1982 congressional races, see Larry Sabato, "Parties, PACs and Independent Groups," in *The American Elections of 1982,* ed., Thomas Mann and Norman Ornstein (Washington, D.C.: American Enterprise Institute for Public Policy Research, 1983), 73-82; see also "The Chairman's Report - 1982," *First Monday,* January-February 1983, 13-20.

71. Leon D. Epstein, "Party Confederations and Party Nationalization," *Publius* 12 (Fall 1982): 86.

72. Conway, "Political Party Nationalization," 8.

73. See Cotter and Bibby, "Institutional Development," 12-13, on the need to conceive of party "nationalization" not simply as the subordination of state and local units but as increased *interdependence* among different levels of party organization.

74. Timothy B. Clark, "The RNC Prospers, the DNC Struggles as They Face the 1980 Elections," *National Journal,* September 27, 1980, 1618-1619.

75. Adamany, "Parties in the 1980s," 86.

76. See Leslie C. Francis, "The Democratic National Committee and the 1980 Elections" (February 1980), a memorandum written by the DNC's executive director, largely in response to criticisms of campaign operations by state chairs and other national committee members. DNC aides questioned this report's claims, according to Adamany, "Parties in the 1980s," 88-91.

77. Martin Schram, "Why Can't Democrats Be More Like Republicans? They're Trying," *Washington Post,* March 23, 1982, A2.

78. On this and other Democratic operations in 1982, see Sabato, "Parties, PACs, and Independent Groups," 82-86.

79. David S. Broder, "The Invalids Are Sitting Up," *Washington Post,* February 9, 1983, A19.

The Parties in Government 3

"For government to function," wrote V. O. Key in an often quoted passage, "the obstructions of the constitutional mechanism must be overcome, and it is the party that casts a web, at times weak, at times strong, over the dispersed organs of government and gives them a semblance of unity."[1] In the previous chapters we examined the extent of party identification and voting in the electorate and the resources possessed and functions performed by party organizations at various levels. We now turn to the parties as networks of coordination and control within and between the branches of government. This party "web," remarkably resilient in some respects but dangerously frayed in others, is sufficiently weakened to prompt doubts about the capacities of our institutions to overcome "the obstructions of the constitutional mechanism" and the threat of governmental fragmentation and immobility.[2]

The Congressional Parties

Party Voting

"Over the course of this century there has been a clear and substantial decline in the strength of party as a determinant of voting," congressional scholar Joseph Cooper concludes.[3] Figure 3-1 shows that "party votes" (votes finding 90 percent of the Democrats on one side and 90 percent of the Republicans on the other) accounted for about 40 percent of all House votes around the turn of the century but only some 5 percent of House votes 50 years later. Use of a less demanding standard of party voting—when a majority of one party votes against a majority of the other—shows an equally significant decline, from the 70 percent range in the earlier period to around 40 percent in more recent years. As Figure 3-1 indicates, the pattern has been somewhat irregular: the decline in party voting was temporarily checked by the landslide election of President Warren G. Harding in 1920 and by the increased polarization of the parties produced by the New Deal realignment in the 1930s. Neverthe-

Figure 3-1   Party Voting in the House, 1895-1953

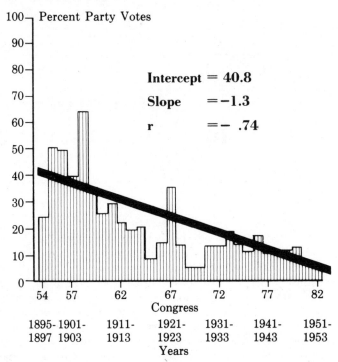

NOTE: "Party voting" here signifies the percentage of recorded votes where 90 percent of the Democrats opposed 90 percent of the Republicans.

SOURCE: David Brady, Joseph Cooper, and Patricia Hurley, "The Decline of Party in the U.S. House of Representatives, 1887-1968," *Legislative Studies Quarterly* 4 (1979): 384-385. Copyright © 1980 by the Comparative Legislative Research Center of the University of Iowa. Reprinted by permission.

less, the overall trend is unmistakable and has been subject only to limited variations in either house since the 1940s.

Party voting reached its height during the speakerships of Thomas B. Reed and Clarence Cannon, the so-called "czars" of the House during the 1895-1910 period of Republican ascendancy. These leaders possessed extraordinary prerogatives and resources: the chairmanship of the Rules Committee, the power to make all committee assignments and appoint chairmen, and wide discretion to refer bills to committees, to grant or deny recognition to members, and otherwise to control the flow of House business. But younger, reform-minded Republicans from the Midwest and West became increasingly frustrated with Cannon's tight control and his use of his position for conservative policy ends. They combined forces with the Democrats and between 1909 and 1911 reduced the powers of the Speaker drastically. He was forbidden from naming members to or serving on the Rules Committee; procedures were established whereby bills could be placed on a "calendar" and considered on the floor without explicit recognition from the Speaker; and provision was made for the election of all standing committees by the full House (upon recommendation by the parties' committees on committees and caucuses).

When the Democrats gained control of the House in 1911, they consolidated the power of the party caucus. All party members were bound to support any position adopted by two-thirds of the caucus, and much of the power formerly held by the Speaker flowed into the hands of Majority Leader Oscar Underwood, who also chaired the Ways and Means Committee and the Democratic Committee on Committees, a function that the party gave to the Democratic members of Ways and Means. Underwood worked closely with President Woodrow Wilson and Senate Majority Leader John Worth Kern in developing party policy and in utilizing the caucuses to mobilize partisan support. These early years of the Wilson administration represent "one of the rare times when party government characterized the political system." [4] But the arrangement did not prove stable: members resisted efforts to bind their votes, and divisions within the party and the leadership made the use of the caucus more and more difficult. Republicans, back in power in 1920, experimented with a steering committee structure but eventually came to rely on an informal leadership group composed of the Speaker, floor leaders, and a few trusted lieutenants. Democratic leadership assumed a similar pattern after the GOP lost control of the House in 1930. As Joseph Cooper and David W. Brady note:

> ...by the late 1920s reliance on party control mechanisms to coordinate action and enforce cohesion had largely passed from the scene. Instead, the majority party was reduced to operating primarily through a small coterie of men, gathered around the Speaker, who met to plan strategy and whose power of direction was much less than that of the caucus or even the steering committee in their heyday. [5]

The decline in party voting was prompted, in part, by these reductions in the powers of the Speaker and other party leaders. But broader societal developments contributed to both trends. The rise of party voting in the 1890s was rooted in an electoral realignment that left the parties ideologically and demographically polarized. Democratic districts were concentrated in the South and West and were mainly agricultural in character, while most eastern and midwestern districts, and those of industrial character, were in Republican hands. By 1900 this polarization and internal party homogeneity were becoming less pronounced. The rise of the Progressive movement in the Republican party strained party discipline and was directly linked to the congressional revolt against Cannon and to the split between William H. Taft and Theodore Roosevelt that gave the presidency to Woodrow Wilson in 1912. Similar developments made Democratic unity more elusive in the post-New Deal period, as the southern wing of the party became increasingly disaffected from the social agenda of Democratic presidents, and the "conservative coalition"—an alliance between Republicans and southern Democrats— became a prominent fixture of congressional voting. Throughout the period the norms and assumptions underwriting party regularity were subjected to periodic attack, and public esteem for the parties waned. [6]

While party ties have declined substantially as a determinant of congressional voting since the 1890s, Figures 3-2 and 3-3 permit a closer examination of the past 30 years. The postwar erosion of the parties-in-the-electorate has been accompanied by a continuing decline of party voting in Congress. Among Democrats, the share of the party's seats held by southerners has declined, and southern members have become less uniformly conservative in their voting. This trend has not produced higher levels of overall Democratic cohesion, however, because northern Democrats concurrently have become *less* party oriented in their voting. The decline seems to have leveled off in both parties since the early 1970s, and the average member's party support score took an upturn (perhaps temporarily) in the early years of Ronald Reagan's presidency. Party polarization was especially evident in the Senate, where the GOP showed its greatest unity since the 83d Congress (1953-1955) when it last controlled the chamber. The same degree of polarization was not present in the House, but the average "party unity" scores of representatives in both parties, which had been edging up since the mid-1970s, reached levels reminiscent of the Kennedy years.

Party voting varies considerably from issue to issue. In the postwar era, voting patterns have been most consistently tied to party on questions of social welfare—labor law, housing, aid to education, health programs—despite the dissent of southern Democratic conservatives. Agricultural assistance also has been a highly partisan issue. Governmental management of the economy, another issue that was central to the New Deal alignment, also has had a polarizing effect. That effect has lessened, however, and splits within the parties have widened as the government-management agenda has shifted from public versus private power, public works, and tax issues to include divisive questions of environmental protection, energy, and inflation control. Party voting generally has been less pronounced on civil rights and civil liberties issues and on questions of international and military policy.[7]

Despite such variations, a member's party affiliation remains the best single predictor of his or her vote. Party voting in the U.S. Congress does not approach the levels it reaches in parliamentary systems, but the average member still votes with his or her party on some 70 percent of the votes that divide majorities of Democrats and Republicans.

What accounts for the persistence of party voting? John Kingdon's careful study of roll-call voting in the House suggests that partisan divisions flow naturally from the contrasting sorts of constituencies that Democrats and Republicans represent. These divisions are reinforced by patterns of association: members generally associate with others of a similar background and viewpoint, and hence of the same party, and such communication with trusted colleagues is a frequent source of voting cues. But Kingdon finds few members identifying party leaders as a direct influence on their votes.[8] Had he focused his inquiry more sharply on votes identified as critical by the party leadership or on members considered to be in a "swing" position, he might have discovered a more significant leadership role. In any event, leadership influence on congressional voting may be less a matter of giving cues on specific votes than of

Figure 3-2 Party Voting in the House and Senate (Percentage of Votes Finding Majorities of Democrats and Republicans on Opposite Sides), 1949-1982

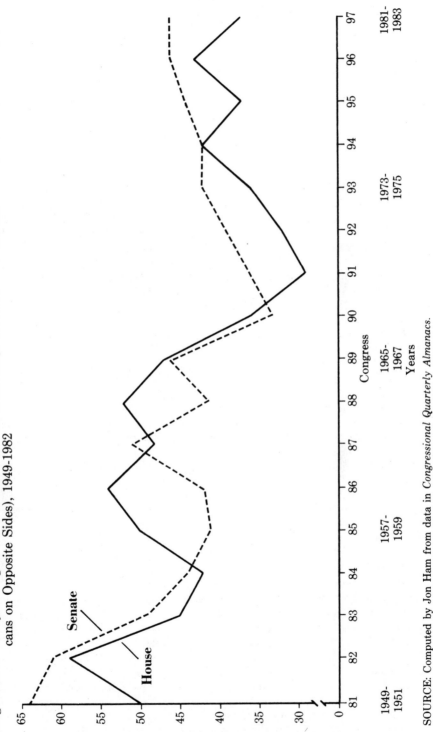

SOURCE: Computed by Jon Ham from data in *Congressional Quarterly Almanacs.*

structuring the way decisions are made and providing certain basic incentives for party regularity. And the parties may influence the shaping of congressional decisions in ways that are imperfectly reflected in roll-call cohesion scores. Thus, it is important to examine the congressional parties as institutions. In what sort of political and organizational environment do they exist? What resources do they command, and what roles do they play? And how promising are the recent changes in procedure that have been designed to enhance their role?

The Electoral Context

House Speaker Sam Rayburn, who served from 1940 to 1961 (except for two Congresses when the Republicans organized the House), and Senate Majority Leader Lyndon Johnson (1955-1961) are often regarded as the strongest postwar party leaders in Congress. Both, indeed, were skillful and persuasive men. But what is most striking about them is the extent to which their leadership was a matter of brokerage and bargaining, concession and compromise. Their formal powers were much less formidable than those of Reed and Cannon, and they were far less able or inclined to use negative sanctions against recalcitrant members. They preferred to traffic in rewards and favors and to rely on personal obligations and loyalties. Rayburn and Johnson did not generally seek to be policy leaders and, as we shall see in Chapter 9, they resisted the efforts of the national party to articulate advanced Democratic positions. Rather, their concern was to find the midpoint among contesting views, to arrange accommodations and restrain conflict. They generally eschewed the use of formal party mechanisms such as the caucus or policy committee, preferring to work informally and to put together ad hoc alliances and agreements that sometimes crossed party lines. This transition from "hierarchy" to "bargaining" as the mode of congressional leadership occurred not because Rayburn was "inherently a less tough or more affective person than Cannon or Reed ... but rather because of his weaker sources of leverage and the heightened individualism of members." [9] That Rayburn and Johnson were masters of the art should not obscure the severe constraints under which they labored and which no leader could have overcome: a party electorate that was badly divided regionally and ideologically, and congressional followers whose interests militated against a disciplined, programmatic party role.

The contemporary Congress has become in many ways even less amenable to party control than it was under Rayburn and Johnson. The most obvious point of linkage between the decline of parties-in-the-electorate, state and local party organizations, and congressional parties is the context in which most members seek reelection. Members are increasingly "on their own" electorally and less dependent on the parties.[10] They face electorates less inclined to vote for them on partisan grounds alone and a public largely unconcerned about their party loyalty once in office. Members are generally nominated, not by party caucuses or conventions, but by direct primaries, and few party organizations retain the power to influence decisively the nomination process. Congres-

Figure 3-3 "Party Unity" Voting in the House and Senate (Average Individual Support for Party on Votes Dividing Party Majorities), 1949-1982

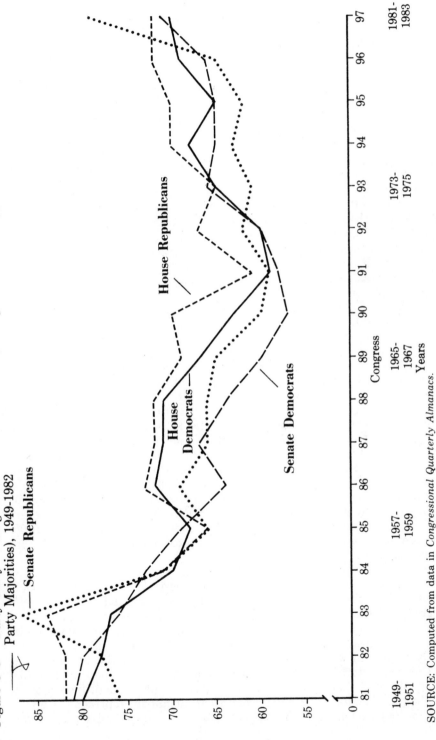

SOURCE: Computed from data in *Congressional Quarterly Almanacs.*

sional candidates must raise their own funds and build their own organization at the primary stage and often for the general election as well. The availability of new campaign technologies, and the threat that their opponents might use them, tempt candidates (especially senatorial candidates, who have more resources and must run statewide) to invest in media, direct-mail, and voter-contact strategies that essentially bypass the parties.

Even in areas where local or state parties are cohesive and well organized, their members are likely to be only casually or sporadically interested in the party's national platform and to offer only limited inducements toward teamsmanship in Washington. National partisan swings have become less and less determinative of election outcomes in most congressional districts, and ticket splitting has become endemic. Understandably, members are inclined to see constituent service and visibility in their districts as more crucial to their electoral fortunes than whatever advantages they might gain from high presidential or party support scores in Congress. It is hardly surprising that when they perceive a conflict between party cues and district interest, members of the U.S. Congress, in contrast to their parliamentary counterparts, frequently defect from their party.

Such an electoral context, volatile and largely unstructured, can increase members' sense of vulnerability. But it also puts a premium on personal electoral entrepreneurship and makes it easier for members to insulate themselves from national partisan trends. The result, at least in the House, has been an enhancement of the electoral advantages of incumbency. In most years, about 90 percent of House incumbents seek reelection, and more than 90 percent of these win. Even in years when a party's fortunes are declining, its members of Congress generally do very well: in the post-Watergate election of 1974, for example, 78 percent of Republican House incumbents survived Democratic challenges; 89 percent of Democratic incumbents survived the Reagan election of 1980; and 85 percent of Republican incumbents prevailed over their challengers in the midst of the Democratic comeback of 1982. Since the 1950s this pattern has been firmly established, and the *margin* by which incumbents typically win has increased substantially. The proportion of House incumbents winning by less than a "landslide" (that is, by less than 60 percent of the vote) has decreased from approximately 40 to 25 percent in a typical year.

The impact of incumbency voting on party voting in House elections is direct and substantial. "Since 1972," Albert Cover observes, "about half of those identifying with the challenger's party have deserted their party's [House] candidate in contested elections involving an incumbent." In 1980, for example, 89 percent of Democrats voted for their party's congressional candidate when he or she was an incumbent, but only 45 percent when he or she was a challenger; Republicans voted at a 93 percent rate for GOP incumbents, but only at a 65 percent rate for Republican challengers. Overall, 48 percent of party identifiers proved willing to abandon their party when their incumbent representative was of the opposite party.[11] Incumbents also enjoy major advantages over challengers in the familiarity of their names and in the opportunities they have to serve voters and impress them favorably. One survey found fully 90 percent of the voters experiencing some form of contact with incumbent members of the House, but only 44 percent reporting any contact with challengers; 23 percent had met the incumbent, but only 4 percent the challenger; 71 percent had received mail from the incumbent, but only 16 percent from the challenger. Overwhelming majorities also report holding a favorable impression of incumbent House members—assessments based more on personal characteristics and on constituency service than on policy or partisan considerations.[12]

Challengers fare better in Senate elections, but not because party-line voting is more common in these races. Senate elections are more volatile. The reelection rate of senators reached a postwar low of 55 percent in 1980, with nine incumbents defeated in the general election and four in primaries, but went up to 93 percent two years later, when only two incumbents were defeated. Senate elections also are more heavily influenced by issues and media images. Party identifiers are no more reluctant to vote against the Senate candidate of their party than against the House candidate, but they are considerably more willing to cast their Senate vote for a nonincumbent. It is harder for senators than for representatives to maintain a favorable image based on constituent service. Senators serve larger numbers of people and receive far more media coverage. Thus their constituents often perceive them in relation to divisive national issues rather than through personal contact or assistance. These factors also influence candidate recruitment. Because senators appear more vulnerable than House members, they often draw stronger and better financed challengers—and this in turn reinforces the pattern of Senate vulnerability.[13]

House and Senate elections thus have evolved in somewhat different directions, but in both cases the result has been to loosen the tie between members and the parties-in-the-electorate and to weaken the incentives for party regularity in Congress. Electoral circumstances also have influenced the way members of Congress have organized the institution. Here, too, the net effect has been to weaken the parties. To an extent, congressional incumbents are "the accidental beneficiaries of behavioral changes they had no part in creating or fostering ... an unraveling of party allegiance among voters and a resulting shift to the incumbency cue in voter decisions."[14] But members have hardly been passive participants in this process. They have not merely adapted to the increased electoral relevance of incumbency, but have acted in ways that heightened that relevance and decreased their dependence on the party even further.

David Mayhew has noted that members seeking to enhance their electoral prospects are likely to engage in three types of activity. They *advertise,* building name familiarity and a favorable image through newsletters, media reports to the district, and huge volumes of mail. They *claim credit,* performing favors for constituents and publicizing their own role in securing funds and projects for the district. And they *take positions,* making speeches, introducing bills and amendments, assuming postures designed for maximum electoral appeal.[15] The rise of television as the dominant medium of political communication has heightened both the importance of such strategies and their potential electoral impact. And the proliferation of governmental agencies and programs has greatly increased the opportunities and political rewards for constituent service and the securing of benefits for the district.

Many of the organizational features of the modern Congress can best be understood in terms of members' quest for electoral security. Resources for advertising, credit claiming, and position taking have increased significantly. Between 1960 and the mid-1970s, authorizations for personal staff more than doubled in both the House and Senate; the percentage of staff assigned to home-district offices increased from 14 to 34 percent; the allowance for expense-paid trips back home went from three trips annually to 26 trips for representatives and 42 to 46 for senators; and the annual volume of franked mail doubled.[16] Obviously, the increased advantages of incumbency have not fallen on members inadvertently. Nor have their efforts to enhance their electability stopped at their own office doors: they have led to organizational "reforms" that have greatly dispersed legislative authority and resources in both chambers. It is this aspect of the congressional quest for electoral security that has affected the current condition of the parties most directly, and to which we now turn.

Parceling Out Power

Committees dominate policy making in the U.S. Congress, in marked contrast to the central role of parties in most parliamentary systems. Committee chairs were the main beneficiaries of the revolt against Speaker Cannon and the decline of the organs of party leadership in the House that followed. Seniority became an almost inviolable norm, giving chairmen and veteran committee members hereditary rights to their positions and making them virtually powers unto themselves. The Senate was even more committee-centered than the House. Because of the strong seniority system that developed in the Senate in the 1880s, party leadership never assumed the dominance that it did during the Reed-Cannon era in the House.[17]

Committee government in both houses was buttressed by an elaborate set of norms that counseled members to focus their legislative efforts on the business of their own committees; to work hard and build up a fund of expertise; to serve a lengthy period of apprenticeship, deferring to their committee elders and keeping a low public profile; to practice the politics of compromise and accommodation within the committee and to remain loyal to its final product on the floor. These norms were not adhered to uniformly on all committees or by all individuals, but most members had far more to gain than to lose from conformity.[18] The committee structure promised cooperative members influence on matters important to their constituencies—both legislative input and leverage with federal agencies—and the system held out the promise of considerable power, eventually, to those who put in their years of service.

All of this changed substantially after the 1950s. More and more members, attuned to a volatile and unstructured electoral environment and anxious to increase their opportunities for advertising, credit claiming, and position taking, came to feel that the parceling out of congressional authority and resources was not proceeding far enough or fast enough. Similarly, congressional "folkways" came under increasing strain; norms dictating policy-area specialization and an extended period of apprenticeship, for example, became far less prevalent. As Rep. John Brademas, a former Democratic chief deputy whip, observed, "1976 is not 1966 and it's not 1956. I don't think, given the changes in American society, that intelligent and highly motivated young men and women will sit back and wait for a few years before speaking out." [19] Highly visible position taking, formerly the province of a few mavericks, became widely engaged in and tolerated, and members worried less about maintaining a facade of committee unity as they took their causes and amendments to the floor. Legislators became more appreciative of the visibility and resources that could come with committee and subcommittee leadership positions and pressed to obtain these advantages earlier in their careers.

Thus did the reform efforts of the 1970s arise—a series of challenges to the powers of committee chairmen that were sufficiently momentous to prompt comparisons with the 1910 challenge to the Speaker.[20] Committee government—relatively stable from the 1920s through the 1960s—gave way to something close to "subcommittee government," although not all the reforms, as we shall see, decentralized authority.

One of the first signs of strain was a proliferation in the number of subcommittees. The Legislative Reorganization Act of 1946 eliminated or consolidated many committees with obsolete or overlapping functions. But its reduction of congressional fragmentation was only temporary, for most of the newly consolidated committees spun off subcommittees in ever-increasing numbers. The number of Senate subcommittees peaked at 174 in 1976, with the average member serving on 14 and the average majority member chairing three subcommittees. The Senate Reorganization Amendments of 1977 effected a modest retrenchment, consolidating some committee jurisdictions and limiting the number of subcommittees members could chair and on which they could serve. But senators in the 98th Congress (1983-1985) are still spread among 113 Senate and joint committee subunits. House members, less thinly spread and more dependent on subcommittee positions for visibility and leverage, have been less inclined to limit subcommittee proliferation, although the Democratic Caucus in 1981 did cap the number of subcommittees on most committees. As of the 98th Congress, 154 subcommittees are available to House members, enough to give chairmanships to well over half of the majority members.

Initially, the number and stature of these subcommittees varied greatly from committee to committee, but between 1970 and 1975 the House Democratic Caucus adopted a "Subcommittee Bill of Rights" and other rules that reduced intercommittee variations and mandated a high level of subcommittee accessability and autonomy. The powers of committee chairs to determine the composition of subcommittees and to name their chairmen were largely removed. Subcommittees were given control over their own meeting schedules and staff hiring, and were assured of an adequate budget.

The caucus also established its right to vote by secret ballot on proposed committee chairs and in 1975 actually deposed three senior chairmen accused of autocratic and/or erratic behavior. Particular attention was focused on the powerful Ways and Means Committee. The "closed rule" procedures that protected its bills from floor amendments were modified, and its Democratic committee-assignment functions were transferred to a reconstituted Steering and Policy Committee. Ways and Means also was the target of a 1974 law requiring all committees to form at least four subcommittees.

Changes in Senate operations were equally significant, although they were accomplished more gradually and with fewer formal alterations in the rules. Majority Leader Johnson adopted certain practices to enhance his own role. For example, the "Johnson Rule" of 1953, which assured each freshman senator of a desirable committee assignment, loosened the grip of committee chairs and gave junior members more visibility and leverage.[21] More and more members pressed for a wider dispersal of authority and resources and came to see the norms of apprenticeship and deference that had buttressed committee government as anachronistic. This resulted in a proliferation of Senate subcommittees, an increased tendency to "go public" with floor amendments, and a general decrease in committee control.

Johnson's successor as majority leader, Mike Mansfield (1961-1977), adopted a permissive style of leadership that was well suited to the new individualistic ethos. Senators thus felt less need than House members in the early 1970s to effect further decentralization. Both parties did adopt procedures that gave their committee and/or chamber caucuses more discretion in choosing committee chairs and ranking minority members. A resolution passed in 1975 provided additional staff members to junior senators to assist with their committee work. And the Reorganization Amendments of 1977 increased the number of subcommittee chairmanships open to junior members. But subcommittee operations were not standardized to the same degree as in the House; Senate committees thus continue to show considerable variation in their degree of decentralization.

Congressional decentralization has served the need of members for influence and power, giving them control of a piece of policy "turf" and leverage for bargaining with their peers and the executive branch. It also has served their reelection needs, increasing their opportunities and resources for effective advertising, credit claiming, and position taking. But has it enhanced the performance of Congress as an institution? It has certainly produced heightened levels of activity, particularly in the early stages of the legislative process—the holding of hearings, the gathering of information, the formulation of policy proposals. Often, however, these efforts go no further, partly because, as Mayhew stresses, the electoral reward is frequently as great for mere posturing as for substantial legislative work.[22] But even when sustained efforts are made, Congress is often difficult to mobilize. The House's Select Committee on Committees (whose proposals for rationalizing and consolidating committee jurisdictions were largely rejected in 1974) found that seven House committees and dozens of subcommittees shared responsibility for energy policy, with the boundaries of their jurisdiction frequently unclear. The major energy proposals of the Ford and Carter administrations ran afoul of this fragmentation of authority, which provided numerous checkpoints for those who wished to kill or alter one provision or another.[23] In earlier years powerful committee chairs, such as Rep. Wilbur Mills of Ways and Means, had frequently been able to hammer out compromise agreements on legislation and make them stick. The weakening of these major committees made their leaders less formidable in their power struggles with presidents and party leaders, but it also greatly complicated the negotiation and accommodation necessary to produce concerted action.

Congressional decentralization, then, increases the likelihood of obstruction and delay, particularly in broad, controversial areas like energy, environmental protection, and tax and welfare reform. In narrower, less controversial policy areas, the effect can be quite different: members can secure positions on subcommittees of particular relevance to their constituencies and, once there, write policies that favor particular interests with little regard for overall spending levels or broad public concerns. Specialized committees and subcommittees in these "distributive" policy areas[24] typically defer to one another, producing legislation on matters such as agricultural price supports and public works projects that exceed the budgets of Democratic and Republican presidents alike. Thus is Congress's policy output apt to appear uncoordinated, unbalanced in favor of those interests that have a firm footing in the committee-subcommittee system, extravagant and unmindful of overall spending constraints, and vulnerable to delay and obstruction in areas of conflict. Both syndromes—the delay and deadlock and the extravagant "particularism"—are rooted in Congress's fragmentation, an organizational characteristic taken to new extremes in recent years by the electoral entrepreneurship of members and the rise of subcommittee government.

Congressional fragmentation and the political dynamics that accompany it threaten the credibility of Congress as a policy-making institution and have given rise to further efforts at institutional reform. The power given to "control" committees such as Appropriations and Ways and Means, frequent reliance on the president for agenda setting and political mobilization, and attempts to strengthen party organs can be seen as correctives (not always compatible with one another) to the shortcomings and excesses of committee/subcommittee government.

The role of the control committees, reinforced by their internal norms and the deference paid them by their parent chambers, has been to trim and dampen costly initiatives and to bring a rough measure of coordination to Congress's policy operations.[25] To this group now must be added the House and Senate Budget Committees, established by the Budget and Impoundment Control Act of 1974. These committees set binding limits to guide other committees as they pass individual authorization, appropriations, and tax bills. The Budget committees periodically have come into conflict with other committees, but "for every confrontation, there have been dozens of legislative decisions routinely made with fidelity to the budget process." [26] The movement of the budget act's "reconciliation" procedures from the end to near the beginning of the budget-making cycle, experimented with in 1980 and put firmly in place as the Reagan administration came to power, greatly increased the constraints placed by the budget process on the authorizing committees and on congressional policy making in general. The Reagan experience demonstrated, however, that under certain political conditions, the new control devices could do more to facilitate control by the executive than to enhance the ability of Congress to coordinate its own decisions.

Party Roles and Resources

The congressional parties operate in this context of countervailing committee powers, and their role reflects the tensions between the reelection and power needs of individual members and the need of Congress as an institution for coordination and control. The net effect of congressional reform has been to make the institution more difficult to manage and mobilize; this is true not only of the decentralizing reforms already discussed, but also of reforms that have aimed at greater openness in the institution. Particularly important in this regard was the provision in the Legislative Reorganization Act of 1970 requiring *recorded* "teller" votes when the House is in the Committee of the Whole (100 or more House members who debate or amend legislation on the floor). Forcing members to go "on the record" may have some advantages, but it certainly reduces their amenability to party persuasion and to party-arranged accommodations on sensitive issues.

There are ways, however, in which reform has enhanced the role of the parties. Some of the effects have been indirect. For example, House Democratic liberals chose their party caucus as the instrument by which they would reduce the powers of committee chairs and institute subcommittee government. This was a strategic decision, not primarily based on a desire to strengthen the congressional parties. The leadership was ambivalent about much of what the caucus did and almost never took the lead. Yet the net result has been a revitalization of the Democratic Caucus. Although caucus decisions contributed to the atomization of congressional authority in the short run, its new role in the long run could strengthen the party attachments of younger members and enhance the place of the leadership. Similarly, the budget reforms were not established to increase the parties' role, but they generally "buoyed the role of party leaders" [27]—both because of the control these leaders assumed over budget committee appointments and because of the necessities for intercommittee and interbranch negotiation the budget process created.

Other reforms were specifically designed to increase the powers of the party leadership. In 1975 the revitalized House Steering and Policy Committee was given the committee-on-committees functions formerly exercised by Ways and Means Democrats, as well as responsibility for nominating committee chairs for caucus selection. Generally, the party leadership effectively controls the committee and the committee-assignment process. Although this power has been diluted somewhat by the increased prominence of subcommittees (whose members and chairs, except on Appropriations, are chosen by committee caucuses, beyond the formal purview of party leaders), the control of committee assignments is nonetheless a key leadership resource. A desire for preferment in committee assignments encourages cooperative behavior by party members, and the appointment power enables leaders to place loyalists on the key "control" committees whose power to promote or to thwart party objectives is greatest.

Other rules changes have substantially increased party leaders' control over the flow of House business. Here the most important change has been in the relationship of the leadership to the Rules Committee, which schedules legislation on the floor and sets the terms for its consideration. The 1910 reforms removed the Rules Committee from party control. From the mid-1930s through the late 1960s, the "conservative coalition" dominated the committee and regularly defied the wishes of Democratic presidents and party leaders. In 1975 the Democratic Caucus gave the Speaker the power to nominate the chairman and the Democratic members of the Rules Committee, thus guaranteeing the transformation of the committee into a reliable ally of the leadership.[28] Meanwhile, the Speaker's discretion at the referral stage had been increased by a 1974 resolution that allowed him to refer bills wholly or in part to multiple committees or to constitute ad hoc committees to consider legislation.

The operations of the Republican party in the House have been much less affected by the process of reform.[29] The dispersal of functions and resources never went quite as far on the Republican as on the Democratic side. After 1910 the minority leader no longer served automatically as ranking minority member of Rules and Ways and Means, and in 1917 his autonomous committee-assignment powers also were removed. But the Republicans, unlike the Democrats, left the committee-assignment function with a party committee chaired by the party leader—although the committee was structured in such a way as to weaken the leader's control. (It consisted of one member from each state having a Republican representative; this member could cast as many votes as there were Republican members from his state.) Ranking Republicans on the standing committees have not been in a position to accumulate powers as formidable as those of their majority counterparts. The power of the Republican Policy Committee (which, in contrast to its Democratic counterpart, is separate from the committee on committees and since 1959 has not been chaired by the minority leader) and the research committee of the caucus have waxed and waned historically. In general, these two committees have played a more active role in discussing and formulating party positions than their majority counterpart. The Republicans' caucus (the House Republican Conference) has adopted some reform measures (for example, prohibiting members of the leadership from serving as ranking members of standing committees [1965] and providing for caucus votes by secret ballot on those nominated to be ranking members of committees [1971]), but it has done less than the Democratic Caucus either to parcel out powers to subcommittees and individual members or to strengthen the leadership's hand.

A shift to GOP control of the House thus might produce marginal changes in the organizational patterns recently established by the Democrats. Party control over the flow of House business probably would change little, but the leadership role in committee assignments might be weakened. And the potential would exist for a much wider divergence in committee-subcommittee functioning because the "Subcommittee Bill of Rights" and related rules changes were enactments of the Democratic Caucus and would have no binding effect on Republican leaders.

Senate decentralization, far advanced by the 1970s, was accomplished less through rules changes than by alterations in leadership and committee practices and changes in institutional norms. Few attempts have been made to increase the leadership's formal powers. Committee fragmentation and the workload of members were marginally reduced by the Senate Reorganization Amendments of 1977; Majority Leader Robert Byrd (1977-1980) actively backed this measure but suggested the deletion of a provision that would have allowed him to appoint ad hoc committees to consider complex legislation. Senate leadership continues to be more informal than House leadership and to vary more with personal style. The Democratic structure is more formally centralized than the Republican, with the party leader chairing the caucus (the Democratic Conference), the Policy Committee, and the Steering Committee (which makes committee assignments). Democratic Majority Leader Byrd employed these powers more assertively than his predecessor, increasing leadership staff resources and making particular use of his skills as a parliamentary tactician. But he proceeded cautiously and with mixed success. As he remarked in 1979:

> I could not run the Senate as [Lyndon] Johnson did.... Johnson could not lead this Senate.... He had cohesive blocs; he had the southern senators.... The members are younger now; they tend to be more independent. We are living in different times now.[30]

Minority Leader Howard Baker took Byrd's job after the 1980 elections shifted the Senate to Republican control. His formal powers were more meager: the Republicans place leadership of the Committee on Committees, the Republican Conference, and the Policy Committee in separate hands. Less the legislative tactician than Byrd, Baker has relied more on interpersonal skills and loyalties built up through political accommodation—and on President Reagan's political capital. But as that political capital has diminished, Baker's job has become increasingly difficult. Legislative deadlocks frequently have occurred and obstructionism, often by small groups or individuals within the majority party, has become more common. "It's every man for himself," observed former Republican senator James Pearson in mid-1982. "Every senator is a baron [with] his own principality. Once you establish that as a means of doing business, it's hard to establish any cohesion."[31]

It is within the Democratic party in the House, then, that the most concerted attention has been paid in recent years to the roles and resources of party leadership. But even here the party's limitations as an integrative force remain at least as impressive as its successes in counterbalancing the centrifugal forces of member individualism and subcommittee government.[32] Most of the changes have given leaders what Charles Jones has called "front-end power"—power, for example, over committee assignments and the referral of legislation—as opposed to the power to achieve "organizational or policy integration."[33] And even front-end power has been employed cautiously. Party concerns seem to have figured prominently only in appointments to key "control" committees—Rules, Ways and Means, Budget—and mainly in the appointment of new members (reappointments still are rarely challenged). And even here the desire to encourage and reward party solidarity sometimes gives way to the need to broaden the party leadership's base and to give less reliable members a greater stake in party operations.

In 1981, for example, the Steering and Policy Committee, at the urging of Majority Leader Jim Wright and with the approval of Speaker Thomas P. O'Neill, Jr., appointed Phil Gramm, a conservative Democratic representative from Texas, to a seat on the Budget Committee (after Gramm supposedly had agreed to support the party's budget position on the floor). House leaders argued that it was necessary to appoint Gramm and two other members of the Conservative Democratic Forum to the Budget Committee because of the thinness of the Democratic margin in the House and the need to woo those members whose votes otherwise might give the Republicans a working majority. Wright took "consolation," he wrote in his diary, in the possibility that Gramm, having been involved in Budget Committee deliberations, would be "less likely to undermine the final product of those deliberations on the House floor."[34] But, as it turned out, Gramm actively collaborated with the Republican leadership and the Reagan administration in devising an alternate budget plan that defeated the resolution reported by the Budget Committee's Democratic majority. Gramm's transgression was serious enough to overcome the caucus's normal reluctance to sanction members: he was denied reappointment to the Budget Committee in 1983. Gramm immediately resigned from the Congress and announced his intention to seek reelection as a Republican. He won the special election handily, apparently persuading many of his constituents that he was being persecuted for following his conscience and/or the wishes of his district.

In reality, the episode illustrates the limits of party discipline. Gramm was not expelled from the caucus, as some urged, nor was he denied his other committee positions; he was denied only a slot on a control committee on which it was essential that the party be represented by members in basic sympathy with the party's goals. The caucus in early 1983 also adopted a new rule providing for the expulsion of members from the caucus who campaigned for Republicans seeking federal office. While these actions clarified the definition of unacceptable behavior— actively collaborating with or campaigning for the opposition—they also indicated that sanctions were unlikely to be employed against members who merely voted with the opposition, even on key measures such as Gramm's budget resolution.

Recent years have seen efforts to increase party resources beyond the "front end" of the process. Bringing the Rules Committee within the party orbit has been a key development, giving the party the ability to schedule its own bills to maximum advantage and enabling leaders to bargain confidently with members who need help in bringing matters to the floor. Noteworthy changes also have occurred in the party's information-gathering and disseminating capacities and in its vote-gathering apparatus.[35] Party staffing has increased considerably; aides now number 27 for the Speaker, 7 for the majority leader, 22 for the majority and deputy whips, 4 for the caucus chairman, and 9 for the Steering and Policy Committee. This has greatly improved the leadership's ability to track legislation, to assist members, and to make the party a dominant and reliable source of information on House business. The most important change in the whip organization has been augmenting the whips elected by the regional caucuses—whose loyalty to the leadership is sometimes in doubt—with a group of appointed whips loyal to the leadership, responsible not simply for polling the membership but for the political tasks of persuasion and accommodation. Greatly expanded in size and functions, the whip operation of the House Democratic party now represents "the most elaborate Whip system that any congressional party has ever possessed." [36]

Also central to party mobilization has been an O'Neill innovation, Speaker's task forces. These ad hoc groups of members are appointed to assist in the passage of bills in which the leadership has a particular interest. The task forces utilize Steering and Policy Committee staff and provide a crucial supplement to the efforts of floor managers (who almost always are the relevant committee or subcommittee chairs) and of the whip organization.

Party involvement in the substance of legislation also has increased, although committees and subcommittees still dominate the process of policy formulation. The party policy committees in both houses meet infrequently, and the party caucuses—despite a few controversial efforts by House Democrats in the 1970s—rarely take votes on legislative matters or attempt to bind their members. Members could be counted on to resist such efforts, and leaders, given the fluctuating and tenuous nature of the coalitions they must put together, are often reluctant to pressure members whose support they may need on another day. In the wake of defeats by Reagan administration forces in 1981, the House Democratic Caucus agreed that the Steering and Policy Committee should identify "litmus test" votes that were particularly important to the party and which would be scrutinized by leaders when members sought committee assignments or other favors. But the caucus also agreed that occasional votes of conscience or constituent interest against the party, even on "litmus test" matters, were permissible (although actively conspiring with the opposition was not), and it offered amnesty to past defectors, inviting them to "return to the fold in good standing." [37]

Beyond such tentative steps toward identifying and pushing the party's policy priorities, there are other ways in which party responsibility for the legislative product is increasing, especially in the House. This is partly the function of the emerging dominance of the budget process in congressional policy making, a process that requires centralized leadership to negotiate intercommittee and interbranch agreements. It is also a function of the new devices—ad hoc committees, Speaker's task forces, expanded whip operations—which require legislative bargains and adjustments as part of the process of mobilizing party forces. And there have been some interesting attempts to increase the party role at the policy-formulation stage as well. During the 97th Congress, Democratic Caucus Chairman Gillis W. Long named a Committee on Party Effectiveness and several issue task forces that worked to formulate Democratic approaches to a wide range of domestic and foreign policy issues. Reminiscent in some ways of Republican caucus and policy committee operations during the Kennedy and Johnson administrations, this endeavor entered a crucial second phase in 1983, when efforts to integrate task force recommendations with the agendas of the standing committees began.[38] Senators Byrd and Baker, who swapped positions as majority and minority leader after the 1980 elections, have taken far more active roles than their predecessors in shaping party policy positions, especially on foreign policy issues. The staffs of both parties' Senate policy committees have greatly expanded in size and in their capacity to develop and disseminate party positions on policy questions.

The slight recent increase in party voting reflected in Figures 3-2 and 3-3 probably owes something to the strengthening of party institutions and the more assertive leadership styles that have been evident in both houses since the mid-1970s. At a minimum, these party efforts have helped prevent the further decline that might otherwise have occurred in an increasingly individualistic and decentralized Congress. Several additional factors also have been at work. The political strength that the Reagan administration enjoyed in the wake of the 1980 elections and the far-reaching character of many of the president's proposals—factors that heightened partisanship on both sides of the aisle—are of obvious importance. The increased role of the parties in candidate recruitment and support, mainly on the Republican side, also is noteworthy. The organizational and fund-raising successes since the mid-1970s of the Republican National Committee and the GOP's House and Senate campaign committees have given many members an additional tie to the party and stronger incentives to cooperate with the party leadership. The Democratic campaign committees have upgraded their operations since 1980, although their financial base is much weaker than that of the GOP. We saw earlier how the reduced dependence of members on state and local party organizations and the emergence of individualistic campaign styles had helped weaken the congressional parties. One of the more hopeful current possibilities is that a renewed dependence on the parties for campaign resources, this time mainly at the national level, might help strengthen these frayed party ties.

The Web of Party

Presidential leadership, like party leadership, is necessary to offset congressional fragmentation and individualism. Our constitutional traditions stress the checking and balancing of the branches of government, but the fact is that Congress and the president are highly interdependent institutions. Congress relies on the president for the setting of priorities, the formulation of authoritative proposals, the marshalling of information, and the mobilization of support within and outside the chambers. And the president finds it necessary to secure the cooperation of Congress if he is to meet the political and policy-making expectations of his office. Dwight D. Eisenhower was the last president to be attracted to "the Whig notion that the legislative branch should legislate and the executive branch should execute," but even he developed a relatively comprehensive legislative program. Eisenhower and those around him found such leadership to be necessary in light of the expectations of the executive departments, interest groups and the broader public, and, not least, Congress itself.[39] Subsequent presidents have attempted through various mechanisms to strengthen the executive capacity for policy co-ordination and leadership.

The political parties traditionally have been the primary means for achieving such coordination, both within and between the branches. Recent experience, however, has prompted doubts as to the parties' adequacy as instruments of governmental integration. In focusing on parties and the presidency, we turn first to the executive as legislative leader and then to problems of coordination and control within the executive branch.

President and Congress: The Party Connection

The conditions under which members of Congress are elected constrain presidential no less than party leadership. We noted in Chapter 1 the steady decrease in party-line voting for Congress, a trend that has tended to insulate House incumbents from national electoral trends (see Table 1-3). Not since 1954 has a Republican president faced a GOP-controlled House. Table 3-1 traces the relation of presidential to congressional voting at the district level since 1940. Increasing numbers of districts are electing a representative of one party and voting for a president of the other. The high point was reached in 1972, when some 44 percent of the 435 districts produced divided results and more than half of the districts voting for Richard Nixon sent a Democrat to Congress.

As the 1976 figures suggest, the number of split districts is apt to be somewhat less when a Democrat wins the presidency, because of the continuing advantage the Democrats have in congressional voting. But it is not clear that such results do much to tie Democratic legislators to their national party, for more often than not it is the representative that leads the ticket. Of the 292 Democrats elected to the House in 1976, only 22 received a smaller share of the vote in their district than did Jimmy Carter; similarly, 20 out of 21 Democrats elected to the Senate in 1976 outpolled Carter in their states.[40]

Studies of presidential "coattails"—the extent to which the vote for a presidential candidate improves the performance of his fellow partisans on the ticket—reveal a steadily declining impact on congressional races in

Table 3-1 Congressional Districts Carried by a Presidential Candidate of One Party and a House Candidate of Another Party, 1940-1980

| | Districts with Split Results | |
Year	Number	Percentage of all Districts
1940	53	14.6*
1944	41	11.2*
1948	90	21.3*
1952	84	19.3
1956	130	29.9
1960	114	26.1
1964	145	33.3
1968	139	32.0
1972	192	44.1
1976	124	28.5
1980	147	33.8

* Data available for only 362 districts in 1940, 367 in 1944, and 422 in 1948.

SOURCE: *Congressional Quarterly Weekly Report*, April 22, 1978, 972; and Gary C. Jacobson, *The Politics of Congressional Elections* (Boston: Little, Brown & Co., 1983), 133.

both parties since the 1950s. The trend was interrupted temporarily in 1980 by the election of Ronald Reagan, which appears to have increased the aggregate Republican House vote by some 3 or 4 percent, the Senate vote by 2 percent—a modest impact by historical standards but greater than that registered in most recent elections.[41] This shift dislodged 27 House Democratic incumbents and enabled the GOP to take 25 of the 43 districts where an incumbent was not running; it also tipped the balance in a number of close Senate races (Reagan outpolled 18 of 21 Republican Senate winners). Certainly the new president's electoral appeal was *perceived* as substantial, partly because the dimensions of his Electoral College victory and of the party turnover in the Senate came as such a surprise,[42] and partly because of his skill in marshalling public support and claiming a popular mandate. That perception substantially increased Reagan's ability to have his way with Congress, especially during his first year in office. But as the 1982 elections approached and the condition of the economy worsened, members—particularly Republicans from relatively liberal northeastern constituencies—came to see solidarity with the president as a dubious electoral asset.

The Republican losses in the House midterm elections of 1982 were not an unusual occurrence. The last time the party of an incumbent president gained House seats at midterm was under the extraordinary circumstances of 1934, when President Franklin D. Roosevelt's popularity swept a wave of New Deal Democrats into office. The 1982 Republican losses in the House (a net 26 seats) would have been greater had not the Reagan coattail effect in the House been rather limited in the first place (a net gain of 33 seats in 1980) and had the national Republican party not been able to pour massive resources into the campaign.

Why is it that the party of the president traditionally loses seats in midterm elections? Voters who are pulled into the electorate and/or away from their normal partisan vote by the presidential election may either fail to vote or return to their normal preference at midterm. In addition, there seems to be a bias toward "negative voting" in midterm elections; those evaluating presidential performance negatively are disproportionately likely both to vote and to let their assessment of the president sway their congressional vote. Such tendencies are strongest when economic conditions are unfavorable or when other factors have reduced the president's popularity; adverse conditions influence not only the way individuals cast their votes, but also tend to bring out a strong and better financed field of congressional challengers.[43]

The ability of presidents to influence midterm electoral outcomes either within their own party's primaries or in the general election has generally proved quite limited. This fact, together with the diminution of the coattails effect, has reinforced the tendency of members of Congress to regard themselves as "on their own" electorally and to discount the importance of fidelity to party or president. Electoral patterns limit both the number of like-minded partisans a president is likely to bring with him into office and the dependence on the president that those who do get elected are likely to feel.

Table 3-2 shows the average presidential "support scores" of Republicans and Democrats in Congress since 1953. It is perhaps surprising, in light of the electoral trends just discussed, that no consistent pattern of decline is discernible, although House Democrats supported Presidents Kennedy and Johnson more consistently than they did President Carter. The highest figure in the table, in fact, is the extraordinary 80 percent average support score registered by Senate Republicans during Reagan's first year. Presidents obviously receive considerably higher levels of support from legislators of their own party than they do from the opposition. These patterns fluctuate, particularly among the Democrats; Democratic support for President Johnson in the Senate, for example, was hardly stronger than Republican support as his second term came to an end. In general, the average member of Congress supports the president about two-thirds of the time when he is a member of his own party and between one-third to one-half of the time when he is not.

To what extent is this voting affinity the result of active party and presidential efforts, and to what extent does it simply reflect the policy attitudes and electoral bases that politicians from the same party are likely to share? The blandishments of the executive seem to have their greatest independent effect in those foreign policy areas where cues from the constituency are generally weakest.[44] John Kingdon, who studied congressional voting early in the Nixon administration, found that Republican House members mentioned the administration some 42 percent of the time in explaining their behavior on key votes. "The administra-

Table 3-2　Average "Support Scores" for Members of Congress on Votes Related to the President's Program, 1953-1982

Year	Party of President	Senate		House	
		Democrats	*Republicans*	*Democrats*	*Republicans*
1953	Republican	46	68	49	74
1954	"	38	73	44	71
1955	"	56	72	53	60
1956	"	39	72	52	72
1957	"	51	69	49	54
1958	"	44	67	55	58
1959	"	38	72	40	68
1960	"	43	66	44	59
1961	Democrat	65	36	73	37
1962	"	63	39	72	42
1963	"	63	44	72	32
1964	"	61	45	74	38
1965	"	64	48	74	41
1966	"	57	43	63	37
1967	"	61	53	69	46
1968	"	48	47	64	51
1969	Republican	47	66	48	57
1970	"	45	60	53	66
1971	"	40	64	47	72
1972	"	44	66	47	64
1973	"	37	61	35	62
1974	"	39	56	44	58
1975	"	47	68	38	63
1976	"	39	62	32	63
1977	Democrat	70	52	63	42
1978	"	66	41	60	36
1979	"	68	47	64	34
1980	"	62	45	63	40
1981	Republican	49	80	42	68
1982	"	43	74	39	64

NOTE: Scores represent the percentage of recorded votes on which members voted in agreement with the president's accounced position.
SOURCE: Relevant volumes of the *Congressional Quarterly Almanac*.

tion is much on the minds of congressmen from the president's party,"
Kingdon concluded. References to the administration were more than
twice as frequent as references to Republican party leadership, suggesting
that "party voting is more a function of the administration than of the
party leadership position." At the same time, Kingdon noted that the
overall correlation between the administration's position and the votes of
GOP members was not particularly high and that the influence of the
administration on voting still fell considerably short of that attributable
to constituencies and fellow representatives.[45]

Presidents of both parties in the postwar years have greatly expanded the White House machinery for influencing Congress. While this
machinery often complements the work of party structures, it also gives
executives the potential to work outside them. Foremost among the new
mechanisms is the Office of Congressional Relations, the White House's
legislative liaison operation. First established under Eisenhower in 1953
to complement the efforts of departmental liaison offices, the office was
upgraded by Kennedy and Johnson and has been a key presidential tool
ever since. Congressional liaison is a kind of executive branch counterpart
to the party whip system—informing, assisting, accommodating, mobilizing. During the Carter years a staff ranging from 7 to 13 professionals
operated under the leadership of Frank Moore. Carter's liaison staff had
numerous handicaps. It was inexperienced; expectations of Democrats in
Congress concerning the assistance the liaison staff would be able to
provide were unrealistically high; and congressional partisans had become accustomed to running their own affairs during eight years of
Republican rule and were alienated by Carter's anti-Washington rhetoric.
Although the operation improved markedly later in the administration, it
never recovered completely from its initial reputation for ineptitude.
President Reagan brought on a more experienced congressional legislative liaison team headed in his first year by Nixon-Ford veteran Max
Friedersdorf and then by Kenneth Duberstein. Aided by a favorable
political climate and a more united congressional party, the office enjoyed
a generally positive reputation and numerous legislative successes. By
1982 congressional liaison involved a White House staff of 27 (12 professionals), whose operations were loosely coordinated with those of 26
departmental and agency liaison offices.[46]

A more recent presidential innovation is the White House Office of
Public Liaison, formed as "an institutional response to the decline of the
party system and the collateral emergence of single-issue pressure
groups." [47] President Nixon appointed Charles Colson, who later left
the White House under the cloud of Watergate, as his liaison with
interest groups; under President Ford, William Baroody, Jr., built the
office into an extensive public relations operation. The office came
into its own as a mobilizer of Congress under Anne Wexler in the second
half of the Carter administration: "Our job," she said, "is to create
lobbyists." [48] To this end, Wexler and her staff coordinated dozens of
briefings of political and opinion leaders on issues ranging from the
formation of a new Department of Education to the Panama Canal
treaties, and they instigated group and constituency communications

with Congress that created a more favorable climate for these and other measures.

Such efforts intensified in the Reagan White House. The public liaison operation (headed by Elizabeth Hanford Dole until she became secretary of transportation in 1983) continued, but the political affairs office directed by Lyn Nofziger (and later Edward Rollins) was more consequential in mobilizing Congress. As one of Nofziger's assistants explained:

> The way we operate, within 48 hours any Congressman will know he has had a major strike in his district. All of a sudden Vice President Bush . . . [or] Congressman Jack Kemp is in your district, ten of your top contributors are calling you, the head of the local A.M.A., the head of the local realtors groups, local officials. Twenty letters come in . . . you're hit by paid media, free media, mail, phone calls, all asking you to support the President.[49]

Such techniques are well-adapted to conditions of political fragmentation. ("We are dealing in a time of very intense single-interest issues," Wexler noted. "New coalitions are being built all the time and are always different." [50]) But these coalitions do little to strengthen the political party structure that historically has served to aggregate dispersed interests. The political affairs office treats party organizations in much the same fashion as other interest groups, and the network of political activists on which it currently relies derives more from Ronald Reagan's "fifteen years of criss-crossing America in the cause of Conservatism" [51] than it does from party ties.

Although legislative liaison, political affairs, and other White House operations may do little to strengthen the congressional parties or national and state party organizations, they are undoubtedly due some of the credit for the stability of party and presidential support scores in Congress in recent years, under conditions that otherwise might have prompted further disintegration. Of course, the mobilization of support for the party's program is only one of the president's roles on Capitol Hill. Equally important is his role as agenda setter and formulator of policy. To say, as a noted political scientist once did, that "the president is now the motor in the system; the Congress applies the brakes" is an exaggeration. Even when activist presidents have enjoyed supportive congressional majorities, Congress and its committees have displayed considerable independence and have undertaken substantial policy initiatives.[52] But the historical trend toward presidential leadership in setting priorities and in defining the base-point of policy deliberations is unmistakable. "Party programs" in the Congress are usually presidential in origin; the congressional parties, majority or minority, who do not hold the presidency are reduced to proposing "alternatives" that have uncertain prospects at best.

James Sundquist has stressed the centrality of party to the president's programmatic role, both in shaping the elements of that program and in marshalling the political support to secure enactment. The period on which he focuses—the Eisenhower, Kennedy, and Johnson years— lends itself to that interpretation. Liberal Democrats in Congress (most conspicuously in the Senate) during the 1950s formulated alternatives to the cautious initiatives of the Eisenhower administration in areas such as aid-to-education and civil rights. They developed ambitious proposals in area redevelopment, manpower training, Medicare, and environmental protection as well. This agenda, promoted by the DNC's Democratic Advisory Council (see Chapter 9), became the basis for the Democratic platform of 1960 and for Kennedy's and Johnson's (ultimately successful) legislative programs. The Democratic party, Sundquist concludes, did precisely those things that loosely organized, nonprogrammatic American parties supposedly have great difficulty doing: "It *did* develop a program to which it committed itself—and which it put into effect after winning office." [53] This interpretation is a bit strained: after all, as Sundquist recognizes, the Democratic leadership in both houses was never at the forefront of, and often resisted, the programmatic thrust of the party's liberal wing.[54] And it took an assassination and the Barry Goldwater landslide—far more than the normal workings of the Democratic majority—to put most of the programs on the books. Still, this example, and others that could be cited from the Nixon and Reagan eras, point up the importance of party to both the content and the political viability of presidential policy leadership. Much of what presidents propose, far more than is generally recognized, has been germinating for years among the president's fellow partisans in Congress. But presidential action often is required to make *party* measures of these proposals and to move them beyond the committee calendars.

Modern growth in the executive office of the president is largely attributable to the increasing importance of these broad policy-making responsibilities. The Office of Management and Budget (OMB) has emerged as the chosen instrument of most modern Republican presidents, oriented as they have been toward programmatic coordination and control, while Democratic presidents, more interested in expansive policy initiatives, have relied more heavily on an augmented White House policy staff. While the development of such staff capacities has been essential to the modern presidency, it has contributed to the parties' further eclipse, often in ways that could and should have been avoided.

President Johnson saw his White House policy operations as a way of reaching beyond traditional congressional and bureaucratic circles and of putting his distinct imprint on legislation; he reportedly was incensed when a political scientist dared suggest that most of his Great Society proposals had been kicking around in Democratic circles for years.[55] President Carter's energy and welfare-reform proposals were more politically vulnerable than they needed to be because of the insulated, White House-centered process by which they were formulated. With Ronald Reagan the problem has been somewhat different. His own policy priorities, together with the potency of OMB within the executive branch and the availability of the new budgetary mechanisms in Congress, have led to what Allen Schick aptly terms the "fiscalization" of policy debate.[56] While consideration of the fiscal implications of certain kinds of policy decisions is long overdue, abstract debates about what levels of defense or social-welfare spending can be sustained all too often ignore the programmatic issues at stake. The fiscalization of presidential policy leadership can bring a measure of coherence to the policy process and even provide the occasion for heightened party cohesion, but in the end it threatens both the quality of policy deliberation and the contribution that the parties as political coalitions can make to it.

An Apartisan Presidency?

"The political party is at best of marginal relevance to the performance of the oval office." [57] Former White House aide and cabinet member Joseph Califano thus describes the "apartisan" nature of the modern presidency. His assessment is something of an overstatement with respect to the executive's dealings with Congress. Nonetheless, as we have seen, numerous factors induce the president to work outside of party channels even in this, the most obvious of his party leadership roles. Party majorities on Capitol Hill are hard to come by, mainly because of limited numbers for the Republicans and internal divisions for the Democrats, making it necessary for mobilization efforts to cross party lines. Interest-group influence, mediated less and less through the parties, and the proliferation of political action committees require direct efforts to influence (or offset) group communications with Congress. And for many members, party identifications and ties to party leaders are weak, offering the White House only limited leverage. Interventions in party primaries are rarely successful, often counterproductive. The disciplining of party mavericks is, at best, weakly supported by congressional and popular norms and may alienate those whose help will be needed in future battles. Members of Congress often behave as independent political entrepreneurs, preoccupied with maximizing the electoral advantages of their incumbency, and the White House often finds it useful to deal with them directly on that basis.

Modern presidents have done little to enhance the role of their national party organizations as instruments of political cohesion and governance. As Chapter 2 indicated, those organizations, particularly the Republican National Committee, have made important strides in recent years, but rarely because of anything incumbent presidents have done to strengthen them. "In my years on Lyndon Johnson's White House staff," Califano recalls, "never once did I hear him say that he wanted to leave behind a strengthened Democratic party." Both the DNC and RNC have fared better as the "out" party than when they had a president in the White House. "If you're Democratic party chairman when a Democrat is president, you're a Goddamn clerk," DNC Chairman Robert Strauss once declared.[58] Some subordination of the national party organization is essential, of course, given the president's role as the party's highest officeholder and his position of policy leadership. But the wholesale displacement of the national party as an instrument for running the presidential campaign, dispensing patronage, staffing the government, and working with Congress has occurred only in the last 25 years.

DNC Chairman James Farley (1932-1940), unusual for his long tenure and national prominence, was rather typical for pre-1960s chairmen in his central role in national campaigns and in his control of patronage positions. (His responsibilities for patronage were underscored by his concurrent appointment as postmaster general; prior to the conversion of the Post Office from a cabinet department to a government corporation in 1971, four chairmen in each party held the two positions either concurrently or in succession.) As late as the 1950s, despite Eisenhower's distaste for partisan leadership, RNC Chairman Leonard Hall (1953-1957) played a central role in the negotiations among congressional and state and local party leaders that were integral to the making of federal appointments at all levels. The campaigns and administrations of John Kennedy, Lyndon Johnson, and Richard Nixon marked a decisive shift in both campaign and patronage functions from the national party to the president's personal organization and the White House.[59]

At least since Roosevelt's day, a tension has been apparent between the party organization and the increasingly prominent White House staff. In the 1960s that tension was conclusively resolved in favor of the president's top aides. Kennedy named (and Johnson retained) John Bailey, one of the last of the old-style state chairmen, as head of the DNC (1961-1968), but the White House gave him only a peripheral role in political decision making. For a time in 1965 Johnson used the national committee as a medium for giving members of Congress help with projects in their districts and backup for their campaigns, but the experiment was ended abruptly after controversies arose over fund-raising techniques. And of course Nixon's centralization of decision making on appointments and other political matters among a few top aides and the personalizing and consolidating of campaign functions in the Committee for the Reelection of the President (CREEP) became notorious as preconditions for the Watergate imbroglio.

While such abuses have not recurred under Carter and Reagan, neither of them has reversed the trend toward the displacement of party organs as a "web" connecting dispersed centers of power. No modern president, in fact, has made less use of his national party organization than Carter. Winning the Democratic nomination and the presidency as a party outsider, Carter and his inner circle seemed to regard the national and state parties more as potential antagonists to be neutralized than as potential allies to be nurtured. Carter's first DNC chairman, former Maine governor Kenneth Curtis, resigned in frustration after a year on the job. Complaints persisted that the White House staff was preempting the party leadership and that the national and state parties had very little say on presidential appointments and political strategy. "The people around him," observed Carter's own state chair, "are concerned with one individual [Carter], not the party organization." [60] The Reagan presidency has not been nearly as damaging to the RNC, partly because the organization was so much more secure financially and had programs of proven worth to leaders and elected officials throughout the party. Nevertheless, GOP Chairman Richard Richards' remarks when he stepped down under pressure in 1982 had all too familiar a ring: "Every clerk at the White House thinks he knows how to do my job." [61]

Finally, what can be said of the role of party *within* the sprawling executive branch? If one simply looks at the party affiliations of presidential appointees, the party connection shows few signs of deterioration. Appointees to major federal positions are drawn overwhelmingly from the 'in" party. Of the major appointees whose party affiliation could be determined, a large proportion (97 percent under Reagan, 89 percent under Carter and Nixon, 81 percent under Johnson) were from the president's party. (About one-third of major appointees, however, typically have *no* prominent party affiliation.[62]) Partisan appointments are most prevalent in departments closely tied to clientele groups—Agriculture, Commerce, Labor—and least prevalent in the departments of State and Defense. Data over time suggest that Democratic presidents slightly increase the partisanship of their appointments as election day approaches as a way of solidifying party support; Republican presidents tend to compensate for their smaller partisan base by making more bipartisan appointments in the election year.[63]

Such figures indicate that those making presidential appointments are dubious concerning the potential loyalty and/or policy compatibility of members of the opposite party. They say very little, however, about the role of party organizations in recommending or clearing these appointees or about the extent to which appointees display party ties that go beyond mere affiliation. Recent data on cabinet appointments are suggestive on this latter point. A primary aim of cabinet appointments traditionally has been to accommodate key constituencies within the president's party. Cabinets typically contain a number of officeholders and other prominent spokesmen for key regions and interests. As Nelson Polsby has observed, this pattern was decisively altered as the Nixon administration progressed:

> After beginning with a group of cabinet appointees that was both politically diverse and reasonably visible, Mr. Nixon increasingly appointed people with no independent public standing and no constituencies of their own. In this shift we can read a distinctive change in the fundamental political goals and strategies of the Nixon administration from early concerns with constituency building to a later preoccupation, once Mr. Nixon's reelection was assured, with centralizing power in the White House.[64]

A number of departments during the Nixon administration saw this sort of transition from a well-known, politically experienced appointee to a person who, while perhaps quite knowledgeable, had far less political standing: from William Rogers to Henry Kissinger at State, Melvin Laird to James Schlesinger at Defense, George Romney to James Lynn at Housing and Urban Development (HUD), John Volpe to Claude Brinegar at the Department of Transportation (DOT).

Although Jimmy Carter did not aim at a Nixonian centralization of presidential power, his cabinet resembled Nixon's last team in important respects. Only the Agriculture secretary, Rep. Robert Bergland, and the Interior secretary, Gov. Cecil Andrus, (and arguably the Transportation secretary, Rep. Brock Adams) could be considered ambassadors from Democratic constituencies. Much more common were subject matter specialists (Cyrus Vance at State, Harold Brown at Defense, Ray Marshall at Labor) and Washington-based careerists (Califano at the Department of Health, Education and Welfare, James Schlesinger at Energy, Patricia Harris at HUD)—together with several Georgians (Griffin Bell at Justice, Bert Lance at the Office of Management and Budget, Andrew Young at the United Nations) and a few conspicuous black and female appointees (Young, Harris, and Juanita Kreps at Commerce). Polsby concludes:

> Of Mr. Carter's top seventeen appointees, how many reached into the constituencies suggested by the old New Deal voting coalition, indeed the coalition which came together to elect him? . . . Perhaps the first clear signal . . . in the way he constituted his administration was to proclaim a disbelief in the reality of the interest group composition of the Democratic party. He understood the need for symbolic gestures, and for satisfying those interest group demands made through the mass media, but there was, clearly, nothing in his experience of the national Democratic party . . . that confronted him with most of the varied components of the grand Democratic coalition.[65]

Reagan has partially reversed this depoliticizing of the cabinet.[66] His cabinet contains substantially more former elected and party officials than did Carter's. But at least one-third of his appointees have no discernible history of party involvement, and in some traditionally "ambassadorial" posts (notably Interior and Labor), his appointments seem designed more to ensure that policy approaches will remain narrowly conservative than to open up channels for political communication and coalition building.

Several factors are responsible for the limited role of the party tie in the executive branch. First, the number of positions available for presidential appointment is relatively small. Jim Farley, Roosevelt's Democratic party chairman, once complained that he had only 15,000 positions exempt from civil service (20 percent of the then-existing federal jobs) to distribute among 10 times that many applicants.[67] Today the number is closer to 5,000—no more than 2 percent of the positions in any federal department and less than 1 percent in most. These positions include some posts exempted from coverage because of the need to hire persons from outside the government who have particular technical or professional qualifications. Moreover, numerous top positions are structured so as to minimize a new president's ability to have a partisan impact; many boards and commissions are required to have an equal number of Democratic and Republican members, and terms are staggered so that they do not coincide with presidential terms. The Civil Service Reform Act of 1978, which created the Senior Executive Service for some 8,500 top civil servants, gave the president and agency chiefs increased flexibility to shift existing appointees among top positions. But the law contains numerous antipartisan "safeguards": such transfers cannot take place during the first 120 days of a new administration, and no more than 10 percent of those in the service may be noncareer political appointees.[68]

The mere existence of "political" positions does not guarantee, of course, that partisan considerations will loom large in filling them. The decline of party ties in the electorate and the persistence of negative public attitudes toward partisanship often make it politically attractive to stress alternative criteria for appointment. The force with which the parties can press their claims has been reduced because of presidents' decreasing dependence on them. Television and modern campaign technologies enable presidents to reach the electorate directly; new modes of campaign finance largely bypass the parties; and large presidential staffs also reduce the need for party assistance. Of particular importance are changes in the presidential nomination process that have greatly reduced the control of party elites and organizations over the nomination (see Chapters 6 and 7). "Nothing in [Jimmy Carter's] experience of the nomination process," Polsby argues, "led him to the view that he needed to come to terms with the rest of the Democratic party"—a fact that helps explain both Carter's apolitical approach to executive appointments and his failings as a leader of Congress.[69]

The trends toward apartisanship in the presidency have been criticized from two perspectives, one rooted in Nixon's presidency, the second in Carter's. The first stresses the role of party in constraining a president, in rendering him accountable. While party networks can greatly extend the reach and the resources of a president, they do not, when healthy, lend themselves to complete subordination. Such ties require a measure of accommodation and responsiveness on the part of a president, giving him a claim on the loyalties and resources of actors based elsewhere in the political system but also opening to them reciprocal channels of influence. It is hard to imagine the Watergate episode occurring without the prior separation of President Nixon's political operations from the party context.[70]

A second, complementary argument is that a revival of presidential partisanship could strengthen the office and increase the coherence and competence of government. This argument must be made with some discrimination. There is a good case for partisan influence in cabinet and other executive appointments—as a means of promoting teamwork and loyalty within the executive branch, cementing electoral and congressional alliances, and increasing inducements to party involvement. But party cannot play a role in the bureaucracy analogous to the role it plays in Congress. Heightened partisanship is no panacea for the problems of coordination and control the president faces in his executive household. Even commentators who are otherwise sympathetic to party renewal often decry the decline of administrative and managerial competence in the executive branch and regard the political basis of top-level appointments as part of the problem.[71] Certainly the machinery for budgeting and policy coordination developed since the 1950s must be evaluated in terms that go beyond its impact on party roles. At the same time, modern presidents seem to have concluded too quickly that the webs of government spun out of the White House and OMB have rendered the web of party obsolescent.

The case for executive partisanship becomes much less equivocal when the president's electoral and congressional ties are considered. Surely Carter's experience bore out the accuracy of this observation by a Democratic state chair: "Party-building and respect toward the party is an insurance policy for a candidate."[72] Both Carter's and Reagan's experiences with Congress powerfully demonstrate that, while strong party ties may be of decreasing importance to one seeking presidential nomination, they are still absolutely essential to legislative leadership. Many factors are conspiring to weaken the web of party on Capitol Hill. But the extent to which the president *chooses* to work with and through the party is itself a crucial factor. To neglect or bypass the party may be understandable in terms of the president's immediate desire for consensus or his need for control, but it is a shortsighted strategy that is likely, in the long run, to reduce the availability and potency of a critical instrument of governance.

A Note on State Government

In some states the party-in-government is considerably stronger than it is at the national level; in others it is much weaker, almost nonexistent. Ample evidence of party decline exists at the state level, but continuing variations give an indication of what the party role might be.

Parties and Legislatures

This variety is nowhere more evident than in roll-call voting in state legislatures. Party voting rates in the U.S. Congress (the percentage of roll calls with majorities of the two parties on opposite sides; see Figure 3-2) have ranged from 29 to 53 percent over the past 25 years. During this period, party-voting rates of more than 70 percent have been registered in one or both houses of the Pennsylvania, New York, Massachusetts, and Ohio legislatures, while rates of less than 25 percent were attained in Wyoming, Utah, and New Mexico. In most states, the parties polarize on between 35 and 65 percent of roll-call votes.

Cohesion within the legislative parties also varies considerably from state to state: the mean "index of cohesion" scores for the strong-party states listed above have been in the 75 to 90 percent range, while it has fallen to 50 percent or below in Kentucky, Florida, Montana, New Mexico, and other states. On this measure almost every state legislature surpasses the U.S. Congress in partisan unity. Few have intraparty divisions as persistent as those producing "conservative coalition" voting at the national level.[73]

Most attempts to explain such interstate differences focus on the regional and demographic patterns associated with them.[74] The highest levels of party voting and of intraparty cohesion are found in those northeastern and midwestern states where two-party competition is strong and where the parties tend to represent relatively distinctive constituencies, divided along rural-urban-suburban, economic, and racial-ethnic lines. In one-party states, or in states where party constituencies are more heterogeneous, intraparty cohesion is generally weaker.

The urbanized, industrialized states where party voting in the legislature is most pronounced tend also to have the best developed state and local party organizations. Strong organizations can help foster legislative partisanship, particularly if they take an active hand in candidate recruitment, preprimary endorsements, and/or the financing and management of campaigns. Legislators from high-cohesion states, such as Connecticut and Pennsylvania, often report a strong party influence in persuading them to run or in helping them get elected, while legislators from lower cohesion states, such as Minnesota, Iowa, Oregon, and Washington, report less indebtedness to the parties.[75] But even in strong-party states, the state organizations are likely to be interested primarily in state-level races, and the local organizations may give priority to races for mayor or county sheriff, where the potential for patronage is greater. Legislative candidates thus are often "on their own" electorally, limited in their ties to the organized party. And even where those ties are relatively strong, they may find that state and local party leaders are interested in only a small portion of those matters considered by the legislature. It seems likely, then, that high levels of party voting owe less to the legislator's relationship to state and local party organizations than to the fact that legislators in strong-party states tend to come from like-minded constituencies and to operate in a cultural milieu that puts considerable value on party regularity.

Incumbent legislators at the state level, as at the national level, typically win reelection handily. In some states reelection rates are as high as 95 percent, and in almost no states do they fall below 80 percent. Such results, of course, may be indicative of party strength, as the organization discourages or defeats primary challenges and delivers the party vote in November. But they often point to a weakened party role. Voters are increasingly splitting their tickets at all levels. This fact, in addition to the limited recruitment and campaign activities of many party organizations, encourages legislators to build their own organizations, to seek a higher public profile, and to specialize in constituent services. In recent years many state legislatures have developed in ways reminiscent of the U.S. Congress—augmented staffs, proliferating committees and subcommittees, more attention to casework and media relations. As incumbents work outside of party channels to enhance their electoral prospects, they may feel less constrained to maintain a record of party regularity. And as their following extends beyond their normal partisan base, they may become cushioned against partisan electoral swings. One eight-state study found the "normal" 16 percent partisan turnover in open seats reduced to 6 percent in seats for which incumbents were running. Even in 1980, when the presidential vote shifted decisively toward the GOP and the RNC involved itself in local races to an unprecedented degree, the shift in state legislative seats was quite limited: the Republicans gained control of only five chambers while losing one, and registered a net gain of some 200 seats out of 5,900 nationwide. In California, Iowa, and Illinois, where Reagan won handily, between 91 and 95 percent of legislative incumbents retained their seats.[76]

Still, the trends toward split-ticket voting and toward nonpartisan campaign styles are not as advanced in the state legislative arena as in congressional races. And at the level of state legislative leadership, party leaders retain powers unheard of at the national level since the days of Reed and Cannon. In general, committees and subcommittees possess fewer resources and less autonomy in the legislatures than in the Congress. Party leaders, or committees under their control, usually appoint committee members and chairs. In making these choices they are not generally bound by strict seniority rules, although they "often select reliable senior members for chairmanships and may use seniority as a device for minimizing intraparty conflict." [77] Most state legislative leaders have considerable discretion in referring bills and in otherwise controlling the flow of legislative business. Many state legislatures also have effective whip operations, although reports concerning how much direct influence leadership blandishments have on roll-call voting vary considerably, even among strong-party states.[78]

Such leadership structures and functions do not guarantee party-centered legislatures. In southern legislatures where the Democratic party is dominant, appointment powers are often used to build a personal or factional following for the leader, as opposed to cementing a broader party coalition. And when majority-party divisions are so severe or majorities so slender that candidates for the leadership are prompted to organize across party lines (which occurred in Alaska, California, and other western states in recent years), leadership appointments are also likely to be bipartisan in nature.

Party caucuses are generally more potent in the state legislatures than in the Congress, but the differences between New Jersey, Connecticut, Pennsylvania, Ohio, and most of the southern and western states are again considerable. According to estimates by Samuel Patterson, in one-third of the states, the legislative caucuses debate and decide policy questions; in one-fourth, votes may be taken in caucus that require party members to vote as a bloc on a particular question on the floor.[79] Committees and subcommittees in recent years have assumed a more prominent role in many legislatures, partly because of the increasing size and complexity of the legislative workload and the desire of members for more power and visibility. Although well-articulated party and committee structures can coexist, it is generally in those assemblies where party voting is weakest and/or the majority party's margin most lopsided, that committees have emerged as the main locus of policy decisions. A recent survey of state legislators nationwide found 27 percent listing committees and subcommittees as the place where "the most significant decisions are made." But party organs ranked higher in most states; 35 percent of the national sample pointed to the offices of presiding officers or majority leaders and another 22 percent indicated party caucuses or policy committees as the most important centers of legislative influence.[80]

Scattered evidence suggests that the electoral relevance of party to state legislators, their inclination to party regularity in voting, and the authority of the party caucuses are undergoing a long-term decline. But there are also accounts of renewed electoral activity by the parties, of new roles for legislative caucuses in some states, and of increases in party voting as formerly one-party states become more competitive.[81] Certainly, whatever decline has occurred has started from a point of party strength in many states that has far surpassed the party's role in the modern Congress. It thus comes as no surprise that recently retired governors from across the country, while downplaying the relevance of partisanship to many of their roles, still regarded the party tie as essential to the task of legislative leadership.[82]

Governors and the Web of Party

In most states the governor, like the president, is the titular head of his party. But governors vary considerably in the extent and the effectiveness of their party and legislative leadership. Although the capacities of many governors for governmental coordination and control have been enhanced in recent years, this has not always strengthened the *party's* role as a "web over the dispersed organs of government."

The circumstances under which governors and state legislators gain election often weaken their party ties, although in somewhat different ways. We already have noted the increased value of incumbency among legislators and the growing importance to them of extrapartisan modes of public relations and constituent service. Governors, like U.S. senators, have been less successful in parlaying the advantages of incumbency, but they (and their opponents) have bought heavily into the "new" campaign techniques and technologies that eschew party appeals and bypass party organizations.[83] Trends in the scheduling of elections also have frayed the party tie among levels of government. More and more states have scheduled their elections so that they do not occur in the presidential election year. In the 1930s, 34 states elected their governor at the same time they voted for president. But as many states shifted from two-year to four-year gubernatorial terms (a trend that, other things being equal, could strengthen the governor's role as party leader), they scheduled state elections at midterm. Only 13 states now vote for governor and president concurrently, and four of these elect their governor only for a two-year term.[84]

This sort of election calendar has appealed to many states as a means of achieving a sharper focus on state issues and candidates and of avoiding the "contaminating" effects of the presidential race. Such a schedule, however, is likely to weaken the party's governmental role in two respects. First, by reducing the impact of national partisan swings, it increases the likelihood of divided party control in the legislatures and statehouses.[85] Second, by reducing the likelihood that the governor and the president will be of the same party, it may impede federal-state coordination. When a sample of governors who had left office since 1976 were asked what relevance the political party had had to their job, they placed the facilitation (or hindering) of communication and cooperation with the national administration near the top of the list. As Florida's Reubin Askew commented:

> I learned quickly the difference when you are of the same party as the president—that's critically important. That is why governors who sit on the sidelines and say that selection of the president doesn't make any difference are misleading themselves. I found that it makes a lot of difference.[86]

In fact, states that schedule gubernatorial elections in the congressional election year maximize the chance the governor and the president will be of opposite parties because gubernatorial races are often influenced by "negative voting" against the president's party at midterm.

Such effects are less pronounced than they once might have been because of the trends away from straight-ticket voting and lessened coattail effects. But those trends have themselves complicated the task of the party-in-government. Gubernatorial, like presidential, coattails are not what they once were in many states. One study finds gubernatorial coattails to have been severely limited in recent California elections, while in Pennsylvania they have remained a "significant factor" in determining the composition of the legislature.[87] Only three southern states (Mississippi, Alabama, and Georgia) plus Nebraska, which has a unicameral nonpartisan legislature, have *not* had the statehouse and one or both houses of the state legislature controlled by different parties for at least two years since 1947. In 20 states, party control has been divided for 14 or more of these 38 years. The 1980 election, which saw a decisive national Republican swing, left 26 states with divided party control. As a result of the 1982 election, 13 legislative chambers and 11 governorships switched party control, but 21 states still had divided government.[88]

Reduced coattail effects and the increased security of legislative incumbents make it more likely that the governor will face legislative majorities from the opposing party; they also may make members from his own party less inclined to link their fate to his. Thus governors, like presidents, have sometimes found it profitable to cross party lines in their courting of the legislature, to establish legislative and group liaison offices apart from the party machinery and to utilize media and public relations strategies that bypass—and sometimes make a point of denigrating—party organs. Such practices represent, in part, an adaptation to the weakening of the party tie among both voters and legislators. But party loyalties and party structures are still strong enough in most states—in the assembly itself, if not outside—to constrain such movements in a nonpartisan direction. The party remains the most promising "basic starting point" governors have in mobilizing support.[89] To go beyond mere ad hoc coalition building, they must lead their parties. In some states, gubernatorial attempts to bypass the party may provoke resentment and prove counterproductive in the end.

In a few states—Connecticut and Rhode Island, for example—governors have been able to use the state party organization to exert pressure and dispense rewards among the party's legislators. Governors sometimes have formed alliances with mayors and other local party leaders who could deliver the votes of legislators from that city or county. In a few instances governors have persuaded local organizations to deny renomination to recalcitrant legislators, although even in strong-party areas this seems to have been regarded as a high-risk strategy. In general, however, the dependence of legislators on state and local organizations has declined, and even where these organizations are relatively well-developed, their members often pay only sporadic attention to legislative affairs. The utility of state and local party organizations as instruments for mobilizing the legislature thus is limited. State chairs often serve as the governor's spokesmen on issues, and some undertake extensive lobbying efforts on behalf of his program. But just as party platforms are one source among many for the governor's program, state and local party organizations are only one instrument among others to be used in moving the legislature.[90]

Party structures *within* the legislature are apt to figure much more prominently in the governor's mobilization efforts. The governor may influence the choice of the assembly's leaders, but it is now quite rare for their selection to be regarded as a gubernatorial prerogative. In states where the lieutenant governor is elected separately from the governor and has extensive legislative functions (about 10 states), the governor may face a natural political rival in the senate leadership. In any event, governors who wish to lead must normally come to terms with party leaders. In most states these leaders possess sufficient resources and authority to play a central role in legislative decision making, and alternative mechanisms whereby the executive might persuade or mobilize the legislature are far less developed than they are at the national level.

While legislative party leaders often bring substantial resources to their dealings with the executive, they have reasons of their own for seeking a cooperative relationship.[91] In many states numerous patronage positions remain under the governor's control. During most of the twentieth century, governors' powers of appointment to top executive positions have grown. At the state level as at the national, the increasing scope and complexity of governmental activity and the need for mechanisms of coordination and control have expanded the executive's policy role. In all but six states, the governor now has sole responsibility for developing the state's budget, and most assemblies now depend on the governor for major policy initiatives and for the setting of legislative priorities. Nor are legislative leaders self-sufficient as mobilizers of the party vote; even in strong-party states, the governor's ability to raise the public's awareness of an issue and to stimulate pressure and support may be essential to party success. Especially in legislatures where one party has been dominant or the parties for other reasons have lacked cohesion in voting, gubernatorial leadership may represent the best hope the legislature and its leaders have to reduce fragmentation and produce a unified party vote. Considerable fragmentation may remain, of course; in many states, "party government" is a sporadic phenomenon at best. But in the states as at the national level, executive leadership is an increasingly important component of whatever success the party enjoys in putting forward an authoritative legislative agenda and marshalling the political resources necessary to enact it.

Many of the same powers and resources that help the governor exercise party leadership in the legislature also increase his capacity for controlling the executive branch. In the management of his executive household, however, the governor is likely to regard partisan considerations and party instruments as much less relevant. The same group of retired governors that regarded party ties and structures as essential to working with the legislature tended to regard partisanship as an outmoded basis for executive branch appointments:

> They cited "qualifications" and "competence" as the overriding considerations in selecting personnel, and they took some pride in appointing

persons from the opposite party, or persons whose party affiliation was unknown. Patronage is in part the victim of [their image of themselves as "managers"] and the emerging conviction that the business of state government is beyond politics.[92]

At the state as at the national level, the vast majority of a governor's appointments go to people who share his or her party identification. But such partisanship is increasingly incidental to the patterns of personal loyalty and policy compatibility that underlie these appointments. Party identification still serves as a threshold condition for appointment, but with the actual extent of party involvement being given little weight.

Here, too, interstate variations are considerable. In most states a larger proportion of positions is subject to "political" appointment than is true at the national level, but the control that state or local parties exercise over such appointments has declined. A sizable fraction of state chairs interviewed in the early 1970s (34 percent of Democrats, 51 percent of Republicans—a disparity that partly reflected the GOP's control of the White House at the time of the interviews) still rated the dispensing of patronage as an important component of their jobs. But over half of the state chairs reported that state-level patronage was completely handled in the governor's office. "Governor _____ doesn't check with us at all," said one. "He makes the appointments and we read about it in the paper the next day." "Sometimes [the governor's staff] calls me and asks what I think of somebody," another chairman indicated; "but it's usually a decision that's already been made and they are simply going through a perfunctory courtesy." [93]

Such gubernatorial control is sometimes defended in terms of a need for competence and for appointments that extend beyond traditional party circles, but the need of governors to maintain their own personal organizations is generally involved as well. The direct primary, particularly in those states that make no provision for party endorsement, requires candidates to develop a cadre of workers and contributors loyal primarily to them—an organization that frequently is difficult to integrate into the party structure for the general election campaign and that often makes rival claims when the time comes to distribute patronage. But nothing dictates that party organizations must be completely bypassed in the appointment process, and governors who do so may forfeit political resources that would have strengthened their position in the long run.

An important limitation on most governors' powers of appointment and bureaucratic control, and one that has been difficult to change, is the practice of independently electing department heads and other executive officers. In 22 states (up from 7 in 1966) the governor and lieutenant governor are now voted on in the general election as a team, and in six states the two must run as a team in the primary as well. But most states still separately elect their secretary of state (36 states), attorney general (43), and treasurer (38), and substantial numbers also elect auditors (25), superintendents of education (18), secretaries of agriculture (12), insurance commissioners (8), boards of education (12), and utility commissioners (11). The parties are of only limited utility in overcoming the problems of executive branch coordination that such arrangements pose. In 1974, 46 percent of elected administrators nationwide were either independents (6 percent) or members of the party opposite of the governor's; this represented a decline from 64 to 54 percent over 10 years in the percentage of administrators who shared their governor's party label. Even among elected administrators of the governor's party, only 17 percent reported that the governor had more control than the legislature over their agency. A very small number (9 percent) attributed their election to the governor's coattails or support, and only slightly more (17 percent, down from 39 percent in 1964) gave the party any credit for their election.[94]

Thus, the "long ballot" grants substantial governmental authority to politicians who are tied only minimally to the governor and may even be his natural rivals. These politicians tend to view the party as less important to their electoral fortunes than their own personal organization and group constituencies. Such arrangements point up both the continuing need for the "web of party" in state government and the conditions likely to limit its effectiveness.

NOTES

1. V. O. Key, *Politics, Parties and Pressure Groups*, 5th ed. (New York: Thomas Y. Crowell Co., 1964), 656.
2. For useful overviews see James Sundquist, "Party Decay and the Capacity to Govern," in *The Future of American Political Parties*, ed. Joel L. Fleishman (Englewood Cliffs, N.J.: Prentice-Hall, 1982), chap. 2; and Morris P. Fiorina, "The Decline of Collective Responsibility in American Politics," *Daedalus* 109 (Summer 1980): 25-245.
3. Joseph Cooper, David W. Brady, and Patricia A. Hurley, "The Electoral Basis of Party Voting: Patterns and Trends in the U.S. House of Representatives, 1887-1969," in *The Impact of the Electoral Process*, ed. Louis Maisel and Joseph Cooper (Beverly Hills: Sage Publications, 1977), 137.
4. Roger H. Davidson and Walter J. Oleszek, *Congress Against Itself* (Bloomington: Indiana University Press, 1977), 34.
5. Joseph Cooper and David W. Brady, "Institutional Context and Leadership Style: The House from Cannon to Rayburn," in *Understanding Congressional Leadership*, ed. Frank H. Mackaman (Washington, D.C.: CQ Press, 1981), 33. For a comparison of how party mechanisms evolved in the House and Senate after the 1870s, see Randall B. Ripley, *Power in the Senate* (New York: St. Martin's Press, 1969), chap. 2.
6. See Cooper and Brady, "Institutional Context"; David W. Brady, Joseph Cooper, and Patricia Hurley, "The Decline of Party in the U.S. House of Representatives, 1887-1968," *Legislative Studies Quarterly* 4 (August 1979): 381-407; and David W. Brady, "Congressional Leadership and Party Voting in the McKinley Era: A Comparison to the Modern House," *Midwest Journal of Political Science* 16 (August 1972): 439-449. On the intertwining of party loyalty and party democracy themes in the 1910 debate, see Charles O. Jones, "Joseph G. Cannon and Howard W. Smith: An Essay on the Limits of Leadership in the House of Representatives," *Journal of Politics* 30 (August 1968): 630-634.
7. See Aage R. Clausen, *How Congressmen Decide: A Policy Focus* (New York: St. Martin's Press, 1973), chaps. 5-6; Aage Clausen and Carl E. Van Horn, "The Congressional Response to a Decade of Change: 1963-1972," *Journal of Politics* 39 (August 1977): 624-666; and Barbara Sinclair, "Coping with Uncertainty: Building Coalitions in the House and Senate," in *The New Congress*, ed. Thomas E. Mann and Norman J. Ornstein (Washington, D.C.: American Enterprise Institute for Public Policy Research, 1980), chap. 6.
8. John W. Kingdon, *Congressmen's Voting Decisions*, 2d ed. (New York: Harper & Row, 1981), 120-123.
9. Cooper and Brady, "Institutional Context," 45. For a study of Johnson and his successor Mike Mansfield that also stresses the situational constraints on leadership, see John G. Stewart, "Two

Strategies of Leadership: Johnson and Mansfield," in *Congressional Behavior*, ed. Nelson W. Polsby (New York: Random House, 1971), chap. 5.

10. This discussion draws on David R. Mayhew, *Congress: The Electoral Connection* (New Haven: Yale University Press, 1974), 17-77; David E. Price, "Congressional Committees in the Policy Process," in *Congress Reconsidered*, 2d ed., edited by Lawrence C. Dodd and Bruce I. Oppenheimer (Washington, D.C.: CQ Press, 1981), 161-170; and Thomas E. Mann, "Elections and Change in Congress," in *The New Congress*, chap. 2.

11. Albert D. Cover, "One Good Term Deserves Another: The Advantage of Incumbency in Congressional Elections," *American Journal of Political Science* 21 (August 1977): 535; Paul R. Abramson, John H. Aldrich, and David W. Rohde, *Change and Continuity in the 1980 Elections*, rev. ed. (Washington, D.C.: CQ Press, 1983), 218-219; and Gary C. Jacobson, *The Politics of Congressional Elections* (Boston: Little, Brown & Co., 1983), 86.

12. See the discussions in Jacobson, *The Politics of Congressional Elections*, chap. 5; Thomas E. Mann and Raymond E. Wolfinger, "Candidates and Parties in Congressional Elections," *American Political Science Review* 74 (September 1980): 617-632; and Roger H. Davidson and Walter J. Oleszek, *Congress and Its Members* (Washington, D.C.: CQ Press, 1981), 79-89.

13. See Jacobson, *Politics of Congressional Elections*, 72-74, 119-221. "Differences between House and Senate elections," he concludes, "must be attributed primarily to the varying characteristics of House and Senate challengers and their campaigns.... Differences among candidates, rather than differences in patterns of voting behavior, are what distinguish House and Senate elections." Jacobson also argues that when partisan swings in the House do occur, they owe less to voters' responses to national forces than to prior expectations of success by potential candidates and contributors, which lead to more and better challengers and better financed campaigns in a number of districts.

14. Albert Cover and David Mayhew, "Congressional Dynamics and the Decline of Competitive Congressional Elections," in *Congress Reconsidered*, 2d ed., 77. See also Walter Dean Burnham, "Insulation and Responsiveness in Congressional Elections," *Political Science Quarterly* 90 (Fall 1975): 412-415. Note the contrasting findings of Keith Krehbiel and John R. Wright, "The Incumbency Effect in Congressional Elections: A Test of Two Explanations," *American Journal of Political Science* 27 (February 1983): 140-157.

15. Mayhew, *Electoral Connection*, 49-77.

16. Morris P. Fiorina, *Congress: Keystone of the Washington Establishment* (New Haven: Yale University Press, 1977), 19-21, 41-49, 56-62.

17. See Nelson W. Polsby, Miriam Gallaher, and Barry S. Rundquist, "The Growth of the Seniority System in the U.S. House of Representatives," *American Political Science Review* 63 (September 1969): 787-807; and Ripley, *Power in the Senate*, chap. 2.

18. Key studies of congressional norms and folkways include Donald R. Matthews, *U.S. Senators and Their World* (New York: Vintage Books, 1960), chap. 5; Richard F. Fenno, Jr., *The Power of the Purse: Appropriations Politics in Congress* (Boston: Little, Brown & Co., 1966), chaps. 3-5, 10; Herbert B. Asher, "The Learning of Legislative Norms," *American Political Science Review* 67 (June 1973): 499-513; Norman J. Ornstein, Robert L. Peabody, and David W. Rohde, "The Contemporary Senate: Into the 1980s," in *Congress Reconsidered*, 2d ed., chap. 1; and Burdett A. Loomis, "The 'Me Decade' and the Changing Context of House Leadership," in *Understanding Congressional Leadership*, chap. 5.

19. James L. Sundquist, "The Crisis of Competence in Our National Government," *Political Science Quarterly* 95 (Summer 1980): 198.

20. Norman J. Ornstein, "Causes and Consequences of Congressional Change: Subcommittee Reforms in the House of Representatives, 1970-73," in *Congress in Change*, ed. Norman J. Ornstein (New York: Praeger Publishers, 1975), 110. For a useful summary of the 1970s reforms, see Norman J. Ornstein and David W. Rohde, "Political Parties and Congressional Reform," in *Parties and Elections in an Anti-Party Age*, ed. Jeff Fishel (Bloomington: Indiana University Press, 1978), chap. 6.3.

21. Rowland Evans and Robert Novak, *Lyndon B. Johnson: The Exercise of Power* (New York: Signet, 1968), 69-76, 105-130. On the distribution of power within the Senate of the mid-sixties, see David E. Price, *Who Makes the Laws? Creativity and Power in Senate Committees* (Cambridge: Schenkman Publishing Co., 1972), 7-8.

22. Mayhew, *Electoral Connection*, 132-136.

23. U.S. Congress, House, Select Committee on Committees, *Report on the Committee Reform Amendments of 1974*, 93d Cong., 2d sess., March 21, 1974, 35-36; Bruce I. Oppenheimer, "Congress and the New Obstructionism: Developing an Energy Program," in *Congress Reconsidered*, 2d ed., chap. 12.

24. See Theodore Lowi, "American Business, Public Policy, Case-Studies, and Political Theory," *World Politics* 16 (July 1964): 690. "Distributive" policies (as opposed to higher conflict questions of redistribution) "are characterized by the ease with which they can be disaggregated and dispensed unit by small unit, each unit more or less in isolation from other units and from any general rule."

25. See Mayhew, *Electoral Connection*, 146-158. Members of the "control committees," Mayhew suggests, are "paid in internal currency for engaging in institutionally protective activities." On the norms prevalent in the taxing and spending committees and the deference accorded them within Congress, see Richard F. Fenno, Jr., *Congressmen in Committees* (Boston: Little, Brown & Co., 1973); and idem, *Power of the Purse*.

26. Allen Schick, *Congress and Money* (Washington, D.C.: The Urban Institute, 1981), 361.
27. Allen Schick, *Reconciliation and the Congressional Budget Process* (Washington, D.C.: American Enterprise Institute for Public Policy Research, 1981).
28. Bruce I. Oppenheimer, "The Changing Relationship between House Leadership and the Committee on Rules," in *Understanding Congressional Leadership*, chap. 7.
29. This summary draws on Charles O. Jones, *The Minority Party in Congress* (Boston: Little, Brown & Co., 1970), 26-39, 150-160.
30. Robert L. Peabody, "Senate Party Leadership: From the 1950s to the 1980s," in *Understanding Congressional Leadership*, 72. See also Richard E. Cohen, "Byrd of West Virginia—A New Job, A New Image," *National Journal*, August 20, 1977, 1292-1299; and idem, "Minority Status Seems to Have Enhanced Byrd's Position Among Fellow Democrats," *National Journal*, May 7, 1983, 758-760.
31. Alan Ehrenhalt, "The Individualist Senate," *Congressional Quarterly Weekly Report*, September 4, 1982, 2181. See also Martin Tolchin, "Howard Baker: Trying to Tame an Unruly Senate," *New York Times Magazine*, March 28, 1982, 17ff.
32. For two competent overviews, the first stressing the "resurgence" of the Speakership and the second the decentralization trends that have "more than countered leadership gains," see Lawrence C. Dodd and Bruce I. Oppenheimer, "The House in Transition: Change and Consolidation," in *Congress Reconsidered*, 2d ed., chap. 2; and Sidney Waldman, "Majority Leadership in the House of Representatives," *Political Science Quarterly* 95 (Fall 1980): 373-393.
33. Charles O. Jones, "House Leadership in an Age of Reform," in *Understanding Congressional Leadership*, 126.
34. Steven S. Smith, "Budget Battles of 1981: The Role of the Majority Party Leadership," in *American Politics and Public Policy: Seven Case Studies*, ed. Allan P. Sindler (Washington, D.C.: CQ Press, 1982), 50.
35. This summary draws on Barbara Sinclair, "Majority Party Leadership Strategies for Coping with the New U.S. House," and Lawrence C. Dodd and Terry Sullivan, "Majority Party Leadership and Partisan Vote Gathering: The House Democratic Whip System," in *Understanding Congressional Leadership*, chaps. 6, 8.
36. Dodd and Sullivan, "Leadership and Vote Gathering," in *Understanding Congressional Leadership*, 228.
37. Smith, "Budget Battles," in *American Politics and Public Policy*, 66-67, 72-73.
38. On the GOP efforts of the 1960s, see Jones, *Minority Party*, 38, 153-160. For the proposals of the Democratic Caucus task forces, see U.S. Congress, House, Democratic Caucus, Committee on Party Effectiveness, *Rebuilding the Road to Opportunity: A Democratic Direction for the 1980s*, 97th Cong., 2d sess., September 1982.
39. James L. Sundquist, *Politics and Policy: The Eisenhower, Kennedy and Johnson Years* (Washington, D.C.: The Brookings Institution, 1968), 489; Richard Neustadt, "Presidency and Legislation: Planning the President's Program," *American Political Science Review* 49 (December 1955): 983-984, 1013-1015.
40. *Congressional Quarterly Weekly Report*, April 22, 1978, 971.
41. See George C. Edwards, III, *Presidential Influence in Congress* (San Francisco: W. H. Freeman & Co., 1980), 70-78; Jacobson, *Politics of Congressional Elections*, 131-137; and Abramson, Aldrich, and Rohde, *Change and Continuity in the 1980 Elections*, rev. ed., 221-223.
42. While winning 51 percent of the popular vote, Reagan carried the Electoral College by a 489-49 margin. The Democrats lost 12 Senate seats, going from a 59-41 to a 47-53 margin, although nationwide they won 53 percent of the total votes cast in Senate races.
43. See Samuel Kernell, "Presidential Popularity and Negative Voting: An Alternative Explanation of the Midterm Congressional Decline of the President's Party," *American Political Science Review* 71 (March 1977): 44-66; Edwards, *Presidential Influence*, 66-70; and Jacobson, *Politics of Congressional Elections*, 124-131, 138-150.
44. Clausen and Van Horn, "Congressional Response," 632, 653; Sinclair, "Coping with Uncertainty," in *The New Congress*, 191.
45. Kingdon, *Congressmen's Voting Decisions*, 2d ed., 183-185.
46. See John F. Manley, "Presidential Power and White House Lobbying," *Political Science Quarterly* 93 (Summer 1978): 255-275; Eric L. Davis, "Legislative Liaison in the Carter Administration," *Political Science Quarterly* 94 (Summer 1979): 287-301; and Stephen J. Wayne, "Congressional Liaison in the Reagan White House," in *President and Congress: Assessing Reagan's First Year*, ed. Norman J. Ornstein (Washington, D.C.: American Enterprise Institute for Public Policy Research, 1982), 44-65.
47. Dom Bonafede, "To Anne Wexler, All the World Is a Potential Lobbyist," *National Journal*, September 8, 1979, 1477.
48. Ibid., 1476.
49. Hedrick Smith, "Taking Charge of Congress," *New York Times Magazine*, August 9, 1981, 17-18.
50. Bonafede, "Anne Wexler," 1478.
51. Smith, "Taking Charge," 17.
52. See Price, *Who Makes the Laws?* 1-9, 289-301.
53. Sundquist, *Politics and Policy*, 391.

54. "Others made the program and initially mobilized the support; . . . [Senate Majority Leader Lyndon Johnson] joined the movement only when it was well underway. But this may be the nature of legislative leadership in the party that does not hold the White House. . . . [P]arty leaders must stand somewhere near the middle of the party spectrum . . . [if they are] to gain and hold power and to use that power effectively. If the party spectrum in the legislature differs from the party spectrum in the nation—as it did in the Senate in the 1950s [because of the prominence of conservative southern Democrats]—then the successful legislative party leader will be out of step with the national party, as Johnson found when he ran for president in 1960." Ibid., 402.

55. See David Broder, *The Party's Over: The Failure of Politics in America* (New York: Harper & Row, 1972), 55-57.

56. Schick, *Reconciliation*, 34-35.

57. Joseph A. Califano, Jr., *A Presidential Nation* (New York: W. W. Norton & Co., 1975), 146. Helpful overviews of the president's party role include Thomas E. Cronin, "Presidents and Political Parties," in *Rethinking the Presidency*, ed. Thomas E. Cronin (Boston: Little, Brown & Co., 1982), chap. 21; and Richard M. Pious, *The American Presidency* (New York: Basic Books, 1979), chaps. 4, 6.

58. Califano, *Presidential Nation*, 159, 153.

59. See Cornelius P. Cotter and Bernard C. Hennessy, *Politics Without Power: The National Party Committees* (New York: Atherton Press, 1964), 67-105, 138-148; Hugh A. Bone, *Party Committees and National Politics* (Seattle: University of Washington Press, 1958), 103-107; Roger G. Brown, "Party and Bureaucracy: From Kennedy to Reagan," *Political Science Quarterly* 97 (Summer 1982): 287-290; Broder, *The Party's Over*, 58-64; and Lester G. Seligman, "The Presidential Office and the President as Party Leader," in *Parties in an Anti-Party Age*, chap. 6.4.

60. Rhodes Cook, "Carter and the Democrats: Benign Neglect?" *Congressional Quarterly Weekly Report*, January 14, 1978, 60.

61. *Congressional Quarterly Weekly Report*, October 9, 1982, 2657.

62. Computed from data in Roger G. Brown, "The Presidency and the Political Parties," in *The Presidency and the Political System*, ed. Michael Nelson (Washington, D.C.: CQ Press, 1983), 324. Brown takes his definition of and information about "major" appointees from the annual listings of confirmed presidential nominees in the *Congressional Quarterly Almanacs*, 1961 to 1982.

63. Brown, "Party and Bureaucracy," 286-287.

64. Nelson W. Polsby, *Consequences of Party Reform* (New York: Oxford University Press, 1983), 91. On the party background of Nixon's initial appointees, see Frank J. Sorauf, *Party Politics in America*, 4th ed. (Boston: Little, Brown & Co., 1980), 363.

65. Polsby, *Consequences of Reform*, 103-104. On Carter's partial reversal of this pattern late in his term, see p. 128.

66. For profiles of Reagan's appointees, see *Congressional Quarterly Weekly Report*, December 20, 1980, 3605-3617; December 27, 1980, 3649-3654.

67. Cotter and Hennessy, *Politics without Power*, 144.

68. James W. Singer, "Changing of the Guard: Reagan's Chance to Remold the Senior Bureaucracy," *National Journal*, November 29, 1980, 2028-2031; and idem, "The Pick of the Plums," *National Journal*, November 29, 1980, supplement.

69. Polsby, *Consequences of Reform*, 129. See also Sundquist, "Crisis of Competence," 193-194: "Jimmy Carter, the outsider, would not have been the nominee in 1976 of an organized political party; he is what can happen when the choice of party leader is taken entirely out of the hands of the party elite and turned over to the people."

70. See Richard Neustadt, "The Constraining of the President," *New York Times Magazine*, October 14, 1973, 38ff; and idem, *Presidential Power: The Politics of Leadership from FDR to Carter* (New York: John Wiley & Sons, 1980), 170-177, 202-207.

71. See Sundquist, "Crisis of Competence," 201-204.

72. Cook, "Carter and the Democrats," 59; see also Brown, "Presidency and Parties," 330-332.

73. The "index of cohesion" is a commonly used measure of party unity, obtained by subtracting the percentage of the party's members in the minority on a given vote from the percentage in the majority; it thus ranges from 100 (for unanimous votes) to 0 (for 50-50 splits). Frank Sorauf (*Party Politics in America*, 4th ed., 340-341) estimates the mean index of cohesion of the congressional parties on party-line votes during the 1970s as 30 to 35 percent, while the range for the weak-party states is more like 45 to 65 percent. Comparative data on party voting in state legislatures are assembled by Malcolm E. Jewell and Samuel C. Patterson in *The Legislative Process in the United States*, 3d ed. (New York: Random House, 1977), 384-385.

74. See Sorauf, *Party Politics*, 344-347; Jewell and Patterson, *Legislative Process*, 382-388; Hugh L. Le Blanc, "Voting in State Senates: Party and Constituency Influences," *Midwest Journal of Political Science* 13 (February 1969): 33-57; and Thomas Flinn, "Party Responsibility in the States: Some Causal Factors," *American Political Science Review* 58 (March 1964): 60-71.

75. See Richard J. Tobin and Edward Keynes, "Institutional Differences in the Recruitment Process: A Four-State Study," *American Journal of Political Science* 19 (November 1975): 667-682; Samuel C. Patterson, "Legislators and Legislatures in the American States," in *Politics in the American States*, 4th ed., edited by Virginia Gray, Herbert Jacob, and Kenneth Vines (Boston: Little, Brown & Co., 1983), 142-147; and Alan Rosenthal, *Legislative Life* (New York: Harper & Row, 1981), 32-33. See

also Robert Huckshorn, *Party Leadership in the States* (Amherst: University of Massachusetts Press, 1976), 102-109. Huckshorn finds 74 percent of state party chairmen nationwide (81 percent of Republicans, 67 percent of Democrats) to be involved in some form of candidate recruitment.

76. Christopher Buchanan, "GOP Makes Modest Gains in State Legislature Contests," *Congressional Quarterly Weekly Report*, November 15, 1980, 3374-3376; Patterson, "Legislators and Legislatures," 147-153; Malcolm E. Jewell and David M. Olson, *American State Political Parties and Elections*, rev. ed. (Homewood, Ill.: Dorsey Press, 1982), 227-232; and Rosenthal, *Legislative Life*, 22-26.

77. Jewell and Patterson, *Legislative Process*, 185. On interstate variations in legislative leadership roles, see 159-161, 183-188; also Rosenthal, *Legislative Life*, chap. 8. For a catalogue of leadership prerogatives in a strong-party state, see John J. Pitney, Jr., "Leaders and Rules in the New York State Senate," *Legislative Studies Quarterly* 7 (November 1982): 491-506.

78. See David Ray, "The Sources of Voting Cues in Three State Legislatures," *Journal of Politics* 44 (November 1982): 1074-1087. Ray has replicated portions of John Kingdon's study of congressional roll-call voting at the state level. He finds party leaders to be the single most important source of voting cues in the Massachusetts House, but this form of party influence seems considerably less important in the New Hampshire and Pennsylvania houses. He does not find sufficient differences in the formal powers of the leadership in the three states to explain these contrasts.

79. Patterson, "Legislators and Legislatures," 163-164; see also Rosenthal, *Legislative Life*, 169-170.

80. Computed from data in Wayne L. Francis and James W. Riddlesparger, "U.S. State Legislative Committees: Structure, Procedural Efficiency, and Party Control," *Legislative Studies Quarterly* 7 (November 1982): 455.

81. Bits of evidence are contained in LeBlanc, "Voting in State Senates," 57; Jewell and Patterson, *Legislative Process*, 159-161, 383-386; and William Pound, "The State Legislatures," in *Book of the States, 1982-83* (Lexington, Ky.: The Council of State Governments, 1982), 185-186.

82. Lynn Muchmore and Thad L. Beyle, "The Governor as Party Leader," *State Government* 53 (Summer 1980): 123.

83. Larry Sabato, "Gubernatorial Politics and the New Campaign Technology," *State Government*, 53 (Summer 1980): 148-152.

84. See Jewell and Olson, *American State Parties and Elections*, 44-45, 158-159; and Table 5-1 in Chapter 5.

85. See Walter Dean Burnham, *Critical Elections and the Mainsprings of American Politics* (New York: W. W. Norton & Co., 1970), 94; and Ronald Weber, "Gubernatorial Coattails: A Vanishing Phenomenon?" *State Government* 53 (Summer 1980): 153. Burnham refers to the practice as "legally prescribed electoral disaggregation." Weber notes, however, that such a schedule is likely to increase the independent pulling power of the *governor's* race within the state.

86. Muchmore and Beyle, "Governor as Party Leader," 124.

87. Weber, "Gubernatorial Coattails," 153-156; see also Jewell and Olson, *American State Parties and Elections*, 235-238.

88. Data from Buchanan, "GOP Makes Modest Gains," 3375; Rob Gurwitt and Tom Watson, "Democrats Recoup State Legislature Losses," *Congressional Quarterly Weekly Report*, November 13, 1982, 2848-2849; and Jewell and Olsen, *American State Parties and Elections*, 233.

89. See Thad L. Beyle, "Governors," in *Politics in the States*, 206-208; and Rosenthal, *Legislative Life*, 238-241.

90. See Huckshorn, *Party Leadership in the States*, 77-89, 97-102, 248-254. Huckshorn apparently did not ask his sample of state chairs to rank the importance of communicating with the legislature in relation to their other functions, but it seems to have been mentioned with moderate frequency, especially by those who regarded themselves as the governor's "agents." See also Jewell and Patterson, *Legislative Process*, 263-264.

91. This discussion draws on Beyle, "Governors," 193-203; Nelson C. Dometrius, "Measuring Gubernatorial Power," *Journal of Politics* 41 (May 1979): 589-610; E. Lee Bernick, "Gubernatorial Tools: Formal vs. Informal," *Journal of Politics* 41 (May 1979): 656-664; and Bernick, "The Impact of U.S. Governors on Party Voting in One-Party Dominated Legislatures," *Legislative Studies Quarterly* 3 (August 1978): 431-444.

92. Muchmore and Beyle, "Governor as Party Leader," 123.

93. Huckshorn, *Party Leadership in the States*, 100, 113-114.

94. Data from *Book of the States, 1982-83*, 168-169; and Nelson C. Dometrius, "State Government Administration and the Electoral Process," *State Government* 53 (Summer 1980): 129-134. See also Table 5-1 in Chapter 5.

The Place of the Party 4

Underlying the previous discussion of the current state of the American parties is a conviction that parties have a crucial role to play in the modern democratic state. In this chapter we will elaborate that theme, with special attention to the ambiguous place of party in the American constitutional order. We first will examine several critiques and defenses of party that have figured significantly in the American political tradition and then explore the party roles of particular importance today.

Evolution of the Party Idea

It was the English publicist and member of Parliament Edmund Burke who in 1770 put forth the classic definition of party as "a body of men united for promoting by their joint endeavors the national interest upon some particular principle in which they are all agreed." Burke mounted his defense of party in a pamphlet expounding the political creed of the Rockingham Whigs, who found themselves, after a brief ministry in 1765 and 1766, in an opposition role in a badly fragmented Parliament. Rockingham's successor as prime minister, William Pitt, denounced parties and sought to organize his ministry around loyalty to himself, picking leaders from a number of parliamentary factions. Burke saw such practices not only as excluding his own group but as removing power from Parliament itself, leaving the king and those around him "unlimited and uncontrolled" in influence. Champions of the court, Burke noted, had propagated the doctrine "that all political connections are in their nature factions, and as such ought to be dissipated and destroyed; and that the rule for forming administrations is mere personal ability, rated by the judgment of this cabal upon it, and taken by draughts from every division and denomination of public men." But for members of Parliament to accept this condemnation of "political connections" would be to relegate themselves to impotence. Their only hope of influence, Burke argued, lay in concerted action:

Whilst men are linked together, they easily and speedily communicate the alarm of any evil design. They are enabled to fathom it with common counsel, and to oppose it with united strength. Whereas, when they lie dispersed, without concern, order, or discipline, communication is uncertain, counsel difficult, and resistance impracticable.... When bad men combine, the good must associate; else they will fall, one by one, an unpitied sacrifice in a contemptible struggle.[1]

Well aware that parties could foster "a narrow, bigoted, and proscriptive spirit," Burke argued that the possibility that they might "degenerate into faction" did not render them any less necessary "for the full performance of our public duty." Public duty, in fact, gave powerful ethical support to party fidelity. Burke was profoundly skeptical of the tendency of politicians to tout their own independence or to portray themselves as motivated by "conscience"; he suspected this was too often a cover for the pursuit of private advantage. Party operations, Burke believed, could leave room for occasional dissent, but the desire to maintain concord would properly nudge fellow partisans toward agreement: "When the question is in its nature doubtful, or not very material, the modesty which becomes an individual, and that partiality which becomes a well-chosen friendship, will frequently bring on an acquiescence in the general sentiment." A public official, moreover, had a positive obligation to "pursue every just method" for putting into practice those principles for which he stood:

It is not enough in a situation of trust in the commonwealth, that a man means well to his country; it is not enough that in his single person he never did an evil act, but always voted according to his conscience, and even harangued against every design which he apprehended to be prejudicial to the interests of his country.... Public duty demands and requires that what is right should not only be made known, but made prevalent; that what is evil should not only be detected, but defeated. When the public man omits to put himself in a situation of doing his duty with effect, it is an omission that frustrates the purposes of his trust almost as much as if he had formally betrayed it.[2]

Assuming that parties could indeed rise above the level of self-interested factions, it thus became incumbent on the politician to maintain the party discipline that alone promised him and his colleagues effectiveness.

"On the subject of party," Richard Hofstadter notes, "Burke was an advanced and prophetic thinker who took a long stride beyond what had been said before him by any of the leading writers."[3] He also took a long stride beyond the realities of British politics of his day. The tendencies toward a two-party system in Parliament that had developed early in the eighteenth century had largely dissipated by the time of George III's reign (1760-1820). There were numerous shifting factions, many unattached members, and an absence of focused, aligning issues. The franchise still was quite restricted and the link between popular partisan sentiments and parliamentary alignments quite tenuous. Britain moved toward an extended electorate of the sort that had been established in the United States only after the Reform Acts of 1832 and 1867, and it was not until 1868 that a prime minister resigned after his party was defeated in parliamentary elections. While Americans in time came to see the British system as exemplary of "responsible" parties, in many aspects of party development it was actually the United States that "proved to be the avant-garde nation."[4]

From Washington to Van Buren

Americans, however, were slow to acknowledge that parties could play a legitimate and constructive role in republican government. Burke had no counterpart among the American founders. The sentiments of Viscount Bolingbroke, England's classic antiparty writer, and of pamphleteers such as John Trenchard and Thomas Gordon,[5] enjoyed much greater currency. George Washington's conception of his role in many ways resembled that attributed by Bolingbroke to his "patriot-king"—a leader above partisan and factional strife whose task it was to embody national unity. Deeply disturbed by the growth of partisan divisions and by opposition to his administration's policies, Washington focused his farewell address in 1796 on the tendency of parties "to render alien to each other those who ought to be bound together by fraternal affection." In monarchical governments, he conceded, parties might serve as a useful check on governmental authority. But in governments "of the popular character," the spirit of party was "not to be encouraged":

> It serves always to distract the public councils and enfeeble the public administration. It agitates the community with ill founded jealousies and false alarms, kindles the animosity of one part against another, foments occasionally riot and insurrection. It opens the door to foreign influence and corruption, which finds a facilitated access to the government itself through the channels of party passion.[6]

Historians differ concerning how conscious Washington was of the partisan character of his own actions and pronouncements. (Federalist leader Alexander Hamilton later described him as "an aegis very essential to me.") What is certain is that, despite his devotion to citizen liberty and popular government, Washington could never reconcile himself to the partisan divisions that were bound to flow from the liberty he championed.[7]

The Jeffersonian Republicans, forerunners of the modern Democratic party, had more reason to claim legitimacy for party operations by virtue of their opposition role. But they, no less than Hamilton, were inclined to portray their own partisanship as a temporary expedient, necessary to return the republic to its true foundations. James Madison, writing in *The Federalist*, used the terms "party" and "faction" interchangeably and acknowledged that both were likely to flourish under conditions of liberty: "Liberty is to faction what air is to fire." To control faction by extinguishing liberty would indeed be a "remedy worse than the disease." But Madison was very far from seeing parties as a positive good: unable to remove their *causes,* he thought it essential to control their *effects,* to remedy those "diseases most incident to republican government."[8] In the *Federalist* his speculations centered on how the most dangerous sort of faction, a tyrannical *majority,* might be checked;

several years later, when he was, in effect, the leader of the opposition party, his emphasis shifted to the perils of minority faction—an appelation he gave the Hamiltonians. In fact he took considerable comfort in the majority status of his own party, for he felt that this would result in its ultimate triumph. He did not conclude that a continuing opposition party would be needed, however, because he did not regard the Republicans, properly speaking, as a faction at all.

Once they had rescued the new nation from the Federalists' subversive designs, the Republicans expected consensus to emerge around sound constitutional principles. The checking of power—among organs of the national government, and of the national government by the states—still would be critical to the preservation of liberty. But these checks were built into the constitutional structure itself; to add to them enduring partisan divisions within governmental organs and extending into the entire body politic would be at once unnecessary and dangerous.

Thomas Jefferson occasionally spoke as if he expected broadly based partisan divisions to endure:

> The same political parties which now agitate the United States have existed through all time. Whether the power of the people or that of the [aristocracy] should prevail, were questions which kept the states of Greece and Rome in eternal convulsions, as they now schismatize every people whose minds and mouths are not shut up by the gag of a despot.[9]

But he could never accept the idea of a continuing party system in the United States, convinced as he was that leading Federalists intended to establish monarchy on the British model and that the public's hostility to such treasonable views assured the final triumph of his own party. Jefferson struck a conciliatory note in his first inaugural address—"We have called by different names brethren of the same principle. We are all republicans; we are all federalists"—and in certain of his policy stances. But as Hofstadter notes, for Jefferson "conciliation was not a way of arriving at coexistence or of accommodating a two-party system, but a technique of absorption: he proposed to win over the major part of the amenable Federalists, leaving the intractables an impotent minority faction rather than a full-fledged opposition party." Less than three weeks after his inaugural address, Jefferson wrote of his determination "to obliterate the traces of party and consolidate the nation, if it can be done without the abandonment of principle."[10]

After his retirement from public office Jefferson became increasingly uneasy about the terms on which the "absorption" of the dying Federalist party was taking place. President James Monroe, who regarded parties as the "curse of the country," rejoiced in 1822 that they had "cooled down or rather disappeared." Jefferson was more wary. The Federalists, he felt, had shed their monarchism but had adopted "the next ground, the consolidation of government." And they had managed to insinuate themselves into Republican ranks and to foment divisions (most notably on the Missouri question) that would work to their own ultimate advantage. "Like the fox pursued by the dog," Jefferson said, "they take shelter in the midst of the sheep."[11] While such apprehensions led Jefferson to reconsider his earlier denigration of partisanship, it did not take him beyond an advocacy of *Republican* restoration. It was left for the next generation to make the case for a full-fledged system of party competition.

Martin Van Buren and many of his collaborators in the rising generation of Republican politicians were the products of years of party contention in New York, Pennsylvania, and other states. They valued partisan politics as a means by which men of humble origins could gain the stature formerly reserved for those from established families. They also were less imbued with eighteenth-century antiparty doctrine than was the generation of the founders and more aware of the potential of party to mobilize a greatly expanded electorate.

Van Buren came to Washington as a senator in 1821, seasoned by years of conflict with the New York Republican faction led by De Witt Clinton, whom Van Buren and other "old Republicans" viewed as a self-serving party wrecker and a Federalist in disguise. Van Buren soon found himself at odds with those heralding the "Era of Good Feeling" and with President Monroe in particular, whom he blamed for the administration's drift from its Jeffersonian moorings and for the increasing fragmentation of Republican forces. "The Republican party, so long in the ascendant, and apparently so omnipotent, was literally shattered into fragments, and we had no fewer than five Republican presidential candidates in the field," Van Buren later wrote of the period from 1821 to 1824. "In the place of two great parties arrayed against each other in a fair and open contest for the establishment of principles in the administration of government which they respectively believed most conducive to the public interest, the country was overrun with personal factions," he lamented. Van Buren particularly criticized Monroe's failure to give firm backing to the party's congressional caucus as the instrument of presidential nomination: "Already weakened through the adverse influence of the administration, the agency which had so long preserved the unity of the Republican party did not retain sufficient strength to resist the combined assault that was made upon it, and was overthrown." [12] Convinced that such an instrumentality was necessary if party unity and discipline were to survive, Van Buren later fastened on the national convention, which the old Republicans (calling themselves Democratic-Republicans and after 1832 simply Democrats) considered having in 1828 and first held to renominate Andrew Jackson in 1832.

Van Buren and others who organized the Jacksonian revolution thus represent a second generation of "founders" who established and legitimated an enduring system of competition between two national parties. In some respects they contravened the intentions of the preceding generation by accepting partisan divisions as a fixed feature of political life and by democratizing electoral competition in a way that the Electoral College and other constitutional devices had been designed to avoid. In other ways, however, they partook of the spirit of the founders, acting to preserve the system under altered conditions.[13] Van Buren's defense of party echoed the founders' apprehensions about the dangers of faction—unchecked power in government and demagogic, divisive electoral appeals. Unlike them, however, he insisted on differentiating partisan divisions from mere factional disputes. In fact it was the *absence* of well-organized parties in the 1820s that raised the spectre of personal factionalism and immoderate appeals. And could not broadly based parties, through their competition, provide a check on the factional abuses of power that otherwise might threaten the republic? Van Buren argued they could:

> Doubtless excesses frequently attend [parties] and produce many evils, but not so many as are prevented by the maintenance of their organization and vigilance. The disposition to abuse power, so deeply planted in the human heart, can by no other means be more effectually checked; and it has always therefore struck me as more honorable and manly and more in harmony with the character of our people and of our institutions to deal with the subject of political parties in a sincerer and wiser spirit—to recognize their necessity, to give them the credit they deserve and to devote ourselves to improve and to elevate the principles and objects of our own [party] and to support it faithfully.[14]

Van Buren was at pains to stress the "principled" character of party divisions, both in distinguishing parties from narrower factions and in opposing the kind of indiscriminate inclusiveness he attributed to Monroe and John Quincy Adams. But his adherence to ideological principle was qualified in two critical ways. First, although he remained a committed Jeffersonian and took comfort in the assurance that his own party, by virtue of its popular character, would generally be ascendant, he differed from his forebears in his acceptance of the legitimacy, even the usefulness, of an organized opposition. He repudiated that "species of cant against parties in which too many are apt to indulge when their own side is out of power and to forget when they come in," and asserted that political parties, not just his own, were "inseparable from free government" and "highly useful to the country."[15] Second, the emphasis of Van Buren and his collaborators on organization and party discipline tended to blur ideological distinctions. Loyalty to the party could not be conditional on its precise correctness on issues, and the imperatives of coalition building and electoral victory in a pluralistic society required a measure of programmatic flexibility.

Van Buren's way of developing the party—"which was to become the American way," Hofstadter notes—"brought with it that lack of consistency and clarity on ideas and issues that is so often the despair of critics of the American party system.... For all their well-meant statements about principles, the very concern of the new politicians for the party as a structure, and for the mechanisms and maneuvers that would strengthen it, tended to displace ideological, and even at times programmatic commitments."[16] Significantly, the controversies that arose toward the end of the nineteenth century concerning party operations on the Van Buren model witnessed not only a revival of antiparty ideas but also a critique of the parties' opportunistic and nonprogrammatic character.

The Two Faces of Progressivism

Eighteenth-century antiparty thinkers in England and America came from all points on the ideological spectrum. Many of them feared parties, in fact, for the democratic excesses they might introduce. But the critiques of the emergent American party system that arose in the nineteenth century increasingly bore a democratic stamp, reflecting the view that party organizations were an obstruction to the direct expression of the people's will. The attacks on legislative and other nominating caucuses were particularly revealing: "I would rather that the sovereignty of the states should be re-transferred to England, than that the people should be bound to submit to the dictates of such an assemblage," wrote a Republican editor in 1824 concerning caucus control of presidential nominations. "The great mass of the American people feel that they are able to judge for themselves; they do not want a master to direct them how they shall vote." [17]

Such attacks reached their zenith in the Progressive Era around the turn of the century. As we saw in Chapter 2, nominating conventions (which initially had been regarded as "democratic" alternatives to legislative caucuses) were replaced by direct primaries in most states. "Abolish the caucus and the convention," admonished Wisconsin's Robert La Follette in an 1897 address titled "The Menace of the Political Machine": "Go back to the first principles of democracy; go back to the people." [18] The quest for democratic reform also led to the direct election of U.S. senators, women's suffrage, the dropping of partisan designations in most local elections, and the widespread adoption of the initiative, referendum, and recall. Behind such measures lay a commitment to human equality, a belief that individual citizens could and should develop and express their political convictions independently, and an expectation that such convictions would naturally coalesce around broad notions of the common good. Profoundly distrustful of political organizations—interest groups and parties alike—many Progressives were attracted by a plebiscitary ideal, whereby the role of intermediate institutions would be thoroughly subordinated to direct and frequent expressions of the popular will. Nebraska Sen. George Norris's defense of the direct primary well represents this view:

> One of the objections that is always made to the direct primary is that it takes away party responsibility and breaks down party control.... Politicians, political bosses, corporations and combinations seeking special privilege and exceptional favor at the hands of legislatures and executive officials, always urge this as the first reason why the direct primary should be abolished. But this objection ... I frankly offer as one of the best reasons for its retention. The direct primary will lower party responsibility. In its stead it establishes individual responsibility. It does lessen allegiance to party and increase individual independence, both as to the public official and as to the private citizen.... Partisanship blinds not only the public official but the ordinary citizen and tends to lead him away from good government.[19]

Not all of the Progressives were as negative about parties as Norris. La Follette frequently declared that it was his intention to purify rather than to abolish the parties and, once in power, he proved to be a statewide machine-master of considerable ability. But in their zeal to make governmental institutions and policies more directly responsive to the popular will, the midwestern Progressives perceived the organized party mainly as a barrier to be overcome. They gave relatively little thought to the functions performed by the parties—such as pulling together scattered personal factions or establishing "political unity" among organs of government—and to how they might be affected by reform.[20]

There was, however, another aspect to the Progressive impulse, particularly in its urban, eastern manifestations: a desire to bring order, efficiency, and rational control to a society where "the network of relations affecting men's lives each year [seemed] more tangled and more distended."[21] "The economic and social changes of the past generation," wrote Herbert Croly, eastern Progressivism's most prominent publicist, "have brought out a serious and a glaring contradiction between the demands of a constructive democratic ideal and the machinery of methods and institutions which have been considered sufficient for its realization." Croly criticized his fellow reformers who conceived of democracy as "essentially a matter of popular political machinery" and whose dominant impulse was "to prevent the people from being betrayed—from being imposed upon by unpopular policies and unrepresentative officials." What the national crisis required was not such "negative" measures but organization and leadership sufficient "to give positive momentum and direction to popular rule." Croly put little stock in mechanisms like the referendum or the direct primary; he thought that the primary, by increasing the number of elections and the "amount of political business to be transacted," might actually *enhance* the powers of professional politicians. Instead Croly advocated a strengthened role for executives (who "are much more representative of public opinion than are the delegates of petty districts") and a professionalized, hierarchically organized civil service.[22]

Such ideas gained wide currency in political, journalistic, and academic circles and were reflected in many pioneering works in the nascent disciplines of sociology and political science. In general they did not prompt a strong interest in the potential of political parties as integrative mechanisms. Indeed, most reformers were inclined to regard parties as part of the problem. "Party government," Croly wrote, "has interfered with genuine popular government both by a mischievous, artificial and irresponsible [i.e., parochial and localistic] method of representation, and by an enfeeblement of the administration in the interest of partisan subsistence."[23] But a few writers, mostly academics, began to suggest that "responsible" parties might serve as instruments both of democracy and of coherent, efficient government. The most prominent among them was Woodrow Wilson, president of Princeton University, who in 1908 described the American parties as "absolutely necessary to ... give some coherence to the action of political forces." He believed they helped overcome the "separation and jealous independence" of the branches of government and, at the electoral level, enabled voters to unite "in truly national judgments upon national questions":

> There is a sense in which our parties may be said to have been our real body politic. Not the authority of Congress, not the leadership of the President, but the discipline and zest of parties, has held us together, has made it possible for us to form and to carry out national programs.[24]

Wilson, no less than Croly, felt that the preoccupations of the founders must now be transcended: "We must think less of checks and balances and more of coordinated power, less of separation of functions and more of the synthesis of action."[25] Accordingly, Wilson's defense of party differed significantly from Van Buren's. Gone is the emphasis on party as an instrument for tempering immoderate factional appeals and for the checking of power; Wilson instead portrayed the party as a vehicle of the majority will and as a device for overcoming constitutional checks and binding the organs of government together. Far from seeing parties as a constraint on democratically chosen leaders, Wilson stressed the role of such leaders in shaping and activating party organizations. "Among a free people," he wrote, "there can be no other method of government than such as permits an undictated choice of leaders and a strong, unhampered making up of bodies of active men to give them effective support."[26] In fact, one could argue that Wilson's notion of popular executive leadership (which led him, as president, to advocate a national presidential primary) left the parties in a subordinate role. But what is certain is that his defense of parties—no less than the case other Progressives were making *against* parties—had shifted to democratic grounds.

Although Wilson and other advocates of responsible parties defended the historical role of American parties, they regarded their traditional mode of operation as inadequate for the tasks that confronted them in the new century. "Such parties as we have," wrote Wilson in an early essay, "parties with worn-out principles and without definite policies, are unmitigated nuisances."[27] Wilson and others took the British parties—supposedly disciplined and cohesive, and unhampered by constitutional barriers in their governing function—as their model of responsible parties, though they disagreed concerning the extent to which British-style parties could or should be transplanted to the American setting. In general, they anticipated that the social and economic upheavals of the day not only would leave the parties with critical tasks of political integration to perform, but also would make them better equipped to do so—less parochial, more programmatic, and more nationally oriented. They were divided and ambivalent, however, about whether the pressures to democratize the parties' internal operations would serve the cause of party responsibility. Some regarded the direct primary as likely to invigorate the parties and increase their legitimacy, while others felt that party cohesion and discipline would be weakened and the likelihood reduced that voters could make coherent choices and have them translated into governmental action. As we shall see, these differences among responsible-party advocates of the Progressive Era prefigured dilemmas that have surrounded the party system ever since.

The Modern "Responsible Party" Debate

Much of the modern debate on the role of American parties has focused on a 1950 report by the Committee on Political Parties of the American Political Science Association entitled "Toward a More Responsible Two-Party System." In stating its basic thesis, the committee grounded its case on both democratic accountability and effective governance:

> Historical and other factors have caused the American two-party system to operate as two loose associations of state and local organizations, with very little national machinery and very little national cohesion. As a result, either major party, when in power, is ill-equipped to organize its members in the legislative and executive branches into a government held together and guided by the party program. This is a very serious matter, for it affects the very heartbeat of American democracy. It also poses grave problems of domestic and foreign policy in an era when it is no longer safe for the nation to deal piecemeal with issues that can be disposed of only on the basis of coherent programs.[28]

The committee put forward a range of proposals designed to increase the coherence of the policy alternatives offered to the electorate by the parties and the capacity of the parties to implement their programs once in office. Among its recommendations were the formation of a central party council, composed of 50 top governmental and party leaders, to exercise broad powers between conventions (including the initial drafting of the national platform and the initial screening of presidential and congressional candidates); the formulation of national platforms "at least every two years"; and the use of the congressional caucuses to bind members to the party's policy positions.

The report touched off a protracted debate within the political science profession. Some regarded responsible parties as basically desirable yet felt that the report underestimated the extent to which American parties approximated that standard. One student of party voting in Congress, for example, argued that "contrary to popular impression, the parties usually maintain their ranks on congressional votes ... with sufficient solidarity so that voters may distinguish between two points of view."[29] Others questioned both the feasibility and the desirability of moving American parties in the responsible-party direction. Responsible-party advocates, it was charged, overestimated the possibility of transforming the parties by intellectual fiat and ignored the social, cultural, and ideological factors that had given the American parties their amorphous shape.

In particular, critics argued, the APSA committee overestimated the electorate's inclination to vote on the basis of issues and ideology; underestimated the barrier that federalism and the constitutional separation of powers posed to party centralization; and failed to understand that the desire to compete effectively in a range of locales, given America's political fragmentation and heterogeneity, required a certain vagueness in the parties' electoral appeals. Moreover, it was asked, might not responsible parties, rather than facilitating responsive government, actually introduce an element of rigidity into policy making, making it more difficult to compromise, to adapt to changing circumstances, or to form supportive coalitions on diverse issues?[30]

The responsible-party debate has had strong ideological overtones. Both sides have claimed to champion majoritarian democracy. E. E. Schattschneider, chairman of the APSA committee and the most influential modern champion of responsible parties, portrayed parties as "the special form of political organization adapted to the mobilization of majorities." "How else can the majority get organized?" he asked. "If democracy means anything at all it means that the majority has the right to organize for the purpose of taking over the government." C. E. Lindblom, by contrast, noted that a majority vote in favor of a party's candidate could not be interpreted as majority approval of each element in the party's platform; in fact, tightly organized parties in government "may be less able to detect and respond to majority wishes on particular elements than can an undisciplined party." [31] (Other critics, however, feared that responsible parties might prove all too willing to disregard *minority* interests.)

In general, critics of the APSA report have accepted the "pluralist" analysis of American democracy, assuming that society's legitimate interests receive a measure of accommodation through the continuing give-and-take within and among decentralized governmental institutions. Nonideological parties have been valued for their facilitation of coalition formation among diverse groups and for their promotion of the system's overall stability: "It is the party system, more than any other American institution, that consciously, actively, and directly nurtures consensus"— by drawing party candidates and workers from all strata of society, by making inclusive and nonideological electoral appeals, and by promising and delivering "to each group *some* but never all of what it wants." [32]

Responsible-party advocates have been less sanguine about pluralist politics, more sensitive to the kinds of interests that get excluded, and more critical of the difficulties the system has in moving beyond "adjustments" among powerful interests to integrated policy approaches. Defenders of the APSA report have regarded their critics as deficient both empirically and ethically, in their high estimate of America's "civil-war potential" and in the priority they give to stability and consensus as social values. Responsible parties, according to their advocates, would be instruments of significant social change, responding not so much to the appeals of powerful organized groups as to widely shared popular sentiments.

The American party system has moved only partially and irregularly in the direction prescribed by the authors of the APSA report.[33] Democratic National Chairman Paul Butler established a Democratic Advisory Council in late 1956 that was modeled in part on the committee's recommendations, but it was boycotted by the Democratic congressional leadership and disbanded in 1960 after the Democrats regained the presidency (see Chapter 9). The 1974 Democratic charter provided for a party conference between quadrennial conventions, but made the calling of the conference optional and did not require that it adopt a platform. The

APSA committee had recommended that the national committees be reapportioned to reflect actual party strength in the states and that their headquarters' operations be upgraded; the Democratic charter effected such a reapportionment (while the RNC has resisted such efforts), but it is the Republicans who have done most to develop their financial and staff capacities. The congressional parties have moved in some directions recommended by the report (increased party control of committee assignments and legislative scheduling, more use of the caucus), but they have not gone nearly as far in consolidating leadership powers, in modifying seniority, or in instituting binding caucus votes as the committee would have wished.

Members of the APSA committee might be encouraged at the slight upturn of party voting in Congress in recent years, at the evidence of heightened issue awareness and issue voting in the electorate, and at indications that the parties are now viewed as more ideologically distinctive than they were in the 1950s. But the weakened linkage between party and issue/candidate preferences (see Figure 1-1), the decline of party coattails, the rise of congressional individualism, and many of the other trends reviewed in Chapters 1-3 would give them small comfort indeed.

Although American parties have retained many of the features criticized by the Schattschneider committee, they nonetheless have undergone significant changes. Many of these changes have been favored by neither the responsible-party advocates nor the defenders of the conventional parties. "Differences between the two schools of thought surely remain, notably over their preferred remedies," Leon Epstein observes, "but the differences [now] tend to be overshadowed by a mutual dissatisfaction with the state of American parties in the 1970s and 1980s." [34] Responsible-party proponents and critics alike have viewed with concern the evidence of party decline and have taken a critical stance toward reform efforts, both inside and outside the parties, which seemed likely to weaken the parties further.

The organizational directions taken since the 1950s by the parties, particularly the Democratic party, owe less to responsible-party ideas than to what has alternatively been called the "representative party structures" and "participatory" school of reform. [35] This perspective, characteristic of challenges to the urban machines as well as of efforts to "open up" the national conventions, has stressed the importance of intraparty democracy—facilitating *participation* by rank-and-file members, ensuring that all segments of the party are *represented* in party councils, increasing the *accountability* of leaders to members. Reformers of this persuasion have been more inclined to work within party structures and less inclined to reject their legitimacy outright than were their Progressive forebears. Nonetheless, they have carried forward much of the distrust of leaders and organization, and the ambivalence about barriers to direct democracy, that characterized the Progressive Era. [36]

The APSA report itself gave considerable attention to intraparty democracy—grass-roots participation in party organizations, a national convention "broadly and directly representative of the rank and file," "safeguards against internal dictation by a few in positions of influence."

It described the direct primary as "a useful weapon in the arsenal of intraparty democracy" and even suggested that a national presidential primary someday might prove "feasible and desirable"! [37] The committee left unexplored the compatibility between this line of reform and the report's stronger emphasis on centralized, disciplined party organizations, capable of fulfilling their policy commitments. Many responsible-party advocates had criticized the direct primary and argued that efforts to democratize the parties internally might actually make the performance of their broader "democratic" functions—projecting coherent electoral appeals and pulling together the machinery of government—more difficult. It was, in fact, the chairman of the APSA committee who had stated the case against intraparty democracy most boldly:

> The sovereignty of the voter consists in his freedom of choice just as the sovereignty of the consumer in the economic system consists in his freedom to trade in a competitive market. That is enough; little can be added to it by inventing an imaginary membership in a fictitious party association. Democracy is not to be found *in* the parties but *between* the parties. [38]

Such a view no doubt underestimates the new life that broadened participation can give to party organizations. But modern champions of reform have rarely focused as sharply as either the responsible-party advocates or those defending the traditional structures on the desirability and the conditions of party strength per se. Accordingly, their recommendations have widely varied in their implications for the health of the parties. It is a central intention of the present study to subject the proposals of this school of party reform to the kind of scrutiny—in terms of their impact on party strength and, indeed, on the parties' ability to implement the reformers' own policy goals—that their advocates have all too often failed to apply.

Making a Case for Parties

Four modern modes of party organization are categorized in Table 4-1 according to their degree of organizational *control* and the importance of *issues* to their internal incentive structure and electoral appeal. [39] Such a scheme helps one visualize the directions in which the "reformers" (quadrants 1 and 3) have wished to move the established party organizations. Responsible-party advocates have wanted to sharpen the policy stances and strengthen the discipline of conventional party structures, particularly at the national level. Modern participatory reformers' attacks on the urban machines often have sought to democratize party operations while committing the party to specific policy positions. Participatory reformers at the national level have wanted to increase national party authority in certain respects, but their underlying goal has been to "open up" the state and local parties to increased participation and to require them (and thus the national conventions) to meet certain standards of representation and inclusion. Like the responsible-party advocates, the participatory reformers have been strongly issue-oriented. They have

Table 4-1 Models of Party Organization

	Strong issue appeal	*Issues vague and/or deemphasized*
Centralized, disciplined	"Responsible" parties	Classic local "machines"
	1	2
	3	4
Decentralized, permeable	Modern "representative structures"/participatory model	Conventional national and state parties

been less inclined, however, to temper their proposals for intraparty democracy in view of the party's organizational needs. "Despite the importance reformers attach to the party's role in promoting issues," Kenneth Janda notes, "they are reluctant to equip the party with an organizational capacity to mobilize support for issue positions among office holders." [40]

Most American party organizations fall into quadrants 3 and 4: they are decentralized, permeable, increasingly populated by issue or candidate enthusiasts, but rarely unified around policy stances with enough clarity or discipline to satisfy the advocates of party "responsibility." There are scattered signs of movement toward increased organizational cohesion and a more articulate and assertive policy role; such trends should be welcomed and encouraged. But it is important to recognize the extent to which parties will remain "responses to their environments." [41] If responsible-party enthusiasts have sometimes forgotten this, so too have defenders of the conventional parties, nostalgic for the days before "amateurism" arose in force. In the remainder of this book, we will be stressing the importance of the party as a potential shaper of the political environment and of the measures that might be taken to enhance that role. But such changes will continue to be constrained by the country's "institutional machinery and political culture." "Those factors that historically have inhibited the development" of ideological, cohesive, disciplined parties, as Gary Orren argues, "are no less powerful today." [42] If the parties are to retain their broad electoral appeal and hold their coalitions together for purposes of governance, they must continue to moderate their ideological appeals, to tolerate considerable organizational "slack," and to practice the politics of bargaining and compromise.

In focusing on the strength of the American parties, we will not be wedded to any of the models presented in Table 4-1. Advocates of each of them have presented themselves as champions of strong parties—some more plausibly than others. But their debates seem increasingly passé, and we will largely bypass them. The crucial question is less whether we should have responsible or pragmatic parties than whether partisan or nonpartisan (or antipartisan) modes of campaigning and governance should prevail. The recommendations of the various schools of party reform must now take their place in a larger context: the case for parties as a vital component of the American political system. In what terms might that case be made?

Parties as Instruments of Democratic Control

By helping voters make rational and consistent electoral choices, parties link the popular base of the political order and the institutions of government. Despite the moderate, coalitional character of the American parties, they differ significantly in their positions on a range of issues, both in their platforms and in the policies they attempt to enact once in office. While the national platforms of the parties generally do not offer point-for-point contrasts, neither do they support the notion that the parties are "Tweedledum" and "Tweedledee." They differ significantly in emphasis and in the groups to which they appeal. Some 69 percent of the pledges appearing in platforms from 1944 through 1976 were made by one party but not the other.[43] Differences in emphasis can be significant: references to unemployoment outnumbered references to inflation at a rate of 48 to 30 in the 1976 Democratic platform, while the Republican platform mentioned unemployment in a context of corrective action only once.[44] Such differences obviously provided a reliable cue to the contrasting policies the Carter and Reagan administrations subsequently would pursue.

Most voters, of course, do not consult party platforms. The party cue is valuable precisely because it serves as a kind of shortcut to identifying compatible candidates and programs. Despite the traditional, habitual character of many people's partisan attachments, there is a general congruence between their socioeconomic status, their ideological and policy views, and their partisan identification. As V. O. Key demonstrated, it is erroneous to assume that consistent partisan voters are "obtuse diehards who swallow their principles to stick by their party." On the contrary, most of them "are already where they ought to be in light of their partisan attitudes." [45]

As we saw in Chapter 1, voters' ideological and issue positions have become considerably more congruent with their partisan perceptions and identifications since the 1950s. At the same time, voters have become less likely to link their issue and candidate preferences to "party" and more inclined to vote on the basis of such preferences independent of the party cue. Walter Dean Burnham described the patterns that have emerged as consistent party voting has declined:

> If decisive minorities of voters do not find party a useful frame of reference of voting decisions, they will seek other kinds of cues for those decisions. At the highest level of salience—say in voting for President, U.S. Senator, or Governor—they will respond to a mixture of candidate appeal, major campaign issues, and, third and last, party.... At lower levels of salience, and especially when this "nonpartisan" minority turns to voting for congressmen, the incumbency effect ... will have overwhelming importance.[46]

One may doubt that such patterns, overall, represent an increase in voter rationality. "Candidate appeal" is often based on the most superficial, contrived kind of media image. "Major issues" are too often a few isolated, symbolically potent issues that happen to be "hot" at the moment—frequently as a result of skilled advertising. And incumbent voting has loosened the link, not only between the issue positions of individual voters and their representatives, but also between national public opinion trends and Congress as a whole.

Given a basic congruence between the interests and attitudes of most voters and their partisan identifications, there is more to be said than is often assumed for the rationality of regular (if not purely reflexive) party voting. Studies of cities where party labels have been removed from ballots for local offices suggest that such nonpartisan elections often heighten the importance of candidates' "celebrity" status, ethnic identity, and incumbency to the vote they receive; increase the campaign role of the media and interest groups; and result in reduced levels of campaigning and voter turnout.[47] Nonpartisanship may be particularly disadvantageous to the poorer and less-educated members of the community, who tend to rely relatively heavily on the party cue to identify candidates who reflect their interests. Willis Hawley demonstrates that nonpartisan balloting is less likely than partisan balloting to produce officials who are attentive to problems of low-income housing, unemployment, and the quality of social services.[48]

But the usefulness of the party label is not limited to poorly informed or marginally involved voters. Amid the powerful and manipulative stimuli of modern campaigns, it is often the party label that offers the best clue to candidates' positions on a range of issues, the interests they will be at pains to accommodate, the cooperative ties they will be able to establish, and the kinds of people they will be likely to bring into government. The idea of voting "for the person and not the party" fits nicely with the individualistic and moralistic strains of American political culture, but neither the virtue nor the rationality of such a stance will bear careful scrutiny.

Parties aggregate the interests and preferences not only of the individual voters, but also of a broad array of groups within the society. The coalitional character of the parties is evident at many levels—from the "balanced" ethnic tickets characteristically put together by urban organizations, to the variegated promises to be found in party platforms, to the "horse-trading" that produces legislative majorities.[49] The parties differ, of course, in the groups to which they are most attentive. Labor, educators, and ethnic/racial minorities figure most prominently in Democratic politics; business and professional groups in the GOP. But both parties have strong incentives to keep channels of communication open with a variety of groups and to become the captive of none.

Today the proliferation of single-interest organizations, the renewal of interest group activity through PACs and other mechanisms, and the weakening of party structures threaten to reduce the party's role in the aggregation of group interests. That role is to be valued, not simply for the access and efficacy it promises to contending groups, but also for the way it balances their demands against broader public interests. It is likely that the array of active organized groups will underrepresent certain kinds of interests—the interests of deviant or disadvantaged groups that are unable or unwilling to jockey for advantage and also those more inclusive interests which, by virtue of their breadth and diffuseness, often are not mobilized effectively.[50] One cannot plausibly identify the public interest, or the majority interest, with the sum of group demands. To aggregate these interests and pressures through strong parties increases the likelihood that they will be balanced not only against one another, but against the presumed interests of an electoral majority. "Pressure politics" and "party politics," as Schattschneider stressed, represent two contrasting ways of aggregating interests; historically, parties have served to "socialize" conflict, to ensure that policy outcomes do not merely reflect "the power ratio among the private interests most immediately involved" but also take into account the interests and concerns of the larger community.[51]

Party aggregation is not without its shortcomings. It is rarely bold or creative, sometimes overly responsive to group pressures and opportunistic in crafting electoral appeals. Parties need leaders whose vision extends beyond the maintenance of the organization, and they often must rely on their candidates and officeholders for policy innovation. The inclusiveness and moderation of the parties has its negative aspects; as Robert Dahl notes, it is often easy "for political leaders to ignore groups of people whose problems lie outside the attention, loyalties, values, and identifications of the great mass of voters, particularly if these groups lack bargaining power because of poor organization, low status, isolation, ignorance, lack of political incentives, and so on."[52] This is one reason that intraparty democracy and the possibility of third-party formation should be valued more highly than either responsible-party advocates, such as Schattschneider, or the defenders of the conventional, coalitional parties have acknowledged.

Parties nonetheless help offset the biases of pluralism, balancing the demands of society's best-organized and best-financed groups with appeals that are more directly responsive to broader public interests. What is at stake in the decline of party is not simply the *presence* of a linkage between government and its mass base, but also the *character* of the mechanisms by which the "public" is organized and its presumed interests are articulated. The historic function of party has been, as Burnham puts it, to "generate countervailing collective power on behalf of the many individually powerless against the relatively few who are individually—or organizationally—powerful."[53] However flawed parties may have been as democratizing, linking institutions, it seems likely that their further demise would leave our politics even more fragmented, more particularistic, and less broadly responsive than it has become already.

Parties as Mediating Institutions

From the beginning, American parties have had a double life as organizers of electorates and governments at the national level and as local associations rooted in "geographically organized wards and precincts

... reflecting closely the characteristics of community life." Historian Samuel Hays recently has argued that many national party victories may have turned less on ostensible "national" issues such as tariffs and trusts than on the ethnic, religious, and cultural values and identifications that mobilized local partisans. In 1928, for example, presidential nominee Al Smith forged a Democratic majority in the country's 12 largest cities primarily by emphasizing ethno-cultural issues. At the same time, economic divisions were becoming more important, as workers began to vote more heavily Democratic. These national trends, rooted less in local communities than in "the technological organization of modern industrial society," became dominant during the depression and the realignment era that followed.[54] But as our earlier chapters have indicated, congressional and local elections often deviate substantially from national trends, and local party organizations show considerable independence and variability in the appeals they make and in the political forces they accommodate.

Local parties, like their state and national counterparts, help structure electoral choice and accountability (although nonpartisan balloting has greatly hindered them in this task in many places). But local parties play a broader role as "mediating institutions," as focal points of community life, and as links between the community and the larger political world. Considerable interest recently has been expressed in the preservation and revitalization of "those institutions standing between the individual in his private life and the larger institutions of public life"— neighborhoods, families, churches, and voluntary associations, for example. Curiously, however, the best-known contemporary defense of these mediating structures does not give parties even passing notice.[55] Certainly such an omission would not have occurred 50 years ago when urban party organizations served as a vital link between neighborhoods and city hall and offered an important means of mobility and influence for ethnic and immigrant groups.

As we have seen, many of the conditions that gave the "machine" its unique mediating function have changed irreversibly. This does not mean, however, that most citizens now are persuaded of government's responsiveness or of the efficacy of the channels of political participation open to them: quite the contrary. The past two decades have seen a widening gap between the public and private spheres of life—an increasing public alienation from remote and vaguely threatening centers of governmental and corporate power, coupled with the deterioration of those intermediate associations and institutions that have enhanced the personal identities of individuals and given them the means of concerted action. "There is abundant evidence," Carey McWilliams notes, "that the contemporary decline of the political party is part of a general political decay." He concludes:

> Americans live lives that are more and more specialized, live in towns and neighborhoods that are less and less stable, live in families that are more and more likely to break up or—increasingly—in casual liaisons, and live in private havens that are more and more penetrated by mass media and mass culture and by the now thoroughly international econ-

omy. The private order is increasingly fragmented, and people are more and more alone in the face of a more gigantic and confusing political world.[56]

The effective functioning of parties as mediating institutions in modern communities requires means and mechanisms considerably different from those of the traditional urban organizations. "Material" incentives generally count for less, and organizations must increasingly provide outlets for the discussion of issues and for the communication of policy concerns to higher organizational and governmental levels. But effective local organizations cannot be disdainful of more mundane concerns—the desire for more flexible residential parking in a downtown ward, the need for signs designating the names of a county's rural roads, the wish to obtain community development funds to improve a neighborhood park. Such concerns still powerfully motivate people, and all too often mechanisms for their effective expression are not at hand. Thus, although local organizations increasingly provide outlets for the broader policy concerns of party "amateurs," their role as a conduit for more conventional, immediate interests is still of considerable importance, both in attracting participants and in prompting governmental responsiveness.

Participation in party organizations has another aspect, however. Party life, like life in other communal structures, is not merely instrumental: it often is intrinsically satisfying, even enriching. And while party organizations help individuals and groups effectively pursue their wants, they also bring them into contact with other values and interests, compelling them to adjust their demands and, ideally, to consider the broader public good. McWilliams suggests that sometimes "our emotions can be charmed out of their preoccupation with self and educated to be allies—if never entirely reliable ones—of reason and community." [57] In fostering such an "alliance," parties differ crucially from interest groups. Mediating structures, properly conceived, are not mere agents of "particularity," not simply mechanisms for the transmission of private wants.[58] They also "mediate" in the other direction, tempering particular interests in light of more general ones, local and parochial concerns in light of those that are more inclusive.

The "give and take of participation," as John Dewey once described it, is "a sharing that increases, that expands and deepens, the capacity and significance of the interacting factors." [59] One need not romanticize the sort of civic virtue fostered by political parties to see in it a vital corrective to the increasingly narrow and fragmented modes of organization and participation that have come to dominate the American political scene.

What might be termed a "communitarian" defense of political parties thus takes its place alongside the more familiar defenses on the grounds of democratic linkage and governmental efficiency.[60] It is a defense that assumes the American political order needs not only structures for the effective pursuit of individual and group interests, but also structures through which those pursuits are tempered and broadened, where the private pursuit of advantage confronts the larger pleasures and demands of citizenship. The communitarian defense also has important implications for current trends in party organization. Certainly it casts doubt on Schattschneider's denigration of intraparty democracy; effective channels of participation and leadership accountability are essential in the contemporary political environment.[61]

This is not to say, however, that the reforms of the representative structures/participatory school have uniformly enhanced the party's mediating role. The communitarian view focuses far more on the quality than on the quantity of participation. It regards as oversimple the view—common among Progressive reformers—that democracy requires an unmediated relationship between independent-minded, public-spirited citizens and their government. The communitarian thus is unlikely to be seduced by the "democratic" credentials of the direct primary; caucuses and conventions will have more appeal as ways of engaging citizens, providing them with effective channels of participation, and putting them in touch with the larger political world. To these and similar questions the communitarian brings an appreciation of the social context of democracy, of the sorts of interaction and communication that are required if political efficacy is to be experienced throughout the society and if unifying notions of the common good are to emerge. Political parties may have filled these needs imperfectly, but nothing currently on the horizon promises to be an effective substitute.

Parties as Instruments of Governance

As we have seen, the defenses of party written by the two American presidents who thought most about the subject were strikingly different. Van Buren mirrored the founders' preoccupation with the checking of power, while Wilson, like others of the Progressive Era, wished to give elected leaders the wherewithal to overcome the tendency toward stasis in checked and balanced government. Although the two views are in tension, they both still bear considerable relevance to the parties' role in government.

The negative role—providing a check against the unpopular or illegitimate use of power—is obviously dependent on the presence of an opposition party or parties. By organizing minority-party forces in the legislature and by contesting elections, the opposition party provides and publicizes a continuing challenge to those in power. Even if the policy differences between the parties are limited, the "out" party provides a mechanism by which the "ins" may be called to account and, by its mere presence, provides a deterrent to careless stewardship. Such opposition, of course, is not always party-based. Recent years have seen increasing numbers of independent operators mounting righteous crusades in legislative halls and on the campaign trail—running "for" Congress by running "against" Congress as an institution, refusing to be a party to political compromise, and so forth. On occasion, such lonely stands may be warranted: recall Sen. Wayne Morse's soliloquies in the 1960s on the country's deepening involvement in Vietnam. In general, however, the mediation of opposition efforts through party mechanisms tends to reduce their idiosyncratic aspects and to increase the likelihood that opposition forces, once successful, will have coherent alternatives to offer and the capacity to put them into effect.

To this traditional role of the opposition party one now must add the importance of party as a check on its *own* officeholders. Although the 1950 APSA report argued, approvingly, that the president's leadership capacities would be enhanced by strengthened parties, it also contained some prescient observations concerning the sorts of presidential "overextension" that might be prompted by party weakness:

> It favors a president who exploits skillfully the arts of demagoguery, who uses the whole country as his political backyard, and who does not mind turning into the embodiment of personal government.[62]

As we noted in Chapter 3, recent critics have emphasized the importance of party as a *constraint* on the president, particularly in analyzing the excesses of the largely apartisan Johnson and Nixon presidencies. Party ties can extend an officeholder's reach, but they also establish a kind of day-to-day accountability to his peers and to the major constituencies that put him in office. It is a need to which the modern champions of plebiscitary democracy, like their Progressive forebears, have paid inadequate attention.

Yet it is equally important to extend the reach of public officials, to develop means of pulling the organs of government together for the achievement of positive ends. The American constitutional system is far better suited to the checking of power than it is to concerted and consistent policy making. Historically, the parties have filled this gap only sporadically and with mixed success. In the twentieth century three periods of strong, unified government stand out, each of them involving electoral landslides and assertive presidents: Wilson's first two years (1913-1914), Franklin Roosevelt's first term (1933-1936), and the first two years of Lyndon Johnson's presidency (1964-1965). Despite predictions to the contrary, Ronald Reagan's first years did not display the same degree of governmental integration. Nor are we likely soon to see a repetition of the Wilson-Roosevelt-Johnson pattern: "If attaining governmental competence has always been difficult in the past," James Sundquist argues, "it will be even more arduous in the future. For in the last decade or two the political scene has changed profoundly, and the changes all militate against governmental effectiveness." [63]

Of the five contributing factors that Sundquist identifies, four are closely linked to party decline: electoral disaggregation, plebiscitary presidential nomination, resistance by Congress to presidential leadership, and heightened centrifugal forces within Congress itself. Politics is increasingly fragmented, volatile, incoherent. Elected in an environment where personal and single-issue factors are as important as the party tie, officials owe little to the party and have few incentives to teamsmanship. As we have noted, the evidence on party decline does not all point in one direction. In Chapter 9 we will find that the parties' track record in fulfilling their national platform pledges is stronger than is sometimes thought. But the overall picture leaves little doubt that party weakness has brought a serious decline in the country's already limited capacity for purposive government. And the decline has occurred precisely at a time when a new generation of economic, energy, and environmental issues has come to the fore—issues singularly resistant to the effortless "adjustments" of pluralistic politics.

Lester Thurow, asking what it would take to forge viable policies in these areas of high conflict, is driven to a pessimistic conclusion because of the weakness of the integrative mechanisms that are needed to do the job. As Thurow aptly concludes, the costs of weak parties are high:

> Our inability to act ... arises because, in a real sense, we do not have political parties.... Instead, we have a system where each elected official is his own party and is free to establish his own party platform. Parties are merely vague electoral alliances. But this means a splintering of power that makes it impossible to hold anyone responsible for failure.... Each individual member of Congress reports to his constituents that his solutions to the problems were killed by someone else, but he is fighting hard.... Since no one has the power to solve the problems, no one can be fired for not solving the problems.

> But not having accountable, integrated political parties fails us in an even more fundamental way. Since all economic solutions require decisions about the distribution of income, we should be voting political parties up and down based on how they are going to allocate the economic losses necessary to solve our problems. Not having political parties with a common position on this issue ... each individual congressman is free to argue that all of the losses should be allocated to someone else's congressional district, and this is exactly what his voters want to hear. Presidential candidates cannot shift the losses quite so easily; therefore they retreat to the position that they can solve the problems without hurting anyone.... To pretend that there are no losses, however, is to guarantee that once elected, a president will not be able to impose the necessary losses.... Every politician with his own platform is the American way, but it is not a way that is going to be able to solve America's economic problems.[64]

Bringing the parties back, then, is critical to achieving democratic accountability and responsiveness, to relating citizens to the broader political community, and to developing a capacity for cooperation and for addressing hard problems within and between the organs of government. The case does not rest on any assumption that strengthened parties could take care of these matters single-handedly or conclusively, or that parties can escape the limitations placed on them by American institutions and political culture. But it is within the power of government and of the parties themselves to strengthen the party system in at least marginal ways, and the performance of critical democratic functions depends on such a strengthening. It has become more rather than less important in recent years for the political system to develop mechanisms of accountability, effective mediation, and policy integration; these are historically the tasks of the parties, and there is little evidence that effective surrogate mechanisms are at hand.

NOTES

1. Edmund Burke, "Thoughts on the Cause of the Present Discontents," in *Works* (London: George Bell & Sons, 1893), vol. 1, 314, 372, 375.
2. Ibid., 373, 376, 378.
3. Richard Hofstadter, *The Idea of a Party System: The Rise of Legitimate Opposition in the United States, 1780-1840* (Berkeley: University of California Press, 1969), 33.
4. Ibid., 42.
5. "There had been no such thing as party now in England, if we had not been betrayed by those whom we trusted," wrote Trenchard and Gordon in *Cato's Letters* (no. 16). "Let neither private acquaintance, personal alliance, or party combination stand between us and our duty to our country." David L. Jacobson, ed., *The English Libertarian Heritage* (New York: Bobbs-Merrill Co., 1965), 48-50.
6. George Washington, "Farewell Address," in *Writings* (Washington, D.C.: U.S. Government Printing Office, 1940), vol. 35, 223-228.
7. See Hofstadter, *Idea of a Party System*, 91-102; and Joseph Charles, *The Origins of the American Party System* (New York: Harper & Row, 1961), 37-53.
8. James Madison, Alexander Hamilton, and John Jay, *The Federalist Papers*, with an introduction by Clinton Rossiter (New York: New American Library, 1961), no. 10.
9. Thomas Jefferson, *Life and Selected Writings*, ed. A. Koch and W. Peden (New York: Modern Library, 1944), 627.
10. Hofstadter, *Idea of a Party System*, 151. See also James Ceaser, *Presidential Selection: Theory and Development* (Princeton, N.J.: Princeton University Press, 1979), chap. 2.
11. Quotes from Ceaser, *Presidential Selection*, 124, 107-108. On the views of Monroe, "an ardent party man with ardent anti-party convictions," see Hofstadter, *Idea of a Party System*, 188-211.
12. Martin Van Buren, *Inquiry into the Origin and Course of Political Parties in the United States* (New York: Hurd & Houghton, 1867), 3-5. On Van Buren's views and strategies, see Hofstadter, *Idea of a Party System*, chap. 6; and Ceaser, *Presidential Selection*, chap. 3.
13. For an interpretation of Van Buren as the founders' "true heir," see Ceaser, *Presidential Selection*, 37-38, 135-136, 168.
14. Martin Van Buren, *Autobiography* (Annual Report of the American Historical Association, vol. 2, 1918), 125.
15. Ibid., 125. When "differences are discussed and the principles of contending parties are supported with candor, fairness, and moderation, the very discord which is thus produced may, in a government like ours, be conducive to the public good," Van Buren wrote in 1814. Ibid., 50.
16. Hofstadter, *Idea of a Party System*, 246-247.
17. Austin Ranney, *Curing the Michiefs of Faction* (Berkeley: University of California Press, 1976), 118.
18. Robert M. La Follette, *LaFollette's Autobiography* (Madison: University of Wisconsin Press, 1960), 86.
19. George W. Norris, "Why I Believe in the Direct Primary," *Annals of the American Academy of Political and Social Science* 106 (March 1923): 23. Note the extensive, approving quotations from Washington's farewell address, 24.
20. For a contemporary critique by an anti-La Follette member of the University of Wisconsin faculty, see Arnold B. Hall, "The Direct Primary and Party Responsibility in Wisconsin," in Ibid., 40-54. See also Richard Hofstadter, *The Age of Reform* (New York: Vintage Books, 1960), 257-271.
21. Robert H. Wiebe, *The Search for Order, 1877-1920* (New York: Hill & Wang, 1967), 42.
22. Herbert Croly, *The Promise of American Life* (1909; reprint, New York: Capricorn Books, 1964), 270, 332, 342; idem, *Progressive Democracy* (New York: Macmillan, 1914), 213. On Croly's dual quest for "social control" and national "community," see David E. Price, "Community and Control: Critical Democratic Theory in the Progressive Period," *American Political Science Review* 68 (December 1974): 1669-1670.
23. Croly, *Progressive Democracy*, 349. See the discussion in Austin Ranney, *The Doctrine of Responsible Party Government* (Urbana: University of Illinois Press, 1962), chap. 8.
24. Woodrow Wilson, *Constitutional Government in the United States* (New York: Columbia University Press, 1961), 206, 217-218. On the views of Wilson and other prominent responsible-party advocates of the period—A. Lawrence Lowell, Henry Jones Ford, and Frank J. Goodnow—see Ranney, *Responsible Party Government*, chaps. 3-6.
25. Wilson, *Constitutional Government*, 221.
26. Ceaser, *Presidential Selection*, 203; for an argument that "Wilson's major objective was to strengthen leadership and not parties," see pp. 197-207. For an insightful interpretation of the Democratic party's performance under Wilson as a case of "executive" rather than "partisan" responsibility, see Croly, *Progressive Democracy*, 337-348.
27. Ranney, *Responsible Party Government*, 33.
28. Committee on Political Parties, American Political Science Association, "Toward a More Responsible Two-Party System," *American Political Science Review* 44 (September 1950 supplement): v.
29. Julius Turner, "Responsible Parties: A Dissent from the Floor," *American Political Science Review* 45 (March 1951): 145.

30. Particularly noteworthy critical discussions include Austin Ranney and Willmoore Kendall, *Democracy and the American Party System* (New York: Harcourt, Brace & World, 1956), chaps. 21-22; Charles E. Lindblom, *The Intelligence of Democracy* (New York: Free Press, 1965), chap. 20; and Evron M. Kirkpatrick, " 'Toward a More Responsible Two-Party System': Political Science, Policy Science, or Pseudo-Science?" *American Political Science Review* 65 (December 1971): 965-990. For latter-day defenses of the responsible-party position, see Gerald Pomper, "Toward a More Responsible Two-Party System? What, Again?" *Journal of Politics* 33 (November 1971): 916-940; and J. Harry Wray, "Rethinking Responsible Parties," *Western Political Quarterly* 34 (December 1981): 510-527.

31. E. E. Schattschneider, *Party Government* (New York: Holt, Rinehart & Winston, 1942), 208; Lindblom, *Intelligence of Democracy*, 327.

32. Ranney and Kendall, *Democracy and Party System*, 508.

33. Compare Pomper's discussion in "Toward a More Responsible Two-Party System," 923-940, and Austin Ranney's accounting of the fate of committee recommendations, *Mischiefs of Faction*, 43-45.

34. Leon D. Epstein, "The Scholarly Commitment to Parties" (Paper delivered at the annual meeting of the American Political Science Association, Denver, Colorado, 1982), 12.

35. See Ranney, *Michiefs of Faction*, 44; and Robert T. Nakamura and Denis G. Sullivan, "Party Democracy and Democratic Control," in *Amerian Politics and Public Policy*, ed. W. D. Burnham and M. W. Weinberg (Cambridge: MIT Press, 1978), 28.

36. For an interpretation of modern reformers as the Progressives' heirs and as the (sometimes unwitting) architects of a plebiscitary presidential selection system that "undermined any role for a party organization," see Ceaser, *Presidential Selection*, chap. 6.

37. APSA, "Toward a More Responsible Two-Party System," 67, 70, 71, 74. The committee, however, opposed "open" primaries, arguing that only registered or declared party members should be allowed to vote; it also advocated preprimary endorsement of candidates by party organizations (71-72).

38. Schattschneider, *Party Government*, 60; see also idem., *The Semi-Sovereign People: A Realist's View of Democracy in America* (New York: Holt, Rinehart, & Winston, 1960), chap. 8. For a study of modern party caucuses in Minnesota that suggests that "grass-roots issue debate among party activists" does *not* lead to "the more rigorous conditions for party responsibility—i.e., to consensus within parties and differences between parties," see Thomas R. Marshall, "Party Responsibility Revisited: A Case of Policy Discussion at the Grass Roots," *Western Political Quarterly* 32 (March 1979): 70-78.

39. For suggestive comparisions of the responsible party to other models along dimensions slightly different from those utilized here, see Gary Orren, "The Changing Styles of American Party Politics," in *The Future of American Political Parties*, ed. Joel L. Fleishman (Englewood Cliffs, N.J.: Prentice-Hall, 1982), 9-30; and Nakamura and Sullivan, "Party Democracy and Democratic Control," 26-31.

40. Kenneth Janda, "Primrose Paths to Political Reform: 'Reforming' vs. Strengthening American Parties," in *Paths to Political Reform*, ed. William J. Crotty (Lexington, Mass.: Lexington Books, 1980), 321.

41. Leon Epstein, *Political Parties in Western Democracies*, rev. ed. (New Brunswick: Transaction Books, 1980), 8.

42. Orren, "Changing Styles," 25-30.

43. Gerald M. Pomper with Susan Lederman, *Elections in America*, 2d ed. (New York: Longman, 1980), 145-150, 167-173.

44. Edward R. Tufte, *Political Control of the Economy* (Princeton, N.J.: Princeton University Press, 1978), 72.

45. V. O. Key, Jr., *The Responsible Electorate* (New York: Vintage Books, 1968), 52-53.

46. W. D. Burnham, "American Politics in the 1970s: Beyond Party?" in *The American Party Systems: Stages of Political Development*, 2d ed., edited by W. N. Chambers and W. D. Burnham (New York: Oxford University Press, 1975), 335.

47. See Fred I. Greenstein, *The American Party System and the American People*, 2d ed. (Englewood Cliffs, N.J.: Prentice-Hall, 1970), 66-70.

48. Willis D. Hawley, *Nonpartisan Elections and the Case for Party Politics* (New York: John Wiley & Sons, 1973), chap. 6.

49. See Gerald Pomper's discussion: "The Contribution of Political Parties to American Democracy," in *Party Renewal in America*, ed. Pomper (New York: Praeger Publishers, 1980), 5-7. On the patterns of "inclusive" compromise characteristic of modern congressional Democrats (and contrasting patterns among Republicans), see David R. Mayhew, *Party Loyalty among Congressmen* (Cambridge: Harvard University Press, 1966), chap. 6.

50. See the essays in William E. Connolly, ed., *The Bias of Pluralism* (New York: Atherton Press, 1969); and, on the disproportionate power narrowly based groups are likely to wield, Mancur Olson, Jr., *The Logic of Collective Action* (New York: Schocken Books, 1968), chap. 5.

51. Schattschneider, *Semi-Sovereign People*, chaps. 2-3.

52. Robert A. Dahl, "The American Oppositions: Affirmation and Denial," in *Political Oppositions in Western Democracies*, ed. Dahl (New Haven, Conn.: Yale University Press, 1966), 64.

53. Walter Dean Burnham, *Critical Elections and the Mainsprings of American Politics* (New York: W. W. Norton & Co., 1970), 133.
54. Samuel P. Hays, "Political Parties and the Community-Society Continuum," in *American Party Systems*, 157-165.
55. Peter L. Berger and Richard J. Neuhaus, *To Empower People: The Role of Mediating Structures in Public Policy* (Washington, D.C.: American Enterprise Institute for Public Policy Research 1977). For a critique, on which the present discussion draws, see David E. Price, "Community, 'Mediating Structures,' and Public Policy," and the ensuing exchange with Berger and Neuhaus, *Soundings* 62 (Winter 1979): 396-416.
56. Wilson Carey McWilliams, "Parties as Civic Associations," in *Party Renewal*, 61.
57. Ibid., 53.
58. Contrast Peter Berger, "In Praise of Particularity: The Concept of Mediating Structures," *The Review of Politics* 38 (July 1976): 399-410; and Price, "Community, 'Mediating Structures,' and Public Policy," 386-388.
59. Dewey, *Individualism Old and New* (1929; reprint, New York: Capricorn Books, 1962), 85.
60. On the origins and variations of the communitarian critique of the American political order, see Price, "Community and Control." Political parties did not fare much better among communitarian thinkers of the Progressive Era than they did among the proponents of "social control." Just as most of the latter were inclined to see parties as barriers to (rather than potential instruments of) concerted national action, many communitarians regarded parties not in their integrative aspect but as particularism exemplified. Josiah Royce, for example, listed partisan alongside sectarian and class loyalties as the sort of "narrow" allegiance a "new and wiser provincialism" would have to overcome. See Royce, *The Philosophy of Loyalty* (New York: Macmillan, 1908), 229, 245, 247-248.
61. McWilliams, "Parties as Civic Associations," 61.
62. APSA, "Toward a More Responsible Two-Party System," 94.
63. James L. Sundquist, "The Crisis of Competence in Our National Government," *Political Science Quarterly* 95 (Summer 1980): 190.
64. Lester Thurow, *The Zero-Sum Society* (New York: Basic Books, 1980), 212-214. See also Morris P. Fiorina, "The Decline of Collective Responsibility in American Politics," *Daedalus* 109 (Summer 1980): 25-28, 39-44.

Parties and the Law 5

Many factors contribute to the current condition of the parties as we have assessed it in earlier chapters: the growth of the welfare state, the advent of professionalism in government, a general decline in citizens' institutional loyalties, and the rise of television as the dominant medium of mass communication. Much of this cannot and should not be reversed. But the state of the parties also owes much to the actions of governments and of the parties themselves. Some overestimate the importance of such laws and rules: "The most important sources of party decomposition," asserts one critic, "are the decisions taken by persons attempting to reform the parties." [1] Yet since the Progressive Era, legislators and rule makers have intervened in the life of the parties at all levels. It is important to understand the impact of their actions on the health of the parties and to assess the potential for constructive change. At the very least, such enactments should not reinforce party-weakening forces in the society. In some instances they may even offset them—freeing the parties to adapt more successfully to a changing political environment.

This chapter addresses the effects of election law on party strength, mainly at the state level. Subsequent chapters will consider other bodies of party and public law, chiefly those regulating presidential nominations and campaign finance. But what exactly is "party strength"? What is it that we are saying laws and rules should promote (or at least should not compromise further)? To what indicators should we look in attempting to gauge the actual or potential impact of a given measure?

Party Strength

Our discussion in Chapters 1-3, like most of the literature on party "decline," assumes that certain indicators reflect party strength or weakness. In discussing party-in-the-electorate, we examined levels of identification with the parties and the extent to which the party cue is utilized in voting. With respect to party organization, we concentrated on trends in party control of key political functions (nominations, campaign management, governmental appointments) and in organizational development (staffing, financial resources, and campaign operations). In considering parties-in-government, we assumed that well-defined partisanship in legislative voting, high levels of support of the executive by fellow partisans in the legislature, party control of key legislative functions (committee assignments, scheduling, mobilization of chamber majorities), and a prominent party role in executive functions (legislative and group liaison, appointments) would be indicative, other things being equal, of party "strength."

Such indicators are plausible measures of what is commonly regarded as strength or weakness in American parties—signs that they are performing or have the capacity to perform the critical tasks outlined in Chapter 4. To a considerable extent, these indicators are free of the normative connotations of "reform." For example, persons who hold quite different views on the possibility and desirability of intraparty democracy might nonetheless agree on what "strong" parties would look like. Insofar as they place importance on party roles—achieving democratic accountability and responsiveness, relating citizens to the broader political community, integrating the disparate organs of government— they might also agree that parties registering higher on all or most of these indicators would be more serviceable institutions. To be sure, they might still attempt to shape the parties in different ways, and certain kinds of "shaping" might be more conducive to party strength than others (party strength, after all, is not an all-sufficient social value). But diagnoses of the parties' current condition and prescriptions to improve their prospects can bypass, at least to a point, the confines in which past debates have placed them.

It is often difficult to link specific governmental policies and party practices directly to general indicators of party strength. For example, could one expect the democratizing of party caucuses to produce more favorable feelings toward parties in the public opinion polls? Would party endorsements of primary candidates produce higher party cohesion scores in the legislature? Perhaps, but the effects would surely be marginal and gradual and, in any case, almost impossible to isolate and measure. What is needed is a set of intermediate concepts or attributes that are more directly linked to the laws and rules in question and also have a plausible connection to the more general indicators of party strength.

For example, the perceived legitimacy and fairness of party operations might be one such attribute—dependent in part on specific procedures adopted by the parties, and also helping to explain levels of public esteem for the parties, attentiveness to party cues, and other indicators of the strength of the party-in-the-electorate. Such attributes generally do not lend themselves to the kind of quantification that public opinion polls or congressional party-voting scores represent. In many cases their relationship, both to the laws and rules being examined and to the broader state of the parties, is more a matter of plausible inference than demonstrated causality. But it is quite important to indicate in a systematic way what we take these linking attributes to be; otherwise the connection between specific enactments and the commonly utilized indicators of party strength will be an unclear and tenuous one.

What attributes, then, might one expect "strong" parties to display in the American context? Eight broad characteristics and conditions seem of particular importance:

(1) perceived legitimacy and fairness;

(2) the ability to control disaffection and conflict among major groups making up the party coalition;

(3) a capacity to limit fragmentation—to deter the proliferation of candidacies at the nomination stage and to unify party factions for purposes of campaigning and governance;

(4) a broad electoral appeal and the ability to retain the loyalty of "mainstream" constituencies;

(5) the possession of attractive rewards and incentives to induce activists and officeholders to work for and cooperate with the party;

(6) an inclination by the party's officeholders to cooperate with the party and with their fellow partisans in government;

(7) party organizations with authority to make decisions of importance to their members and identifiers, especially regarding party nominations, and with considerable autonomy in making these decisions;

(8) sufficient resources to perform their functions adequately and to successfully adapt and expand their role in response to a changing political environment.

Some of these attributes pertain most obviously to the parties' electoral base, others to party organizations or parties-in-government. Some are more directly linked to our general indicators of party strength than others, and some will be easier than others to relate plausibly to specific laws and rules. Some of the conditions may not prove totally compatible. Our discussion of national party rules, for example, will raise the possibility that attempts to placate one or another group in the party coalition may jeopardize the party's broader mainstream appeal. Laws designed to enhance the legitimacy of party operations may reduce the authority of party organizations. Some tradeoffs will be necessary. Nevertheless, other things being equal, each of these conditions will render the parties better equipped to perform their basic functions.

Organizations as multifaceted and complex as the parties must possess a wide variety of resources: mass appeal and legitimacy, organizational cohesion and stability, adequate human and financial capital, and political authority and power. Conversely, a party will be weakened by voter disregard and disaffection, organizational fragmentation, the absence of inducements to involvement and cooperation, the removal or displacement of decision-making authority and discretion, and an inadequate base of resources. This diverse list of attributes and conditions, which will loosely structure the discussions to follow, should help us think more clearly about the ways public policy and party rules augment or reduce the strength of the parties and hence affect their capacity to perform their various tasks.

Election Law

In no Western democracy are parties regulated as closely as they are in the United States. As Leon Epstein observes, "Americans are now so accustomed to legal control of party candidate selection, along with a host of other governmental controls over parties, that it is hard to appreciate how unusual it is among Western democratic nations." [2] Such regulation is much looser at the national than at the state level; recent Supreme Court decisions have confirmed the considerable latitude the national parties have in governing themselves. But such latitude does not exist in most states. "By 1920," Austin Ranney notes, "most states had adopted a succession of mandatory statutes regulating every major aspect of the parties' structures and operations." Ordinarily, the first step was to require the use of secret ballots in intraparty elections. Many states then stipulated who could and could not participate in these elections. Next came statutes specifying the composition and powers of party conventions and committees. The climax of this line of reform came with the adoption in almost every state of the direct primary. [3] This process went further in some states than others. In general, parties in the midwestern and western states where Progressivism was strongest are the most regulated, and parties in the southern states are the least regulated. The general pattern, however, is one of extensive statutory control.

California, where laws covering party organization and campaign practices cover several hundred pages, is an example of the lengths to which such regulations can go. It is also a good example of the way state laws can constrain parties and prevent their successful political adaptation. [4] California law places county and municipal elections on a nonpartisan basis and prohibits party participation in them. It mandates selection by direct primary for those offices for which the party does nominate candidates and forbids the parties to make preprimary endorsements. Until 1959, it even permitted a candidate to file in the primaries of both parties. Under this "cross-filing" provision, Earl Warren received *both* the Republican and Democratic nominations for governor in 1946.

California law also dictates how the parties are to be organized. It gives each party's state legislators (and defeated legislative nominees) the power to name a majority of members on the state central committees. In 1979, the legislature gave assembly-district caucuses and county committees the right to choose 45 percent of the Democratic state committee. Until then, the automatic membership of county chairs on the central committee was the only structural link between the state and county levels of organization; this is still the case for the GOP. County organizations thus have been unable either to run candidates for local office or to have a substantial impact on the state organization. The state party organization has been placed under the control of assembly members and has been subject to other restrictions on its leadership structure (for example, a requirement that state party chairmanships be limited to nonconsecutive two-year terms and that they rotate between northern and southern California). Such constraints have encouraged the development of party clubs and associations outside of the official structure.

These groups have gained some influence through their volunteer work and candidate endorsements, but their exclusion from official party operations has weakened their effectiveness.

Legal challenges, based in part on recent Supreme Court decisions affirming the prerogatives of the national parties (discussed later in this chapter), are being mounted against many such state and local restrictions. The northern California chapter of the Committee for Party Renewal, an organization characterizing itself as "scholars, political practitioners, and other citizens interested in strengthening our political parties," has filed suit to remove three particularly onerous restrictions from California law: the ban on preprimary endorsements and on participation in nonpartisan elections, laws governing the composition and selection of state central committees, and the two-year limitation and rotation requirement for state chairs. These restrictions, the committee argues, not only compromise constitutional guarantees of free expression and association, but also "greatly weaken the parties . . . depriving [them] of leadership and talent, forbidding vital powers, and preventing them from organizing on a grass-roots, integrated, functional basis."[5] Such deregulation efforts have been encouraged by some recent lower court decisions; for example, a Rhode Island statute prescribing the size and method of selection of local party committees was ruled unconstitutional. The Supreme Judicial Court of Massachusetts in a 1982 advisory opinion voided a state law that attempted to override the state party charter's requirement that a statewide candidate must receive at least 15 percent of the state convention's vote to be placed on the primary ballot.[6]

The constitutional case for dismantling state laws that constrict the associational freedoms of party members and constrain the parties in the performance of their functions is a strong one.[7] It seems quite likely that at least some of the more blatant restrictions will be struck down in the next few years. As desirable as deregulation might be, however, it does not represent a comprehensive solution to the problems state laws pose for the parties. Although one might make a convincing constitutional argument against compelling the parties to nominate their candidates in primaries, it is unlikely that either the courts or the legislatures will carry deregulation to such lengths. Even if they did, many state parties no doubt would still elect to hold primaries, and questions concerning how they should be structured and conducted would remain. Moreover, a number of state laws, while they are not primarily designed to regulate the parties, nonetheless can have an appreciable impact on party cohesion and strength. It is not sufficient, therefore, to argue simply that fewer laws are better than more. One also must attempt to discriminate among existing laws and ask what *kinds* of statutes and rules are more or less damaging or helpful to party prospects.

Laws Affecting the Party Role in Nominations and Elections

We now will examine specific laws and practices in the states, concentrating on measures that are directly relevant to party strength and that reveal substantial interstate variations. Some regulatory statutes—for example, the required use of the secret ballot in primaries—are so universally accepted and easily justified that, even if one could demonstrate that they weaken parties in certain respects, changing them would be out of the question. Therefore, we will focus on measures that have not been universally accepted and thus might be reconsidered, at least in some states, in terms of their effects on the parties.

Table 5-1 provides a summary view of party-strengthening laws and practices in each state. Eleven laws and practices are presented in the table. We turn first to the six measures that mainly affect the party's role in nominations and elections.

(1) Does the party partially or potentially make its nominations through conventions? Today, no state relies totally on the convention system for party nominations. A few states—New York, Delaware, Connecticut, Indiana—held out until recent decades, but in all of them state law now provides for primaries for congressional and major statewide offices. There are still, however, significant differences among the states. Nominations for various minor offices, for vacancies created by the death or resignation of candidates, and for special elections are often made by conventions. Three southern states still permit the parties to nominate for major offices by convention if they wish. This option mainly has been utilized by the GOP in circumstances where the chances for victory in the general election were minimal. As elections have become more competitive, Republican leaders, like Democratic, have increasingly found it politic to open up the process to the primary electorate. Only in Virginia have conventions been employed with any frequency by both parties in recent years; both parties nominated their gubernatorial candidates in 1981 and their U.S. Senate candidates in 1982 by this method. The convention method has some potential for dampening factionalism and promoting party unity, but in situations where the party is already divided among strong rival candidates, party leaders generally have seen primaries as the safer course.

As Table 5-1 indicates, several states employ a mixed system, with party conventions playing a decisive role in granting access to the primary ballot. As already noted, the Massachusetts Democratic party recently has adopted a rule requiring statewide candidates to receive 15 percent or more of the state convention's vote before being placed on the primary ballot, and the courts have held that such a rule supercedes state law. Most states employing such a system, however, have written it into their statutes. Utah, for example, has a preprimary convention at which two gubernatorial candidates are selected for the primary ballot (although if one candidate receives 70 percent of the convention vote, he is declared the nominee). In Colorado, only candidates receiving 20 percent of the convention vote are placed on the primary ballot. New York's primary law, adopted in 1970, requires a candidate to receive 25 percent of the convention vote to get on the primary ballot (although it also provides alternative access to the ballot via nominating petitions). In Connecticut, a primary—called a "challenge primary"—is held only if a convention winner is challenged by a candidate who received at least 20 percent of the convention vote.

(2) Does the party regularly make preprimary endorsements? In many states party leaders responded to the adoption of the direct primary by scheduling preprimary conventions at which the organized party could make formal or informal endorsements. Such a convention, argued the Republican chairman from Illinois in 1923, "is one way of restoring party responsibility." [8] In some states such endorsements are still required or encouraged by law. In Colorado, for example, the winners at the convention are placed first on the primary ballot; in Rhode Island, although no convention vote is required to place a candidate on the primary ballot, state law dictates that convention winners be placed first on the ballot with asterisks beside their names. In a few states, such as California, state law actually prohibits such endorsements. In most, state law is silent and whether state parties endorse or not is left to their own discretion and custom. In the southern states, where winning the Democratic primary often has been tantamount to election, party organizations and leaders generally regard "neutrality" as the appropriate stance to take, at least publicly, in primary contests. By contrast, in Illinois, Indiana, Pennsylvania, and Minnesota, party organizations regularly endorse statewide and/or legislative candidates.

Such gate-keeping and endorsing roles for party conventions appear to reduce party fragmentation. Sarah Morehouse has demonstrated that the share of the primary vote won by gubernatorial nominees tends to be substantially higher in states that hold preprimary endorsing conventions.[9] Such a role in nominations also increases the authority of party conclaves, strengthens the incentives for party involvement, and ties officeholders more closely to the organized party. Its effects will partially depend upon circumstances: in areas where party neutrality is a widely accepted norm, endorsements could reduce party legitimacy, and where factional conflict is intense, party unity might best be served by foregoing a convention fight. Nor should one overestimate the likely impact of such gate keeping: the party's success in playing such a role may be as much a result as a cause of its organizational cohesion and strength. In general, however, measures giving party conventions a decisive role in the nomination process buttress both the organized party and the party-in-government. A widespread return to pure systems of convention nomination would not necessarily prove successful or desirable. But mixed systems of the sort Colorado and Connecticut have adopted combine some of the presumed virtues of primaries—popular legitimacy, provision of a "safety valve" for conflict and dissent—with the retention of an authoritative party role. They deserve close examination and emulation.

(3) Does the state use a caucus-convention system rather than a primary for choosing and allocating its delegates to the national conventions? Table 5-1 includes information on delegate selection in the states because of its obvious relevance to the decision-making power and autonomy of party organizations and to the incentives they can offer for serious involvement. But we will reserve discussion for Chapter 7, where the presidential nomination process will be treated in detail.

(4) Do the laws governing voter participation in primaries adequately protect the integrity of the parties? Laws mandating presidential

Table 5-1   Party-strengthening Laws and Practices in the States

	NORTHEAST										BORDER				SOUTH										
	Conn.	Del.	Maine	Mass.	N.H.	N.J.	N.Y.	Pa.	R.I.	Vt.	Ky.	Md.	Okla.	W.Va.	Ala.[3]	Ark.	Fla.	Ga.	La.	Miss.	N.C.	S.C.[3]	Tenn.	Texas	Va.[3]
1. Party conventions help choose major state-level nominees[1]	X	X		X			X								[3]							[3]			[3]
2. Official party bodies regularly endorse candidates for statewide and/or legislative races	X	X	X	X	X	X	X					X	X												
3. Caucus-convention system used for choosing and allocating national delegates[4]	X	X	X	X		X	X	X	X																
4. Primary voting limited to persons preregistered by party	X		X	X	X	X	X			X	X		X	X		X	X			X	X	X		X	X
5. "Sore loser" or "disaffiliation" statute: primary loser cannot run as independent in general election				X				X			X	X		X		X					X	[5]	X		
6. State has public funding of campaigns, channeled totally or in part through parties			X								X		X	X			X				X				
7. Ballot form permits straight-party vote	X							X	X												X				
8. Governor elected for four-year term in presidential election year											X		X	X	X			X			X	X		X	
9. Governor elected at same time as entire legislature	X	X	X	X	X	X	X	X	X	X	X	X	X	X	X			X	X	X	X	X			
10. Governor-lieutenant governor elected as a ticket in general election	X	X	[6]		[6]	[6]	X	X			X	X		[6]	X		X	X	X	X					
11. State has four or fewer statewide executive offices on ballot		X	X	X	X	X	X		X													X	X		X

[1] Includes states where the convention vote places a candidate on the primary ballot or where primary is held only if convention nominee is challenged by candidate who received a threshold percentage of convention vote.

[2] Postprimary party convention makes nomination if no candidate receives more than 35 percent of the primary vote.

[3] State law permits parties to nominate by primary or convention.

[4] Includes states where only one party uses caucus-convention system. Data as of November 1983.

[5] Primary candidates must sign a pledge not to run under other auspices in general election if they lose the primary.

[6] State has no lieutenant governor.

	MIDWEST												WEST												
	Ill.	Ind.	Iowa	Kan.	Mich.	Minn.	Mo.	Neb.	N.D.	Ohio	S.D.	Wis.	Alaska	Ariz.	Calif.	Colo.	Hawaii	Idaho	Mont.	Nev.	N.M.	Ore.	Utah	Wash.	Wyo.
1. Party conventions help choose major state-level nominees[1]	X	X	2						X		2					X					X		X		
2. Official party bodies regularly endorse candidates for statewide and/or legislative races					X	X						X				X							X		
3. Caucus-convention system used for choosing and allocating national delegates[4]				X	X	X	X					X	X	X	X	X	X	X	X	X	X	X	X	X	X
4. Primary voting limited to persons preregistered by party			X	X				X			X			X	X	X				X		X			X
5. "Sore loser" or "disaffiliation" statute: primary loser cannot run as independent in general election		X			X	X	X	X	X	X	X	X		X	X	X		X	X		X		X	X	X
6. State has public funding of campaigns, channeled totally or in part through parties			X														X	X							
7. Ballot form permits straight-party vote	X	X	X		X		X		X	X	X	X									X		X		
8. Governor elected for four-year term in presidential election year		X					X		X		X								X					X	
9. Governor elected at same time as entire legislature					X	X			X					X				X							
10. Governor-lieutenant governor elected as a ticket in general election	X	X		X	X	X	X	X	X	X	X	X	X	6		X	X		X		X	6	X	X	6
11. State has four or fewer statewide executive offices on ballot													X				X								

SOURCE: *Book of the States* (Lexington, Ky.: The Council of State Governments), vol. 23, 1980-1981, 70-71; vol. 24, 1982-1983, 103-104, 108-110; Thad Beyle, "The Governors' Power of Organization," *State Government* 55 (Summer 1982): 82-83; *Comparative State Politics Newsletter* 4 (May 1983): 17; Malcolm Jewell and David Olson, *American State Political Parties and Elections*, rev. ed. (Homewood, Ill.: Dorsey Press, 1982), 110, 115; Sarah McCally Morehouse, "The Effect of Preprimary Endorsements on State Party Strength" (Paper delivered at the annual meeting of the American Political Science Association, Washington, D.C., 1980); and personal inquiries at party headquarters and with secretaries of state. "Sore loser"/disaffiliation data furnished through the courtesy of George Frampton, Jr., counsel to the John Anderson campaign.

primaries generally have been accompanied by provisions defining the eligible primary electorate. Here, too, the interstate variations are considerable, with some kinds of laws going much further than others in removing powers of decision not only from party leaders but also from the party's rank-and-file adherents. The "blanket" primaries held in Alaska and Washington, for example, are party contests in name only: voters are given ballots containing the names of both parties' candidates and may choose among the Republicans running for one office and among the Democrats for another. Louisiana's "nonpartisan" primary goes a step further, listing all primary candidates on a single ballot.

More common and only slightly more restrictive is the "open" primary, used for state-level offices in Vermont, Michigan, Minnesota, North Dakota, Wisconsin, Hawaii, Idaho, Montana, and Utah. Here voters can vote in only one party's primary, but they are given ballots for both parties and choose which one to mark in the privacy of the voting booth. A variant of this type, sometimes called the "same-day declaration" system, is in use in most southern and several midwestern states. Here, too, voters are not registered by party and can vote in whichever primary they please. They must request, however, a specific party ballot (sometimes in writing) at the polls.

As Table 5-1 indicates, true "closed" primaries are in effect in about half the states. Here voters register by party in advance of the election, although in Iowa and Wyoming they can change that registration on election day. For members of one party to cross over and vote in the primary of another, they ordinarily would have to change their registration status several days or weeks in advance of the election.

A number of open-primary states employ a slightly different system in their presidential primaries. This is mainly because the national Democratic party since 1974 has required that only Democratic voters "who publicly declare their party preference and have that preference publicly recorded" shall be eligible to vote in primaries that choose or allocate national convention delegates.[10] Later we will examine Wisconsin's defiance of the national party on this issue. But most open-primary states have elected to abide by the national rule. For some, the problem has not arisen because they have continued to use a convention system at the presidential level. Others either have adopted some variant of same-day declaration for their presidential primary or have converted their presidential primary into a "beauty contest" preference poll, using a caucus-convention system to allocate delegates.

Had the national party truly wished to protect the integrity of the primary, it should have prohibited not only the pure "open" primary but the same-day declaration primary as well, which is only slightly less vulnerable to crossover voting (although in some states the parties at least gain access to a list of declared partisans through the same-day system). But with 13 states utilizing same-day declaration (8 of which hold presidential primaries), the national party has been reluctant to push its case further. In fact, the protracted Wisconsin battle has pointed up the difficulties of using party rules to challenge state law and has led many to ask whether such expenditures of party resources and political capital promise a net gain.

The parties, however, do have a stake in preregistration and the closed primary system. Both open-primary and same-day states have seen instances of crossparty "raiding"—where the word was passed to members of one party to vote in the other's primary, sometimes for the express purpose of choosing the nominee who would be easiest to beat in the general election. More often, crossover voting occurs simply because independents or members of the opposite party find a primary contest or candidate of particular interest. Studies of Wisconsin's presidential primaries from 1968 through 1980 suggest that only about 55 percent of the voters were party identifiers voting in the primary of their own party; some 35 percent were independents, and about 10 percent were partisan crossovers. By contrast, in Florida and California (where preregistration by party is required), more than 70 percent of the presidential primary voters were partisan identifiers voting in their own primaries, and less than 5 percent were partisan crossovers.[11] In other words, the preregistration requirement was a substantial deterrent to voting in the "wrong" primary by partisan identifiers.

Crossover participation can decisively influence primary outcomes. Studies of open primaries in Wisconsin and Michigan consistently have shown that the candidate preferences of crossover and independent primary participants differ significantly from those of partisan identifiers voting in their own primary. If only Democratic identifiers had voted in the 1968 Wisconsin Democratic presidential primary, President Lyndon Johnson's vote would have been increased, and Eugene McCarthy's decreased, by as much as 9 percentage points each. In 1972, Hubert Humphrey was the candidate most obviously disadvantaged by open primary provisions in Wisconsin and Michigan; George Wallace was the major beneficiary in both states. In recent years the effects on the Democratic side, at least at the presidential level, have been less pronounced, but Republican contests have been substantially affected. In 1976, Ronald Reagan did considerably better and President Gerald Ford worse (about 4 percentage points each) in Wisconsin than they would have under a closed primary. But in 1980 Reagan was the main victim, while the participation of independent and Democratic voters in the Republican primary doubled John Anderson's share of the vote from 14 to 28 percent.[12]

Do the parties have anything to gain from open primaries? In states where they are a time-honored tradition, legitimacy perhaps. But the disadvantages to the parties from open primaries are more pronounced than any potential benefits. Some claim that persons drawn into a party's primary are more likely to cross over on that party's behalf in the general election. Evidence for this proposition, however, is inconclusive at best. One might expect open primaries to attract a range of voters more representative of the general electorate than those voting in closed primaries and thus to prompt the nomination of candidates with broad appeal. But the Wisconsin results cast considerable doubt on this proposition as well. *No* primaries attract a majority of the electorate nowadays. And those voters that are prompted to cross over often seem to be those inclined to leave the mainstream, such as supporters of McCarthy, Wallace, and Anderson. Their presence may make it harder rather than easier for parties to nominate candidates with broad appeal.

Open primaries dilute the impact of the parties' core constituencies and substantially reduce the role and influence of party leaders and organizations. Although they have a superficial "democratic" appeal—allowing individuals to vote for anyone they please at every electoral stage—they make the party label less significant for voters and candidates alike. The primary loses its character as a *party* nomination and becomes little more than the first round of the general election. This may make individual voters feel less restricted, but insofar as it reduces the meaning of the party label and weakens the party ties of elected officials, the result hardly enhances the functioning of democracy.

Closed primaries, by contrast, help preserve the integrity of the party system. Preprimary registration requires a modicum of commitment from partisan identifiers, and the lists thus generated are invaluable tools for parties as they undertake voter registration and get-out-the-vote drives and other efforts at communication and organization. Candidates and officeholders have stronger incentives to work with party organizations and to support party positions. Hostile crossparty "raiding" becomes quite difficult, and the nomination process is made less vulnerable to freewheeling candidate and issue appeals based outside the parties. The Wisconsin experience suggests that national party rules are not an effective or efficient vehicle for moving large numbers of states toward closed primaries. But party leaders and legislators in states with open-primary and same-day systems would do well to examine their debilitating effects on parties and to consider corrective action.

(5) Do the laws governing access to the general election ballot adequately protect the integrity of party nominations? The general election ballot should remain open to independents and third-party nominees as well as to the nominees of the two major parties. But should a Republican or Democrat who runs in his or her party's primary be able, having lost, to run under another banner in the general election? The question arose in 1980 when Anderson, having finished far behind in the Republican presidential primaries in a number of states, then sought a place on the general election ballot as an independent candidate. In several states he ran afoul of so-called "sore-loser" laws and other statutes designed to prohibit such a second chance for defeated party candidates. Because of certain features of his case (particularly his attempts to take his name off the primary ballot before election day in some states) and because of certain ambiguities in the state laws as applied to presidential primaries, Anderson was able to place his name on the general election ballot in every state. But his battle prompted heated discussion about those obscure statutes by which about half the states have sought to prevent "abuse of the party primary and . . . distortion of the general election outcome." [13]

The Supreme Court in 1974 upheld two such California laws: a "sore-loser" statute that prohibited candidates who had lost a primary from subsequently running as independents and a "disaffiliation" statute that

prohibited persons from running as independents who had been registered with a party during the year preceding the primary. "The state's
general policy," the Court explained,

> is to have contending forces within the party employ the primary
> campaign and primary election to finally settle their differences. . . .
> [The "sore loser" law] effectuates this aim, the visible result being to
> prevent the losers from continuing the struggle and to limit the names
> on the ballot to those who have won the primaries and to those indepen-
> dents who have properly qualified. The people, it is hoped, are presented
> with understandable choices, and the winner in the general election with
> sufficient support to govern effectively.
>
> [The "disaffiliation" statute] carries very similar credentials. It protects
> the direct primary process by refusing to recognize independent candi-
> dates who do not make early plans to leave a party and take the
> alternative course to the ballot. It works against independent candida-
> cies prompted by short-range political goals, pique, or personal quarrel.
> It is also a substantial barrier to a party fielding an "independent"
> candidate to capture and bleed off votes in the general election that
> might well go to another party.[14]

The Court linked these California laws to the state's 1959 repeal of
"cross filing": the state thereby made its primary "not merely . . . a warm-
up for the general election, but an integral part of the entire election
process," and gave it a decisive role in winnowing out candidates and
structuring the choice to be made in the general election. "California,"
the Court concluded, "apparently believes with the Founding Fathers
that splintered parties and unrestrained factionalism may do significant
damage to the fabric of government"[15]—a strong endorsement of the
direction the state's laws had taken, albeit a somewhat ironic one in light
of the extensive antiparty legislation that remained on the books in
California.

The Court recently has drawn a distinction between the laws it
upheld in the California case and the early filing deadlines used by Ohio
to achieve the same end. In a case brought by John Anderson, the Court
held that requiring prospective independent candidates to file for inclusion on the November ballot by the same deadline (March 20) that
applied to party candidates running in the *primary* placed an unconstitutional burden on the voting and associational rights of such candidates'
supporters. Although it reaffirmed the legitimacy of efforts to maintain
"the integrity of various routes to the ballot," the Court argued that Ohio
had simply chosen inappropriate means: the early filing law burdened
genuine independent candidates and their supporters in a way that the
California laws did not.[16] While one could argue, as did the Court's four
dissenters, that the Ohio and California statutes were essentially identical
in purpose, the "sore-loser" approach does seem more efficient and open
to fewer objections.

Opponents of sore-loser laws, like defenders of the open primary,
ostensibly appear to be on the side of "democracy." Why should anyone
be denied access to the ballot? To answer, one must consider the roles
parties play in structuring electoral choice: they reduce the number of

contenders, tie individual candidates to one another and to a range of policy positions, and enable scattered popular preferences to coalesce in a majority decision. Parties cannot perform these functions—indeed, conclusive choices that meet democratic criteria cannot be made—if access to the ballot is unlimited at successive stages. The sore-loser statutes reflect the conviction that limits should be set in a way that enhances *party* performance of the winnowing-out function. Without such laws, candidates may be less inclined to take the primary seriously as an intraparty contest that requires them to come to terms with the organized party and its main constituencies; they may be tempted to reserve the right to launch an independent candidacy or even to exploit the primary as a launching pad for such an effort. At the general election stage the absence of sore-loser or similar laws heightens the risk that primary battles will be continued in the general election and, indeed, that parties and candidates will encourage independent candidacies to draw votes from their opponents. The cost, in party fragmentation and distorted electoral outcomes, could be substantial.

Although rarely invoked, sore-loser and disaffiliation statutes strengthen the presumptions that favor the party nomination route to the ballot and may deter abuses of that process. As the independent, individualistic style in voting and campaigning becomes more prevalent, the protections such laws offer the parties may become more important.

(6) *Does the state provide public funding for campaigns, and do the monies go partially or entirely to the parties?* Table 5-1 contains information on public funding because of its relevance to the resources state parties can command and the campaign role they can assume. Chapter 8 will address this question and other aspects of campaign finance law in detail.

Laws Affecting Party Cohesion in Government

By tying candidates and officeholders more closely to the party, the measures just discussed can strengthen the party-in-government. But other election laws are more directly related to the likelihood of party cohesion and teamwork. We now turn to the last five provisions in Table 5-1, laws that have less to do with party organizations or with the nomination process than with the circumstances under which party nominees gain election.

(7) *Does the ballot facilitate straight-ticket voting?* As Table 5-1 indicates, some 21 states now use a ballot that permits a straight party vote. Increasingly in vogue since the Progressive Era has been the "office-block" ballot, which organizes candidates' names by the offices they seek and generally does not permit one to vote for the party ticket by marking a single square or pulling a single lever. A party-column ballot is particularly important in facilitating gubernatorial-legislative coattailing and in increasing the numbers of people voting for lesser known offices. One study showed that "poorly educated, peripherally involved" voters were especially likely to leave their ballot unmarked for less-advertised races under the office-block system.[17] The ballot form influences voting less at the top of the ticket. But overall, the party-column ballot can facilitate

the use of the party cue in voting and increase the likelihood that those elected will share a party tie.

(8) and (9) Are elections timed to facilitate party voting and reduce the likelihood of divided government? In every state except Kentucky, the governor and the lower house of the legislature are elected at the same time, although in most states, house members must stand again for election midway in the governor's term. Only in Virginia, South Carolina, Kentucky, Kansas, and New Mexico is the election of the state senate completely separated from the governor's election, but a number of states elect only half of their senate in the gubernatorial year.[18] Table 5-1 identifies two sorts of electoral arrangements that may enhance the coattail effect and strengthen the party tie between levels and branches of government: the election of the governor (for a four-year term) in presidential election years (item 8) and the election of the governor and all members of both legislative houses at the same time (item 9). Twenty-three states meet neither condition. The only state that meets both conditions is North Carolina, but what it gives with one hand it takes away with the other; it is also the only state to deny the governor the most rudimentary tool of legislative leadership, the veto.

Structuring the election calendar to maximize the coincidence of choices cannot, in isolation, prompt party cohesion. But if other conditions of strong partisanship are present, such a coincidence can help ensure that these conditions are reflected in the composition and operation of government.

(10) and (11) Do electoral arrangements foster unified party leadership within the executive branch? Historically, two of the most important constraints on governors have been their short terms and frequent ineligibility for reelection. These constraints have now been loosened considerably: only four states still forbid consecutive four-year terms (Kentucky, Mississippi, New Mexico, and Virginia); four others still elect to two-year terms, but with no limit on reelection (Arkansas, New Hampshire, Rhode Island, Vermont). The other 42 states elect to four-year terms with at least one reelection permitted.

Table 5-1 presents state-by-state data on another condition of leadership, the consolidation of executive power. As we saw in Chapter 3, gubernatorial leadership of the legislature and within the executive branch is often made more difficult by the multiplicity and the independence of statewide elective offices. Although governors vary in the extent to which their leadership utilizes and serves the party, party accountability and cohesion are rarely served by the fragmentation of executive authority.

Twenty-two states now elect their governor and lieutenant governor as a ticket. (Kansas, Florida, Maryland, Minnesota, North Dakota, and Montana also require the two to run as a team at the primary stage, and Ohio and Utah permit the gubernatorial candidate to select the candidate for lieutenant governor.) Nationwide, the legislative powers of lieutenant governors have declined. While this trend has reduced the significance that team election otherwise might have had for executive-legislative relations, it also has lessened the likelihood that lieutenant governors will develop independent bases of power.

Our final measure, the number of statewide offices listed on the ballot, has seen far less movement. Well over half the states still elect seven or more statewide officials—a situation that encourages factionalism within the parties and a government divided between the parties. Only in a few states, mainly in the Northeast, does the long ballot not complicate the governor's leadership of the executive branch and of the legislature.

Conclusion

The 11 measures presented in Table 5-1 are not of equal importance, nor is their correlation with broader indicators of party strength exact. Nonetheless, certain patterns do appear. It is in the northeastern states, where party organization inside and outside the government is strongest, that the laws and practices favorable to parties are most prevalent—no doubt an effect as well as a cause of the parties' strength. These states rank highest on what are probably our most important measures: retaining a significant role for party conventions (except, curiously, in presidential nominations) and protecting the integrity of the primary ballot. They also rank relatively high on measures promoting party cohesion in government. By contrast, the laws in southern states have done the least to promote party strength. Virginia is the only southern state to give conventions a significant role in state-level nominations, and only North Carolina and Florida have adopted the closed primary. Five southern states have retained the party-column ballot, but in no other region is there more evidence of executive branch fragmentation.

The greatest interstate variations occur in the Midwest and West, both in the provisions of state law and in the role played by the parties. Many of these states have retained a significant role for party conventions at the state level and in presidential nominations, but an equal number also have embraced the open primary (a few, such as Michigan, Minnesota, and Utah, actually have done both). A closer look at the states of these regions would be of particular interest, both for estimating the comparative effects of specific measures and for understanding the conditions of successful policy innovations.

The Parties and National Law

Election law is primarily the province of state and local governments. In a few areas, most notably campaign finance, Congress has passed laws that directly affect party operations. In general, however, the national parties labor under far fewer restrictions and regulations than their state and local counterparts. Our discussion of the impact of national law on the parties will focus on the Supreme Court. This will point up the constitutional norms the parties must observe but also the constitutional defenses that protect the parties against certain kinds of legislative intrusion.

Constitutional Constraints

In a few critical cases the Supreme Court has invalidated party nomination rules and procedures deemed to violate the constitutional rights of voters. In the early 1940s, for example, the Texas Democratic party was prohibited from allowing only whites to vote in its primary. In 1963 the Georgia Democratic party was restrained from using a county-unit system (rather than one person-one vote) in tabulating the primary vote for U.S. senator.[19] In most such cases the Court has determined that party practices were closely intertwined with state regulation and control, thus constituting "state action" for purposes of the Fourteenth Amendment. Occasionally, however, the courts have hinted at a broader criterion, regarding party nominations as "simply one stage of the unitary governmental process of election" and thus as constituting "state action" by definition.[20]

Such reasoning could justify judicial scrutiny of nomination practices comparable to that given elections per se. In ruling on challenges to the national Democratic party's formula for allocating convention delegates among the states, the U.S. Court of Appeals (D.C. Circuit) in 1971 held that the "state action" prohibitions of the Constitution applied to nominating conventions:

> The major parties' nomination procedures play such an important role in the presidential selection process that they can hardly be said not to be "integrally related" to the subsequent general election. . . . By placing the nominees' names on the ballot, the states, in effect, have adopted this narrowing process as a necessary adjunct of their election procedures. Therefore, every step in the nominating process—especially the crucial determination of how many delegates each state party is to be allowed—is as much a product of state action as if the states themselves were collectively to conduct such preliminary conventions.[21]

The court declined, however, to require a precise one person-one vote, or one Democrat-one vote, representation formula of the party and found the existing formula (which allocated 54 percent of the delegates to the states in proportion to their voting strength in the Electoral College) constitutionally acceptable: "Absent unconstitutional classifications based on race, religion, sex or economic status, deviations from mathematically precise equality of voting power may be allowed to further some reasonable countervailing policy." [22]

Four years later the same court likewise refused to invalidate the apportionment formula—a scheme giving states "victory bonus" delegates—used by the national Republican party. But by this time the Supreme Court had handed down its *Cousins* v. *Wigoda* decision, affirming the national parties' autonomy in determining delegate credentials (see discussion, p. 139). Accordingly, the Court of Appeals defended its deference to the GOP's apportionment rule in stronger terms than it had in the Democratic cases, invoking a constitutional right "not only to form political associations but to organize and direct them in the way that will make them most effective." On the question of "state action," the court acknowledged that the answer was "less clear" than it had seemed earlier and expressly declined to decide whether the party's actions could be so classified.[23] Thus there have been some indications of judicial second thoughts about the thoroughgoing application of the state action concept to party rules and practices. But the Supreme Court has yet to define sharply the constraints the parties must observe in carrying out their electoral role.

In a larger group of cases, the Supreme Court has scrutinized state election laws designed to protect or strengthen the parties. As the California disaffiliation case demonstrated, preventing "splintered parties and unrestrained factionalism" has been treated as a legitimate interest of the state. California therefore was upheld in its attempts to ensure that only genuine independents be allowed to run as independents in the general election. The Court earlier had upheld New York's lengthy waiting period for those who wished to switch their party registration, on the grounds that the state had a legitimate interest in preventing crossparty "raiding" in primary elections.[24]

Such deference has not been unlimited, however. We already have noted the John Anderson case in Ohio in which an early filing deadline for independent candidates was declared unconstitutional. In an earlier Ohio decision the Court ruled that the state's excessive petition requirements for parties that wished to gain a place on the ballot placed unacceptable burdens on "the right of individuals to associate for the advancement of political beliefs, and the right of qualified voters, regardless of their political persuasion, to cast their votes effectively." The state, the Court acknowledged, could "validly promote a two-party system in order to encourage compromise and political stability," but its restrictive statutes went too far in their tendency to give to the two dominant parties "a permanent monopoly." [25] In another case involving antiraiding statutes, the Court determined that Illinois had overstepped constitutional bounds in prohibiting persons from voting in one party's primary if they had voted in another party's primary within the past 23 months.[26] Thus, while sanctioning statutory efforts to strengthen the parties, the Court has placed such laws under closer scrutiny than it has the rules and practices of the parties themselves.

It is in a third group of cases—concerning the use of patronage in filling governmental jobs—that the courts have made their farthest and potentially most damaging intrusion into party affairs. In a landmark 1976 decision the Supreme Court ruled unconstitutional the dismissal of two employees by the Cook County, Illinois, sheriff because of their partisan affiliation: "The cost of the practice of patronage is the restraint it places on freedoms of belief and association." [27] The Court acknowledged that in the case of policy-making or "confidential" employees, the state's interest in maintaining governmental effectiveness and efficiency might properly override the First Amendment interests of the dismissed employees. But a subsequent decision enjoined a county public defender from dismissing two assistant public defenders of the opposite political party and thus raised questions concerning the appropriateness of partisan considerations in filling positions such as United States attorney. The court adopted a vague new standard that left it quite uncertain how far judicial restrictions on governmental staffing decisions might extend:

> The ultimate inquiry is not whether the label "policymaking" or "confidential" fits a particular position; rather, the question is whether the hiring authority can demonstrate that party affiliation is an appropriate requirement for the effective performance of the public office involved.[28]

Justice Lewis Powell wrote the dissenting opinion in both cases. He questioned whether the First Amendment rights of the plaintiffs had been jeopardized: "Such employees assumed the risks of the system and were benefited, not penalized, by its practical operation." And he argued that the Court should give greater weight to the state's interest in a healthy party system, as it had in the California disaffiliation case. "Patronage appointments," he stressed, "help build stable political parties by offering rewards to persons who assume the tasks necessary to the continuing functioning of political organizations." The parties, in turn, facilitate rational electoral choice and coherent, effective governance after the choice is made. Powell concluded:

> Patronage—the right to select key personnel and to reward the party "faithful"—serves the public interest by facilitating the implementation of policies endorsed by the electorate.[29]

These decisions represent a threatening area of uncertainty in the law. They already have weakened the hand of those state and local parties that still bear some responsibility for governmental appointments, and they seem likely to inhibit the reconstitution of the party "web" among disparate centers of power.

The Judicial Defense of Party

In other circumstances the courts have turned the First Amendment to the parties' defense. With the "procedural nationalization" of the parties has come an increased likelihood of conflict between national party rules and state law. The Supreme Court, in dealing with these conflicts, has created a powerful presumption in favor of national party rules. But the implications of the decisions for other areas of dispute—conflict between state law and state party rules or the permissible limits of federal legislation—are still uncertain and unsettled.

The Supreme Court first squarely faced the question of whether state law was superior to national party rules in *Cousins* v. *Wigoda,* a case arising out of the refusal of the 1972 Democratic National Convention to seat the delegates from Cook County, Illinois.[30] The convention's Credentials Committee found that the 59 Chicago delegates were elected in violation of several guidelines that had been formulated by the party's McGovern-Fraser Commission and incorporated into the Call to the convention—for example, prohibitions against "slate making" and requirements for minority participation. Accordingly, the convention seated a rival delegation that had been elected in private caucuses after the state-sponsored primary. The Illinois courts enjoined these non-elected delegates from seeking recognition, and after the convention contempt proceedings were brought against them for their failure to obey the injunction. The Illinois court acknowledged that the delegates and the party enjoyed "fundamental constitutional rights of free political association," but argued that the state had an overriding interest in protecting the efficacy of its primary. The Supreme Court reversed this judgment:

> The states themselves have no constitutionally mandated role in the great task of the selection of presidential and vice-presidential candidates.... The convention serves the pervasive national interest in the selection of candidates for national office, and this national interest is greater than any interest of an individual state.

To let each state determine the eligibility of convention delegates, the Court reasoned, "could seriously undercut or indeed destroy the effectiveness of the Convention as a concerted enterprise." Accordingly, decisions concerning the seating of delegates must be left to the convention itself.[31]

Among those narrowly interpreting the *Cousins* decision was the Supreme Court of Wisconsin. At issue in 1980 was that state's open primary, which under national Democratic party rules could not be used to allocate the state's national convention delegates. In *Democratic Party of the U.S.* v. *La Follette* (1981), the U.S. Supreme Court reversed the state court's decision, grounding the supremacy of national party rules in the "First Amendment freedom to gather in association for the purpose of advancing shared beliefs." The Court concluded:

> The State argues that its [open primary] law places only a minor burden on the National Party. The National Party argues that the burden is substantial, because it prevents the Party from "screening out those whose affiliation is . . . slight, tenuous or fleeting," and that such screening is essential to build a more effective and responsible party. But it is not for the courts to mediate the merits of this dispute. For even if the state were correct, a state, or a court, may not constitutionally substitute its own judgment for that of the Party. A political party's choice among the various ways of determining the makeup of a state's delegation to the party's national convention is protected by the Constitution. And as is true of all expressions of First Amendment freedoms, the courts may not interfere on the ground that they view a particular expression as unwise or irrational.[32]

The Illinois and Wisconsin decisions are not as conclusive in practical terms as they seem. The Democratic National Convention in 1980 seated the Wisconsin delegates, not because it lacked the authority that the *La Follette* ruling would later confirm, but because it lacked the time and resources to select an alternative slate of delegates from the state. To set up alternative primary or caucus procedures can be very difficult and expensive, and the state can hardly be denied representation altogether.[33] Good law does not necessarily make good politics: national party authority can quickly run up against the practical and prudential limits of coercion.

It would be a mistake to regard the Wisconsin situation as typical. State laws have not represented a major barrier to the procedural nationalization of the parties. Compliance has been the norm. The main significance of the *La Follette* decision is not in furnishing a workable solution to specific conflicts, but in legitimating an increasingly autonomous and assertive role for the national parties in the presidential nomination process and other aspects of party life.

Exactly how far the Court's reasoning in the *La Follette* case might be extended is unclear. Is one bound to conclude, as Justice Powell asked in his dissenting opinion, "that every conflict between state law and party rules concerning participation in the nomination process creates a burden on associational rights"? [34] Certainly the case supports such a presumption in instances where national party rules conflict with state law, even when (as in Wisconsin) the *state* party supports the state law. But the implications for conflicts between state law and state party rules and practices have yet to be developed.

In the Massachusetts opinion cited earlier, the state's Supreme Judicial Court argues that the party has "a substantial interest, implicit in its freedom of association, to ensure that party members have an effective role" in determining who will appear as the party's nominee on the general election ballot. The requirement of the party charter that a candidate must receive 15 percent of the convention vote to compete in the primary, the court reasons, serves party interests in two ways: it limits the number of candidates on the primary ballot (a party interest parallel to the interest of the state upheld in the California disaffiliation case), and it ensures that persons will not be nominated who have "little or no support from the regular party membership." Thus, without any demonstration by the state of a "compelling interest" in its contrary provisions, the party's charter requirement must stand. [35]

The California and other deregulation cases may result in further limitations on the rights of the states to ban party endorsements, to dictate organizational arrangements, or otherwise to intrude in party affairs. But state parties surely will not be able to claim the same degree of autonomy from state regulation as have the national parties. That regulation is pervasive and well-buttressed by judicial precedent. Moreover, one of the Court's main justifications for freeing the national parties from state constraints—the confusion and contradictions that would result from subjecting the parties to the laws of 50 states—is not relevant at the state level.

The implications of the *Cousins* and *La Follette* decisions for national legislation affecting the parties is similarly unclear. Congress already regulates federal elections in many respects—corrupt practices, campaign financing (which extends to party primaries and conventions), and prerequisites of voting, for example. As the Court declared in its ruling on the Federal Election Campaign Act, "The constitutional power of Congress to regulate federal elections is well established and is not questioned by any of the parties to this case." [36] But the Court's recent rulings may have limited the extent to which such an argument could justify further interference in *party* affairs; "Congress would be required to justify the abridgement of the fundamental right of association in favor of the fundamental right of voting," asserts one group that has studied the matter. [37] Congress almost certainly has the authority to regulate existing presidential primaries in their timing and other aspects, but whether it could constitutionally compel nomination by primary or establish a national primary is a more difficult question. The issue does not appear to be a particularly pressing one at present. Congress seems inclined to defer to the wishes of the national parties for control over their own rules and procedures. But as Chapters 6 and 7 will show, continuing problems with the presidential nomination process could prompt renewed calls for congressional intervention.

The absence of extensive federal legislation regulating the parties and the limits *Cousins* and *La Follette* have placed on state regulation mean that an examination of "parties and the law" at the federal level must mainly focus on the "laws" of the parties themselves. Accordingly, we turn in the next two chapters to that area where party rule making during the past two decades has been most extensive and has had the greatest political impact: presidential nominations. As we have seen, state law has had a decidedly mixed and often negative impact on the strength and viability of the parties. Have the parties done any better when legislating for themselves?

NOTES

1. Jeane J. Kirkpatrick, *Dismantling the Parties: Reflections on Party Reform and Party Decomposition* (Washington, D.C.: American Enterprise Institute for Public Policy Research, 1978), 2. For a critique of such assumptions of "party primacy" that imply that parties "are more a product of political will and ingenuity than of the social and political environment," see Frank J. Sorauf, "Political Parties and Political Analysis," in *The American Party Systems: Stages of Political Development*, 2d ed., edited by W. N. Chambers and W. D. Burnham (New York: Oxford University Press, 1975), 49-50. See also the exchange between Everett C. Ladd, Arthur Schlesinger, and James Sundquist in *The American Constitutional System Under Strong and Weak Parties*, ed. Patricia Bonomi, James M. Burns, and Austin Ranney (New York: Praeger Publishers, 1981), 84-89, 124, 140-141.
2. Leon D. Epstein, *Political Parties in Western Democracies*, rev. ed. (New Brunswick, N.J.: Transaction Books, 1980), 44.
3. Austin Ranney, *Curing the Mischiefs of Faction: Party Reform in America* (Berkeley: University of California Press, 1976), 81. See the overview by John F. Bibby et al., "Parties in State Politics," in *Politics in the American States*, 4th ed., edited by Virginia Gray, Herbert Jacobs, and Kenneth Vines (Boston: Little, Brown & Co., 1983), 69-75.
4. The account that follows draws on Kay Lawson, "California: The Uncertainties of Reform," in *Party Renewal in America*, ed. Gerald M. Pomper (New York: Praeger Publishers, 1980), chap. 8; and on two memoranda issued by the California Committee for Party Renewal: "Seeking Legal Relief from Excessive Regulation of California's Parties" (July 1982); and Robert Girard, "Litigation to Deregulate Political Parties" (1982).
5. Girard, "Litigation to Deregulate," 1.
6. *Fahey* v. *Darigan*, 405 F. Supp. 1386 (1975); *Opinion of the Justices*, 385 Mass. 1201 (1982).
7. For an argument that the courts historically have been remiss in permitting the passage of direct primary laws and other regulatory statutes and a rationale for thoroughgoing deregulation, see Stephen E. Gottlieb, "Rebuilding the Right of Association⹀The Right to Hold a Convention as a Test Case," *Hofstra Law Review* 11 (Fall 1982): 191-247.
8. Schuyler C. Wallace, "Pre-primary Conventions," *Annals of the American Academy of Political and Social Science* 106 (March 1923): 103.
9. Sarah McCally Morehouse, "The Effect of Preprimary Endorsements on State Party Strength" (Paper delivered at the annual meeting of the American Political Science Association, Washington, D.C., 1980). For an overview of endorsement practices and evidence on the frequency of challenges, see Malcolm E. Jewell and David M. Olson, *American State Political Parties and Elections*, rev. ed. (Homewood, Ill.: Dorsey Press, 1982), 111-120; and Malcolm E. Jewell, "The Impact of State Political

Parties on the Nominating Process" (Paper delivered at the annual meeting of the Midwest Political Science Association, Chicago, Ill., 1983).

10. This wording from the report of the Winograd Commission replaced a less specific provision in the 1976 rules. See Commission on Presidential Nomination and Party Structure, *Openness, Participation and Party-Building: Reforms for a Stronger Democratic Party* (Washington, D.C.: Democratic National Committee, 1978), 68-70.

11. Ronald D. Hedlund, Meredith H. Watts, and David M. Hedge, "Voting in an Open Primary," *American Politics Quarterly* 10 (April 1982): 201-204. David Adamany, defining independents who report "leaning" toward a party as partisans for purposes of this analysis, obtains higher estimates of both same-party (70-80 percent) and crossparty (around 15 percent) voting in Wisconsin presidential primaries. "Communication: Crossover Voting and the Democratic Party's Reform Rules," *American Political Science Review* 70 (June 1976): 537-538.

12. Hedlund, Watts, and Hedge, "Voting in an Open Primary," 204-214; Adamany, "Communication," 538-540; and James I. Lengle, *Representation and Presidential Primaries* (Westport, Conn.: Greenwood Press, 1981), 98-103.

13. Walter E. Dellinger, "Should Anderson Be on the Ballot?" *The Chapel Hill (N.C.) Newspaper,* October 5, 1980, 3C.

14. *Storer* v. *Brown,* 415 U.S. 724 (1974), at 735.

15. Ibid., at 734-736.

16. The Court also distinguished the presidential contest from the state races at stake in the California case, arguing that in the presidential case the state had a lesser interest in limiting political fragmentation and its laws were less capable of doing so. *Anderson* v. *Celebrezze,* 51 LW 4375, at 4381-4382. The Court was closely divided (5-4); for the dissenters' argument in terms of the *Storer* precedent, see 4383-4385.

17. Ronald E. Weber, "Gubernatorial Coattails: A Vanishing Phenomenon," *State Government* 53 (Summer 1980): 155; Jack L. Walker, "Ballot Forms and Voter Fatigue: An Analysis of the Office Block and Party Column Ballots," *Midwest Journal of Political Science* 10 (August 1966): 460.

18. Data from *Book of the States* (Lexington, Ky.: The Council of State Governments), vol. 23, 1980-1981, 70-71; vol. 24, 1982-1983, 108-109, 151, 189; and from personal inquiries.

19. *Smith* v. *Allwright,* 321 U.S. 649 (1944); *Gray* v. *Sanders,* 372 U.S. 368 (1963).

20. Antonin Scalia, "The Legal Framework for Reform," *Commonsense,* vol. 4, no. 2 (1981): 41-42. See also Ranney, *Curing the Mischiefs,* 82-94.

21. *Georgia* v. *National Democratic Party,* 447 F. 2d 1271 (1971), at 1276.

22. *Bode* v. *National Democratic Party,* 452 F. 2d 1302 (1971), at 1305.

23. *Ripon Society* v. *National Republican Party,* 525 F 2d. 565 (1975), at 574-576, 585 (certiorari denied, 424 U.S. 933 [1976]). In concurring opinions, four judges argued that the Republican Convention's practices did *not* in fact constitute state action (at 598-600, 605-609). See, however, the dissent by Chief Judge Bazelon at 616-617.

24. *Storer* v. *Brown,* 415 U.S. 724 (1974); *Rosario* v. *Rockefeller,* 410 U.S. 752 (1973).

25. *Williams* v. *Rhodes,* 393 U.S. 23 (1968), at 30-32.

26. *Kusper* v. *Pontikes,* 414 U.S. 51 (1973). Note the distinctions drawn between this and the New York case, 60-61.

27. *Elrod, Sheriff* v. *Burns,* 427 U.S. 347 (1976), at 355.

28. *Branti* v. *Finkel,* 445 U.S. 507 (1980), at 518, 523-525.

29. Ibid., at 526-529.

30. *Cousins* v. *Wigoda,* 419 U.S. 477 (1975); compare *O'Brien* v. *Brown,* 409 U.S. 1 (1972), in which the Court refused to intervene on behalf of the California and Illinois delegations denied seating. The Court did not venture a judgment on the merits but, in staying a Court of Appeals decision favoring the California delegates, stated a presumption, based on "vital rights of association," that "the convention itself is the proper forum for determining intra-party disputes" (4). The discussion that follows draws on Scalia, "Legal Framework," 44-46; and on a memorandum prepared by Albert J. Beveridge, Counsel to the Commission on Presidential Nomination, Democratic National Committee, August 19, 1981.

31. *Cousins* v. *Wigoda,* at 489-491.

32. *Democratic Party of the U.S.* v. *La Follette,* 450 U.S. 107 (1981), at 121, 123-124.

33. Michigan Democrats, however, did set up an alternative selection system for 1980 after the legislature refused to change the state's open primary law. The Court of Appeals for the Sixth Circuit subsequently ruled that such an alternate plan, prepared by a state party in compliance with national party rules, took precedence over a noncomplying scheme specified in state law. *Ferency* v. *Austin,* 666 F. 2d 1023 (1981).

34. *Democratic Party* v. *La Follette,* at 130.

35. *Opinion of the Justices,* 385 Mass. 1201 (1982), at 1204-1206. The Massachusetts Supreme Judicial Court elaborated its views in a case brought by a candidate denied access to the ballot under the 15 percent rule: *Langone* v. *Secretary of the Commonwealth,* 388 Mass. 185 (1983). The U.S. Supreme Court denied certiorari and a dissent signed by three justices suggested that the state court had improperly extended the *La Follette* precedent. 51 LW 3719 (1983).

36. *Buckley* v. *Valeo,* 424 U.S. 1 (1976), at 13; see also *Burroughs* v. *United States,* 290 U.S. 534 (1934).

37. Committee on Federal Legislation, "The Revision of the Presidential Primary System," *The Record of the Association of the Bar of the City of New York* 33 (May-June 1978): 325. The committee goes on to argue that "the requisite justification is lacking" to require the states to hold presidential primaries or to establish a national primary, although legislation to regulate the timing of existing primaries and to maintain their "integrity" (for example, prohibiting crossover voting) could be constitutionally justified (319-329). Compare Scalia, "Legal Framework," 46-49.

Presidential Nomination and Party Reform 6

The most important function of the national parties is to nominate candidates for president and vice-president of the United States. It is thus understandable that ambivalence about the parties and attempts to reform them often have had as their focal point the process of presidential nomination. This chapter will provide an overview of the nomination reforms adopted since the late 1960s, and Chapter 7 will assess the nomination system that has emerged in terms of its impact on the parties. Critics claim that in this more than in any other single area modern practices and policies have wounded the parties and hastened their decline. We will attempt to assess this charge, to examine correctives that the Democratic party recently has applied, and to ask what further changes in the laws and rules governing presidential nomination might contribute to bringing the parties back.

Reform in the Democratic Party

The last two decades of American party history display a bewildering array of committees and commissions charged with the examination of some aspect of the presidential nomination process. Table 6-1 provides a summary account of these groups and their missions. In the Democratic party, where the debates have been more intense and the changes farther-reaching, "reform" was a direct outgrowth of the two issues that divided the party and the country most seriously during the 1960s: civil rights and the Vietnam War.[1]

The Credentials Committee of the 1964 Democratic National Convention was faced with a highly publicized challenge filed by the Mississippi Freedom Democratic party against the all-white Mississippi delegation. This was only one extreme example of a more general pattern: many southern delegations had almost no black members, and blacks accounted for only 2 percent of the 1964 convention delegates overall. More significant than the specific concessions made to the Mississippi challeng-

145

ers (two of them were given at-large delegate seats, and the others were designated honored guests of the convention) were two other actions that barred such discrimination in the future and affirmed the national party's authority to deal with the problem: the convention resolved that the Call to the 1968 convention should require state parties to give "voters in the state, regardless of race, color, creed, or national origin ... the opportunity to participate fully in party affairs," and a Special Equal Rights Committee was established to develop antidiscrimination standards that the convention's Credentials Committee presumably would enforce. This Equal Rights Committee, chaired by New Jersey Gov. Richard Hughes, recommended a set of guidelines, designated the "six basic elements," which forbade discrimination and required the publicizing of party meetings and procedures. The Democratic National Committee incorporated these rules into the Call for the 1968 convention, and they have been a part of the party's delegate selection rules every since.

In the meantime opposition to incumbent president Lyndon Johnson, centering on his Vietnam War policies, led to the insurgent candidacies of Sens. Eugene McCarthy and Robert Kennedy. Vice-President Hubert Humphrey, the favorite of most of the party's leaders after Johnson announced in early 1968 that he would not seek reelection, delayed his announcement of candidacy until late April, thus avoiding the filing dates for most primaries. Humphrey's strategy—to rely mainly on the support of the party regulars in the nonprimary states—frustrated the McCarthy activists, whose organizational efforts in the nonprimary states had been "too little or too late" [2] and who were inclined to regard a candidate who did not fight on their chosen turf as fearful of the judgment of "the people." Kennedy and Humphrey (with a stand-in slate) did square off in the crucial winner-take-all California primary on June 4, but Kennedy was assassinated on the evening of his triumph. McCarthy's faltering campaign was unable to pick up the pieces; in the end he could claim only 601 of the convention's 2,008 votes.

As the primary season drew to a close, a group of leading McCarthy strategists, frustrated and angered by the irregularities of the delegate selection process in many states and by their own difficulties in gaining representation, formed the ad hoc Commission on the Democratic Selection of Presidential Nominees. Chaired by Iowa Gov. (later senator) Harold Hughes, the commission issued a report on the eve of the 1968 convention. "State systems for selecting delegates to the national convention and the procedures of the convention itself display considerably less fidelity to basic democratic principles than a nation which claims to govern itself can safely tolerate," the commission concluded. Its proposals were highly influential in shaping the agenda for reform. They included placing an "affirmative obligation" on state organizations to achieve racial representativeness, prohibiting the unit rule (the rule requiring all members of a state to vote in accord with the choice of the majority), ensuring "fair representation" of runner-up candidate preferences at all stages of the delegate selection process, and requiring the "timely selection" of delegates through processes beginning no earlier than six months before the convention.[3]

Table 6-1 Chronology of Democratic and Republican National Commissions Dealing With Presidential Nomination, 1964-1982

Dates	Official Designation	Chair	Areas of Responsibility
DEMOCRATIC			
1964-1968	Special Equal Rights Committee	Gov. Richard Hughes	Develop antidiscrimination guidelines to be enforced by Credentials Committee of 1968 convention.
1968	Commission on the Democratic Selection of Presidential Nominees	Gov. Harold Hughes	Ad hoc, unofficial group; brought views on nomination process to 1968 convention.
1969-1972	Commission on Party Structure and Delegate Selection	Sen. George McGovern (1969-1971); Rep. Donald Fraser (1971-1972)	Develop delegate selection guidelines to be enforced by Credentials Committee of 1972 convention.
1969-1971	Commission on Rules	Rep. James O'Hara	Review convention rules; report to DNC.
1972-1973	Commission on Delegate Selection and Party Structure	Baltimore Councilwoman Barbara Mikulski	Propose delegate selection rules; report to DNC.
1973-1974	Charter Commission	Former governor Terry Sanford	Propose new charter to 1974 midterm conference.
1975-1978	Commission on Presidential Nomination and Party Structure	Michigan State Chair Morley Winograd	Initially to examine role of primaries; then to review delegate selection rules; report to DNC.
1981-1982	Commission on Presidential Nomination	Gov. James Hunt	Review delegate selection rules; report to DNC.
1981-1982	Commission on Low and Moderate Income Participation	Rep. Mickey Leland	Review low-income participation in convention and party affairs generally; report to DNC and 1982 midterm conference.
REPUBLICAN			
1966	Committee on Convention Reforms	RNC Committeeman Robert Pierce	Review convention rules; report to RNC.
1969-1971	Committee on Delegates and Organization	RNC Committeewoman Rosemary Ginn	Review convention and delegate selection rules (especially antidiscrimination); report to RNC.
1973-1975	Rule 29 Committee	Rep. William Steiger	Review rules governing delegate selection and the RNC; report to the RNC.
1977-1980	Rules Review Committee	RNC Committeeman Perry Hooper	Review delegate selection and convention rules; report to RNC.
1981-1982	Committee to Study Election Reform	RNC Committeeman Ernest Angelo	Review election reform generally; report to RNC.

The tumultuous Chicago convention of 1968 confirmed the insurgents' sense of the illegitimacy of party operations and also left many regulars convinced of the need for fundamental change. The Credentials Committee, which had faced 17 challenges alleging racial discrimination and other unfair and exclusionary practices, proposed the establishment of a "special committee" to study delegate selection, to "recommend improvements" that would broaden participation, and to "aid the state Democratic parties in working toward relevant changes." The convention's Rules Committee recommended the appointment of a commission to investigate the advisability of changes in the convention's rules of procedure. And a minority report from the Rules Committee, narrowly adopted by the convention, provided that the Call to the 1972 convention should forbid the unit rule and should ensure that delegates were selected by procedures "open to public participation within the calendar year of the national convention." [4] These resolutions together laid the groundwork for two commissions: Rules, and Party Structure and Delegate Selection.

The McGovern-Fraser Commission

National Democratic Chairman Fred Harris appointed the 28-member Commission on Party Structure and Delegate Selection in early 1969, with Sen. George McGovern as chairman. Within a year the commission had adopted ambitious "guidelines" to govern state delegate selection processes. These included provisions that:

- Mandated representation of blacks, women, and young people, requiring "affirmative steps" by the state parties to ensure that each group's share of delegate slots would bear a "reasonable relationship to the group's presence in the population of the state." (guidelines A-1, A-2)
- Required the adoption of written rules governing the process of delegate selection in each state, uniform statewide times and dates for all meetings related to delegate selection, and adequate public notice of such meetings. (A-1, A-5, C-1)
- Required state parties to remove any mandatory assessments of delegates, to set filing fees for delegate candidates at no more than $10, and to set petition requirements for delegate candidates and presidential candidates at no more than 1 percent of the Democratic electorate. (A-4)
- Required candidates for national delegate to indicate their presidential (or uncommitted) preference. (C-1)
- Banned the unit rule. The commission declined, however, to move decisively against California's winner-take-all primary, recommending only that the 1972 convention deal with the question of the representation of runner-up preferences. (B-5, B-6)
- Forbade proxy voting in meetings related to delegate selection and required party committees involved in the process to set their quorum at 40 percent or more. (B-1, B-3)
- Standardized the apportionment of delegate slots within states through a formula giving equal weight to the district's population and its Democratic presidential vote in the previous election. Convention states were required to select at least 75 percent of their delegates in a decentralized fashion, at or below the congressional district level. (B-7)

- Limited the number of delegates that could be chosen by party committees to 10 percent of a state's delegation and recommended that committee selection be eliminated entirely. (C-5)
- Prohibited party or public officials or committees who were elected before the calendar year of the convention from nominating or selecting delegates, thus taking the 1968 convention's "timeliness" requirement a major step further. (C-4)
- Required that public notice be given of the meetings of groups making up slates of nominees for delegate and that opportunity to challenge official slates be guaranteed. (C-6)
- Prohibited the ex officio designation of delegates to caucuses or conventions at any level. (C-2)

The most obvious effect of these rules was to reduce the ability of party leaders to influence or control the delegate selection process. But they did more than this; in effect, they abolished whole systems of delegate selection.[5] One of these was the "party caucus" system, what Byron Shafer describes as "the oldest and most widely used delegate selection institution in American history." Under this system party officers (usually precinct committeemen and committeewomen) constituted the first level in the process; they elected representatives to the next level in a hierarchy of conventions that eventually chose national delegates. Also banned was the "delegate primary" in which candidates for delegate ran under their own names only—a system used for half a century by states such as New York and Pennsylvania. Acceptable systems were narrowed to a "participatory convention" in which first-stage participation was open to any party member; a "candidate primary" in which the names of presidential contenders (or of delegate candidates with their presidential preferences) were placed on the ballot; or some combination of the two.

The commission made some compromises designed to accommodate state practices, and at several critical points it elected to recommend rather than to require that a standard be met. Nevertheless, the changes envisioned were momentous—"the greatest goddamn changes since [the advent of] the two-party system," as Larry O'Brien, Harris's successor as national party chairman, put it.[6] McGovern commented in retrospect:

> The shattering impact of the Chicago convention had everybody in more or less of a humble mood. Those key factors—the unpleasantness of the past and the fear of further division . . . enabled us to get together and make some rather bold changes.[7]

Rep. Donald Fraser, who assumed the commission chairmanship after McGovern became an active presidential candidate in 1971, proved to be a persistent and effective advocate of reform. O'Brien, despite some ambivalence, gave the commission crucial backing. Joseph Califano, counsel to the Democratic National Committee, issued an opinion in mid-1970 that buttressed the commission's authority and the binding nature of its guidelines. And the DNC ordered the state parties in its Call to the 1972 convention to "make all efforts to comply." In the end, 45 of the 55 state and territorial parties achieved full compliance, and the remaining 10 could be declared in "substantial" compliance—a remarkable achievement but one open to divergent interpretations. Had the party proved its resilience and responsiveness? Or did the magnitude of change simply bear witness to how weak the party's state and local substructures had become, leaving a vacuum which zealous reformers were all too eager to fill?

The Rules (O'Hara) Commission operated in the shadow of the McGovern-Fraser Commission; its mandate was less open-ended and its impact more limited. Revising the formula allocating convention votes to the states was its most sensitive task. The commission's proposed allocation, based on population and on Democratic voting performance in the three most recent presidential elections, was sharply attacked in the Democratic National Committee and consequently was substantially revised.[8] The commission left the overall size of the convention at its 1972 level of 3,000 delegates, renovated the convention's standing committee system, and made numerous changes in convention procedure.[9]

Time ran out on one remaining item from the 1968 convention's reform agenda: the development of a party charter. Both the McGovern-Fraser and O'Hara commissions claimed the authority to draft such a document, and each disputed the claim of the other. The two commissions eventually cooperated in producing a draft charter on the eve of the 1972 convention. But the issues were too complex, the document too controversial, and the party's divisions too deep to permit the convention to deal with the proposal. Instead, a new commission was authorized to develop a party charter and to bring it to a midterm convention in 1974.

Post-1972 Adjustments

"My nomination is all the more precious," said George McGovern in his acceptance speech at the 1972 convention, "in that it is the gift of the most open political process in our national history."[10] How essential the rules changes were to McGovern's nomination is debatable. So is the question of how much better a more conventional candidate might have fared against the incumbent president. But the devastating magnitude of the party's defeat made it difficult to maintain a vision of reform as the party's salvation. For a time it seemed as though the Coalition for a Democratic Majority,[11] the AFL-CIO, and party regulars from state and local organizations might be able to prompt a thorough reconsideration of the rules changes in light of their impact on the party's strength. As it developed, however, the McGovern-Fraser guidelines were only incrementally altered.

The difficulties and controversies surrounding the implementation of the guidelines prompted the 1972 convention to set up another delegate selection commission. But the convention adopted some measures—prohibiting, for example, the future use of winner-take-all primaries[12]—that carried the McGovern-Fraser reforms forward. And the new Commission on Delegate Selection and Party Structure, chaired by Baltimore Councilwoman (later U.S. representative) Barbara Mikulski, was basically controlled by advocates of reform. In fact, because of the enhanced role it gave presidential candidates in slating potential delegates, the Mikulski Commission weakened the hand of party leaders even further.

The most controversial issue facing the commission was demographic quotas. A footnote in the McGovern-Fraser Commission's report had stated an "understanding" that the representation of minority groups was "not to be accomplished by the mandatory imposition of quotas."[13] But a subsequent statement by Fraser, endorsed and circulated by National Chairman O'Brien, served notice that the presence of women, minorities, and young people in a delegation in percentages smaller than "the proportion of these groups in the [state's] total population" would constitute prima facie evidence of violation of the antidiscrimination guidelines.[14] This led to the challenge of some 20 delegations and to widespread demands for change. The Mikulski Commission's solution was to state the prohibition against quotas more strongly (although expressly permitting states to divide their delegate positions equally between men and women) and to specify the affirmative action obligations of the states in much greater detail. The new rules also stated that the demographic composition of a state's delegation would neither provide prima facie evidence of discrimination nor shift the burden of proof to the state party. "If a state party has adopted and implemented an approved Affirmative Action Program, the party shall not be subject to challenge based solely on delegation composition. . . ."[15]

The Mikulski Commission implemented the 1972 convention mandate that runner-up preferences receive a fair share of a state's delegate slots with a rule requiring that any presidential candidate receiving as much as 10 percent of the primary or convention votes in a given district (or statewide) be given a proportionate share of the delegates to be elected at that level. (The DNC subsequently raised the "threshold," below which candidates would not be entitled to any delegates, to 15 percent.) The commission prudently decided, however, not to move against states, such as Illinois, Pennsylvania, New York, Ohio, and New Jersey, where individual delegates were voted for directly on the primary ballot. Such direct-election primaries—termed "loophole" primaries by their detractors because they offered a "way out" for states that did not wish to adopt proportional representation—generally produced winner-take-all results. This was because voters favoring a given presidential candidate were likely to vote for all (or as many as possible) of the delegate candidates pledged to that preference. A full slate of delegates pledged to the winning candidate would thus be likely to win a plurality, leaving no slots for the runner-up preferences. The Mikulski rules merely required that candidates for delegate in such contests be clearly identified as to presidential preference and that they should not be chosen statewide, but at or below the congressional district level.[16]

The 1972 convention, reacting to instances where state delegations had failed to vote for the candidate (for example, George Wallace) who had won their primaries, required that "any delegate mandated to vote for a presidential candidate be selected in a manner which assures that he or she is in fact a bona fide supporter of that candidate." The rule adopted by the Mikulski Commission to implement this resolution brought back slate making with a vengeance, but this time the power to select delegates was given to candidate organizations rather than to party leaders:

> A presidential candidate shall have the right to approve any candidate for national convention delegate identified with that person's candidacy.[17]

There was nothing in the rules to prevent a candidate from approving only one candidate for each delegate slot to which he or she was entitled. The commission did not seem to appreciate the paradox: the fidelity of the convention to rank-and-file preferences was being sought through a mechanism that effectively could deny the rank-and-file any choice as to who represented them as delegates.

The other rules changes made by the commission were less momentous; their general effect was to loosen some of the more stringent of the McGovern-Fraser provisions. The prohibition against ex officio delegates was retained, but convention "privileges" (except voting rights) were extended to governors, members of Congress, and DNC members not elected as delegates. The election of such leaders was given some encouragement by raising from 10 to 25 the percentage of a state's delegation that could be appointed by party committees; no state, however, could select more than 25 percent of its delegates at-large. The "timeliness" guideline was loosened to permit state party committees elected as recently as 1974 to participate in the choice of delegates in 1976. Additional options were provided for apportioning delegates within states. The prohibitions against proxy voting and slate making were qualified. And compliance procedures were altered considerably: the appointment of a Compliance Review Commission (CRC) was authorized for early 1974. Described as a "preliminary Credentials Committee," the CRC was to work with the states in developing delegate selection and affirmative action plans and to hear challenges alleging noncompliance.[18]

The Charter Commission, chaired by former governor Terry Sanford of North Carolina, proved generally willing to accept the work of the McGovern-Fraser, O'Hara, and Mikulski commissions and enshrined a number of reform principles in basic party law.[19] Some commissioners, however, dissented strongly. AFL-CIO representatives led an attempt to weaken or to eliminate from the charter altogether the Mikulski compromise on quotas and affirmative action, the ban on the unit rule, the requirement that the allocation of delegate slots "fairly reflect" the division of preferences, and the requirement that delegate selection processes begin within the calendar year of the convention. This prompted an angry walkout by blacks and liberals and necessitated extensive efforts—ultimately successful—by National Chairman Robert Strauss to preserve a document that reinforced the consensus that had developed around the Mikulski rules.[20]

The Winograd Commission

In 1975 Strauss appointed another commission to examine a development arising out of the reform era: the proliferation of primaries. The

Commission on the Role and Future of Presidential Primaries, chaired by Michigan State Chairman Morley Winograd, was given a broadened mandate by the 1976 convention, and its name was subsequently changed to the Commission on Presidential Nomination and Party Structure. The Winograd Commission thus became a full-fledged successor to the Mc-Govern-Fraser and Mikulski commissions, but its agenda was less ambitious, and it aroused less interest within and beyond the inner circles of the party. "Both the reform mood and its emotional backlash had long since passed," concluded one observer of the earlier battles.[21] But a number of the commission's debates demonstrated the continuing capacity of the old issues to stir party passions. And its deliberations were given a distinctive cast by its being the first of the delegate selection commissions to operate under a Democratic president. The White House augmented the Winograd Commission with members supportive of the president and strongly influenced its deliberations.

In two areas, both covered by 1976 convention resolutions, the commission gave reform advocates additional victories. First, the convention had taken a major step toward reinstating quotas with a charter amendment requiring that affirmative action programs contain "specific goals and timetables"; the Winograd Commission added this language to the rules and specifically identified women, blacks, hispanics, and Native Americans as the objects of "remedial action to overcome the effects of past discrimination." The commission declined by a 31-23 vote to require the states to divide their delegate slots equally between men and women, but the DNC reversed this decision and included an equal division requirement in its Call to the 1980 convention. Second, the 1976 convention also had directed the commission to interpret the charter's "fair reflection" language "to bar the use of delegate selection systems in primary states which permit a plurality of votes at any level to elect all of the delegates from that level." The Winograd Commission thus eliminated the reprieve that the Mikulski rules had granted direct-election ("loophole") primaries.[22]

Champions of proportional representation fared less well in debates over what "threshold" a candidate would have to reach to be entitled to a share of delegate seats. The White House had an obvious interest in seeing the threshold raised, so that challengers to the president would find it more difficult to gain a convention foothold. The issue prompted heated debate and an esoteric series of proposals. The scheme adopted by the commission provided for a threshold that would escalate from 15 to 20 to 25 percent as the season progressed, on the theory that while long-shot candidates should be given a fair chance early in the campaign, a device was needed to narrow the field later on. The DNC rejected the escalating threshold in favor of a compromise proposal that set the district-level threshold in primary states at 100 percent divided by the number of delegates to be chosen in the district (but no more than 25 percent); the threshold at the district level in caucus states and for at-large selection in all states was to be no lower than 15 and no higher than 20 percent. This was compromised further, as it turned out, by the Compliance Review Commission. Instructed to "adopt regulations to prevent winner-take-all outcomes" at the district level, the CRC, in effect, reinstated a 15 percent threshold in the event of a two-candidate contest—which, of course, is exactly what the Democrats had in 1980.[23]

The White House's interest in discouraging challengers was also evident in a proposal requiring state filing deadlines to be at least 55 days before a primary. The DNC responded to criticisms of this proposal by allowing filing deadlines to fall within a broad 30- to 90-day range.

"I think it was clear that a majority of the Winograd Commission would have liked to do something about the proliferation of presidential primaries," commission member Donald Fraser later complained, "but then President Carter was elected and a large number of members were added to the commission. The work of the commission was diverted to rewriting the rules in order to protect the incumbent." [24] The commission's report merely reviewed the caucus-versus-primary debate, and a few proposals for limiting the impact of primaries, in noncommittal terms. It criticized proposals to standardize the system through devices such as national or regional primaries, and it strongly opposed any federal legislative involvement. But on the key question of proliferation, the commission could not report a consensus, much less recommend any specific course of action. The report simply noted that "about half of the members of the commission would prefer a larger proportion of state caucus systems in the present national 'mix' of caucus and primary systems." [25]

The commission, however, had more to say about other aspects of the primary system. The idea of shortening the nomination season, and reducing the impact of small, early states that gave a platform to long-shot candidates (such as Jimmy Carter in 1976), had obvious appeal to an incumbent president. But there was a more general case to be made for shortening and reducing the fragmentation of the process; some even supposed that this might reduce the attractiveness of primaries for certain states and thus halt or reverse proliferation. The commission finally settled on a "window" extending from the second Tuesday in March to the second Tuesday in June, during which all primaries and first-stage caucuses must be held. The CRC could permit exceptions only where state law set a different date and the state party had taken "provable positive steps" to change the law. As it happened, the effect of the "window" rule was appreciably reduced when the CRC granted exemptions to two primary states (New Hampshire and Massachusetts) and to three that held caucuses (Iowa, Maine, and Minnesota).

The Winograd Commission also moved much more boldly than its predecessors against open primaries. Although opposition to open primaries cut across the ranks of party regulars and reformers, their use in key states such as Michigan and Wisconsin had discouraged definitive party action. The Mikulski Commission had required state parties to "take all possible steps to restrict participation in the delegate selection process to Democratic voters only"—with little apparent effect. The Winograd panel made the prohibition absolute, going so far as to rule out exemptions even when the state party had taken "provable positive steps" to change state law; under such circumstances the party would be compelled to implement an "alternative party-run delegate selection system." It was this rule that led to the Wisconsin challenge in 1980 and the Supreme Court's *La Follette* decision.[26]

Two final rules recommendations by the Winograd Commission are worthy of note. Each state was given additional at-large seats numbering 10 percent of its base delegation. The purpose of this change was to encourage the selection of top party leaders and elected officials. Although some advocates of earlier reforms saw this new rule as a threat to the domination of the convention by "ordinary Democrats," the commission approved the "add-on" by a vote of 41 to 13.[27] It rejected, however, proposals to enlarge the increment, to permit these delegates to come to the convention not pledged to a candidate, or to give delegate seats ex officio to governors, members of Congress, and state party chairs and vice-chairs.

The Winograd panel also refined the procedures established by the Mikulski Commission for candidate approval of prospective delegates. The new rule required that presidential candidates approve at least three candidates for delegate for every slot to which they were entitled. The effect of this change was to discourage exclusive slate making by candidate organizations while leaving them with the power to veto any prospective delegate who wished to run under their banner. A new provision required that a candidate's delegates at the district level be selected by a caucus of persons who were themselves pledged to that candidate; district party conventions were therefore forbidden to vote as a unit for the delegates they sent to the national convention. And in a provision little discussed at the time but hotly debated in connection with Sen. Edward M. Kennedy's challenge at the 1980 convention, the commission required delegates "to vote for the presidential candidate they were elected to support for at least the first convention ballot" and gave candidate organizations the right to replace them with alternates if they sought to violate this obligation. "You will get your printout of the convention [outcome] as soon as the Secretary's office certifies the delegates," Commissioner Scott Lang wryly remarked. But the Winograd Commission passed without dissent the rules binding delegates to candidates that had been developed and presented as a package by White House representatives.[28]

"The main triumph of the Winograd Commission," observed commission member Austin Ranney, "[was] keeping the party from being weakened further."[29] Perhaps. The "add-on" for party leaders and elected officials and the ban on open primaries could be regarded as party-strengthening moves, although the rules binding convention delegates and giving candidate organizations more control over their selection went in the opposite direction. Still, the impact of the rules on party strength was clearly identified as an area of concern, and some possibilities were suggested that a commission more focused on party renewal could pursue four years later. That account will be developed presently. For now we turn to the milder sorts of reform that in the meantime had been pursued in Republican ranks.

Republican Reforms

Prior to the 1960s the Republicans had done more than the Democrats to assert national party authority in the presidential nomination process and to codify their convention and national committee rules. The GOP's ban of the unit rule, for example, dates to the party's first conventions in the mid-nineteenth century. The party's Committee on Convention Reforms, appointed in 1966, addressed proposals to streamline convention procedure that would later be on the agenda of the Democrat's O'Hara Commission. Thus in 1972 RNC Cochairman Anne Armstrong could claim with some validity that "many of the reforms the Democrats are just now getting around to discussing were accomplished without fanfare years ago by our own party." [30] But once the Democratic party abandoned its traditional deference to state law and party practice, it went far beyond anything the Republicans had ever attempted.

The Republican response to Democratic reform initiatives was sometimes imitative but more often reactive, as party leaders warned against "McGovernizing" the party and wrote the principle of state discretion and autonomy more explicitly into national party law. And it was in part defensive. Republicans soon realized that, no matter what rules they adopted, they would be affected by state laws that were altered to accommodate Democratic reforms. Thus in recent years they have monitored Democratic rules changes closely, attempting to anticipate their effects and to help their state party and public officials respond appropriately.

For several reasons the Republican party has not felt pressures to reform the presidential nomination process as strongly as the Democrats have. Insurgent elements in the party did not find the rules a barrier to working their will in the 1964 convention, and the 1968 and 1972 conventions were relatively consensual affairs, followed by electoral victory. The party has far fewer blacks and other minorities who might press for increased representation. Its conservative ideology has discouraged strong affirmative action measures and has placed a burden of proof on those who would intervene in state and local matters. And while the Democrats have given their national committee (and, in some cases, individual commissions) the power to recast nomination rules between conventions, the Republicans have retained a system that, in reserving final authority over such matters to the national convention itself, makes it impossible to change the rules for the next convention in the wake of the last.

Other forces impelled the Republicans to make at least a modest effort at reform. Many party leaders wanted to broaden the party's demographic base and, in particular, to reach out to newly enfranchised young voters. Some were looking for ways to loosen the hold that Vice-President Spiro Agnew seemed likely to have on the 1976 convention. And there was a widespread view that the party should take some action to discourage discrimination. President Richard Nixon was widely quoted: "I want the Republican party to be the party of the open door." [31]

The 1968 Republican National Convention authorized the appointment of a committee to consider ways of implementing the party rule prohibiting discrimination in the delegate selection process. The national chairman subsequently appointed a 16-member Committee on Delegates and Organization (the "DO" Committee), which was entirely drawn from the RNC and chaired by Rosemary Ginn, committeewoman from Missouri. The committee's first recommendation, designed "to implement the Republican Party's Open Door policy," provided that meetings at the first stage of the delegate selection process should be open to all party members. The committee also recommended banning automatic or ex officio delegates at any level to avoid giving undue advantage to a "few select people"; to make the process responsive to current political sentiments, all delegates should be "required to stand for election." The 1972 convention approved these recommendations and others that forbade the use of proxies in electing national delegates, limited the imposition of fees or assessments on delegates, and required each state to "endeavor" to have "equal representation of men and women in its delegation." The convention balked, however, at a DO Committee recommendation that would have required each state to include in its delegation "delegates under 25 years of age in numerical equity to their voting strength within the state." [32]

The 1972 convention also strengthened the rule requiring the party to take "positive action" to end discrimination and broaden participation, and authorized the appointment of a committee to work with the state parties in reviewing and implementing this and other rules. This "Rule 29 Committee" (named after the bylaw that created it) was appointed in 1973 with 57 members and Rep. William Steiger of Wisconsin as chairman. The work of this committee represented the high point of reform efforts in the Republican party, but its rebuff at the hands of the RNC in early 1975 clearly served notice that the GOP was not going to follow the McGovern-Fraser-Mikulski pathway to reform.

The Rule 29 Committee's most important recommendation was that each state Republican party be required to implement "positive action" through a specific plan and that the RNC review such programs and recommend any needed changes. These plans were not to include quotas, nor was failure to submit or implement an acceptable plan to be grounds for unseating a state's delegation. But even this pale reflection of the Democrat's compliance review procedures proved too strong for the RNC. "We're emulating the majority party on the very thing that took it down to defeat," said Mississippi State Chairman Clark Reed.[33] The RNC adopted a compromise proposal that urged rather than required the submission of "positive action" plans and provided for national party review only when the state party requested it. But the 1976 convention declined to institute compliance procedures of any sort.

Many of the questions addressed by Democratic reform commissions—proportional representation versus winner-take-all, the apportionment of delegates within states, the timing of delegate selection events, the candidates' role in approving or slating delegates—received little or no attention by Republican rules-writing bodies and hence remained matters of state discretion (see Table 7-1). The 1976 convention did adopt a milder version of the Democrats' open primary rule, providing that only voters "deemed to be Republicans" in light of state law or party rules could participate in Republican primaries or caucuses "except where state law otherwise mandates" (Rule 31[n]).

The 1976 Republican convention also prefigured the 1980 Democratic debate on the binding of delegates, and under similar circumstances. Supporters of the incumbent, President Gerald R. Ford, secured the adoption of a rule that provided for the automatic recording of a state's vote in accordance with the result of any binding primary. The 1980 convention, controlled by supporters of the 1976 challenger, Ronald Reagan, dropped this section from Rule 18, leaving it to the states to enforce their own binding rules.

On the question that tripped up the O'Hara Commission—the apportionment of delegates among the states—Republican debates were more protracted and no less heated than Democratic. The 1966 Committee on Convention Reforms and the DO Committee skirted the subject, but the case for reapportionment was pressed at the 1972 convention. Conservatives and small-state forces secured the retention of the "victory bonus" in the rules for 1976, thereby granting states a number of extra votes, regardless of their size, if the party's presidential, gubernatorial, and/or congressional candidates carried the state in the last election. The Ripon Society, an organization of moderate-to-liberal young Republicans, urged the adoption of a formula similar to that recommended by the O'Hara Commission and pressed a suit claiming that the victory bonus denied large states their just share of convention votes. The matter was resolved by the 1975 *Ripon* decision that gave the parties broad discretion in allocating delegates.[34] The victory bonus has remained in the rules ever since, although debate over allocation formulas continued at Rules Committee meetings prior to the 1976 and 1980 conventions.

Committees appointed by the GOP to consider rules changes since 1976 have been low-key affairs. The Rules Committee of the 1976 convention rejected appeals to prolong the life of the Rule 29 Committee, authorizing only the appointment of a Rules Review Committee within the RNC. Chaired by RNC Committeeman Perry Hooper of Alabama, the committee recommended removal of the 1976 binding rule but otherwise left delegate selection procedures intact.

Two additional committees were appointed to review the rules after the 1980 convention. At the instigation of the Convention Rules Committee, a Technical Amendments Subcommittee was formed to report to the RNC and to the Rules Committee of the 1984 convention. This group has largely limited itself to reordering and clarifying existing convention and delegation selection rules. Its report suggests new language to reflect the *La Follette* decision, stating that rules of the national party "have preeminence insofar as they choose to assert that preeminence" over state laws. But it recommends no changes in existing provisions for deference to state laws when they conflict with party rules on such matters as the openness (to all Republicans) of first-stage caucuses, the limitation of primary participation to bona fide Republicans, the assessment of delegate fees, and the timeliness of delegate selection.[35]

A second committee was given a broader mandate to review "all areas of election reform." This Committee to Study Election Reform, chaired by Committeeman Ernest Angelo of Texas and containing nine other RNC members, was named by National Chairman Richard Richards in mid-1981 and issued its final report a year later. The report mainly concerns proposed changes in the Federal Election Campaign Act and the conditions under which the Voting Rights Act of 1965 should be renewed. The committee's consideration of the presidential nomination process was largely limited to its participation in a bipartisan conference on the subject at Harvard University in December 1981.[36] In its report the Angelo Committee simply endorses what it takes to be that conference's main recommendations:

> ...that political parties should [themselves] determine how their nominees are chosen; state party organizations should have the authority to adjust the delegate selection process to fit their local political traditions; national, time zone, or regional primaries should not be imposed; and changes in party rules which require state legislative action should be drafted in a manner which would permit rather than require a party to adopt the change.[37]

The Hunt Commission

We now return to the Democrats and to the fourth of their quadrennial rules-writing bodies—the Commission on Presidential Nomination, chaired by Gov. James B. Hunt, Jr., of North Carolina, which completed its work in early 1982. The Hunt Commission, on which the author served as staff director, is of particular relevance because of its conscious focus on party renewal. It also furnishes an occasion to look at the political context in which the parties may attempt to help themselves—a context that provides significant opportunities for party renewal but also substantial barriers to change.

The 1980 Democratic National Convention passed two vaguely worded resolutions mandating a review of the presidential nomination process.[38] Had President Carter been reelected, the rules review probably would have been a low-key affair, perhaps carried out entirely within the Democratic National Committee. As it happened, however, the rules became a focal point for those attempting to diagnose the troubles of 1980 and wishing to "do something" about the party's condition. Outgoing DNC chairman John White announced in late 1980 his intention to appoint a rules-writing commission with Hunt as chairman. Incoming chairman Charles Manatt had a healthy skepticism about the tendency of Democrats to place excesses of both blame and hope on party rules. But faced with widespread expectations that a rules-writing commission would and should be named, and finding commission posts useful bargaining chips in his own election bid, Manatt carried White's plans forward.

Manatt found White's choice of Hunt, a long-time friend, a compatible one. Hunt wanted the assignment, and his credentials were impeccable. He had served on the O'Hara Commission, headed the panel that rewrote North Carolina's party rules in the wake of the McGovern-Fraser Commission, and was known as one of the most party-oriented of the Democratic governors. Hunt was an attractive southern moderate whose appointment was acceptable to the broad range of constituencies within the party. Manatt appointed as vice-chairmen United Auto Workers President Douglas Fraser and Dorothy Zug, vice-chair of the Pennsylvania State Democratic Party.

On July 2, 1981, Manatt announced the appointment of the commission, directing it to "undertake a complete review of the presidential nomination process for the purpose of making specific recommendations to the Democratic National Committee." [39] While avoiding specifics, Hunt and Manatt stressed at their press conference the importance of giving party professionals and elected officials an enhanced role at the convention. They also emphasized the party's interest in shortening the nomination season and in easing the rules that bound delegates to vote in a predetermined fashion. Like the McGovern-Fraser, Mikulski, and Winograd commissions (but unlike all of the Republican commissions except the Rule 29 Committee), the membership of the Hunt Commission extended far beyond the national committee, conspicuously including people whose main identification was with candidate and constituency groups. The 70-member commission included 22 members of the DNC and 7 people who were chairs, vice-chairs, or executive directors of state parties—a substantial group but a much smaller force proportionately than they represented within the DNC. The large number (15) and active participation of commissioners identified with organized labor contrasted markedly with the near boycott of earlier reform efforts by major segments of the labor movement. Several governors, members of Congress, and mayors were appointed to the commission, but the failure of some to appear at even one meeting created some embarrassment for proponents of a more active role for elected officials in party affairs.

Manatt guaranteed that candidate orientations would play a major role in the commission's deliberations by inviting Walter Mondale and Edward Kennedy, generally regarded as the party's most likely 1984 presidential contenders, to name two members each. Beyond this, those assembling names at the DNC were attentive to the past and present candidate affiliations of those being asked to serve. In general, a scrupulous balance was observed, but Kennedy's associates were especially successful in getting commissioners named whose *first* allegiance was to the senator—some seven members. This was to prove important later in helping the Kennedy group resist commission action on matters they judged adverse to their interests. Mondale's associates, finding themselves in closer agreement with the directions they saw labor and the state parties taking, felt less constrained to secure the appointment of supporters beyond those already being named to the commission for other reasons.

To work with the commission, Manatt appointed a 22-member Technical Advisory Committee (TAC), primarily composed of staff members from previous campaigns and rules experts spawned by 12 years of party reform. Faced with a heavy demand for commission slots, Manatt knew that to appoint one group's or candidate's experts would frequently necessitate the appointment of another's. Setting up a separate advisory group thus had considerable appeal. It would reduce the demand for commission seats while giving the experts a constructive role to play. To ensure that the TAC's work would be subordinate to and coordinated with that of the commission, Manatt appointed Hunt to chair the TAC and preside over its meetings. As cochair he named former DNC executive director Mark Siegel.

Some of the early talk about the TAC as a "neutral" source of expertise proved unrealistic. Many TAC members had conspicuous candidate affiliations, most had strong ideas about the form the rules should take, and some wanted to use the TAC as a base of influence. By the time the commission was ready to make its major decisions, some, including Cochairman Siegel, were referring to ideas generated by groups of TAC members as "TAC proposals" or "TAC recommendations." A degree of rivalry with the staff and with the commission itself was inevitable. Hunt attempted to minimize this by presiding over TAC meetings when possible, by ruling out TAC votes on specific proposals, and by holding relatively few meetings of the full TAC; specific assignments instead were given to individuals and committees within the group. In the end, the TAC experiment could be deemed a qualified success. It solved difficult political problems for Manatt and probably made for a less Washington-based and candidate-oriented commission. TAC members provided the commission with information and analysis that otherwise would have been very difficult to obtain, given the small size of staff operations.

The first meeting of the commission on August 20-21 left the leadership and staff duly impressed with the sensitivity of their task. Every panel or set of presentations had to be scrupulously "balanced," not only demographically but also with respect to the past and present candidate allegiances of participants and their attitudes toward party reform. Rumblings already were being heard concerning the role and the neutrality of the TAC. And commissioners let it be known that they wanted all decisions made in plenary sessions—no subcommittees or drafting committees or like devices.

The first TAC and commission meetings also made it clear that, despite all the talk about the need for change, it was entirely possible that the commission would be able to accomplish very little. There was hardly a rule in which some powerful or vocal group did not perceive it had a vital stake. Many people who either had a hand in writing the rules or who made their living by interpreting them for candidates proved quite reluctant, when it got down to specifics, to consider significant changes. Perhaps the best example of this attitude was a lengthy paper prepared by Carter pollster and TAC member Patrick Caddell. Caddell confessed to having a bias in favor of primaries, suggested that the early New Hampshire contest be preserved, argued that proposals to seat Democratic members of Congress and other elected officials as ex officio delegates were "fraught with many potential dangers," suggested that all the talk about "thinking delegates" and a "deliberative convention" threatened to deny "the people" their sovereign power—and then concluded with a challenge to the commission to act "boldly"! [40] It became clear that if the chairman contented himself with nothing more than a brokering role, the opposing forces might do little more than cancel one another out. "If you don't watch it," Hunt observed after an early meeting, "these people will bargain you out of *anything* you want to do!"

After its initial meeting the commission turned to a series of regional hearings in Des Moines, Chattanooga, Los Angeles, and Washington. These hearings made clear the high salience of three clusters of issues— affirmative action and equal division, the role of party leaders and elected officials, and the enforcement of the timing "window"—to a broad range of groups within the party. The positions that were staked out on these issues—or at least on the latter two—did not reveal any emerging consensus, but the boundaries within which debate and bargaining would take place became considerably clearer. By contrast, questions of fair reflection/proportional representation and of the candidates' role in delegate selection came to the fore only sporadically. The hearings thus revealed to persons interested in those issues what kind of effort would be required to put them on the agenda.

The timing of the Harvard University Institute of Politics' December 4-6 conference on "The Parties and the Nominating Process" was fortuitous. The conference did not assume the same importance for the Democrats that it did for the Republicans, whose 10-member Angelo Committee attended the conference and incorporated its conclusions into their final report. But a number of Hunt Commission and TAC members did attend, and the conference proved particularly important to Hunt, who was becoming increasingly concerned about the crossfire surrounding the proposal in which he placed greatest stock—the bringing of larger numbers of party leaders and elected officials to the convention as unpledged delegates. He decided to use his luncheon address to articulate the basic principles he felt should guide the commission's work and to develop a convincing rationale for the inclusion of more party and elected officials in particular.

Hunt's speech, much of which eventually made its way into the commission's report, placed the work of the commission squarely in the context of party renewal. While confirming his desire to preserve the reforms that had "opened up the process," Hunt stressed that "representativeness" was not to be achieved "simply by opening up channels of mass and group participation." The rules, he argued, bore considerable responsibility for the proliferation of primaries, the reduced participation of public officials, and the emergence of a "rubber stamp" national convention—all of which had weakened the party. The governor suggested three "fundamental goals" for those recasting party rules: (1) "strengthening the party as a cohesive force in government and within the electorate"; (2) making the nominating process more *representative* of the Democratic party's "broad constituency"; and (3) increasing the likelihood that the party's nominee could campaign and govern effectively. While the party and elected official proposal was no "panacea," Hunt said, it did relate directly to each of these goals and was thus of particular importance.[41]

The commission held three working sessions after its regional hearings, concluding its work on February 5, 1982. At the first of these on November 6-7, 1981, Hunt was able to elicit a consensus on retaining the affirmative action and equal division rules, continuing the open primary ban, and softening the 1980 rule that allowed candidates to remove "unfaithful" delegates from the floor. But on other major questions it was evident that wide differences remained. Hunt thus set in motion intensified discussion among the four major voting blocs on the commission—labor, state parties, and Kennedy and Mondale loyalists. These groups seriously disagreed on several matters, but the cleavages were less severe than on earlier commissions and all felt that it was in their interest to keep bitter battles off the floor. This process of negotiation largely succeeded; by the time the commission next convened on January 14, compromise resolutions containing precise rules language were assured of easy passage in most areas under dispute.

The commission's ability to do its work expeditiously and without divisive conflicts seemed to many like "a breath of spring air" after the reform battles of the past and the 1980 debacle.[42] Its contribution to the party's short-run peace and harmony was valuable. But how well did it serve the party's long-range interests? How effectively did it counter the party-weakening aspects of reform? To answer these questions we will examine more closely the decisions the commission made and then analyse in Chapter 7 the implications for party strength of these changes in the presidential nomination system.

Affirmative Action and Equal Division

The party's affirmative action rule should remain intact: on this virtually everyone involved with the Hunt Commission agreed from the beginning. Occasional complaints were heard from labor and state party quarters that the "specific goals" required by the rules were no different, in practice, from quotas, and several black members criticized the provision (dating from the Mikulski Commission compromise) that the composition of a delegation alone could not provide sufficient grounds for a challenge. In general, however, there was great reluctance to tamper with the rule. Hunt identified affirmative action as first on the list of matters on which he assumed consensus existed at the November 7 meeting. For several reasons, no one questioned that judgment. Most importantly, the affirmative action program seemed to have worked well. It had addressed an obvious injustice and seemed to have struck about the right balance— strong rules with effective guidelines and sanctions, but without the rigidities of a pure quota system. And politically, almost everyone recognized that the costs of reopening questions upon which the party had carefully and painfully reached agreement would far exceed any anticipated benefits.

The requirement that delegate seats be equally divided between men and women has posed considerably greater difficulties for state parties (see Chapter 7). The rule nonetheless provoked relatively little controversy on the Hunt Commission. The proponents of equal division on the DNC had managed to get the principle written into the charter as well as into the 1980 rules, so an abandonment of the standard would have required a two-thirds majority on the DNC to amend the charter. Several women from the state parties, labor, and the traditional Democratic women's organizations had spoken out strongly against equal division—as "a rigorous and strict rule [that] can only be self-defeating"—when it was considered by the Winograd Commission.[43] But by 1981 these women either had changed their minds or were maintaining a prudent silence. Many who were not enamoured of the rule still worried about the symbolism of appearing to weaken or dismantle it, particularly at a time when the Republican party had abandoned the Equal Rights Amendment and the polls showed women to be turning increasingly to the Democrats. And the champions of equal division were relentless: the National Organization for Women and the National Women's Political Caucus testified at every hearing, did their homework, and communicated effectively with commission and DNC members.

It was thus a foregone conclusion that equal division would remain in the rules. What was less certain was how it would relate to the various proposals to bring more party leaders and elected officials to the convention as unpledged delegates. Some suggested that the equal division and affirmative action requirements should not apply to them, particularly if top officials came to the convention ex officio: they would be there because of their office, regardless of gender or race or candidate preference, and therefore should be treated as true "add-ons," and not included in the demographic breakdowns applied to regularly selected delegates. To this some added a practical argument: since most of the elected officials were likely to be white males, to require the states to compensate for them demographically would put considerable strains on the at-large portion of the delegation, perhaps making it impossible to include other males that it was politically important to accommodate.

Equal division proponents not only rejected these arguments but also expressed considerable skepticism about the party leader-elected official proposal itself. Some acknowledged that it would put pressure on state parties, claimed women would become the scapegoats for the ensuing difficulties, and opposed it for those reasons. Others fastened on the special status that might accrue to add-on delegates by virtue of their being unpledged. TAC member and Kennedy adviser Susan Estrich put the matter starkly in an early memorandum to the commission: equal numbers were not enough; what equal division required was rather equal *power!* Even if equal division calculations included all convention delegates, the convention would only "look" representative:

> Virtually every woman and virtually every minority group member would be a "committed" delegate. The "uncommitted" delegates ... would be, almost to a man, white men. Power would not be shared, fairly

and equally, among men and women and minorities. It would—unequally—be placed in the hands of white men.[44]

For some, this kind of thinking led to outright opposition to the party leader-elected official idea. For others, it led to attempts to require that the group of unpledged "superdelegates" *itself* be equally divided.

The commission leadership, aware of the intense feelings of equal division advocates and wary of jeopardizing the elected officials measure, decided early on to try to defuse the issue. If assurances could be given that equal division would continue to apply to delegations as a whole— i.e., that any imbalances created by the addition of more elected officials would be compensated for elsewhere in a delegation—then perhaps the women's groups might relax and other proposals would appear less threatening. Thus Hunt asked for "consensus" on equal division as well as affirmative action on November 7, and commissioners proved willing to confine their misgivings to private discussions. This move did not totally dispose of the issue, but it did clear the air at a critical juncture and contributed measurably to the agreement the commission was able to achieve.

The affirmative action rule adopted by the commission also included language from the 1980 Call that required state parties to devise plans to help defray the expenses of delegates who otherwise would not be able to attend the convention.[45] This action was taken with an eye to the Commission on Low and Moderate Income Participation, which had been charged by the 1980 convention with finding ways of providing financial support for low-income delegates and recommending rule changes that would "ensure fair representation of low and moderate income Democrats" in the delegate selection process and at the convention.[46]

The Association of Community Organizations for Reform Now (ACORN), a federation of state and local community action groups, had made the formation of such a commission the focal point of its activities during the 1980 campaign season. The DNC leadership and the Carter and Kennedy campaigns had found it in their interest to support the convention resolution authorizing the commission, but without any clear sense of what such a commission might produce or how it would relate to broader rules-writing efforts. By the time the Hunt Commission was named, a 16-member Commission on Low and Moderate Income Participation, chaired by Rep. Mickey Leland of Texas, was already in place, and the potential for conflict between the two commissions was evident. Their mandates clearly overlapped, and the Leland Commission resolution required a report to the 1982 party midterm conference, long after Manatt hoped to have the 1984 rules adopted by the DNC.

DNC Deputy Chair Ronald Brown, under whose jurisdiction both the Leland and Hunt commissions fell, devised a plan whereby the reports of both would be considered at the same March 1982 meeting of the DNC. (The required Leland "report" to the midterm conference in June thus became an accounting of decisions already made.) The Hunt Commission's move to require state financial assistance plans was intended as a gesture of support to the Leland Commission and a demonstration of sensitivity to its concerns. But it also implied that the Hunt

Commission considered low-income participation to be within its own jurisdiction and that it had given due consideration to the range of suggested remedies. Commission and DNC leaders had a firm idea of what remedies were *not* acceptable. Any attempt to superimpose goals or quotas based on income on those already existing for gender, race, and nationality would, as one of them put it, "sink this ship for good." For a time it looked as though the Leland Commission would not recommend such a course, but in the end Leland himself and a majority of the commission's members voted to recommend the inclusion of "low and moderate income persons" as an affirmative action target group. The commission was late in getting its report approved and issued, so there was little time to work out a compromise before the DNC convened on March 26.

The Leland proposal particularly alarmed the state chairs, a group Manatt needed to accommodate in light of their complaints about being insufficiently consulted on the party leader-elected official compromise (see pp. 169-170). Commission leaders were convinced that the proposed Leland rule was neither politically nor administratively feasible, but they were anxious to signal their concern about low-income participation and to give Leland a basis for claiming to have strengthened affirmative action. A compromise was thus crafted that added "low and moderate income persons" to the list of groups targeted for party "outreach" and made the Hunt Commission's financial assistance provision part of a broader requirement "to encourage the participation and representation of persons of low and moderate income." [47] This prompted a charge from ACORN that "last minute compromises" had "gutted" the Leland report of "its most important provision." But Leland defended the compromise as a necessary one, and it cleared the way for unanimous DNC acceptance of his commission's report.

Party Leaders and Elected Officials

Nothing commanded more attention or excited more controversy on the Hunt Commission than proposals to reserve unpledged delegate slots for party leaders and elected officials (the "PL/EO" issue). There was wide agreement that the rules had discouraged the participation of these leaders and a sense, rooted in the Carter presidency, that the party tie between the White House and Congress must be strengthened. Manatt and Hunt stressed in all of their early pronouncements that this item would head the commission's agenda, and labor and state party spokesmen did likewise. But there were also early signs that agreement would not come easily. Some defenders of reform argued that giving special status to public and party officials would give the convention an "elitist" cast and would dilute the influence of women and minorities in particular. At the commission's first meeting supporters of Senator Kennedy cited CBS News figures (see Table 7-4) to show that some 64 percent of the 1980 delegates were already public or party officials of some sort, implying that the problem had been exaggerated. [48]

Kennedy and his spokesmen decided early that their interests were threatened by the PL/EO proposals and particularly by the prospect of large numbers of representatives and senators attending the convention as unpledged delegates. Their preferred strategy, as in the senator's challenge of President Carter in the 1980 primaries, was to pose as the defenders of Democratic orthodoxy and the champions of reform. They did not attack the elected official idea directly; rather they insisted that no delegates should be unpledged. Their strategy thus could be seen as a defense of reform principles—delegate preferences should "fairly reflect" those of the electorate; men and women and grass-roots and official delegates should have "equal power." But attacking the elected officials' unpledged status was, in effect, little different from attacking the proposal itself. Many officials simply could not and would not serve if they were required to make an early pledge of candidate support. Rep. Geraldine Ferraro put the matter starkly:

> The bottom-line question is whether you want them to go. Either they're going to go as uncommitted delegates or they won't go.[49]

Walter Mondale was less threatened than Kennedy by the PL/EO idea. "Everybody seems to think that these will be our people," said one commissioner with close Mondale ties. "We aren't sure that it's true, but we certainly aren't going to act like we don't *think* they'll be with us!" In truth, some of the Mondale operatives on the TAC were hardly more enamoured of the idea of unpledged delegates than their Kennedy counterparts. But Mondale and his representatives on the commission told Hunt that he could count on their support for whatever proposal he wished to endorse.

The first skirmish on the PL/EO issue centered on the preparation of an "option paper" before the commission's November 6-7 meeting. A group of TAC members, asked by Hunt to develop alternative proposals, decided instead to put forward a preferred solution. "We worked up this model, and then we realized: This is it; this is the solution," as one of them put it later. They recommended that the 10 percent PL/EO "add-on" to each state's delegation adopted by the Winograd Commission be supplemented by a second 10 percent add-on, with only this second group—about 300 delegates or 8 percent of the total convention—being unpledged. Hunt and the commission staff were distinctly unenthusiastic about both this "solution" and the role the TAC subcommittee had assumed. Labor and state party representatives were also alarmed. Viewing the TAC subcommittee's "10-10" proposal as what the candidates would be willing to settle for, they decided to testify in favor of a higher and less flexible PL/EO percentage than they might otherwise have suggested. The AFL-CIO began its testimony with a proposal that "a *minimum* of 30 percent of the national convention delegates be elected and party officials" and that all of them be allowed to remain unpledged. The president of the state chairs, Marge Thurman, also led off with a recommendation "that at least *30 percent* of the convention be composed of *uncommitted* party leaders and elected officials." And Senate Democratic Conference Chair Alan Cranston suggested 25 percent as a "reasonable" percentage for elected officials, "totally uncommitted."[50]

The November hearings also confirmed that a proposal for the selection of congressional delegates by the House and Senate Democratic caucuses, which was being pushed by House caucus chairman Gillis Long, was attracting growing support. Long presented a caucus resolution recommending "that at least two-thirds of the Democratic members of the House, upon election by our caucus, become uncommitted, voting delegates" to the 1984 convention—adding that he wished "to stress the necessity for this uncommitted status." This proposal was part of a more general effort to strengthen party cohesion in the House. Long's main concern was to bring congressional influence to bear on presidential selection and platform-writing and to bridge the presidential-congressional gulf that had plagued the Carter presidency. He was also interested in expanding and diversifying the functions of the caucus and the rewards it had to offer cooperative members. Long was strongly backed by the leaders of organized labor, who favored caucus selection because they regarded it as more likely than state party selection to "screen, challenge, or discourage" those who had not supported national party positions.[51]

The main objections to caucus selection, naturally, came from the state parties. Commissioner Dominic Baranello, New York's state chair, portrayed this as only one of a number of rules that threatened the "extinction" of party organizations.[52] Marge Thurman was convinced that in a state like hers (Georgia) the caucus might refuse to choose conservative members of Congress who were important to the state party's strategy of "inclusion." She was never fully reassured by Long's insistence that the caucus's powers of exclusion were likely to be used sparingly and that the number of slots would be large enough to include virtually everyone who wanted to attend the convention. A number of commissioners, including Hunt, who in the long run would have preferred state party selection, nonetheless became convinced that for the present the party should make the most of the congressional caucuses' interest in intraparty bridge building. Moreover, it seemed likely that a push by the caucuses could do more than selection by scattered state parties to bring congressional participation quickly back to its prereform levels and beyond.

One of Hunt's main objectives in setting in motion the bargaining process among the four major commission blocs after the November meeting was to try to reach an agreement on the size and committed-uncommitted status of the PL/EO contingent. His own preferred approach was to compromise on the number of PL/EO delegates but to leave the entire group unpledged. The idea of selecting the add-on in two stages, part unpledged and part pledged, seemed overly complex and administratively unworkable. Thus the staff developed a "20 percent compromise." A single 25 percent add-on would be calculated on a base of 3,000 delegates, producing 750 unpledged delegates, or 20 percent of the convention (of 3,750) overall. The 20 percent figure was derived from a state-by-state calculation of what minimum figure would allow *every* state (save two) to include its "core" officials (governors, members of Congress, large-city mayors, and party chair and vice chair) and would allow *most* states some discretion to choose other key officials and to choose enough female and black officials to ease the demographic pressures on the at-large portion of the delegation. While state party leaders viewed 20 percent as barely enough, labor and Mondale spokesmen did not hesitate to accept it. But the Kennedy group dug in, perhaps sensing that labor and the Mondale group had not yet reached their bottom line. Thus, while the meetings of the bloc spokesmen moved toward consensus on some issues, no progress was made on the PL/EO question; a major floor fight on January 14 seemed likely.

Hunt and John Perkins, who as director of the AFL-CIO's Committee on Political Education was handling labor's informal negotiations, calculated that the 20 percent compromise could count on 45 firm "yeas" and only 13 "nays." They agreed, however, that a bitter battle could have a disruptive effect on the consensus that was emerging in other areas. Therefore, they decided to ask National Chairman Manatt, who had involved himself only sporadically in commission matters thus far, to work with them in making one final effort at accommodation.

In the meantime, Rep. Geraldine Ferraro, wary of being caught between contending forces on the commission, decided to see if she could devise a PL/EO proposal that would break the deadlock. She turned to TAC Cochair Mark Siegel for help. The Ferraro-Siegel draft was based on the TAC subcomittee's double add-on proposal, but it provided for a considerably larger number of unpledged delegates. Each state would receive slots for its chair and vice-chair, and 400 additional slots would be allocated among the states in proportion to the size of their base delegations to accommodate other party leaders and elected officials. The House and Senate caucuses would name up to two-thirds of their members as delegates, forwarding those names to the states. State caucuses or conventions would then fill out the rest of the unpledged PL/EO slots, giving first consideration to governors and big-city mayors, and then to DNC members and members of Congress not already selected and to other party and public officials. The states could then fill a second pledged add-on, numbering 10 percent of their base delegation, just as they had in 1980.

Manatt, Hunt, and Perkins agreed that Ferraro's initiative might be what was needed to revive the prospects for agreement, and Manatt set out to bring the major blocs on board. Labor, anxious to avoid a battle and preferring not to alienate either Mondale or Kennedy, readily agreed to the Ferraro plan. The Mondale group, many of whom were none too enthusiastic about unpledged delegates in the first place, followed suit. Kennedy's spokesmen, knowing they were unlikely to get a better deal, did likewise. But Manatt did not seek out Thurman's views or those of any other state party leaders. Why he chose this course is not entirely clear. He may have regarded Hunt's views as an adequate representation of state party interests, though Hunt himself insisted otherwise. Manatt knew that it would be difficult to get Thurman to agree to a number of unpledged delegates as low as Ferraro had proposed and that bringing Thurman into the negotiations, given her strong feelings about caucus selection, might reopen that issue as well. And perhaps he assumed that the state party people, being good "regulars," could be counted on eventually to go along with whatever the leadership proposed.

The way Manatt structured his consultations, with the state parties essentially out of the picture, meant that it was Hunt who expressed the most substantial reservations about the Ferraro-Siegel draft. He insisted that it be revised in two respects. First, the number of unpledged delegate slots in each state should be sufficient to accommodate all that state's "core" officials. (The Ferraro plan had left 15 states without enough positions.) Thus the proposal was revised to provide "bonus" unpledged slots to a state when needed to make its first add-on large enough to accommodate the state chair and vice-chair, governor, Democratic members of Congress, and Democratic mayors of cities with over 250,000 population. This eventually added 52 unpledged delegates to the 1984 convention, making for a total of 566 (14.4 percent of all delegates). Second, the pledging procedure for the second add-on should be altered to reduce the disincentives the required pledge would pose to party leaders and elected officials who might seek these positions. The Ferraro proposal therefore was amended to allow state parties to set up later and less formal procedures for pledging and for candidate approval for persons running for pledged PL/EO positions.[53]

While Hunt's amendments made the plan considerably more palatable to state party leaders, they still anticipated that the reduced numbers of unpledged delegates would make it quite difficult for them to include key leaders outside the "core" group or appreciable numbers of blacks and women. (In over half the states, the number of unpledged PL/EO slots would not exceed the number of "core" officials.) After some initial angry exchanges, however, most state leaders went along with the Ferraro compromise. After all, the party had come a long way since the Winograd Commission had provided a small add-on, entirely pledged to candidates; now the states would be entitled not only to these slots but to another increment, almost twice as large, entirely unpledged.[54] The number of unpledged delegates, even in the Ferraro plan, was almost twice the number contained in the TAC subcommittee proposal that had been touted as an obvious "solution" just two months before. And while splitting the add-on into pledged and unpledged components promised major headaches, the second add-on (with Hunt's amendment relaxing pledging procedures) did give the states a "safety valve" for key officials who could not be included in the unpledged group.[55]

The most spirited attempt to alter the Ferraro plan came from a quite different direction, as feminist leaders proposed that any bloc of unpledged delegates should be required to meet affirmative action and equal division requirements. Convinced that being unpledged would confer a kind of "superdelegate" status, they regarded equal division among *all* delegates (which the commission had already accepted) as inadequate representation for women. But requiring the unpledged PL/EO bloc itself to be equally divided would eliminate many of those public officials the add-on was originally designed to accommodate. As Ferraro pointed out, "If you are looking for participation of elected officials and if you are looking to keep [down] the number of uncommitted delegates ... to mandate equal division [of the uncommitteds] is absolutely numerically impossible." [56]

The major voting blocs united to defeat the equal division amendment handily. But a number of commissioners, including Ferraro and several labor members, continued to explore ways of including more women and minorities in the unpledged group. Reducing the number of delegates that the congressional caucuses would select was the main option that was considered. At its final meeting the commission agreed that commission, congressional, and DNC leaders would arrive at a lower figure and insert it into the text to be submitted to the DNC for approval on March 26.

There was, of course, a much simpler and more effective way to increase the number of unpledged positions available to minorities and women: provide the states with enough slots to let them choose more than the bare minimum of "core" officials. But this alternative posed a dilemma for equal division advocates who, as reformers, feared a brokered convention and, as supporters of Senator Kennedy, wanted to keep the number of unpledged delegates at a minimum. So they advocated instead a reduction in the number of members of Congress to be included in the *existing* add-on, investing their fight with great symbolic significance although even a large cut in the fraction of members named (say from two-thirds to one-half of the Democratic representatives and senators) would free up an average of less than one additional unpledged slot per state.

At several junctures, Manatt, Hunt, and Long floated the idea of creating additional unpledged slots. "We'll soon see," an aide remarked at one point, "whether they're more interested in getting more places for women or in looking out for Kennedy's interest." The answer was not long in coming. Almost all of the advocates of reducing the congressional number refused to consider an overall increase in the number of unpledged delegates. The credibility of their position was further reduced by the prominence of Kennedy aides and associates in promoting it. The suspicion grew that Kennedy was simply using the women's issue as a means of reducing the number of congressional delegates.

At the meeting of key commission and congressional spokesmen that Manatt called to resolve the issue, Long argued that substantially cutting the number of members of Congress would make the party appear ambivalent about the elected official participation it supposedly wanted to encourage. Manatt then announced his preferred solution: reducing the number of congressional participants only slightly by providing for caucus selection of "up to three-fifths" rather than "up to two-thirds" of Democratic members. Some were displeased, but none felt compelled to take a fight to the floor. With this last piece in place, the party leader-elected official rule was ready for approval by the national committee.[57]

Proportional Representation's Demise

The only rules changes made by the Hunt Commission that rivaled the PL/EO proposal in importance were its thorough rewriting of the "fair reflection" rules governing the allocation of delegates to candidates.

Even more than the PL/EO changes, these were consciously designed to reverse a course taken earlier in the name of reform. They were less straightforwardly related, however, to the theme of party renewal; proponents were primarily motivated by state and candidate interests. And while the fair reflection changes provoked intense opposition within the commission and the DNC, they did not divide the major voting blocs.

Mondale supporters made their interests known early in an August 1981 *Washington Post* article. Proportional representation, they argued, "prolonged divisive campaigns and inhibited consensus building"; direct-election ("loophole") primaries should again be permitted.[58] The Kennedy group was more divided and ambivalent. To endorse a return to any form of winner-take-all was difficult for many of the senator's supporters who had a history of reform involvement; certainly it squared poorly with the Kennedy attempt, on other issues, to pose as the guardian of reform.[59] But Kennedy's harder-headed advisers eventually prevailed. The proportional representation (PR) rule had blunted the impact of Kennedy's victories in New York, California, and New Jersey in 1980. The advantages of giving victories in large industrial states a greater impact in 1984 seemed obvious. Therefore, by the time the commission's voting blocs were ready to talk business in December, the Kennedy and Mondale views on PR were virtually indistinguishable.

Organized labor was also interested in modifying the system to give an increased advantage to primary and caucus winners in large industrial states. Some labor leaders had a lingering dislike for direct-election primaries, where their candidates for delegate, not well-known beyond labor circles, had sometimes been at a disadvantage. Thus their initial testimony was quite cautious, endorsing only a raising of thresholds "to prevent a glut of candidates from crowding the field." [60] But they realized that because of the post-1968 rules—the required listing of a delegate candidate's presidential preference, for example, and candidate right of approval—the credentials of a prospective delegate affected the vote he or she received much less than they once had. Labor thus eventually accepted direct-election primaries as one of several means to their desired ends: letting winners win more and large-state delegations count for more.

The state parties as a whole did not give top priority to fair reflection questions, but they were generally inclined to minimize the constraints on the states' traditional ways of selecting delegates. And many individual states were intensely interested in reinstating the direct-election systems that the 1980 rules had forced them to abandon. Three of these states— Pennsylvania, New York, and Maryland—were represented on the commission by spokesmen who argued, with considerable success, that direct-election primaries should be permitted as a matter of state discretion.

Thus the question confronting the bloc leaders in their discussions prior to the January 14 meeting was not whether substantial modifications of PR were desirable or feasible, but rather what options should be opened up and how they should be presented. Hunt was sympathetic to states that wanted to return to direct-election systems, and he felt that changes in PR could be justified in terms of reducing party fragmentation and expanding state options, quite apart from the interests of front-running candidates. The matter was therefore brought to the floor via a leadership resolution introduced by the vice-chair of the commission and of the Pennsylvania state party, Dorothy Zug.

This resolution, approved by all of the bloc spokesmen, essentially returned to the 1976 fair reflection rule: the direct election of district-level delegates on the ballot by plurality vote would again be an acceptable option (but only at the district level and with a requirement that each delegate candidate's presidential preference be indicated). Other states would continue to employ PR, but with higher thresholds: thresholds in caucus states would be uniformly set at 20 percent at the district level and, more importantly, the 1980 rule requiring the CRC to adopt regulations to prevent winner-take-all outcomes would be dropped. All states would continue to use PR in awarding at-large delegates to candidates, and here too the threshold would be set at 20 percent.

Hunt indicated his willingness to consider additional options but suggested that they be introduced from the floor. Thus an AFL-CIO representative proposed what became known as the "winner-take-more" or "bonus delegate" option. One delegate per district would be awarded to the winner in that district; the remaining delegates in that district would then be allocated as under PR, but with thresholds in primary states that could go as high as 30 percent.[61] This alternative seemed increasingly attractive to many commissioners as a possible middle way for states wishing to avoid the fragmentation of pure PR but without the complexities and undiluted winner-take-all effects of direct-election.

Both the resolution permitting the direct election of delegates and the amendment adding the bonus delegate option passed overwhelmingly. A few veteran reformers, including former representative (now Minneapolis mayor) Donald Fraser, voiced strenuous opposition, but recognizable spokesmen for the major voting blocs chimed in their assent, demonstrating that on this, as on the PL/EO question, modal opinion on the Hunt and Winograd commissions differed markedly.[62] "[We have] no 'ideal' allocation system to recommend to all states," the commission concluded in its report. "Each option has its strengths and shortcomings. What we propose is rather to open a range of possibilities, all falling within the standards of fair reflection, from which the states may choose in light of their own preferences and traditions."[63]

Although reform-oriented members from Texas and several mid-western states attacked the fair reflection rule in the DNC, it passed by a 4-1 margin. Opposition from potential challengers to the presidential front-runners was never a significant factor. Sen. John Glenn's administrative assistant, who served on the TAC, monitored the situation closely, and Sen. Gary Hart expressed mild reservations about the threshold increases in a letter to Hunt.[64] But a defense of PR could not have seemed very promising to such prospective candidates, given the inside track Kennedy and Mondale had on the commission and the attraction that direct-election primaries and the winner-take-more plan held for many states. Some of them no doubt realized that the new rules, while placing some burdens on long-shot candidates in general, could help

specific candidates in specific instances. Glenn's state of Ohio, for example, traditionally has held a direct-election primary, and the reinstatement of such a system could conceivably give a home-state senator a
significant bloc of delegates. And it was only a few weeks after the Hunt
Commission completed its work that the Florida legislature, at the urging
of supporters of former governor Reubin Askew, became the first to take
advantage of the new rules by adopting a direct-election primary.

Candidate Control

Despite considerable talk about the need for a "deliberative convention" and scattered complaints about candidate abuses of the right to
disapprove prospective delegates, the commission moved only tentatively
to loosen the ties binding delegates to candidates. Candidates and labor
interests successfully resisted changes in the devices by which candidates
slated "their" delegates, and commissioners in debate often revealed—by
negative references to a "brokered convention," for example, or referral
to delegates as "candidate representatives"—how far they had gotten
from any conception of the convention as an assembly of representatives
from state and local party organizations.

Mondale and Kennedy representatives wished to retain both the
candidate's right to approve/disapprove prospective delegates and the
1980 rule (11F) providing that only persons themselves pledged to a given
candidate could vote for that candidate's national delegates at the district
level. They were willing to drop the controversial 1980 provision allowing
candidates to remove from the convention floor any delegates "seek[ing]
to violate" their pledge. But they were reluctant to drop first-ballot
binding entirely unless they could return to the one-for-one slating
prerogative they enjoyed in 1976 (that is, unless the 1980 rule requiring
them to approve three names for each slot were dropped). In all this they
were backed by organized labor. The AFL-CIO testified that the dele-
gate-removal rule should be repealed because it made delegates into
"messengers for candidates instead of independent deliberators." [65] But
subsequent discussions revealed that labor found candidate slating a
convenient means of securing delegate slots for their members; any
significant loosening of the candidate-approval rule, they reasoned, could
increase the competition they faced and could greatly complicate the
processes of negotiation required to secure delegate positions.

Of course, such a complicating of the process was precisely what
many state parties sought. Although it was hardly realistic to contem-
plate a return to old-fashioned slating by party leaders, they did seek to
increase their role in the selection of delegates and to increase the
selection chances of persons who had earned their spurs as party workers
rather than as candidate loyalists. A good number of states, moreover,
had had negative experiences with candidate right-of-approval (CRA);
Georgia chair and state chairs' president Marge Thurman could claim the
dubious distinction of having once been struck from the list of "bona fide
supporters" by Jimmy Carter himself. In focusing on abuses of CRA,
however, state party spokesmen sometimes seemed to be generalizing on
the basis of isolated episodes rather than articulating a coherent view of

the delegate's and the convention's role. In any event, CRA was the component of Rule 11 the candidates were most determined to preserve; in focusing on that, the state parties perhaps overlooked opportunities to loosen the rule in other respects.

Hunt, while sympathetic to the state parties' views on Rule 11, recognized early that the chances of repealing CRA were small. He did insist that the 1980 rule requiring the approval of three names for each slot remain in place. For this reason, as well as a concern for public appearances, the candidates and labor refrained from pushing for a return to the one-for-one slating they preferred.[66] Hunt then structured discussion to focus on two additional issues: Rule 11F and first-ballot binding. Rule 11F's requirement that candidate caucuses be used to elect national delegates at the district level had been the most problematic of all the 1980 rules for the Democratic party in Hunt's home state. The North Carolina chairman's testimony called it a "confusing and divisive" requirement:

> We were faced with the prospect in 1980 of splitting our district conventions into three groups—Carter delegates in one room, Kennedy delegates in another, and uncommitted in yet another—when the time to nominate national convention delegates and alternates arrived. This division was avoided only by adopting a complex scheme of color-coded ballots. But we didn't like it![67]

Because of the Carter-Kennedy battle over "freeing the delegates" in 1980, first-ballot binding represented the most visible symbol of the "rubber stamp" convention. Hunt saw the modification or removal of this rule as the most tangible way of addressing the concern he and Manatt had initially expressed for increasing the convention's decision-making flexibility.

Realizing that any attempt to firm up an agreement would probably lock most of Rule 11 in place, Hunt proposed instead that the several components of the existing rule be debated and voted on seriatim. But solid Mondale, Kennedy, and labor opposition assured the defeat of a nonmandatory version of Rule 11F. "The caucuses of presidential candidates have a right to select whom they want to be their delegates at the convention," argued a labor spokesman in opposing the amendment. "People from another caucus who are supporting another candidate do not have the right to select who best represents candidate X." But was it not true, asked one former state chair, that delegates also represented members of the *party* in their district? And another chair testified to the "hostility and anger generated by the requirement that [convention delegates] identify themselves as supporting one presidential candidate or another before they can vote for a delegate." But pleas for state autonomy and diversity—which Mondale and Kennedy partisans were to make so freely in the PR debate—fell on deaf ears when Rule 11 was at issue.[68]

Labor and candidate spokesmen then decided to reconsider their earlier insistence on first-ballot binding. Their defense of CRA and candidate caucuses had been successful, and they felt indebted to Hunt and other critics of Rule 11 for the agreements that had been worked out on the fair reflection and PL/EO questions. They also realized that the "rubber-stamp" convention had become an important symbol of the party's weakness. Thus they accepted substitute language for the entire binding/delegate-removal rule (11 H):

> Delegates elected to the national convention pledged to a presidential candidate shall in all good conscience reflect the sentiments of those who elected them.

This compromise was politically important. It helped defuse the "superdelegate" argument; now neither pledged nor unpledged delegates were completely "bound." And it let Manatt and Hunt claim to have removed the rule that, more than any other, had divided the party in 1980. The move was of substantive as well as symbolic importance. The repeal of the national binding rule (which cast doubt upon the authority of state laws and rules binding delegations), when combined with the addition of a substantial number of unpledged delegates, promised to restore to the convention an appreciable measure of decision-making discretion and flexibility. By leaving the rest of Rule 11 intact, however, the commission forfeited a chance to encourage a stronger *party* as opposed to *candidate* orientation among delegates or to strengthen the role of party organizations in the selection process.

The "Window" Reconsidered

Public awareness of the work of the Winograd and Hunt commissions has focused on the length and disorderliness of the nomination season and the disproportionate influence of the first contests, particularly the New Hampshire primary and the Iowa caucuses. Manatt's charge to the Hunt Commission urged "particular emphasis on shortening the primary season," and many commissioners in their early comments indicated a desire to eliminate the exemptions that had compromised the Winograd Commission's attempt to establish an early March to early June campaign "window." But the issue did not provoke as much intense feeling on the commission as the media emphasis suggested, and it quickly brought commissioners up against the limits of party authority and the political risks of attempted coercion. In the end, therefore, the commission struck a compromise with the "early" states, who felt very intensely indeed. And while the terms of that compromise did not please the commission's major voting blocs equally well, they did not let their differences on timing mar the prospects for agreement in other areas.

If commissioners had any doubt that the issue was salient to Iowans, that impression was dispelled by the Midwest Regional Hearings in Des Moines. The Iowa state party orchestrated a parade of some two dozen witnesses who testified to the party-building effects of the early Democratic caucuses and the advantages that their abandonment would give the opposition. Only two in-state witnesses, both affiliated with the United Auto Workers, acknowledged that the isolated early contest in Iowa could give the national process an unrepresentative cast. A team from New Hampshire, headed by Gov. Hugh Gallen and Rep. Norman D'Amours, made a shorter but equally forceful presentation at the Eastern Regional Hearings on November 5: "New Hampshire is a last outpost where hard work can get one's ideas and one's name around without the backing of the well-financed image makers." [69]

In both New Hampshire and Iowa, Democrats could argue that they were in no position to dictate the scheduling of election-year events. New Hampshire's law, which decrees that the primary in that state will be held "on the Tuesday immediately preceding the date on which any other state shall hold a similar election," is unlikely to be changed by the state's Republican-controlled legislature. Scheduling the Iowa caucuses later than the second Monday in February would also require a statutory change, and in 1982 that state's legislature was also under Republican control.[70]

But in both states, Democrats are no less supportive than Republicans of the tradition of "going first." There would be fierce resistance within the party to conforming to the national rule; if the "window" were shut tight, the likelihood that the state parties could not or would not comply would be great. "If the [commission's] only solution is to close the window and thus [abandon the field] to the Iowa Republican Party," warned Iowa's representative on the Hunt Commission, "it is a price that will simply be too great for us to pay.... [I can assure] the commission of one thing: in January of 1984 the Republicans will not caucus alone." [71] Some expressed resentment at such implied threats of defiance, but few doubted their credibility. The *LaFollette* decision had strengthened the party's hand legally, but it had done little to reduce the political damage such a showdown could produce.

The most outspoken opponent on the commission of the early contests was Rep. Morris Udall, whose 1976 run for the presidency had left him with many funny stories about grass-roots campaigning in Iowa and New Hampshire but also with a strong conviction that reducing the disproportionate influence of these isolated early states was "the key reform needed in both parties." [72] Udall earlier had proposed legislation requiring states to hold their presidential primaries on one of four designated dates within the "window" period, but he made no effort to organize Hunt Commission members around his point of view or to influence the bargaining process. More ominous for New Hampshire and Iowa was organized labor's insistence that all exceptions to the 1980 timing limits be eliminated. Labor regarded the prominence of both states, where labor was relatively weak, as detrimental to its own influence; the AFL-CIO's testimony thus placed a high priority on "diluting the impact of the early trend-setting primaries" and suggested not only "rigorous enforcement" of the window rule but additional measures such as designating specific primary dates and giving bonus delegates to states choosing later dates.[73]

Naturally, prospective candidates' positions coincided with their calculations of likely advantage. Kennedy wanted the window shut. While the primary in the senator's home state of Massachusetts might again be exempted, the earlier New Hampshire contest was more visible. It was likely to be considered by the media as Kennedy territory, with the result that anything less than a smashing victory would be portrayed as a defeat. Kennedy had lost to Carter in New Hampshire in 1980, and in all three pre-window caucus states—Iowa, Maine, and Minnesota—as well.

The Mondale forces recognized the perils early contests could pose for front-running candidates and initially signaled an interest in deemphasizing them in favor of later contests in larger states.[74] But they evaluated their prospects in Iowa and Minnesota quite favorably and were well aware of the pitfalls New Hampshire, considerably more conservative than neighboring Massachusetts, held for Kennedy. Mondale commissioners thus became leading advocates of "flexibility" in dealing with the early states. Senator Hart also argued against closing the window, but from the standpoint of an underdog who valued the "opportunity to compete" which the early contests offered to "candidates from all parts of the country, with a variety of backgrounds and different ideas." [75]

State party representatives on the commission were divided on the question. While some resented the early states for reducing their own influence, many were reluctant to see strong sanctions imposed against any state. There was also considerable admiration for the party-binding successes of Iowa and Minnesota, to which the early caucuses seemed to have contributed, and a desire to preserve the politics of personal contact and precinct organization, in which the small early states specialized.

Hunt shared many of these inclinations. He regarded it as essential for the commission to shorten the official campaign season, but saw little gain in tightening the rule to a point that was sure to provoke defiance. It would be far better to set a date slightly outside the window that would be honored than to shut the window entirely—given the likelihood that New Hampshire and Iowa would then hold their events as early as they had in 1980 and the party would have nasty challenges on its hands in the bargain. Hunt thus encouraged New Hampshire and Iowa representatives to confer with their own constituents and with their Republican counterparts to determine what dates might prove feasible. His own inclination was to leave open the possibility of exemptions for the five states that were eligible for them by virtue of having been allowed to go early in 1980, but to provide that none of these could hold their primary or caucuses more than one, or at most two, weeks before the window period began.

The word that eventually came back from New Hampshire and Iowa was that bipartisan agreement could probably be secured on scheduling the New Hampshire primary one week in advance of the second Tuesday in March and first-stage Iowa caucuses 15 days in advance—one week and five weeks later, respectively, than these events had been held in 1980. They preferred writing specific exemptions for themselves, and only themselves, into the rules—partly to avoid the possibility of a later adverse decision by the Compliance Review Commission (CRC) and partly because the viability of the compromise, especially for New Hampshire, depended on other states not being allowed to go on the same dates. The proposal represented a substantial concession, particularly for Iowa, and it came close to what most of the bloc spokesmen had privately said might be an acceptable solution. But consensus eluded the negotiating partners in their December and January meetings, and the window rule ended up being the only major issue to be subjectd to an up-or-down vote on the floor of the commission without prior agreement.

It was particularly important for Manatt to be a party to the window agreement because assurances about future CRC action were likely to figure into the bargain. He shared Hunt's inclination to seek an accommodation with Iowa and New Hampshire, but one that would still let the party claim to have shortened the season substantially. He also saw the advantage of writing Iowa and New Hampshire into the rules specifically, for this would relieve the pressure on him to promise and produce a specific CRC decision later. By the same token, he would have welcomed a rule decreeing that the CRC could *not* grant exemptions to the three additional states that remained eligible for them. But because these states had not been brought into the negotiating process, leaders of the commission were reluctant simply to dictate what their status would be.

In early December, with serious negotiations getting under way and the commission's major decision-making meeting only a few weeks away, Iowa and New Hampshire representatives counted only 10 sure votes on the commission in their favor. But their chances were helped by the failure of the group representatives to agree on a compromise. Mondale's supporters decided to take full political advantage of their position as defenders of the early states, insisting on writing a 15-day exemption for Iowa and a 7-day exemption for New Hampshire into the rules. This posed a painful dilemma for Kennedy supporters, who faced the prospects not only of losing the rules battle but also of alienating party leaders in two bellweather states. The senator's partisans could afford to take their opposition to New Hampshire and Iowa only so far; their negotiating partners knew this, of course, and it strengthened their resolve to hold out for the 15 day/7 day proposal.

When the timing rule came up for consideration on January 15, a close ally of the leadership proposed a general limit on CRC exemptions of 15 days before the second Tuesday in March for caucus states and 7 days for primary states. A Mondale representative then amended the motion to write such exemptions for New Hampshire and Iowa directly into the rules. It was in this form that the proposal was finally approved.[76] Weakening amendments supported by labor, Kennedy, and some state party representatives came close to passage, but the final vote on the motion was deceptively lopsided (47-16)—mainly because the Kennedy group, knowing what the outcome would be, had no desire to offend Iowa and New Hampshire further.[77]

Unfinished Business

On two major questions the commission was able to do little more than raise warning flags in its final report. The first of these, the proliferation of primaries, had been given extensive attention by the Winograd Commission, albeit to very little effect. The dimensions of the second problem, the early concentration of primaries and caucuses within the window period (dubbed "front-loading"), had become apparent only in 1980. TAC-staff task forces examined both issues in some detail before the commission's final meetings, but they identified few solutions that did not seem forbiddingly complex or coercive.

A majority of commissioners, especially those with labor and state party connections, no doubt felt that the national mix of primaries and caucuses had become unbalanced, to the party's detriment. But for few was it a matter of intense concern. The national trend seemed to have leveled off, and many had learned to live with primaries in their own states. Repealing primary laws was a very difficult and costly political prospect in most places, and few commissioners relished the attempt to impose constraints on the states sufficient to induce them to take such action. Mayor Fraser lamented that what he had hoped would be "the number one concern of this commission" seemed instead "to have been relegated to an afterthought. . . . I fear we are not going to come to grips with this issue." [78]

Fraser's preferred remedy was to limit the percentage of a state's delegates who could be chosen or allocated by primary. The simplest variant of such a rule would make the percentage of delegates allocated by the primary equal to the percentage to be chosen at the district level. Then all the at-large and pledged PL/EO delegates would have to be allocated in some other fashion, presumably through some sort of parallel caucus/convention procedure. Such a rule indeed would give added weight to party conventions, and its complexity might induce some states to abandon primaries altogether. But few commissioners were ready to take a step of this magnitude, and other prospective remedies appeared even less promising. A "freeze" that forbade any new primaries would risk numerous challenges and might actually "lock in" states fearful of abandoning their primary lest they lose any possibility of reinstating it in the future. The task force also discussed more positive incentives, but the ones that might have been effective (bonus delegates for caucus states, for example) posed serious problems of interstate equity (and charter violation), while those that did not pose serious problems of equity (various convention perquisites) generally seemed too weak to induce the desired primary-to-caucus shift.

There were, in short, no attractive remedies at hand for the proliferation of primaries, and those most concerned about the problem did not make a concerted effort, formally or informally, to overcome the reluctance of the bloc spokesmen and of most commissioners to take major steps in this area. The commission did manage to make a less equivocal statement of principle than had the Winograd Commission: the national party, it said in its final report, should "use whatever incentives and persuasive power it has at its disposal to encourage more states to shift from primaries to caucuses so that a better overall balance might result." [79] Some of its rules—the strengthening of the window rule and of the ban on open primaries—made primaries less attractive or feasible for some states and bore some responsibility for the slight reduction in their number in 1984 (see Chapter 7). But the commission foreswore any effort to deal directly with the problem. If this suggested a flagging of concern, it also reflected the fact that "many of the solutions appear to be worse than the problem," as the head of the TAC-staff task force put it. [80]

The front-loading problem proved equally intractable. The task force's report, presented to the commission in January, noted that some of the actions it was about to take could ease the problem. Adding unpledged delegates to the convention could make it more difficult to lock up the nomination early and thus give more significance to later contests. Allowing states to deviate from PR would give large, closely contested states the prospect of having a greater impact and thus should relieve some of the pressure they had felt to schedule their primaries and caucuses earlier. But the rules changes also could exacerbate the problem because states determined to increase their impact could do so with a vengeance, moving early *and* moving toward winner-take-all. As the head of the task force argued:

> One can easily draw a rather nightmarish scenario of big states moving into March or early April *and* adopting loophole primaries, thereby increasing the likelihood that a factional, flash-in-the-pan candidate, riding the crest of free media from upsets in Iowa and New Hampshire, could sweep to nomination, and giving us a nominating system unable to deliberate reasonably among candidates and issues. It is much more difficult judging how likely such a scenario is. States may have other reasons for staying where they are on the calendar. And major, mainstream candidates rather than factional ones could perhaps profit most from a winner-take-more, front-loaded system. (Representatives of Mr. Kennedy, Mr. Mondale, and the labor movement apparently believe this to be the case.) But prudence argues for a serious attempt to prevent the nightmare scenario from developing and to provide insurance against the most extreme sorts of unintended consequences.[81]

"This combination of factors," added another TAC member, could "enhance the ability of an early winner to ... wrap up the nomination in early April.... The result could well be a *de facto* national primary before Easter." [82]

Some of the possible remedies identified by the task force—a "freeze" whereby a state could move its primary later but not earlier, for example, or the awarding of bonus delegates to late states—seemed no more appealing as an antidote to front-loading than to the proliferation of primaries. But there were some less drastic possibilities, and two of them received serious consideration, although neither was finally adopted.

The first possibility was to tie the reinstatement of direct-election primaries and/or the availability of the new bonus delegate scheme to the calendar. States wishing to exercise these options could do so only after a certain date; the date most often mentioned was the third Tuesday in April, the traditional date of Pennsylvania's direct-election primary. Such a rule would require few states to change, for most direct-election states had a tradition of late primaries already. The proposal had a kind of equity about it: a state could enhance its impact either by holding its primary or caucus early, or by moving toward district-level winner-take-all, but not by both. The proposal did threaten some traditionally early direct-election states, most notably Illinois, and other states did not relish having their options restricted. Moreover, the Kennedy, Mondale, and labor groups, for whom the relaxation of PR was at or near the top of their priority lists, felt that tying either of the new winner-take-more options to the calendar cast a stigma on these plans, implying that they needed to be hemmed in with restrictions and making their widespread adoption less likely. In the negotiations preceding the January meeting, therefore, the idea of tying the new fair reflection options to the calendar attracted no strong advocates and was dropped from consideration.

The issue got a new lease on life during and after the January meeting, as TAC and staff members considered the possibilities for accelerated front-loading that the commission's actions had created. Hunt was willing to amend the new fair reflection rule to provide that the direct-election (and perhaps also the bonus-delegate) option would be available only to states that did not schedule their primaries earlier than they had been held in 1980. This proposal, made by Commissioner Jay Hakes, seemed more politically viable than earlier proposals tying PR modifications to the calendar because it would not have affected Illinois or other states that already held their primaries early. But it was not a general solution to the front-loading problem. It offered nothing to states not attracted by the winner-take-more options and would have affected the movement toward the front of the calendar that actually occurred in 1984 only to a limited extent (see Chapter 7). But it did seek to ensure that the situation would not be made worse by the new rules.

The Hakes amendment got nowhere because Manatt and most of the bloc spokesmen were hostile to the proposal. As head of the California party, Manatt had repeatedly urged that the state's primary be scheduled earlier, and he was not inclined, as national chairman, to support restrictions on the states' abilities to pursue what they regarded as their own best interests. Moreover, Manatt argued, it was not clear that there was a problem. The most recent word from California—at that point the large state most likely to move its primary—was that legislative leaders were backing away from scheduling an early, separate presidential primary because of its projected costs. Nor did Manatt take seriously the spectre of states rushing to the front of the window; he tended to dismiss such scenarios (and complex rules to deal with them) as typical products of the kind of Washington-based "technicians" he had relegated to the TAC.

For these reasons Hakes decided not to offer his amendment. Mayor Fraser, never one to shy away from lost causes, offered the proposal anyway, but after a brief debate it was defeated by voice vote. The commission did pass a resolution "urging" party leaders and candidates "to discourage states from scheduling their primaries or first stage caucuses earlier than they were scheduled in 1980."[83] It was not such exhortations, however, but yet-to-be-determined calculations of state and candidate interest that would effectively determine whether the troubling trend toward early scheduling would continue in 1984.

An Improved Process?

"Building the party" was the "common thread" running through its proposals, the Hunt Commission claimed in its final report.[84] To a considerable extent, this claim was credible. A renewal of party organiza-

tions was not necessarily uppermost in the minds of commission members all or even most of the time, but many of their actions seemed likely to promote the conditions of a revitalized party as outlined in Chapter 5—maintaining the party's public legitimacy, heightening its likely responsiveness to its broad constituencies, controlling internal disaffection and conflict, bolstering party loyalty among public officials, increasing the autonomy and authority of party organizations and decision-making bodies, and strengthening its structure of incentives and rewards.

As the next chapter will make clear, however, the reformed and counter-reformed presidential nomination process still is destructive of party strength in many respects. And if the Hunt Commission story points up the more hopeful possibilities for change, it also shows some of the constraints under which the parties, especially the Democratic party, labor as they attempt to help themselves. The commission's most conspicuous party-strengthening moves—enhancing the role of party leaders and elected officials and (partially) unbinding the national convention—represent rather modest changes, changes that would have been even more modest had Hunt simply assumed the neutral "broker's" role that many urged upon him. It is still politically perilous to question the idea of demographically-based representation, with the feminist caucuses being perhaps the most vigilant guardians of reform orthodoxy at present. The leading presidential candidates were also in a position to deflect any commission moves that might have threatened their interests. The commission was able to alter the rules in constructive ways because certain interests of labor, Kennedy, and Mondale supporters converged with the interests of the party. But where that convergence was lacking—most notably on candidate slating and other aspects of Rule 11—significant change proved impossible. Certainly the state and local parties were in no position to protect their interests single-handedly, and on crucial matters labor and candidate forces were quite willing to unite against them.

In short, intraparty politics are not likely to permit a single-minded pursuit of the party's interest in delegate selection. But the Hunt Commission's deliberations revealed some willingness to identify that interest and to explore the common stakes various elements in the party have in enhancing the organized party's role. In the next chapter we will analyze the impact of the current nomination system on party strength and the possibilities that remain for making that relationship a more positive one.

NOTES

1. The account that follows draws on Carol F. Casey, "The National Democratic Party," in *Party Renewal in America*, ed. Gerald M. Pomper (New York: Praeger Publishers, 1980), chap. 6; William J. Crotty, *Decision for the Democrats: Reforming the Party Structure* (Baltimore: The Johns Hopkins University Press, 1978); Crotty, *Party Reform* (New York: Longman Publishing Co., 1983); Austin Ranney, "The Democratic Party's Delegate Selection Reforms, 1968-76," in *America in the Seventies*, ed. Allan Sindler (Boston: Little, Brown, & Co., 1977), chap. 4; and Nelson W. Polsby, *Consequences of Party Reform* (New York: Oxford University Press, 1983), chap. 1.

184 *Bringing Back the Parties*

2. William R. Keech and Donald R. Matthews, *The Party's Choice* (Washington, D.C.: The Brookings Institution, 1976), 198.
3. Commission on the Democratic Selection of Presidential Nominees, *The Democratic Choice*, reprinted in *Congressional Record*, 90th Cong., 2d sess., October 14, 1968, 31544-31560.
4. Commission on Party Structure and Delegate Selection (McGovern-Fraser Commission), *Mandate for Reform* (Washington, D.C.: Democratic National Committee, 1970), 52-53.
5. The balance of this paragraph is drawn from Byron Shafer, *The Party Reformed*, as quoted in Polsby, *Consequences of Party Reform*, 34-35.
6. Andrew J. Glass and Jonathan Cottin, "Democratic Reform Drive Falters as Spotlight Shifts to Presidential Race," *National Journal*, June 19, 1971, 2393.
7. Ibid., 1295.
8. See the account and the comparison of allocation schemes in Crotty, *Decision for the Democrats*, 174-181, 190-196. The alternative formula substituted voting strength in the Electoral College for the direct population measure. It was this scheme that the Court of Appeals upheld in the *Georgia* and *Bode* cases, footnotes 21 and 22, chap. 5.
9. The report of the Rules Committee is reprinted in *Congressional Record*, 92d Cong., 1st sess., October 21, 1971, 37361-37367.
10. *Congressional Quarterly Weekly Report*, July 15, 1972, 1781. For an argument that McGovern's challenge might have succeeded even without the reforms, see Keech and Matthews, *Party's Choice*, 207-212. Focusing more specifically on the rules that discouraged winner-take-all primaries, James Lengle and Byron Shafer find McGovern to have been the main beneficiary; see "Primary Rules, Political Power, and Social Change," *American Political Science Review* 70 (March 1976): 25-30. Their analysis is flawed, however, by the omission of California, where the *retention* of winner-take-all rules benefitted McGovern. See the recomputation by Gerald Pomper, "New Rules and New Games in Presidential Nominations," *Journal of Politics* 41 (August 1979): 792.
11. The Coalition for a Democratic Majority (CDM) was a group of moderate-to-conservative Democrats, many of them identified with the presidential aspirations of Sen. Henry Jackson, who developed a systematic critique of the reform guidelines. Rules Commission Chairman James O'Hara cochaired the group and political scientist Austin Ranney, who had served on the McGovern-Fraser Commission, was a prominent spokesman. Another founder was Ben Wattenberg, coauthor with Richard Scammon of *The Real Majority* (New York: Coward-McCann, 1970), a widely read book urging the Democrats to back away from the politics of protest and to focus their appeal on the majority of Americans who are "unyoung, unpoor, and unblack."
12. California's winner-take-all primary, won by McGovern, prompted the most bitter battle between McGovern and Humphrey forces at the 1972 convention. McGovern advocates accurately pointed out that the commission had deliberately declined to ban such primaries, but the convention's Credentials Committee supported the Humphrey group's contention that the California primary violated the guideline (B-6) that urged the fair representation of minority views. The convention reversed this decision and seated the California delegation, but it also resolved that delegates to the next convention should be selected in a manner that "fairly reflected" the division of preferences among all participants in the nominating process.
13. McGovern-Fraser Commission, *Mandate for Reform*, 40.
14. Crotty, *Decision for the Democrats*, 124.
15. Commission on Delegate Selection and Party Structure (Mikulski Commission), *Democrats All* (Washington, D.C.: Democratic National Committee, 1973), 22.
16. Ibid., 18. Kenneth Bode, research director for the McGovern-Fraser Commission and a strong reform advocate on the Mikulski Commission, later explained to the Winograd Commission that many were reluctant to require the proportional representation of preferences in direct-election states "because they felt that it would be so controversial that it would jeopardize the mandate of the whole commission. They simply could not get compliance in those states." Democratic National Committee, *Transcript of the proceedings of the Commission on Presidential Nomination and Party Structure* (Winograd Commission), May 9, 1977, 67.
17. Mikulski Commission, *Democrats All*, Rule 10A, 17. For a critique of the cure as "much worse than the disease," see Casey, "National Democratic Party," 96-97.
18. Mikulski Commission, *Democrats All*, 11-13, 22-24.
19. See Articles 2, 10, and 11 of the charter, reprinted in *Official Proceedings of the 1974 Conference on Democratic Party Organization and Policy* (Washington, D.C.: Democratic National Committee, 1974), 238-245.
20. See the accounts by William Crotty in *Political Reform and the American Experiment* (New York: Thomas Y. Crowell Co., 1977), 247-255, and in *Decision for the Democrats*, 240-250. Affirmative action emerged as the most divisive issue at the midterm conference. On the debates there and the marginal changes made in the Mikulski/Sanford language, see Denis Sullivan, Jeffrey Pressman, and Christopher Arterton, *Explorations in Convention Decision Making* (San Francisco: W. H. Freeman & Co., 1976), 32-34, 84-88.
21. Crotty, *Decision for the Democrats*, 251.
22. See Committee on Rules, *Report to the 1976 Convention*, sections 3, 9, 12; and Commission on Presidential Nomination and Party Structure (Winograd Commission), *Openness, Participation and*

Party Building: Reforms for a Stronger Democratic Party (Washington, D.C.: Democratic National Committee, 1978), 89-91, 94-95. The commission did let one "loophole" remain: permitting states to elect delegates from single-member districts. Such systems were in effect in Alabama and Georgia. They obviously gave "all" to the winner in a given district and made it difficult to achieve proportional representation of candidate preferences or of demographic groups in the state's delegation. The DNC reversed the commission and banned the use of single-member districts in the Call to the 1980 convention.

23. See Democratic National Committee, *Delegate Selection Rules for the 1980 Democratic National Convention* (Washington, D.C.: Democratic National Committee, 1978), Rule 12B. The regulation, drafted and redrafted many times, finally read as follows: "At the congressional district or other smaller national delegate selection unit, if only one candidate reaches the threshold, the next highest vote-getter shall be awarded one delegate, except in the following situations; (a) if one preference receives 85 percent or more of the vote, or (b) if the frontrunner is 50 or more percentage points ahead of the second place preference and the second place preference has 15 percent or less of the vote. In either situation (a) or (b) the frontrunner shall be awarded all the delegates." Regulation 6.15, Compliance Review Commission, Democratic National Committee, 1980.

24. Patricia Bonomi, James MacGregor Burns, and Austin Ranney, eds., *The American Constitutional System under Strong and Weak Parties* (New York: Praeger Publishers, 1981), 99.

25. Winograd Commission, *Openness, Participation, and Party Building*, 29-36. For the commission's extensive discussions of the effects of primaries and of various reform proposals, see Winograd Commission, *Transcript*, August 11, 1977; September 9-10, 1977; and January 21, 1978, pt. 1.

26. Winograd Commission, *Openness, Participation, and Party Building*, 68-70. For debate of the "window" and open primary rules, see Winograd Commission, *Transcript*, January 21, 1978, pt. 2.

27. Ibid., January 22, 1978, 72, 74, 125.

28. Ibid., January 21, 1978, pt. 3, 51, 54; and Winograd Commission, *Openness, Participation, and Party Building*, 80-85.

29. *Congressional Quarterly Weekly Report*, June 3, 1978, 1393. For an interpretation of the Winograd rules as an "180-degree turn" away from reform, see Crotty, *Party Reform*, 75.

30. *Congressional Quarterly Weekly Report*, April 29, 1972, 943. See the discussion in Cornelius P. Cotter and Bernard C. Hennessy, *Politics Without Power: The National Party Committees* (New York: Atherton Press, 1964), 16-20.

31. See *Congressional Quarterly Weekly Report*, August 12, 1972, 1998. Brief overviews of Republican reform efforts may be found in Ranney, "Democratic Party's Reforms," 195-197; Crotty, *Party Reform*, chaps. 17-18; and John F. Bibby, "Party Renewal in the National Republican Party," in *Party Renewal*, ed. Pomper, 103-107.

32. Delegates and Organizations Committee, *Progress Report*, Part II, "The Delegate Selection Procedures for the Republican Party" (Washington, D.C.: Republican National Committee, 1970), 5, 7, 9.

33. *Congressional Quarterly Weekly Report*, August 16, 1975, 1814. On the importance of the less noticed recommendations of the Rule 29 Committee that formalized RNC procedures and restricted the national chairman's authority—adopted by the RNC and the 1976 convention—see Bibby, "Party Renewal in the National Republican Party," 105.

34. See footnote 23, Chapter 5.

35. Technical Amendments Subcommittee, *Report* (Washington, D.C.: Republican National Committee, 1982), 10-11 and proposed rules 33(a), 33(b) (6), 33(c), 35(c).

36. Papers prepared for this conference were printed in the RNC journal, *Commonsense*, vol. 4, no. 2 (1981); for a full report on the conference, see vol. 5, no. 1 (1982).

37. Committee to Study Election Reform, *Report* (Washington, D.C.: Republican National Committee, 1982), 7-8.

38. The 1980 convention resolutions are reprinted in *Report of the Commission on Presidential Nomination* [Hunt Commission] (Washington, D.C.: Democratic National Committee, 1982), 58-59. See also the *Report of the Rules Committee to the 1980 Democratic National Convention*, July 21, 1980, 15, 22.

39. For a reprint of the charge to the commission, see Hunt Commission, *Report*, 60.

40. Patrick H. Caddell, "Some Thoughts on the Presidential Nominating System," September 17, 1981, 26, 38, 39, 43, 47. Caddell's paper was one of several prepared by TAC members in response to Hunt's invitation at their first meeting to put their initial thoughts on paper.

41. The contrast with a plebiscitary view such as Caddell's was direct and intended. Compare Caddell's "first principles": (1) to *preserve* the sovereignty of "the people," and (2) to *preserve* "the ability of 'one man and the truth' to prevail ... regardless of recognition level or the paucity of resources." Caddell's and Hunt's third goals were similar—effective campaigning and governance—but Caddell immediately turned the question to one of legitimacy: any system that allowed the convention "to deny an obvious winner the nomination" would invite "electoral repudiation." See Ibid., 18-25; and James B. Hunt, Jr., "Remarks" at the Conference on the Parties and the Nominating Process, Institute of Politics, John F. Kennedy School of Government, Harvard University, December 5, 1981, 1-5.

42. Elaine C. Kamarck, "What Next? A Look at Changes in the Presidential Nomination Process Passed by the Hunt Commission" (Paper delivered at the annual meeting of the National Capitol Area

Political Science Association, February 27, 1982), 15. For another useful overview of the commission's work, see Rhodes Cook's accounts in the *Congressional Quarterly Weekly Report,* December 26, 1981, 2563-2567; January 23, 1982, 127-128; April 3, 1982, 749-751.

43. The quotation is from the AFT's Rachelle Horowitz; see also comments by Evelyn Dubrow of the International Ladies Garment Workers and Patty Evans of the Indiana state party: Winograd Commission, *Transcript,* January 21, 1978, vol. 2, 161-183.

44. Susan Estrich, "Unintended Consequences" (Memorandum prepared for the Commission on Presidential Nomination, September 9, 1981), 2.

45. The conventions of both parties are indeed highly unrepresentative of their rank-and-file in terms of economic status. The 1972 Democratic convention adopted a potentially far-reaching solution, providing that 8 percent of party revenues be used to defray the expenses of low-income delegates. But because the party was never subsequently out of debt, and also because of a Federal Election Commission ruling (discreetly sought by party leaders) that the parties' federal convention subsidies could not be used to defray the expenses of individual delegates [11 CFR 9008.6(b) (1)], the resolution was not implemented. The Winograd Commission took note of the problem only to the extent of recommending that the DNC make funds available to state parties "for the sole purpose of establishing and implementing affirmative action programs." Winograd Commission, *Openness, Participation, and Party Building,* 40. But the 1980 Call and a subsequent CRC regulation (6.18) went a major step further, requiring states to devise specific plans to assist needy delegates. Only rarely did this result in direct state party subsidies for low-income delegates, but many states made extensive efforts to help delegates obtain support from individuals and from candidate organizations. It was this kind of assistance that the Hunt Commission decreed should continue.

46. 1980 Rules Committee Report, 17.

47. Hunt Commission, *Report,* 33, 36. Other "outreach" groups include "ethnics, youth, persons over 65 years of age, workers, persons with a high school education or less, the physically handicapped, and other groups significantly underrepresented in party affairs" (Rule 5C).

48. See remarks by Carl Wagner, *Transcript of Meetings of the Commission on Presidential Nomination,* Democratic National Committee, August 21, 1981, 98-100.

49. Michael J. Malbin, "Democratic Rule Makers Want to Bring Party Leaders Back to the Conventions," *National Journal,* January 2, 1982, 27.

50. Statements submitted to the Commission on Presidential Nomination (Hunt Commission), November 6, 1981, by the AFL-CIO, 2; the Association of State Democratic Chairs, 2; and Sen. Alan Cranston, 8-9. Emphasis in original.

51. Statements submitted to the Hunt Commission, November 6, 1981, by Rep. Gillis Long, 3-4; and the AFL-CIO, 2. See also the remarks of Commissioners Douglas Fraser and Rachelle Horowitz, Hunt Commission, *Transcript,* November 7, 1981, 136, 144-146.

52. Ibid., January 14, 1982, 150; February 5, 1982, 49.

53. Hunt Commission, *Report,* 18, 40-41 (Rule 8B [3]).

54. In "add-on" terms, unpledged PL/EO delegate would number some 17 percent of the base delegation in most states, and more in those states entitled to bonus unpledged delegates. For an astute comparison of the politics surrounding PL/EO proposals on the Winograd and Hunt Commissions, see Malbin, "Democratic Rule Makers," 25-28.

55. The debate was interesting for the assumptions it revealed about the nature of the national convention. Ferraro tried to draw a distinction between a "flexible" and a "brokered" convention, the former desirable, the latter not, and suggested that to have more than between 12 and 15 percent of the delegates unpledged might tip that balance. Maryland's state chair scoffed at such distinctions: "I hear these words getting bandied about—'brokered convention.' There is no magic number—10, 12, 13, 15. Somebody just decided 12 is better than 22, and the votes may or may not be there...." To which a former California chairman added: What was so bad about a convention that "brokered" Adlai Stevenson? Hunt Commission, *Transcript,* January 14, 1982, 130, 160-161, 198.

56. Ibid., 144.

57. The only challenge to the rule at the DNC meeting came from Michigan committeeman and former commission chairman Morley Winograd, who was deeply offended by Manatt's bypassing of the state chairs and their association, which he had formerly headed. By then, however, most state party representatives on the commission had agreed to unite behind the commission's report, and Manatt had lobbied the national committee heavily. Thus Winograd's proposal, to provide unpledged delegate positions for all DNC members, received little support.

58. Robert Torricelli and Tom Donilon, "Reforming the Democrats' Reforms," *Washington Post,* August 24, 1981, A17; see also the paper by TAC member Elaine Kamarck, "Comments on the Democratic Party's Delegate Selection Process," August 13, 1981.

59. On the early reluctance of Kennedy commissioners to tamper with PR, see David Broder's account, *Washington Post,* August 22, 1981, A7.

60. AFL-CIO statement, 6.

61. For primary states the commission retained the variable district-level thresholds contained in the 1980 rules. Under the PR option, the threshold would be 100 percent divided by the number of delegates to be elected in the district, but not more than 25 percent. Under winner-take-more, the

threshold would be 100 percent divided by the number of delegates to be elected in the district minus one, but not more than 30 percent.

62. On several marginal provisions, those wishing to loosen PR overplayed their hand. (1) They wrote an extraordinary high maximum threshold, 33 percent, into the bonus delegate option and were willing to accept no more than a token reduction to 30 percent. (2) A rule providing that the bonus delegate option would not be available for districts electing fewer than three delegates—where obviously it would have a pure winner-take-all effect—passed only with difficulty. Mondale and labor representatives refused to make even this small concession to PR advocates, but the Kennedy group broke ranks and tipped the balance on the commission in favor of the amendment. (3) Siegel wrote into the Ferraro draft a provision allocating at-large delegates according to the presidential preferences of delegates previously elected at the district level—a procedure that obviously would have compounded whatever winner-take-all or winner-take-more effects were present at the district level. The commission staff altered this to provide that at-large delegates should be allocated to presidential candidates directly in proportion to their statewide primary or state convention vote, and the spokesmen for the commission's voting blocs accepted the change. See Hunt Commission, *Transcript*, January 14, 1982, 236-242; January 15, 1982, 154, 163, 181-183; and February 5, 1982, 144-151; and Hunt Commission, *Report*, 19, 21-22, and Rules 9C and 12A(2).

63. Hunt Commission, *Report*, 22.

64. Hart acknowledged that "too often . . . a winning candidate [receives] far fewer delegates than seems an appropriate reward," but argued against setting thresholds higher than 15 percent. Letter to Gov. James B. Hunt, December 21, 1981, 4.

65. AFL-CIO statement, 6.

66. The rules did make explicit an exception sanctioned by the CRC in previous years: One-for-one slating by candidate organizations was permitted in states where delegates were to be elected directly on the primary ballot. Otherwise, a candidate's vote could be diluted by being spread among a large number of delegates pledged to him. See Hunt Commission, *Report*, Rule 11D.

67. Statement of Russell G. Walker, chairman, North Carolina Democratic Party, October 3, 1981, 2-4.

68. Hunt Commission, *Transcript*, January 15, 1982, 9, 13, 14, 17, 19, 32.

69. Statement submitted to Hunt Commission by Rep. Norman E. D'Amours, November 6, 1981, 2.

70. New Hampshire Revised Statutes Annotated, 653:9; Iowa Code, 43.4. The 1982 elections shifted both houses of the Iowa legislature to Democratic control.

71. Hunt Commission, *Transcript*, November 7, 1981, 162-164.

72. Transcript of Harvard Conference on "The Parties and the Nominating Process," *Commonsense*, vol. 5, no. 1, (1982): 42. See also Hunt Commission, *Transcript*, August 20, 1981, 65-66; November 6, 1981, 71-77.

73. AFL-CIO statement, 5.

74. See Torricelli and Donilon, "Reforming the Reforms": "The process must promote individuals of national reputation and broad appeal. By limiting the length of the process and having a variety of states in various regions express their preferences on the same day, we can avoid the distortions of the current process. Press attention and public awareness can be shifted to significant contests."

75. Hart letter to Hunt, December 21, 1981, 3.

76. While the Mondale spokesman, Robert Torricelli, at first appeared to be *limiting* the exemptions to New Hampshire and Iowa ("a decision of this magnitude should be made here . . . not in the CRC"), he later acknowledged that the remaining three early states from 1980 could also be granted exemptions at the CRC's discretion. Hunt Commission, *Transcript*, January 15, 1982, 49.

77. Supporters of the January 15 decision narrowly escaped a setback at the commission's final meeting on February 5, when Rep. Morris Udall, in an apparently unpremeditated move, proposed that the rule exempting New Hampshire and Iowa be amended to expire after 1984. With many commissioners absent or away from their seats, the amendment failed by only 23-24. Ibid., February 5, 1982, 114-118.

78. Ibid., January 14, 1982, 81.

79. Commission Vice-chairman Douglas Fraser, another strong critic of primary proliferation, moved that this sentence be followed with another in the final report: "We urge the Democratic National Committee to undertake an immediate review of the steps required to implement this policy." Hunt Commission, *Report*, 10-11; Hunt Commission, *Transcript*, February 5, 1982, 166-167.

80. Ibid., January 14, 1982, 73.

81. Memorandum to Gov. James Hunt and Chairman Charles Manatt from Thomas E. Mann, February 1, 1982, 2. See Hunt Commission, *Transcript*, January 14, 1982, 50-71.

82. Letter to Hunt Commission members from Patrick H. Caddell, February 5, 1982, 6. See also Michael J. Malbin, "The Democratic Party's Rules Changes: Will They Help or Hurt It?" *National Journal*, January 23, 1982, 165.

83. Hunt Commission, *Transcript*, February 5, 1982, 125-136, 172-173; Hunt Commission, *Report*, 11-12, 57.

84. Hunt Commission, *Report*, 8.

Presidential Nomination and Party Strength 7

The rules and procedures governing the Democratic and Republican parties as they enter the 1984 presidential nomination season differ considerably (see Table 7-1). The previous chapter highlighted the political dynamics that helped produce these differences. Yet the post-1968 era of "reform" has affected both parties profoundly, in similar as well as dissimilar ways. In this chapter we will assess that impact. What are the most important features of the nomination system? In what ways do they strengthen or weaken the parties?

Who Participates?

It is appropriate to begin with the question of participation because it is that value which reformers have invoked more than any other. The 1970 report of the Commission on Party Structure and Delegate Selection (McGovern-Fraser Commission) opened with a selective reading of party history that placed the commission squarely in the "representative structures"/participatory school of reform: "From the days of Jefferson and Jackson, the Democratic Party has been committed to the broad participation of rank-and-file members in all of its major decision-making." This tradition, the commission concluded, had not always been "adequately expressed":

> After a lengthy examination of the structures and processes used to select delegates to the national convention in 1968, this is our basic conclusion: meaningful participation of Democratic voters in the choice of their presidential nominee was often difficult or costly, sometimes completely illusory, and in not a few instances, impossible.

The tone of the 1970 report by the GOP's Committee on Delegates and Organization was more muted but its priorities were no less clear: "The DO Committee wants to be sure that the door is open in every state for those who wish to participate in the procedures that lead to the selection of an individual for president." [1]

189

Table 7-1 Comparison of Democratic and Republican Delegate Selection Rules

Issue	Democratic Rule	Republican Rule
Open or crossover primaries.	Prohibited, but same-day declaration sufficient to certify voter as a Democrat. (2)	Prohibited unless mandated by state law. (31n)
Participation in primaries or first-stage caucuses.	Open to all Democrats in the jurisdiction. (2D; 4 [1])	Open to all Republicans in the jurisdiction, unless state law provides otherwise. (32a) Not consistently enforced.
Participation of minorities.	Affirmative action plans with specific goals required. (6) Discrimination forbidden. (5B)	"Positive action" required, but without specific plans or goals. Discrimination forbidden. (32a)
Participation of women.	"Equal division" of delegate seats required. (6C)	States required to "endeavor" to achieve equal representation. (32c)
Apportionment of delegates within state.	Base delegation: 75 percent chosen at or below congressional district level, 25 percent at large. "Add-on" for party leaders and elected officials. (7)	No national rule. Entire delegation may be chosen at-large. (31f)
Party leaders and elected officials.	"Add-on" seats allocated among states: approximately 566 for unpledged, 300 for pledged PL/EO. Congressional delegates chosen by caucuses. Automatic delegates (except state chairs and vice-chairs) prohibited. (8)	No special provisions. Automatic delegates prohibited. (31n)
Timing.	No primaries or first-stage caucuses before first Tuesday in March. Limited exemptions for Iowa and New Hampshire. (10)	No limits on first-stage events.
Timeliness.	All steps in delegate selection process must take place within election year. (10B)	Delegates to conventions selecting national delegates must be elected subsequent to national call, unless state law provides otherwise. (31o)
Candidate preference.	Prospective delegates must declare preference. Candidate has right to disapprove. District-level delegates chosen by caucus of persons pledged to given candidate. (11)	No national rule.
Bound delegates.	National rule establishes nonbinding presumption of fidelity to declared preference. (11H)	No national rule.
Allocation of delegates to candidates.	Three options at district level: proportional representation, bonus delegate plan, direct-election primary. At-large allocation follows PR. Thresholds range from 17 to 30 percent. (12)	No limits on district-level or statewide winner-take-all.
Unit rule.	Prohibited at all levels. (16A)	Prohibited in vote for nominations at national convention. (18b)

SOURCE: Hunt Commission report; rules adopted by the 1980 Republican National Convention.

Trends Since 1968

Without question, meetings related to delegate selection are more open and better publicized than they were before 1968. Both parties require their state organizations to prepare and distribute instructional material on the delegate selection process. Both require that the first-stage caucus or convention be open to all party members in the relevant jurisdiction, and both prohibit ex-officio delegates at all levels of the process. In the Democratic party these rules have ensured access to party members who wish to participate at the precinct level. Republican practice has moved in the same direction, although less uniformly. The GOP's open-meeting rule contains a loophole for states with contrary laws, and a number of states—despite the ex-officio prohibition—still make precinct committee members automatic delegates to county or district caucuses or even give them or other local party officers the power to select those who will serve as delegates at the next stage.[2] Nevertheless, the overall trend is toward increased rank-and-file participation in caucuses. And the increase in the number of primaries has enabled larger numbers of party adherents to participate, albeit in a minimal way, in the selection of presidential nominees and/or national delegates in both parties.

Participation also has become, as the reform-commission jargon would have it, more "timely." As the McGovern-Fraser Commission noted:

> More than a third of the convention delegates had, in effect, already been selected prior to 1968—before either the major issues or the possible presidential candidates were known. By the time President Johnson announced his withdrawal from the nomination contest, the delegate selection process had begun in all but twelve states.[3]

As we have seen, the Democratic party has taken the timeliness principle quite far, allowing sitting party committees to choose only a limited number of delegates and then only if the committee itself was elected within two years of the election year. Republican rules are less restrictive, requiring only that delegates to district and state conventions be elected after the Call to the national convention is issued (generally around the middle of the previous year) unless state law requires otherwise. But several GOP rules—opening up first-stage meetings, for example, and eliminating ex-officio delegates—also have facilitated participation by persons who become active only within the election year.

Attempts to broaden participation by previously underrepresented groups also have met with considerable success, particularly within the Democratic party. As Table 7-2 shows, the imposition of the McGovern-Fraser guidelines produced a dramatic increase in the representation of all three targeted groups—blacks, women, and young people—in the 1972 convention. The Mikulski Commission's relaxation of the quota system brought these numbers down somewhat in 1976, although nowhere near their 1968 levels. The requirement in 1980 of specific "goals" for affirmative action programs and of equal division between men and women apparently had the desired effects. Hispanics comprised 6 percent of the 1980 convention participants, and black representation returned to the 15

Table 7-2   Blacks, Women, and Young People as Percentages of National Convention Delegates, 1964-1980

Year	Democratic Delegates			Republican Delegates		
	% Black	% Women	% Under 30	% Black	% Women	% Under 30
1964	2	13	*	1	18	*
1968	6	13	4	2	17	1
1972	15	40	22	3	32	7
1976	11	33	15	3	31	7
1980	15	49	11	3	29	5

* Figures not available.

SOURCE: CBS News Surveys, DNC and RNC records, and other sources, as presented in Thomas R. Marshall, *Presidential Nominations in a Reform Age* (New York: Praeger Publishers, 1981), 46; and James W. Ceaser, *Reforming the Reforms: A Critical Analysis of the Presidential Selection Process* (Cambridge: Ballinger Publishing Co., 1982), 52. Figures are averaged where estimates are discrepant.

percent level. This compares favorably with the percentage of blacks and hispanics in the total population— 12 and 6 percent, respectively. But black representation still has fallen short of the percentage of blacks among Democratic identifiers (20.5 percent in 1980) and the contribution blacks have made to the Democratic presidential coalition (nonwhites comprised 16 percent of the Carter vote in 1976; 22 percent in 1980).[4] The share of convention seats going to persons under 30 in 1980 was still three times what it had been in 1968, but it was down by half from the extraordinary 1972 figure of 22 percent. This reflected the fact that the Compliance Review Commission, while insisting on affirmative action goals for minority groups that realistically mirrored their "presence in the Democratic electorate," permitted state parties uniformly to set a goal of 10 percent for youth.

Republican participation moved in the same directions but less dramatically. The share of convention seats claimed by women doubled between 1968 and 1972 and has hovered around 30 percent since then. Since 1972, blacks have accounted for some 3 percent of GOP delegates; this, of course, is far below the black percentage of the general population, but it actually exceeds the black share of the Republican presidential electorate (1 percent in both 1976 and 1980).

It seems clear, then, that new party rules have increased the numbers of people participating in some fashion in the nomination process and that relatively greater numbers of those participating in the national convention (and no doubt at earlier stages as well) are drawn from the ranks of women, minorities, and the young. This is not necessarily to say, however, that the *quality* of participation is higher than it used to be or that the process more adequately *represents* the party rank and file—much less that the net result of the changes has been stronger parties.

Even if one assumes that the goal of reform has been simply to maximize the number of participants, the evidence of success is mixed. Of course, caucus systems are bound to compare poorly with primaries on a purely quantitative measure. The Iowa caucuses, first in the nation and attended by extensive media coverage and campaign activity, involved an estimated 200,000 people in 1980—almost 10 percent of the state's voting age population, 18 percent of its registered Democrats, and 22 percent of its registered Republicans. For most caucus states the figures were considerably lower; one analyst estimated that the number of participants in Democratic caucuses reached 3 percent of the state's voting age population in only five of the 20 states for which data were available in 1976.[5] Thus even "participatory" caucuses do not compare with primaries as instruments of mass participation. But turnout in the primaries themselves is often quite low. The United States' general election turnout in presidential years—approximately 54 percent of the voting age population in 1976 and 1980—is considerably lower than that of most other Western democracies, and turnout in presidential primaries is generally about half of the general election figure.

Only 24 percent of the voting age population voted in the two parties' presidential contests in primary states in 1980; for 1976 the figure was 28 percent. State-by-state variations were great, but nowhere reached 50 percent in either year. Turnout in 1980 ranged from highs of 45 percent in Wisconsin, 40 percent in New Hampshire, and 35 percent in California and Montana, to lows of 7 percent in Rhode Island, 14 percent in Kentucky, and 15 percent in New Jersey, Tennessee, Louisiana, and the District of Columbia. Turnout tends to be higher in states with a longer history of presidential primaries, and it is strongly related to how much money the candidates spend in the state. Primaries that allocate or select delegates tend to attract more voters than "beauty contest" preference polls. The evidence relating turnout to the competitiveness of the race is mixed, however, and primaries held early in the nomination season do not generally attract more voters than those held in May and June.[6]

How representative of the parties' rank and file are the participants in the modern nomination process? Here, too, the evidence does not favor primaries as much as their defenders might like. Several studies have found the primary electorate to be better educated and wealthier than either the general election electorate or rank-and-file party identifiers, and to underrepresent minorities, blue-collar workers, the young, and the elderly (but not, in most cases, women). Most of these studies have focused on the Democratic party, and the patterns are of particular concern there because the underrepresented groups are precisely those who tend to support the party most faithfully in general elections. Data collected by the Winograd Commission showed that in each of the 13 primary states examined, the primary electorate comprised substantially smaller percentages of noncollege-educated, low- and moderate-income, black, and elderly voters than did the November electorate.[7]

Demographic unrepresentativeness sometimes has skewed ideology and/or candidate preference among primary voters. For example, James Lengle found primary turnout patterns within the California Democratic party to favor segments of the electorate that were liberal in ideology and policy views; his simulation of alternative turnout patterns led him to a dramatic conclusion:

> Had the 1972 California Democratic primary electorate been demographically representative of the party rank and file, Hubert Humphrey, not George McGovern, almost surely would have won the primary and captured all of California's delegates.... Undoubtedly, had Hubert Humphrey won the California primary, he would have been the presidential nominee in 1972.[8]

However, a study comparing 1972 primary and general election voters in a national sample found similar distributions of policy views in the two groups. And a team from the Center for Political Studies, comparing primary voters and all party identifiers in the 1972, 1976, and 1980 elections, found "little to support ... the argument that primary voters are ideologically unrepresentative of the party identifiers in primary states." [9] While these studies do not directly examine the distribution of candidate preferences, they do suggest that the extent to which demographic unrepresentativeness makes for unrepresentative primary outcomes is still an open question.

Little systematic data has been gathered on first-stage caucus participants. One Minnesota study found a demographic skew among caucus participants somewhat more pronounced than that displayed by the state's primary electorate. The author concluded, however, that this imbalance and the relatively small number of caucus attenders "apparently had *not* led to misrepresentation much greater than that typically found in primary elections—at least in policy, candidate, and party-related attitudes." [10] Such findings do not make a particularly inspiring case for the caucus system, nor do they gainsay the possibility of caucuses being packed by highly unrepresentative issue or candidate enthusiasts—given the rules mandating open participation. It does appear, however, that the presidential primaries spawned by the reform era are something less than an unqualified success in terms of participation and representation and that their superiority to caucuses on these criteria is less than might have been supposed.

A "Representative" Convention?

Reformers in both parties placed a high priority on broadening participation at the first stage of the delegate selection process (although most of them did not expect this to be accomplished by moving from caucus to primary systems). They gave as much or more attention, however, to patterns of participation at the last stage, at the national convention. As we have seen, they enjoyed remarkable success in altering the convention's demography. But here, too, critics have suggested that altering patterns of participation may make for a less rather than a more "representative" convention.

Not all demographic groups have fared as well as women, blacks, and youth. Disparities between the income and education levels of delegates and of rank-and-file voters have remained largely unchanged during the era of reform. Some 63 percent of the 1968 Democratic delegates had a college degree; this declined slightly (to 57 percent) in the 1972 convention but reached the 65 percent level in 1976 and 1980.

This contrasts markedly with the 14 percent of all Democratic identifiers who have a college degree. Figures for Republican conventions also suggest little change between earlier conventions and the 65 percent figure recorded for 1976 and 1980; this compares with 22 percent of Republican identifiers with a college degree.[11]

Income figures tell a similar story. At a time when 50 percent of all American families had incomes under $10,000, only about 13 percent of Democratic delegates and 5 percent of Republican delegates to the "reformed" conventions of 1972 were in this income bracket. And while only 5 percent of the American public had an income over $25,000, 59 percent of the Republican delegates and 35 percent of the Democratic delegates made this much or more.[12] By 1980, when the median U.S. family income was $21,000, the median income among Democratic delegates was $37,000 and among Republicans $47,000.[13]

Occupational patterns among national convention delegates have reflected the rules changes more directly, but they have not uniformly moved in a more "representative" direction. Some 12 percent of the 1972 Democratic delegates were lawyers, compared with 28 percent in 1968; the percentage of business people also plummeted, from 27 to 8. By 1980, the figures had leveled off at 13 percent for lawyers and 14 percent for business people, still well below 1968 levels. Republican patterns were similar: 15 percent lawyers in 1980 compared with 22 percent in 1968, and 18 percent business people in 1980 compared with 40 percent in 1968. These trends are no doubt partially attributable to rules that have mandated the inclusion of more women, minorities, and young people and have encouraged participation beyond traditional circles of party leaders and contributors. But other trends are the result of other changes in the rules—particularly Democratic provisions that have given candidates an increased role in slating delegates. The number of teachers (15 percent of all delegates) and union members (27 percent) at the 1980 Democratic convention reached all-time highs, partly because of the assistance and approval given by President Jimmy Carter and Sen. Edward M. Kennedy to the members of national organizations that had supported them. Yet the blue-collar workers and farmers to whom Democrats directed their general election appeals could claim only 4 percent and 2 percent of the convention seats respectively.[14]

Turning from demographics to ideology and issue positions, one finds even less grounds for regarding the national conventions as "representative" of rank-and-file voters. A convenient prereform benchmark is provided by Herbert McCloskey's study of delegates and alternates to the 1956 conventions. McCloskey and his associates presented their findings as a refutation of the "Tweedledee-Tweedledum" view, which holds that the two American parties do not differ significantly from one another.

Leaders of the two parties, they found, were "obviously separated by large and important differences." Rank-and-file party identifiers, however, differed far less sharply; on only five of the 24 issues probed did substantial divergences of opinion appear between Democratic and Republican identifiers in the electorate. Democratic convention delegates were more liberal and Republican delegates more conservative than their respective constituencies. The gap was particularly wide for the GOP; the views of the Republican rank and file, in fact, were "much closer to those of the Democratic leaders than to those of the Republican leaders." [15]

A study by Jeane Kirkpatrick after the 1972 convention argued that the McGovern-Fraser reforms had exacerbated the differences between leaders and followers that McCloskey had identified, reversing the positions of Democratic and Republican elites. The Democratic elite, she asserted, was now "odd man out," farther from its own rank and file in many of its attitudes than were the leaders of the opposing party. The differences were most pronounced on "new" issues such as the war in Vietnam, law and order, political protest, and busing; Democratic activists and voters were in closer agreement on most economic issues. [16]

Kirkpatrick's picture of ideological extremism among Democratic activists parallels her account (noted in Chapter 2) of a national convention dominated by "amateurs" and purists, and needs to be interpreted with similar caution. It is particularly difficult, as she recognizes, to sort out the enduring effects of rules changes from the shorter term impact of the antiwar movement and the George McGovern presidential candidacy. By 1976, Democratic delegates were more likely to characterize themselves as political moderates, and the gap between delegates and party identifiers on a range of policy issues fell back to a point midway between the differences identified by McCloskey in 1956 and Kirkpatrick in 1972. [17] But this gap again widened in 1980—a development probably attributable, in part, to the imposition of equal division and of specific "goals" for affirmative action.

It seems likely, despite the results of the 1980 election, that Kirkpatrick's characterization of the Democratic elite as the "odd man out" was exaggerated. Her account of a "close correspondence" between Republican mass and elite attitudes was not fully borne out by her own data, and subsequent years have seen an activist-identifier gap reopen among Republicans that approaches the differences found among Democrats. Figure 7-1, based on Center for Political Studies survey data, compares the ideological orientations expressed by delegates and rank-and-file identifiers in the 1972, 1976, and 1980 presidential elections. Clearly, Republican differences increased after 1972, mainly by virtue of the activists' steady drift rightward. By the same token, the Democratic electorate no longer could be described as having a closer affinity to the opposing party's leadership than to its own. [18] Other studies have found Republican elites and followers to be more homogeneous in their conservative identification, but when specific issues are broached, the Republican rank and file are considerably more likely than their leaders to respond as "operational" liberals, favoring programs and benefits traditionally championed by Democrats. [19] This makes any explanation of unrepresentativeness in

Figure 7-1 Comparisons of Ideological Orientations of Convention Delegates and Party Identifiers, 1972-1980

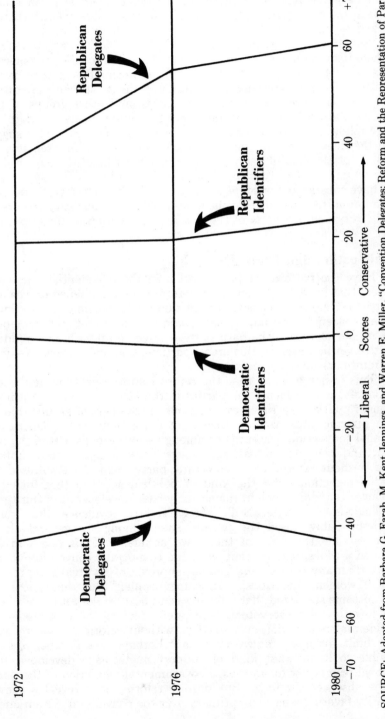

SOURCE: Adapted from Barbara G. Farah, M. Kent Jennings, and Warren E. Miller, "Convention Delegates: Reform and the Representation of Party Elites, 1972-1980" (Paper prepared for the Conference on Presidential Activities, College of William and Mary, 1981), 22.

terms of party reform problematic, for while there is a "symmetry" between the two parties' patterns of elite-mass disagreement,[20] there is a marked asymmetry in the kinds of rules they have adopted.

Numerous studies, therefore, have built on McCloskey's work, many of them inspired by debates over party reform. But confident generalizations about the role of rules changes in prompting divergences between the national conventions and their rank-and-file constituents are difficult to make. Gaps are present in both parties, and other groups of party leaders—national committee members and state chairs—deviate from party followers almost as much as convention delegates.[21] This suggests that the rules are not the only factor at work. But the fact remains that, in the post-1968 era of party reform, the activist-identifier gaps in ideology and policy views that McCloskey identified have not only remained but have substantially widened, particularly in the Democratic party. At a minimum this suggests that the relationship of broadened *participation* to the *representativeness* of the national convention is highly problematic.

Participation and Party Strength

Have the patterns of participation in the presidential nomination process that have developed in the reform era strengthened or weakened the parties? No simple answer to this question is possible: precise indices of party strength are not at hand, and, in any event, the evidence is mixed. But one would be hard-pressed to come up with a resoundingly positive verdict, even in this area—participation and legitimacy—where the reformers invested most.

This is not to deny that the reforms addressed some of the most serious difficulties facing the parties in the 1960s—a time of turmoil in national politics and rising expectations on the part of groups that had been discriminated against. Dozens of delegations were challenged at national conventions, resentment among various groups within the party grew, and the party's national image became increasingly unfavorable. Without reform, the Democratic party might have suffered substantial defections, and the kind of political activism that fueled the McGovern candidacy might increasingly have developed into third-party or single-issue efforts. Still, there is little evidence that reform has appreciably raised the parties' stock among the general electorate or among the mass of their own adherents. Polls taken in 1972 revealed a widespread perception of the Democratic convention as more "open than any before" and general approval of its greater representation of women, minorities, and young people.[22] But that year's election outcome suggested that reform was, at best, irrelevant to the choices and loyalties of most voters. Some defenders of the commissions on presidential nomination suggest that, without reform, pressures would have built for more radical changes.[23] Perhaps this is true: it is impossible to know what kind of support might have developed for a national primary or for increased governmental regulation of the parties in the absence of reform. But despite reform, polls reveal a growing majority favoring a national primary over the convention system and, as we saw in Chapter 1, a continuing decline in public esteem for the parties.[24]

How might one assess the impact of the patterns of representativeness/unrepresentativeness produced by reform? In concentrating on the representation of women, blacks, and hispanics, the Democrats have no doubt dealt with the best-organized groups and those it was politically most important to accommodate. Reform has not measurably affected the participation of low-income people or of blue-collar workers and farmers, and it seems likely that these groups would be as distinctive (or more so) in their policy and candidate preferences as those the party has been at such pains to include. But the effect of such omissions is not as great as it once was because the decision-making discretion of national convention delegates has been greatly reduced. Paradoxically, the same rules that required the inclusion of previously underrepresented groups rendered that inclusion far less significant by constricting the discretion of *all* delegates. As James Ceaser notes:

> When a delegate is already bound on the central issue facing the convention, the interest he represents has already been defined, and it is of no importance, except perhaps for symbolic purposes, whether the delegate is white, black, male, female, old, or young.[25]

This slightly overstates the case, for neither party's convention is totally bound, and candidates can rarely exercise total control over platform decisions. Delegates, through their actions and pronouncements, also help create a national media image of the party. Thus, the composition of the convention does affect the stances the party assumes and the appeal it projects. Moreover, ideological and policy views are likely to figure more prominently among delegates' motivations now than previously. In the prereform convention system the effects of demographic and ideological unrepresentativeness were mitigated to some extent by the desire of professional politicians to *win*. Representativeness was achieved—more effectively, it might be argued—not by bringing various groups into the convention in proportion to their share of the population, but by party leaders calculating which candidate and platform would have maximum voter appeal and mobilizing their delegations accordingly. But even party professionals did not always behave in this fashion, and as the proportion of issue "purists" in conventions increases, the likelihood that their unrepresentativeness might result in decisions that reduce the party's legitimacy and electoral appeal increase as well.

Turning from the party in the electorate to the party as an organization, one comes to a similarly mixed assessment of the participatory regime. The rules requiring that first-stage meetings be open and that the selection process be "timely"—the first adopted by both parties, the second by the Democrats—have greatly reduced the role of party committees and officers in many states. In addition, the Democrats have put explicit limits on the number of delegates that may be elected at large and/or by a state committee. These changes have been of some benefit to the parties. They applied needed correctives to a system that had reached a dangerous level of unresponsiveness. The horror stories recited by the

Hughes and McGovern-Fraser commissions—20 states without rudimentary procedural guidelines for delegate selection, several delegations entirely handpicked by governors or party chairs—pointed to a system on the brink of illegitimacy. Participatory caucuses, moreover, could and did become an important recruitment channel for state and local parties at a time when the traditional inducements to involvement were less effective. All in all, however, the advocates of participation, especially among the Democrats, showed little regard for the party as an ongoing organization.

The debates over "timeliness" and the role of party committees were especially revealing. The McGovern-Fraser Commission found it scandalous that some one-third of the 1968 convention delegates had been chosen, in effect, before the calendar year 1968. By the same token, it found delegate selection by state committees unresponsive almost by definition, since these committees would have been chosen before candidates and issues came sharply into focus. Most of the commission's guidelines, as one participant-observer noted, uncritically assumed that the type of participation to be maximized was that involving "persons who were enthusiasts for a particular presidential aspirant or policy *in the year of the convention.*" [26] Few would dispute the contention that channels of rank-and-file participation and influence needed to be opened up in many states. But the commission was hardly required to go as far as it did in giving the delegate selection process a plebiscitary character.

Why should one assume that persons serving on party committees, or delegates sent forward from one level of the party organization to another, will be unrepresentative and unresponsive if they are not selected in the heat of the presidential campaign? Such members of the ongoing party organization, in fact, may prove *more* responsive than "representatives" whose only role is to reflect a one-shot caucus or primary verdict—more responsive to late campaign developments, more responsive to those voters not participating in the caucuses and primaries, more sensitive to the qualities of the candidates and the requisites of victory.

There is much to be said for a mixed system that contains plebiscitary elements (selecting and committing delegates in response to the unfolding events of the campaign), but that also gives a measure of decision-making power and discretion to the occupants of ongoing structures of representation within the party. The rules on participation and timeliness, going as far as they have in reducing the role of party officers and committees, actually may have reduced the parties' capacity to make responsive and credible electoral appeals. Certainly they have weakened the party structures in question, reducing their functional importance and the incentives they have to offer for serious and sustained involvement.

What, finally, of the "quotas" about which so much controversy has raged? The health of the parties, and elementary fairness as well, required that the participation of women and minorities in the nomination process be enhanced. The convention's capacity to make decisions that were seen as legitimate and worthy of support otherwise would have been in jeopardy. Nonetheless, there have been some tradeoffs from the standpoint of the organized party, particularly on the Democratic side, where affirmative action rules are most stringent. Convention seats are both a device for drawing in leaders of key elements of the party coalition and a reward for the faithful. Reform commissions cannot change the fact that many of these key people, under present circumstances, are white males; they can only dictate that white males can have so many seats but no more. Thus does affirmative action, while strengthening the party by increasing the stake of previously excluded groups, restrict the availability of a key organizational resource.

The negative impact of affirmative action can be mitigated by relaxing absolute percentage requirements and providing a "safety valve" so that every stage of the process need not be hamstrung by representation requirements. This the Democratic party has largely achieved in its rules for minority representation: the substitution of affirmative action "goals" for quotas affords a measure of flexibility, and the possibility of "balancing" delegations through the use of at-large seats removes the necessity of requiring specific demographic breakdowns at the district level. Unfortunately, the requirement of "equal division" between men and women does not have these mitigating features. The 50 percent quota is absolute. And since the at-large safety valve comprises only 25 percent of a state's base delegation, there is no way to ensure equal division without requiring equal male-female representation at the district level. In district after district, then, selection processes and the judgments of party leaders are constrained by the equal division requirement. The price that the party pays—in confusion, resentment, and the distortion of incentive and reward structures—seems particularly excessive in light of the fact that comparable results usually could be achieved by less Draconian means.

The Role of Public and Party Officials

One trend in convention participation is clear: the role of top-level elected officials has been reduced substantially by changes in the rules governing delegate selection. The problem is mainly a Democratic one, as Table 7-3 shows. Participation among top Republican officeholders, while fluctuating somewhat, has generally remained near the level attained by both parties in the 1960s; the GOP's ban on ex-officio delegates had little apparent effect. But the numbers of members of Congress serving as Democratic delegates fell by more than half in the wake of the McGovern-Fraser reforms. Gubernatorial participation plunged 37 percentage points between 1968 and 1972; by 1976 only 16 of 37 Democratic governors were serving as delegates. The Winograd Commission's provision of a 10 percent "add-on" to encourage the inclusion of key elected and party officials brought gubernatorial participation back to 76 percent. (As Table 7-4 shows, the 23 governors at the 1980 Democratic convention all came as part of their state's 10 percent increment.) But congressional participation sank lower than ever: only 14 percent of the Democrats in the Senate and 13 percent of the party's House members served as delegates.

Table 7-4 suggests that while the problem is most acute at the congressional level, there are some interesting gaps in participation down

Table 7-3 Percentages of Governors and Members of Congress Serving as Voting Delegates in National Conventions, 1968-1980

	Percentage of Democratic:			Percentage of Republican:		
Year	Governors	Senators	Represen-tatives	Governors	Senators	Represen-tatives
1968	96	61	32	92	58	31
1972	59	28	12	80	50	18
1976	44	18	14	69	60	36
1980	72	15	13	72	63	41

SOURCE: Computed from CBS News data in Warren Mitofsky and Martin Plissner, "The Making of the Delegates, 1968-1980," *Public Opinion* 3 (October/November 1980): 43.

the ranks as well. In both parties a considerable number of state chairs and over half of the national committee did not serve as delegates in 1980. A substantial majority of delegates—64 percent for the Democrats, 73 percent for the Republicans—did hold some public or party office. But the fact that more than one-fourth of the GOP delegates and well over one-third of the Democratic delegates held no such position, not even membership on a state or county committee, suggests that candidate or issue or group activists often found access with ease.

These trends can be explained only partially by the encouragement that rules changes and political developments in both parties have given to issue and candidate enthusiasts. Of greater importance in the Democratic party have been the *disincentives* to participation that officeholders have faced. Some of these are related to reform only indirectly. For example, the emergence of insurgent candidates and of single-issue groups pushing their causes often have made the convention seem like a political mine field, replete with no-win dilemmas for elected officials who choose to participate. But the new rules have added some powerful disincentives of their own. Top public and party officials often have faced the prospect of competing with their own constituents and local workers for delegate slots, and to be eligible, they have had to make an early declaration of preference for a presidential candidate. Some of them, of course, have been denied slots because the candidate to which they were pledged lost in their state or district. But many more have been deterred from seeking a delegate slot in the first place. The Republican case suggests that the mere prohibition of ex-officio slots has not been the problem. Rather, top public and party officials have been asked to seek delegate positions through means that they regard as politically disadvantageous and/or inappropriate to their role.

The provision of a 10 percent add-on for party and elected officials did not change this situation appreciably. It enabled many states to elect their governor and state chair separately from other delegates, but the add-on was not large enough to include most states' congressional delega-

Table 7-4 Public and Party Officeholders Serving as Delegates, Republican and Democratic National Conventions, 1980

| | | Democratic | |
	Republican	All Delegates	10 Percent Add-On
Total Delegates	1,994	3,383	290
Public Officials	504 (25%)	797(24%)	174
Party Officials	1,170 (59%)	1,759(52%)	163
All Officials (public and/or party)	1,465 (73%)	2,186(64%)	288
Public Officials			
U.S. Senators	26	8	6
U.S. Representatives	64	37	17
Other U.S. Officials	4	3	0
Governors	13	23	23
Lieutenant Governors	4	15	12
Attorneys General	5	6	6
State Legislators	164	238	46
Other State Officials	33	74	17
County Officials	58	113	10
Mayors	29	60	15
City Councilors, Aldermen	23	99	14
Other Local Officials	79	108	8
Judges	2	13	0
Total	504	797	174
Party Officials			
State Chairs	39	37	25
State Vice-chairs	32	28	12
Other Nat'l. Comm. Members	55	97	41
National Finance Council	5	6	1
Other State Comm. Members	301	469	41
State Fin. Comm. Members	27	11	3
District Chairs & Vice-chairs	67	31	1
Other District Comm. Members	20	25	0
County Chairs and Vice-chairs	196	184	14
Other County Comm. Members	123	321	14
Local Party Officials	223	473	11
Others (includes Democratic and Republican Women's Club Officers)	82	77	0
Total	1,170	1,759	163

SOURCE: CBS News.

tions, much less other top officials. Many states, moreover, did not fill even the few extra slots they had with top officials; the Winograd Commission's rules, as amended by the DNC, gave unclear signals concerning the priorities the states were to observe in making their selections.[27] Table 7-4 suggests that the state parties took full advantage of this ambiguity. Thus, most officials were still faced with the prospect of competing for a delegate seat, if not with the rank and file, then with their own party peers. And the add-on rule did nothing to change the required early declaration of presidential preference.

The deliberations of the Hunt Commission revealed a growing consensus among Democrats that the party had indeed been weakened by the falloff in official participation. The trend, however, hardly had been inadvertent. The McGovern-Fraser Commission's report made the case against ex-officio delegates in terms that suggested public and party officials should be given no preferred position whatsoever:

> Delegate selection by a process in which certain places on the delegation are not open to competition among Democrats is inconsistent with a full and meaningful opportunity to participate.[28]

But displacing party and elected officials for the sake of candidate and issue activists is not likely to produce a more representative and responsive convention. Public and party officials, after all, have *constituencies,* and in most cases their constituencies are a good deal broader than those of people who seek delegate status as group spokesmen or candidate loyalists. They often have gotten where they are because they are attuned to the interests and sentiments of rank-and-file Democratic voters. If one's concern is to strengthen the party-in-the-electorate—to moderate its public image and increase its legitimacy, to make convention decisions more representative of mainstream voters and to heighten their electoral appeal—bringing top public and party officeholders back to the convention in substantial numbers is an important first step.

The case is even more compelling when one considers the organized party and the party-in-government. As late as 1978, Rep. Donald Fraser argued against the Winograd Commission's minimal "add-on" for party leaders and elected officials: "One of the measures of the strength and health of political parties," he said, "is their ability and willingness to be independent of and not dominated by public officials." But Fraser is also one of those who has argued most eloquently for deemphasizing primaries and restoring the organized party as an instrument of "peer review," whereby candidates could be screened by those who know them best:

> Members of the organized party . . . are in the best position to take into account a myriad of considerations affecting electability and performance and to make recommendations to the party voter accordingly. To deny the party voter and ultimately the total electorate the benefit of this knowledge is a disservice to the community.[29]

Effective peer review strengthens the party, both in giving weight to its conventions and councils and in helping it nominate able and electable candidates. It is difficult to see how the inclusion of the party's top elected officials in the national convention could fail to enhance that process.

Peer review, however, is only part of the picture. In fact, such an emphasis risks portraying the process of selection—and the role of party and public officials in it—as a good deal more disinterested and deliberative than it is. The process is and will continue to be fundamentally *political,* and it is mainly for political reasons that it is important to have substantial numbers of top public and party officials at the convention. Their presence requires candidates to reach beyond their own enthusiasts, to make alliances and build coalitions to ensure their own success and the adoption of a congenial platform. Candidates might find such negotitions onerous; they might even regard it as unfair, after having survived the primary process, to have to undertake a second round of persuasion with the party's leaders and officeholders. But such a process enhances both the candidate's electability and his ability to govern once in office. To the extent the process deteriorates or becomes unnecessary, both the party and its candidates are poorly served.

Consider David Broder's portrayal of the contrasting political dynamics of John Kennedy's and Jimmy Carter's nominations:

> After Kennedy won [in the crucial West Virginia primary], he still had to persuade the leaders of his party—the governors, the mayors, the leaders of allied interest groups, particularly organized labor—that they could stake their reputation on his qualities as the best man to be the standard bearer for the party. Contrast that with Jimmy Carter, who never had to meet, and in fact in many cases did not meet, those similar officials until after he had achieved the Democratic nomination. The significance of the difference for the presidency is that in the [earlier] case, the man, if he was elected, came with the alliances that made it possible for him to organize the coalitions and support necessary to lead a government.[30]

The contrast Broder draws is not solely attributable to the reduced role of officials in conventions; it also points up the decline of the kind of local and state organizations that can *command* attention and the reduced decision-making autonomy of the national convention itself. But the decline in official participation contributes to the party's organizational weakness. Elected officials and even some party leaders are likely to feel a more tenuous identification with the party's platform and with the nominees leading the ticket. And the process of alliance formation within the party, still necessary for effective campaigning and coherent governance, has been rendered more difficult. It is for these reasons that the devices adopted by the Hunt Commission to reverse the decline in party leader/elected official participation represent a significant contribution to party renewal.

The Proliferation of Primaries

The most familiar hallmark of the reform era, and a trend with clear implications for the health of the parties, was neither envisioned nor intended by the architects of reform: the doubling of the number of state presidential primaries. Table 7-5 encapsulates the story. The number of states electing or allocating their delegates through primaries rose by six in both parties between 1968 and 1972 and again between 1972 and 1976. The trend continued for the Republicans in 1980, but leveled off for the Democrats: four states added or reinstated Democratic primaries; but Texas let its primary law lapse, and Idaho and Michigan, faced with rules banning their "open" primaries, elected to allocate their delegates through caucus-convention procedures and to regard the primary as a nonbinding preference poll.

Current indications are that 1984 may see a slight reduction in the number of primaries that elect or allocate delegates in both parties. Although the Hunt Commission declined to move directly against the primary system, Democrats in six states have nonetheless returned to caucus-convention selection (and a seventh state, Tennessee, would have, had the Republican governor not vetoed the bill repealing the presidential primary). In two of these states, Wisconsin and Montana, the national party's decisive ban on the open primary (together with the *La Follette* decision) have compelled the state party to devise an alternate selection system if it wants its delegates to be seated. In the remaining four states (Arkansas, Kansas, Kentucky, and Nevada) party and/or legislative leaders have decided to simply terminate their states' short-lived presidential primary experiments. These shifts, plus the Hunt Commission's addition of unpledged delegates to every delegation, could result in as few as 54 percent of the 1984 delegates being directly allocated by primary results (see Table 7-5). A similar shift seems likely to occur on the Republican side, but it will probably be less pronounced—partly because in several "open primary" states the GOP will continue to use the primary to allocate its national delegates.

Primaries and Reform

As we have seen, primaries were promoted by Progressive Era critics of the parties as a means of "lessening party spirit and decreasing partisanship." [31] The adoption of presidential primaries often accompanied the adoption of primaries at other levels, although presidential primaries were less widespread and often less firmly rooted than primaries for state and local offices. The first laws establishing primaries for selecting national delegates and/or ascertaining the electorate's presidential preferences were adopted by Florida, Wisconsin, Pennsylvania, and Oregon between 1901 and 1910. By 1912, 12 states had presidential primary laws of some description. That year's nomination battle between William H. Taft and Theodore Roosevelt led to widespread calls for further democratization. Congress did not act on President Woodrow Wilson's proposal for a national presidential primary, but several additional states adopted primary laws. By 1916, the movement had reached its high point, with laws on the books in 26 states. But reform sentiments ebbed in the postwar years, and state legislators became disillusioned by the high costs of holding primaries, the frequent disinterest of presidential contenders, and low voter turnout. Six states repealed their primary laws between 1917 and 1929; by 1936 presidential primaries were being held in only 16 states.[32]

To what extent can the resurgence of the presidential primary in the 1970s—and its extension far beyond the 1916 high-water mark—be attributed to rules changes adopted by the reform commissions? This question has been hotly debated, for unlike the proliferation of primaries during the Progressive Era, their current spread was neither sought nor anticipated by most reformers. Somewhat defensively, reform advocates stress that primaries have been adopted for all sorts of reasons—as vehicles for home-state candidates (for example, Lloyd Bentsen in Texas and Jimmy Carter in Georgia), as a way of attracting interest to a state or strengthening the electoral clout of a region (the West in 1976 and the South in 1980).[33] Moreover, there is some evidence that primaries were on the way back before the McGovern-Fraser Commission completed its work. Primaries usually have been adopted in the wake of hard-fought nomination battles. This was the pattern between 1912 and 1916, and it recurred on a smaller scale after the Republican contests of 1948 and 1952 (although a reverse effect was also possible: Estes Kefauver's victory over the organization slate in the 1956 Democratic primary in Minnesota led the legislature to repeal the law). In the wake of the 1968 Democratic contest (and before the adoption of the McGovern-Fraser Commission guidelines), primary laws were introduced in 13 states; some of the six primaries that eventually were added might have been established even without the new rules.[34]

Nevertheless, it is impossible to separate the proliferation of primaries from the workings of reform.[35] The stress on participation and on reducing the control of party leaders created a climate favorable to primaries as the simplest mechanism for involving large numbers of people and responding directly to their preferences. And the complexity of the rules and the seeming likelihood of challenge led many state organizations to look favorably on primaries as the simplest way of achieving compliance. The new rules also created incentives to separate the allocation of national delegates from the conduct of other party business. The new timetables and procedures required by the rules threatened to disrupt established routines, and the prospect of an influx of candidate and issue enthusiasts threatened the role of the established party leadership. Primaries thus gained appeal as a means of "spinning off" the national delegate selection process and of insulating state and local organizations and conventions from the disruptions of presidential politics. This reaction was intensified in a number of states in 1972 when McGovern forces took over the caucus-convention apparatus; party regulars, historically suspicious of primaries, began to see how presidential primaries might help them retain organizational control.

Rationales for primaries thus could be developed from reform and antireform perspectives—as a means of expanding participation but also of limiting the effects of participatory caucuses—and both arguments played a role in their adoption. Unlike some other changes linked to reform, this one affected Republicans and Democrats equally. Many of the appeals of primaries crossed party lines; Republicans in South Caro-

Table 7-5 States with National Convention Delegates Chosen or Allocated by Primaries, 1968-1984

1968	1972	1976	1980	1984
Alabama	Alabama	Alabama	Alabama	Alabama
California	California	California	California	California
D.C.-D	D.C.-D	D.C.	D.C.	D.C.
Florida	Florida	Florida	Florida	Florida
Illinois	Illinois	Illinois	Illinois	Illinois
Indiana	Indiana	Indiana	Indiana	Indiana
Massachusetts	Massachusetts	Massachusetts	Massachusetts	Massachusetts
Nebraska	Nebraska	Nebraska	Nebraska	Nebraska
New Hampshire	New Hampshire	New Hampshire	New Hampshire	New Hampshire
New Jersey	New Jersey	New Jersey	New Jersey	New Jersey
New York	New York	New York	New York	New York
Ohio	Ohio	Ohio	Ohio	Ohio
Oregon	Oregon	Oregon	Oregon	Oregon
Pennsylvania	Pennsylvania	Pennsylvania	Pennsylvania	Pennsylvania
South Dakota	South Dakota	South Dakota	South Dakota	South Dakota
West Virginia	West Virginia	West Virginia	West Virginia	West Virginia
Wisconsin	Wisconsin	Wisconsin	Wisconsin	Wisconsin (*D)
	Maryland	Maryland	Maryland	Maryland
	Michigan	Michigan	Michigan (*D)	
	New Mexico		New Mexico	New Mexico
	North Carolina	North Carolina	North Carolina	North Carolina
	Rhode Island	Rhode Island	Rhode Island	Rhode Island
	Tennessee	Tennessee	Tennessee	Tennessee
		Georgia	Georgia	Georgia
		Idaho	Idaho (*D)	Idaho (*D)
		Vermont (*)	Vermont (*)	Vermont (*)
		Montana (*R)	Montana (*R)	Montana (*)
		Texas	Texas (*D)	Texas-R

	1968	1972	1976	1980	1984
	Louisiana-D	Louisiana	Puerto Rico	Mississippi-R	Louisiana
	Arkansas	Arkansas-D	Connecticut	North Dakota (*)	
	Kentucky	Kentucky			
	Nevada	Nevada			
		Kansas			
		Puerto Rico			
		Connecticut			
		South Carolina-R			
		Mississippi-R			
Number of primaries choosing or allocating delegates					
Democratic	17	23	30	31	25
Republican	16	22	28	34	29
Percent of all convention votes cast by delegates chosen or allocated by primaries					
Democratic	37.5	60.5	72.6	71.4	54 (approx.)
Republican	34.3	52.7	67.9	76.0	66 (approx.)

D   Democratic primary only
R   Republican primary only
(*)   Both parties hold "beauty contest" primary that does not choose or allocate delegates.
(*D) Democratic primary does not choose or allocate delegates.
(*R) Republican primary does not choose or allocate delegates.

NOTE: District of Columbia and Puerto Rico are counted as "states."

SOURCE: Adapted from data prepared by Herbert Hedden for the Commission on Presidential Nomination, Democratic National Committee, 1981; James W. Ceaser, *Reforming the Reforms: A Critical Analysis of the Presidential Selection Process* (Cambridge, Mass.: Ballinger Publishing Co., 1982), 33–35; Richard Scammon and Alice McGillivray, eds., *America Votes*, vol. 14 (Washington, D.C.: Elections Research Center, 1981), 21–39; and relevant issues of the *Congressional Quarterly Weekly Report*. Prospective data for 1984 obtained from the Democratic and Republican National Committees, December 1983, and *National Journal*, October 29, 1983, 2218-2220.

lina in 1980, for example, calculated (correctly, according to most reports) that a primary would attract candidates to the state and would promote local interest in and publicity for the party. And in those situations where primaries were adopted in response to Democratic rules changes, the means was often a state law that dictated an identical change in Republican practice.

Although the proliferation of primaries was not intended by reformers, a major reversal of this trend would prove more difficult now than it did in the 1920s.[36] Primary proliferation has gone much further, and there is now a large bloc of states in which presidential primaries are a well-established tradition. While primaries were never established as the main route to nomination in the earlier period, they now play that role. The participatory rhetoric surrounding primaries makes legislators wary of removing them, and the weakening of party organizations and of party ties in the electorate has rendered the caucus alternative less credible. Some of the alternatives to outright repeal that were available earlier (for example, forbidding candidates for delegate from listing their presidential preference on the ballot) are now prohibited by party rules. And finally, many of those ambivalent about primaries view the participatory caucus—the only alternative now permitted under the rules—with equal or greater skepticism.

At the same time, it seems unlikely that a great many more primaries will be added, at least in the near term, and a few more states may follow the pattern set in 1984, returning to caucus systems. As already noted, Democratic rules prohibiting certain kinds of primaries—"open" primaries, some varieties of winner-take-all, and primaries earlier than the "window" period—have made them less attractive for some states. As more states have adopted primaries, they have become devalued as a way of attracting money or media and candidate attention. Many primaries in 1976 and 1980 received very little national notice, much to the dismay of their promoters. The list of nonprimary states contains many states with relatively strong party organizations and well-established caucus traditions. Moreover, the fading of participation and openness as dominant themes in political debate—as well as the dismal performance of most new primaries in actually stimulating turnout—have reduced their appeal, while the idea of state party organizations and public officials reasserting themselves in the nomination process has gained some currency.

Primaries and Party Strength

The prospect of stabilization can offer only small comfort to proponents of party renewal, for there is little doubt that the current number and role of primaries sap party strength. We already have touched on some of the implications for the party-in-the-electorate. Primaries have brought more people into the nomination process, and primary participants have generally mirrored the makeup and the views of the wider Democratic electorate somewhat more accurately than have caucus and convention participants. But primaries have not lived up to their billing as instruments of either participation or representation. The proliferation of primaries has prompted no discernible increase in public identification with or approval of the parties. In the mixed system of caucuses and primaries that prevailed from the Progressive Era through the 1960s, primaries no doubt played a useful role, increasing the parties' ability to respond to the electorate and the perceived legitimacy of their procedures. It does not follow, however, that the present system, in which primaries dominate the "mix," has realized these capacities to a greater degree. Useful as a limited means of testing public opinion, primaries tend to become inflexible and irrational mechanisms when utilized as the definitive process for choosing the nominee.

In the prereform selection system, convention delegates were able to take account not simply of which candidates were the first choice of this or that primary electorate, but also of which candidates were anathema to one group or another and which might be widely acceptable although they were not the first choice of sizable factions. Of course, primary outcomes can register only first-place choices, and with those choices duly made and delegates irrevocably bound to them, the convention may have no alternative to ratifying a factional candidate as "the people's choice," despite the fact that other candidates have a much greater potential for uniting the party and appealing to the general electorate. As Nelson Polsby notes,

> What is missing in the relatively automated processes of choice involved in the simple allocation of securely pledged delegates, allocated according to the results of a ballot in which first choices only are allowed, are devices for arranging compromises. Second choice candidates enjoying widespread approval are unable to get into a game in which only first choices are counted. This becomes problematic because not all first choice candidates of some voters are minimally acceptable to other voters—conceivably even to large numbers of voters to whom the party wants to appeal in the general election. Processes of deliberation ought in principle to be able to smooth out some of the difficulties that arise when a plurality first choice candidate causes divisions of this sort in the party electorate. Primary elections simply do not deal with the problem at all, leaving it to fester until the general election.[37]

Such rigidity could be alleviated if primary states changed to schemes such as "approval voting," whereby voters could cast a vote for each candidate they found acceptable and the winner would be the candidate with the broadest approval.[38] But since movement in this direction is improbable, the obstacles to rational decision making that the dominance of primaries poses for the parties seem likely to remain.

Do caucus-convention systems under the current rules really offer a better way? Does not the ease with which caucuses can be packed with issue and candidate enthusiasts make it equally likely that they will produce unrepresentative and unpopular outcomes? It is precisely this possibility that has led some party regulars and antireform commentators to rethink their antipathy to primaries and even to a national primary.[39] Moreover, the reformed caucus system, at least in the Democratic party, has built in many of the same decision-making rigidities that we have attributed to primaries. Often delegates from caucus states have been no less pledged and bound—and no more able to seek out compromise candidates with maximum electoral appeal—than their counterparts in primary states.

Such considerations suggest that a shift from primaries to caucuses would be most beneficial in states where the party already has a modicum of organizational strength. Caucuses and conventions there would be less susceptible to takeover by "candidate organizations, manned by candidate and issue activists with few if any links to dominant social, economic, or political interests within the community." [40] It is also clear that decision-making inflexibility is not solely attributable to primaries. Serious questions need to be raised about rules that tend to make all national delegates the ciphers of candidate organizations.

Such caveats notwithstanding, the case for caucuses is still a strong one. An influx of participants, after all, can be a sign of public interest, and under the normal circumstances of a multicandidate race and reasonably well-developed local party structures, it need not produce wildly unrepresentative outcomes.

The 1972 Democratic caucuses were atypical; in 1976 and 1980 party regulars regained much of their influence in caucus states. Moreover, studies comparing delegates selected through caucus systems with those chosen in primary states reveal few differences, either demographic or ideological, in either party (1972 was one of the few years when significant differences appeared among Democrats, but it was the delegates from *primary* states that were most atypically liberal). Caucus states, however, are more likely to select party officeholders as delegates, and delegates from caucus states, even in 1972, have been consistently more inclined to see themselves as representatives of the party (as opposed to representatives of a candidate) at the convention.[41] The face-to-face nature of caucus meetings makes crossparty "raiding" less likely than in primaries and permits communication far superior to that characteristic of most primary campaigns. Although caucus outcomes can put delegates in a straitjacket almost as confining as primary outcomes, the caucus system does make possible a degree of deliberation and a reconsideration of preferences at successive tiers of the process that is impossible in a primary system. Both the public expectations and the state laws that accompany caucus systems are less likely to require a national delegate merely to reflect the first choice of a plurality of voters.

These advantages are compounded when one focuses more explicitly on the organizational needs of the parties. Even if the primaries could claim to involve large numbers of people (which they generally cannot), the caucuses would have a clear advantage in terms of the *quality* of participation. Caucuses are far superior to primaries as a recruitment device, a means of engaging people in party affairs. Many caucus participants, of course, are never heard from again, but reports from several states suggest that a good number work actively for the ticket and otherwise become involved in party affairs—even if they were initially attracted by a single candidate or issue. The fact that party meetings actually decide something of national significance increases incentives for involvement, and the interest and the lists generated by caucuses are obviously valuable organizational resources for state parties. Critics are legitimately concerned that weak party structures might be overrun by caucus enthusiasts, but it is just as important to stress how caucuses can invigorate state and local organizations.

Primaries remove decision-making powers and functions from party organizations and meetings. As Michael Walzer argues:

> Once primaries are established ... the state and local organizations lose their hold. The candidate makes his appeal not through an articulated structure but through the mass media. He doesn't negotiate with local leaders, speak to caucuses, form alliances with established interest groups. Instead, he solicits votes, as it were, one by one. And he solicits votes among all the registered voters, without regard to their attachment to the party, interest in or loyalty to its programs, or willingness to work for its success. In turn, the voters encounter the candidate only in their living rooms, on the television screen, without political mediation. Voting itself is lifted out of the context of parties and platforms. It is more like impulse buying than political decision-making.[42]

Candidates in recent years have employed campaign techniques in the caucus states that increasingly resemble those used in the primary states—media promotions and phone banks, for example. But a crucial difference remains: in caucus states this activity is channeling participants into party functions and party structures. And the candidates still must create alliances with those party leaders and public officials likely to play an influential role in those meetings and organizations.

In many states, party leaders have acquiesced in the adoption of presidential primaries, either as a way of giving their state a place in the sun, or of helping a candidate, or of avoiding uncertainty and challenge, or of separating presidential from state and local politics. But the price of these short-term advantages has been high: a presidential nomination process in which party leaders and party organizations have become less important and candidate organizations and the media more influential.

The Character of the Convention

Candidates and Delegates

Another characteristic of the reformed presidential nomination process, and one as consequential for the strength of the parties as the proliferation of primaries or the withdrawal of elected officials, is the loss of decision-making discretion by national convention delegates. At the same time, presidential candidates and their organizations have gained substantial control over delegate selection. These trends are partly attributable to the overall decline in the power of party organizations and the rise of candidate-centered campaign technologies, but party rules have played a major independent role. These consequences of reform, like many others, were not fully intended or anticipated by reformers.

The McGovern-Fraser Commission report mentioned candidate prerogatives only in a proviso that "any slate presented in the name of a presidential candidate in a primary state be assembled with due consultation with the presidential candidate or his representative."[43] But the commission required that the presidential preference (or uncommitted status) of each candidate for delegate be indicated at each stage of the process. This was presented as a key aspect of giving "adequate public notice" to voters and caucus participants; moreover, such a firm indication of delegate commitments was necessary if delegate slots were to be allocated to candidates in proportion to the distribution of presidential preferences among all participants.[44] Tying delegates to candidates thus was not an end in itself, but a byproduct of the quest for informed participation and the "fair reflection" of candidate preferences. As we have seen, however, there continued to be some slippage between primary outcomes and convention votes, and candidates—including President Carter as he looked toward 1980—had reasons of their own for tightening the link. The Mikulski and Winograd commissions tried to ensure that prospective delegates were bona fide supporters of the candidates to whom they were pledged. In so doing, however, they erected an edifice of candidate control that drastically reduced the ability of rank-and-file Democrats to elect delegates of their own choosing and helped make the convention itself what Austin Ranney has called a "rubber stamp electoral college."[45]

The most critical move was made in 1973 when the Mikulski Commission instituted the candidates' right of approval (CRA) of persons who wished to run for delegate under their banners. The Winograd Commission prohibited the one-for-one slating of delegates and required candidates to approve at least three names for each slot to which they were entitled. But it tightened the link in other respects—dictating that district-level delegates pledged to a candidate be chosen by caucuses of persons who were themselves pledged to that candidate (current Rule 11F) and giving candidates the right to pull delegates from the floor who wavered from their first-ballot commitments. Such provisions reflected a thoroughgoing shift away from any notion of the convention as a representative or deliberative body and toward a plebiscitary view: delegates were faithfully to reflect the array of preferences in the Democratic electorate as it existed at the moment of their selection. As a national panel sponsored by Duke University concluded:

> The binding of delegates has transformed what had been an election of party representatives into a fixing of a vote to be held far in the future, at the convention. The bound delegate, once selected and committed to his or her candidate, is no longer a person of any importance, no longer a target of persuasion or speculation. . . . Delegates thus "represent" nothing; rather they go to the national convention simply to cast an automatic vote for the candidate who approved them. . . . If, as is the usual case, a candidate accumulates a majority of bound delegate votes before the convention opens, there is in essence no reason to have a convention. These predetermined results inevitably encourage the trend among both public officials and party leaders to pass up the national convention— why bother, when there is nothing significant for a delegate to decide?[46]

The Republican party has erected nothing comparable to the candidate-control mechanisms adopted by the Democrats, but it too has moved in a plebiscitary direction. National GOP rules do not require prospective delegates to indicate a candidate preference; nor do they contain anything comparable to CRA or Rule 11F. A number of caucus states elect their delegates as individuals, requiring neither caucus participants nor candidates for delegate to specify their presidential preference. In 1980 three primary states (Illinois, New York, and Pennsylvania) still listed prospective delegates on the ballot without candidate identification. Reports of dissatisfaction with this practice continue, however. In primary and caucus states alike, candidate organizations have developed reasonably effective means of communication with their supporters about which delegates they prefer. One study, in fact, found the "intensity of candidate organization identification" to be greater among Republican delegates in 1976 than at either the 1972 or the 1976 Democratic conventions.[47]

As we have seen, the Republicans experimented in 1976 with their own binding rule for national convention delegates. And Republicans no less than Democrats have been affected by the plebiscitary expectations accompanying the proliferation of primaries. Most states adopting primaries have explicitly required delegates to both conventions to vote, at least on the first ballot, in accord with the primary outcome and/or their declared preferences.[48]

How have the tightened bonds between delegates and candidates affected the parties? On balance, parties are well served by requirements that candidates for delegate indicate their presidential preference. It is true that to elect delegates on their own recognizance is to maximize their autonomy and underscore their representative role. (Party regulars realized this in the 1920s when they forbid candidate preferences to be listed alongside delegates' names on the ballot in many states.) But such an extreme view of the delegates' independence is no more tenable than to regard them as mere ciphers; their presidential preferences are the most critical bits of information about them for many of those doing the selecting, and the party risks illegitimacy and voter alienation if it does not provide such information. Moreover, if one wishes to retain any provision for allocating seats in proportion to the spread of preferences among convention or primary participants, there must be some mechanisms for registering delegate preferences. Countervailing considerations are compelling only in the case of top party and public officials, whose roles and/or interests often militate strongly against making an early pledge to a candidate, yet whose participation is vitally important to the party. Here, as the Hunt Commission recognized in 1982, it is important that an exception be made.

Making a case for the additional paraphernalia that the parties, especially the Democrats, have erected to tie delegates to candidates is more difficult. Some have argued that candidate approval/disapproval can strengthen the party in certain instances: it can weed out opportunistic delegates who would break faith with their constituents; it has contributed to the meeting of affirmative action goals in some states and has taken some of the onus of these programs from the state parties; and the involvement of candidate organizations in delegate recruitment can have the salutary effect of stimulating interest and bringing new blood into the party. But CRA is hardly necessary to the achievement of any of these objectives. Delegates who have announced a preference and have been elected on that basis will be reluctant to vote otherwise at the convention (unless they have good reason to think that a shift would meet with the approval of those who sent them—in which case they probably *should* vote otherwise). Candidates are amply protected by the required declaration of preference and the political costs delegates would incur in reneging on such a commitment.

A prospective delegate with a record of party service and broad contacts within the organization *ought* to have substantial advantages over a newcomer interested only in a particular candidate or cause. The party's incentive/reward structure depends on the capacity of organizational loyalists to get elected, just as its ability to mount an effective campaign depends on their active involvement. The parties are ill-served by any system that allows candidates and their operatives to deny seats to such people. The candidates, for that matter, are often ill-served as well; under short-term pressures to reward their own campaign stalwarts, they may exercise CRA in a way that generates considerable ill will and sacrifices opportunities to broaden their base within the party. In some states in 1976 and 1980 the candidates were smart enough and/or the state parties strong enough to avoid self-defeating and divisive uses of CRA. But there were enough contrary instances to suggest that the party had gone too far in turning over critical aspects of delegate selection to candidate organizations. The 1980 requirement that three names be approved for each slot prevented the most blatant forms of slating, whereby caucuses and conventions could be denied any choice whatsoever. But candidates could still get around the rule and in several states did so by arranging for the filing of "dummy" candidates who were on the list only to permit the requisite number to be approved without choosing serious contenders who were not on the preferred slate.

The case for the additional candidate safeguards adopted by the Winograd Commission is even weaker than that for CRA. It hardly seems necessary, after having provided for delegates' declarations of preference and all the political constraints that puts in place, *and* having given candidates the right to veto any candidates for delegate that they please, to protect the candidates further by providing that only persons who are themselves pledged to them will be permitted to vote for "their" delegates at the district level. Surely this additional mechanism for weeding out weak or devious supporters is of marginal importance at best. But its negative consequences for state parties who have strong district-level organizations or a tradition of holding inclusive district conventions are by no means negligible. State parties are left with unpalatable choices, all of which transfer authority and prestige and incentives for involvement from the party to candidate organizations. The most drastic alternative is to forego a district convention altogether and to turn the delegate-selection function over to separate candidate caucuses. If the convention retains this function, it must be divided into candidate caucuses for the purpose of nominating and/or electing delegates.

Finally, there is the *coup de grace:* the binding of delegates. This transforms the required declaration of preference, which began as a device for helping primary and caucus participants choose delegates in an informed manner, into a requirement that delegates cast an automatic vote for the candidate they designated as their first choice at the time they were selected. While both parties have experimented with the binding of national delegates—the Republicans in 1976, the Democrats in 1980—neither now has such a rule at the national level. But most primary states still bind their delegates to the primary outcome. It is not clear exactly how these state-level binding statutes could be enforced, but enforcement is hardly a major concern: the plebiscitary expectations that surround the process and the various mechanisms tying delegates to candidates have made defections from declared commitments quite rare.

Thus does a binding rule make an already inflexible system only slightly more so. The point is not that conventions should overturn primary and caucus verdicts with impunity; on the contrary, there should be a presumption in favor of delegates remaining faithful to their declared commitments. But the preferences of both delegates and their constituents are likely to be more complex than simply registering a single first choice would indicate. Moreover, first choices and views concerning what other candidates might be acceptable or electable are likely to evolve as the campaign progresses. Delegates required by law to act as mere ciphers—or locked into that role by virtue of the control over their selection exercised by candidates' campaign operatives—can hardly act as responsible representatives of those party members who selected them. Nor is such a delegate role adequate to the tasks of choosing the best nominee and strengthening the parties' capacities for campaigning and governance. Delegates need to be free to respond to changing circumstances, to take account of the assessments of those party leaders and public officials who know the contenders best, to make decisions in the interest of party unity and victory. It is not desirable that candidates take "their" delegates totally for granted. It is in the shoring up of support and the cementing of alliances that the sinews of the party are strengthened— ties that will serve the candidates far more effectively than could a network of purely personal followers once they start to campaign or attempt to govern.

Such an assessment does not require any romanticizing of the convention as a "deliberative" body, nor does it envision a return to "smoke-filled rooms." What is essential is that the delegates retain some decision-making discretion and flexibility. If the party's decisions are to be legitimate and responsive, delegates must be accountable to those who elected them—accountable in the sense of acting in their constituents' and the party's best interests rather than in mechanically casting a single predetermined vote. Requiring prospective delegates to indicate their presidential preference (or perhaps preferences) at the time of selection helps establish such accountability. Beyond that, the parties should rely on the normal, informal political forces that tie representatives to constituents. The national Democratic party, and both parties in many primary states, have not been content to rely on political constraints; in single-minded attempts to ensure that delegates *genuinely* support the candidates to whom they are pledged and that rank-and-file preferences are *precisely* reflected by the national convention, they have turned slate making over to the candidates and have made the national conventions analogous in many respects to the Electoral College. The adverse consequences for party organizations are unmistakable: reduced decision-making powers, reduced incentives for serious involvement, a reduced capacity to influence who attends the convention (and hence to discipline and reward party members), and a weakened position from which to deal with candidates and their organizations.

The Fair Reflection of Preferences

High on the agenda of the McGovern, Mikulski, and Winograd commissions were questions concerning the fair representation of runner-up presidential preferences—first the unit rule and then winner-take-all and "loophole" primaries. It may be, as James Ceaser suggests, that the rules requiring the "fair" allocation of delegate slots have had their "greatest effect not in the way they have divided delegates among the candidates but rather in forcing most delegates to be committed to a particular candidate." [49] The allocation system erected by the Democrats has given candidates a dominant role in securing and validating delegate commitments; "binding" rules have been widely adopted; and voters in primary states, given a choice, have generally proved reluctant to vote the "uncommitted" line or for uncommitted delegates. The result has been a much larger percentage of committed delegates and commitments that permit delegates much less flexibility. Although early reformers often displayed little solicitude for the decision-making discretion of delegates, it is not clear that they fully intended this result. What most of them clearly *did* intend was to make the convention mirror more accurately the presidential preferences of caucus and primary participants and, in particular, to give fair representation to runner-up candidates. Thus has "fair reflection" become a hallmark of modern Democratic conventions, with the Republicans moving, though less rapidly or uniformly, in the same direction.

The exact meaning of "fair" representation has been subject to continuing debate. Although the McGovern-Fraser Commission was constrained to leave California's winner-take-all primary untouched, it did "urge" state parties to "provide fair representation of minority views on presidential candidates" and suggested two specific means to this end: dividing at-large positions among candidates "in proportion to their demonstrated strength" and/or choosing all or most delegates "from fairly apportioned districts no larger than congressional districts." [50] The 1972 convention battle over the seating of the California delegation sealed the doom of statewide winner-take-all, but the Mikulski Commission did not leave it at that: at least 75 percent of a state's delegates had to be elected "at the congressional district level or lower," and delegates chosen at that level (as well as at large) had to be allocated in proportion to the distribution of presidential preferences among district voters or convention participants. A major "loophole" was left for states that permitted primary voters to elect delegates directly, although it was provided that such elections could take place only on the district level and that the presidential (or uncommitted) preference of these candidates must be indicated on the ballot. The 1976 convention and the Winograd Commission took this line of reform to its logical conclusion, outlawing the direct-election primary. In place of the earlier, vague criterion of "fairness" stood a full-blown system of proportional representation (PR), qualified only by the 15-25 percent "thresholds" that candidates had to reach to be entitled to delegate slots. But the Hunt Commission again relaxed this standard, permitting both direct-election primaries and a hybrid "bonus delegate" scheme as alternatives to PR at the district level.

The Republican party has never permitted the unit rule, and its delegate selection processes have been altered in a number of states as primary elections have been brought into conformity with Democratic rules. In its national rules, however, the GOP has not gone down the "fair reflection" path of the Democrats. By 1980, 17 of the Republicans' 34 primary states allocated at-large and/or district-level delegates in proportion to the number of votes received by candidates, an increase from 12 PR systems out of 28 primary states in 1976. But 11 states still gave all delegates to the winner of the primary, by district and/or at large, in 1980. Nine additional primary states elected delegates directly; particularly in the six of these where the presidential preference of delegate candidates was indicated on the ballot, these contests also tended to produce winner-take-all outcomes. There was a similar variety among caucus states. Many still elected delegates as individuals without requiring them to declare a presidential preference. In practice, this often led to winner-take-all outcomes as participants voted for delegates informally sponsored by candidate organizations.[51]

Democratic systems have become more standardized, although the relaxation of proportional representation by the Hunt Commission has encouraged renewed diversification. Caucus states operated under proportional representation in 1976 and 1980; participants at each level were required to specify their candidate (or uncommitted) preference, and delegates being elected for the next higher level were apportioned according to this breakdown of preferences. Thirteen states took advantage of the reprieve given direct-election ("loophole") primaries by the Mikulski Commission in 1976. Ironically, another of the reform rules—requiring that the presidential preferences of prospective delegates be specified on the ballot—made the winner-take-all outcomes that the reformers decried even *more* probable in these "loophole" states, for voters became less likely to vote for delegate candidates as individuals and more likely to vote for a presidential candidate's entire slate.

Two of these states, Illinois and West Virginia, were allowed by the Compliance Review Commission to retain direct-election primaries in 1980, while in a third state, Texas, Democrats elected to hold only a nonbinding preference poll and returned to a convention system. The remaining 10 states, many of them under vociferous protest, altered their primary laws or rules to conform to the PR standards laid down by the

Winograd Commission.[52] Some, but not all, of these have taken advantage of the Hunt Commission's relaxation of PR; six traditional "loophole" states (Illinois, West Virginia, Pennsylvania, Maryland, Ohio, and New Jersey) and two new states (Florida and California) plan direct-election primaries for 1984. The "bonus delegate" option has been adopted for four primaries (New York, Georgia, Puerto Rico, and North Carolina) and six caucus-convention systems (Hawaii, Arkansas, Kentucky, Montana, Colorado, and Idaho). The remaining 34 Democratic primaries and caucuses will still adhere to PR.

What potential does "fair reflection" have for strengthening or weakening the party? Reformers were no doubt correct in asserting that the unit rule and statewide winner-take-all contributed to some voters' sense of disenfranchisement and undermined the system's legitimacy. To these problems the McGovern-Fraser Commission's suggested remedies (disaggregating selection to the district level and/or applying proportional representation to at-large delegates) were a useful antidote. As with so many other remedies, however, the reformers made the mistake of taking this one to its logical conclusion. When a requirement that most delegates be elected at the district level is *combined* with the application of proportional representation *at that level,* the resulting distortions can match those the rules set out to remedy. Consider the case of a four-delegate district: a candidate could receive as much as 61 percent of the vote in a two-candidate race and still only break even in the allocation of delegates. Or in a five-delegate district, candidate A could receive 49 percent of the vote, candidate B 30 percent, and candidate C 21 percent, but a PR formula would give A no more delegates than B (two each). The proportional allocation of delegates makes sense at the statewide level, where a large number of seats are being allocated. But at the district level it can produce distorting effects of its own—making it difficult for winners to win anything and even tempting candidates to write off districts selecting an even number of delegates. In terms of fairness or the legitimacy of party processes, it is hard to argue convincingly for such a rule.

Both proponents and opponents of proportional representation anticipated that it would encourage runner-up candidates to remain in the race and often might delay the emergence of a decisive favorite. Critics saw this as likely to fragment the party and to damage its prospects for an effective and unified campaign. Defenders, however, sometimes saw in this an opportunity to revitalize the party at another level, to increase the likelihood that the national convention would be faced with an inconclusive primary-caucus verdict and thus would resume a decisive decision-making role. As one party official was heard to remark after proportional representation was adopted, "What the reformers have done is put the nomination back into the back room—where it belongs." [53]

Thus far, the "brokered" convention sought by some and dreaded by others has not materialized. While it has become more difficult for candidates to capture whole state delegations, it also has become more difficult for delegates to come to the convention uncommitted. And commitments have become more ironclad, less subject to control by party organizations. Candidates are dealing with fewer uncommitted delegates, and with committed delegates often recruited through and controlled by their own organizations. Moreover, the proliferation of primaries and heightened media coverage have made it easier, in certain instances, for candidates to achieve a momentum that wipes out their rivals' natural bases of financial and electoral support. Thus have other aspects of the system—the precise effects of PR notwithstanding—actually helped leading candidates narrow the field and lock up the convention.

Nevertheless, the effect of PR, other things being equal, is to heighten the possibility of an inconclusive outcome. Is the role that the convention then could assume something that a strong-party advocate should welcome? Numerous analysts and party leaders have their doubts. There are questions of legitimacy. Given the plebiscitary expectations that now surround the process, could the party overturn even a narrow popular choice without inviting electoral disaster? And there are questions concerning the impact of such a convention on party organizations. Might not the anticipation of convention bargaining heighten the tendency of PR to encourage fringe candidacies, as individuals and interest groups seek to gain a foothold in the fray? Given the way delegates now are selected and the reduced power of state and local party organizations, might not the actual bargaining units turn out to be narrowly based candidate and constituency groups? It is not certain that party organizations would dominate the brokering at a brokered convention or that convention bargaining would draw candidates closer to party organizations. "It may seem paradoxical," Paul David and James Ceaser acknowledge, "that a 'pro-party' position would want to avoid a convention decision, but the type of convention likely to take place would bear little resemblance to the managed affairs of previous times."[54]

Such apprehensions, although well-founded, are somewhat exaggerated. Convention bargaining would surely give national and state party leaders an opportunity to mediate the relationships of constituency groups to candidates and among candidate loyalists as well, particularly if the role of these leaders is further strengthened by including more of them as unpledged delegates and by loosening the grip of candidate organizations on delegates. The party would give up a great deal were it to conclude that such brokering was beyond its capacities and that a convention that required such exertions was therefore to be avoided. Movement toward "fair reflection" in both parties has made such a convention role marginally more likely; on balance, that gives the argument for fair reflection added strength.

Arguments about party fragmentation have implications that go beyond the probability of a brokered convention, however. If the field of contenders is broad and evenly matched, the party may be better served by a convention battle than by premature closure on a weak or factional nominee—and it is important to have a convention equal to the task. On the other hand, if an able and attractive candidate clearly dominates the field, the party is well-served by a nomination system that permits that person to build a decisive lead and to consolidate broad support. Prolonged and divisive nomination contests are damaging to both the party's organizational cohesion and its electoral prospects.[55] In assessing the implications of fair reflection, one must not simply calculate the likelihood of a brokered convention but also assess the likely effects when and if a strong candidate has the potential to lock up the nomination before the end of the primary-caucus season.

Fair reflection rules have made building such a lead more difficult and in other ways have had a dubious impact on party organizations. First, presidential candidacies in both parties have proliferated in the postreform era, a trend to which fair reflection rules, as well as the structure of federal campaign funding (see chapter 8) and the spread of primaries, have contributed.[56] Second, fair reflection has given candidates incentives to enter races in all states, for even third- and fourth-place finishes can net substantial numbers of delegates. One might expect this fielding of a fuller list of candidates to heighten the interest in each state's primary or caucuses by bringing these contests more closely into line with the choice to be made nationally. It also could help a front-runner obtain a strong delegate base in a large number of states. But PR also has reduced the leverage of state parties and delegations, rendering the selection of favorite-son candidates or uncommitted delegates far more difficult. Proportional representation has tended to replace the traditional kind of convention fragmentation, based on the bargaining strength of state and local party organizations, with fragmentation of a different sort—the dispersal of power among candidate and constituency groups—which has far different implications for party strength.

Finally, in addition to prompting more candidacies and giving candidates incentives to enter more contests, the demise of winner-take-all has encouraged losing candidates to stay in the race longer. Candidates can continue to amass delegates, even while losing, and the prospect of possessing a bound bloc of delegates as a bargaining resource at the convention has obvious attractions as well. Studies of the 1976 nomination suggest that the stronger candidates, Carter and Edmund G. Brown, Jr., would have done far better in primary states under direct-election or district-level winner-take-all systems than under PR, while their challengers would have fared considerably worse—thus "confirming once again ... the 'concentrating' effect of a plurality system relative to a proportional system." [57] Figures compiled in 1981 for the Hunt Commission suggest that the effects of PR in 1980 varied a great deal by state: in New Jersey, Kennedy's 68-45 delegate edge under PR would have increased to 99-14 under district-level winner-take-all; in Illinois, Carter's 165-14 lead under the direct-election system would have been cut to 115-64 under PR;[58] and in Maryland, the results would have changed little, from 32-26 in Carter's favor under PR to 34-25 under winner-take-all. Overall, proportional representation slightly reduced the advantage of Jimmy Carter, the front-runner and incumbent president.

Thus, just as the advantages of PR in terms of "fairness" are often exaggerated by its defenders, so have its detractors exaggerated the capacity of winner-take-all systems to "pick a winner" and prevent party fragmentation. On balance, however, the adoption (or retention) of winner-take-all or other schemes qualifying strict PR at the district level (assuming that winner-take-all statewide is no longer a realistic option for the Democrats or, in most states, for Republicans either) should make it easier for the party to consolidate around front-running candidates. Such modifications also would have some advantages in terms of the representativeness of the national convention, at least for the Democrats; their normal effect would be to increase the impact of the large industrialized states where the bulk of the traditional Democratic electorate is to be found.

Some have claimed additional virtues for direct-election primaries in particular. The selection of party leaders and public officials as delegates is more common in these systems. Direct election also can give delegates more stature and independence from candidate domination, although the required indication of presidential preference on the ballot (and the process of candidate approval within the Democratic party) have made these contests more like other presidential preference polls and have reduced the importance of the credentials of individual candidates for delegate.[59] The direct-election feature perhaps gives democratic *bona fides* to this kind of primary that other winner-take-all schemes lack. But direct-election schemes also have some substantial drawbacks: voters often find them complex and confusing, and they remove not only the allocation of the state's delegates but also the choice of who should fill the seats from party caucuses and conventions.

While it is therefore difficult to argue that the advent of fair reflection and PR has, on balance, strengthened the parties, one cannot identify deleterious effects comparable to those inflicted by other rules changes. Arguments in terms of fairness, legitimacy, party fragmentation, and the role of the national convention lead to a mixed verdict. Clearly, however, the parties have been better served by the rules changes that prohibited statewide winner-take-all than by those that went on to impose strict PR at all levels of the selection process. Consequently, the Hunt Commission's relaxation of PR at the district level was consistent with its overall stress on building party strength.

Timing

A final hallmark of the reformed nomination process is an earlier, longer, and more media-dominated campaign season. This is ironic, for one of the main concerns of the reformers was to make the process more "timely." It was true, of course, that committees naming delegates and officials assured of delegate seats were often in place well before the election year. But the processes by which most delegates were chosen or allocated actually occurred in closer proximity to the convention then than they do now. In 1968, for example, New Hampshire's March 12 presidential primary was the only one occurring that month, and 13 of the 17 primaries were held in May or June. A handful of first-stage caucuses were held in February or March, but most occurred considerably later in the spring. Moreover, since caucus participants generally were not selecting delegates who were publicly committed to candidates, their actions were often difficult to interpret or cover in relation to the impending campaign.

In 1976, by contrast, New Hampshire held its primary on February 24, and the primaries in Massachusets, Florida, and Illinois (plus Vermont's preference poll) were held by mid-March. Caucuses began on January 19 in Iowa and were held in nine additional states by mid-March.[60] And since delegates to these caucuses, particularly on the Democratic side, were declaring a presidential preference and voting for delegates to the next-level caucuses on that basis, these meetings clearly influenced the standing of the individual candidates and were covered by the media accordingly.

Recent Trends

The Winograd Commission established, and the Hunt Commission maintained, a "window" extending from the second Tuesday in March to the second Tuesday in June, during which all first-stage delegate selection events must be held. The impact of the rule was reduced by a decision to allow states that had been outside the window in 1976 to apply to the Compliance Review Commission for an exemption in 1980. ("You're not only rewarding sin," argued Commissioner Austin Ranney, "you're making it monopolistic.")[61] But the Hunt Commission rule was considerably more restrictive. The earliest of the 1980 states were given guaranteed but limited exemptions: the New Hampshire primary could be held no more than one week before the window period and the Iowa caucuses no more than 15 days before. Only the three additional states given waivers in 1980 could even apply for an exemption (and only Maine did so).

The only primaries affected by the window rule have been those of New Hampshire (and they have threatened noncompliance in 1984 if Vermont's "beauty contest" poll—over which the delegate selection rules have no control—is scheduled on the same date as their primary) and Massachusetts (which will move one week later in 1984). The caucus scene is somewhat more complex. Five Democratic caucus states were constrained to hold their caucuses later in 1980 than in 1976, more than a month later in three cases, and three additional early caucus states have moved later for 1984. The Republicans have followed suit in some but not all cases; in 1980, for example, the GOP scheduled first-stage caucuses in seven states before the opening of the Democratic window.

While marginal changes have occurred at the beginning of the primary/caucus season, equally significant trends in timing *within* the window period have continued unchecked—and perhaps have even been aggravated by the window rule. Table 7-6 documents what has become known in the trade as "front-loading": the general movement of delegate selection events earlier and earlier in the year. The number of states scheduling primaries on or before the third Tuesday in March increased substantially, from three in both parties in 1976 to 7 Democratic and 8 Republican primaries in 1980. The percentage of Democratic primary-state delegates whose primaries had been held by the third Tuesday in April was 7 percent in 1968 and 17 percent in 1972, but had jumped to 44

Table 7-6   "Front-loading": Percentage of Delegates from Primary States Whose Primaries Were Held in Successive Weeks in the 1968-1980 Campaigns

Primary Held on or Before:	1968		1972		1976		1980	
	D	R	D	R	D	R	D	R
Last Tuesday in February	0	0	0	0	1	1	1	2
First Tuesday in March	0	0	1	2	5	4	6 xxx	5
Second Tuesday in March	2	1	6	7	9	8	14	16
Third Tuesday in March	2	1	13	15	16	15	24	24
Fourth Tuesday in March	2	1	13	15	19	18	38	36
Fifth Tuesday in March					19	18		
First Tuesday in April	7	6	17	19	33	31	42	41
Second Tuesday in April	7	6	17	19	33	31	44	41
Third Tuesday in April	7	6	17	19	33	31	44	41
Fourth Tuesday in April	17	17	31	32	41	38	52	48
Fifth Tuesday in April	23	22					52	48
First Tuesday in May	41	40	45	50	56	53	62	58
Second Tuesday in May	46	45	54	57	58	57	65	63
Third Tuesday in May	46	45	63	67	67	65	67	65
Fourth Tuesday in May	54	53	66	71	74	76	71	68
Fifth Tuesday in May			66	71				
First Tuesday in June	76	76	86	88	77	79	100	100
Second Tuesday in June	85	85	86	88	100	100	xxx	
Third Tuesday in June	100	100	100	100				

States holding "beauty contest" primaries not included.
Heavy line indicates 50 percent breakpoint among primary states; dotted line, 30 percent breakpoint.
xxx = Boundaries of Democratic "window," 1980.

SOURCE: Adapted from data prepared by Herbert Hedden for the Commission on Presidential Nomination, Democratic National Committee, 1981; and from relevant issues of the *Congressional Quarterly Weekly Report*.

percent in 1980. The Republican figures were similar. And the end of the primary season, which had extended into mid-June in 1968 and 1972, came two weeks earlier, on June 3, in 1980.

The front-loading trend has continued between 1980 and 1984, concentrated this time in the caucus states. One additional primary (Rhode Island) has moved into March. But five of the six states anticipating a shift from primary to caucus on the Democratic side have scheduled their first-stage caucuses for March; in four of the states this represents a movement forward of at least 10 weeks. The number of states scheduling caucuses on or before the third Tuesday in March has increased from 12 in 1980 to 15 in 1984 for the Democrats and from 9 to 13 for the Republicans. Overall, jurisdictions accounting for 37 percent of the Democratic delegates will have held their first-stage event by this date, compared with 28 percent in 1980. The comparable figures for the Republicans are 28 percent in 1980 and 36 percent in 1984.

What explains this movement toward the beginning of the season? Television has brought more coverage to primaries (and, increasingly, caucuses) and has heightened the "momentum" effect, whereby the outcomes of earlier races affect those coming later. Therefore, states wishing more extensive exposure and a greater electoral impact are tempted to schedule their events early, ahead of the pack. This temptation has become stronger as primaries have proliferated; states adding primaries, or wishing to retain the influence of their existing primaries, faced heightened competition for visibility and impact. Only one of the four states adding or reinstating Democratic primaries in 1980, and only two of the seven states on the Republican side, scheduled their primaries after the first week in April. At the same time, states moving in the other direction—from primaries to caucuses—also have tended to move concurrently to earlier dates. In part, this reflects the fact that a multitiered caucus process takes several weeks to complete and thus must begin relatively early in the season. But it also reflects the quest for influence: one way of compensating for the reduced visibility a return to the caucus system might bring is to attempt to become an early bellwether state.

The increased number of pledged and bound delegates also has encouraged early scheduling by heightening the possibility that the contest might be locked up early. One might expect the abolition of winner-take-all and, more recently, the addition of unpledged delegates, to have an offsetting effect, making it *more* difficult for candidates to amass a majority and thus promising a decisive role to states coming late in the process. This no doubt partially explains the willingness (thus far) of states such as California and New Jersey to hold June primaries. But the larger states have begun to look at "fair reflection" from another angle: since it reduces their capacity to deliver a large bloc of votes, they should perhaps move earlier to ensure that their impact is not reduced.

Several factors inhibit the front-loading trend. Perhaps the most important is the relationship of the presidential primary to state and local contests. Cost-conscious state legislators are increasingly unwilling to authorize a separate primary election, and they often have no desire to push primary contests for their own or other in-state offices into March or April. Moreover, as more states schedule primaries and caucuses near the beginning of the window period, the exposure and impact gained by such a move is diminished. As we have seen, large states have expressed considerable frustration, not only with New Hampshire and Iowa, but with the numerous other (generally small) states moving to early dates. The system continues to hold out to them, however, the prospect of a pivotal role in May or June. Finally, the window rule itself has erected barriers against the drift of primaries and caucuses into February and January, at least in several caucus states, although it also has encouraged a rush to the second Tuesday in March in 1980 and 1984 by states wishing to share the distinction of kicking off the season.

It is thus difficult to predict how much further the front-loading trend will go. It already is quite advanced and has been addressed only peripherally by the window rule. Nor does the window rule decisively deal with the problem for which it was specifically designed: the *lengthening* of the season. Too many other forces are at work—heightened television coverage accompanied by a search for early trends and indicators; year-round polling, which can greatly affect candidates' financial and political prospects; the proliferation of candidates, each looking for a way to gain an initial advantage; campaign finance laws that require early efforts to enlist small donors in a number of states; pledged-delegate and PR rules that make it more and more disadvantageous for candidates to sit out the first contests; and the increased interdependence of primary and caucus contests, whereby momentum from early contests is often a crucial ingredient of later successes. All of these factors have conspired to put candidates in the field earlier and to gear up media coverage of the "campaign" months before the first caucuses.

The period preceding the 1984 campaign showed how group and candidate interests could contribute to these trends. As a part of its attempt to heighten its influence in nomination politics, the AFL-CIO decided to endorse a candidate at its October 1983 national convention. The National Education Association followed suit, reasoning that to do otherwise would risk a relative loss of influence. These early endorsements were actively encouraged by Walter Mondale, their presumed beneficiary. Seeking to wrap up the nomination early, Mondale forces also encouraged early scheduling within the window period. "We're all for front-loading and are encouraging it whenever we can," acknowledged one Mondale operative in mid-1983. The most conspicuous case in point was Michigan, where the movement of the caucuses forward by six weeks seemed likely to serve both labor's and Mondale's interests.

The Hunt Commission, as noted in Chapter 6, tended to use "shortening the season" as a euphemism for reducing the disproportionate impact of the earliest contests. If one's concern is not simply the earliness of the campaign but also its *focus* (for example, whether New Hampshire continues to get 170 times as much coverage per vote on the evening news as New York),[62] then the remodeled window rule can be regarded as a modest success. The snows of New Hampshire and living-room meetings in Iowa farmhouses still will figure prominently in the opening scenes of campaign '84. But the closer proximity of these contests to the window period makes it more likely that they will be considered in conjunction with other contests, both in candidate strategies and in media interpretation. The movement of New Hampshire and Iowa actually may have exacerbated the problem of a lengthy season, however. Candidates can no longer anticipate a hiatus of several weeks after these early contests, during which they could capitalize on their successes there to raise funds and build organizations in other states. They must be at work in a number of states simultaneously. The relative impact of the contests in New Hampshire and Iowa has been reduced, but candidates now must get an earlier start in other states.

The Parties' Interest

The lengthened season and the New Hampshire and Iowa contests are not without their defenders. Apologists stress the interest the unfolding campaign generates in the electorate, the prolonged scrutiny candidates undergo, and the openness of the process to lesser known contenders. But all of these supposed assets appear somewhat dubious from the standpoint of party strength. Against claims of heightened voter interest must be weighed the evidence of alienation from the parties and low turnout. Of course, a prolonged campaign provides a kind of testing, particularly of the candidates' physical endurance, but the media too often focus on minor personal gaffes or the "horse race" aspects of the campaign—assessing who is ahead and who is behind at every bend. The momentum generated by the coverage and interpretation of early events often preempts or displaces the kind of scrutiny that otherwise might occur in succeeding states or in party councils. And surely the advantage given outsiders to break into the process should be weighed against the interest the parties normally have in nominating a tested candidate with a broad base of party support.

Despite the failure of the window rule to halt the trend toward earlier campaign activity, the shortening of the official primary/caucus season has served the parties well. Reducing the impact of the scattered, often unrepresentative "early" states on media coverage, on candidate strategy and appeal, and on the outcome of succeeding contests is desirable. As James Lengle argues:

> As a result of more primaries and caucuses per week, contenders would be forced to face large, more diverse constituencies; that is, constituencies more representative of the party membership and the general election electorate.... Although a shortened primary season would not eliminate momentum, it would confer it upon those candidates with the political skills and broad appeal that make the party competitive in the general election.[63]

A condensed process should discourage the proliferation of long-shot candidacies while conferring advantages on candidates who have broad enough financial and political support, not simply to make a splash in Iowa and New Hampshire, but also to organize effectively in a number of states simultaneously. The new calendar also makes it more difficult for candidates to move their personal campaign apparatus from state to state in succession. This could make them more dependent on existing party leaders and organizations, although it also might encourage them to rely more heavily on television advertising and to forego some of the work within the party that has been one of the most appealing features of early caucuses in states such as Iowa and Minnesota.[64]

It will be important after the 1984 campaign to assess the impact of the earliest contests under the new rules and to consider the advisability of closing the "window" completely. Interestingly, one of the strongest reasons for retaining a couple of early events may turn out to be the need to avoid the further concentration of primaries and caucuses in the second and third weeks of March. "Front-loading" within the window period now represents a more serious problem than the few remaining exceptions to the window rule. It is in the interest of the parties to avoid further concentration and, indeed, to reverse the trend that manifested itself in 1980 and 1984.

The parties are best served by a system in which large, electorally diverse states retain a decisive role late in the primary/caucus season. Democratic rules changes relaxing proportional representation (and the GOP's failure to adopt PR) should facilitate such a role and help the parties consolidate around candidates with strong appeal to their major constituencies. But that consolidation should not be premature. It could take place around a front-runner from the party's mainstream, as Mondale supporters assumed in welcoming front-loading in 1983. But it also could favor a factional candidate who made a splash in the earliest contests, received sensational media coverage, and achieved enough momentum to sweep to sudden victory in the larger states. The "anchoring" role of the larger states can be most reliably performed late in the season.

Front-loading already threatens the balance and stability of the process. Although many states still have good reasons not to schedule their primaries early, moves by a few large states could alter those calculations in fairly short order. If it suddenly appeared not only possible but probable that the nomination would be locked up in March or April, most states might conclude that a May or June primary was untenable and a rush to the front of the window could ensue. Such a development would particularly disadvantage caucus states. As we have seen, caucus states need 8 to 10 weeks to complete their multitiered series of conventions. Democratic and, in some states, Republican rules requiring delegates to declare their presidential preferences at successive caucus stages have made it possible to project state convention outcomes on the basis of first-stage caucus results. But these precinct-level results do not determine allocation of the state's national delegates as decisively as does a primary; the likelihood of choosing uncommitted delegates is greater, and delegates may shift their preferences and votes at various stages. This is one reason front-loading by caucus states is somewhat less alarming than the early scheduling of primaries. It also means that caucus states have a great deal to lose if it is perceived that the last stages of their delegate-allocation process are taking place after the national convention outcome already has been determined.

Some have argued that the parties could gain from an earlier and shorter season. A decisive outcome would be reached sooner, fragmentation and divisiveness would be minimized, and the parties would have more time to heal their wounds and marshal their forces for the general election. But there are a number of less attractive possibilities. As already noted, the consolidation of the parties around their candidates could be premature, predicated on little more than the momentum gained in a few early contests. If an early season produced a deadlocked outcome, the parties could be left with no late contests capable of tipping the balance and with a long and divisive period of preconvention jockeying and uncertainty. Or the early season could produce a decisive outcome but, given the limited flexibility of the convention, leave the parties largely unable to respond to new developments over a long three-to-four-month period.

Therefore, the parties have a stake in shortening the nomination season to something like a three-month span, but they also have a stake in maintaining an even spread of caucuses and (especially) primaries over the entire mid-March to mid-June period. This spread is essential if the caucus-convention option is to remain viable. It is essential if the larger states are to continue to "anchor" the process. And it is essential if all of the states are to see the process as affording them some influence over the outcome. Undoubtedly, the role of state parties in presidential nomination has declined, but such power as they have retained is highly dependent on the sequential, state-by-state nature of the process. Contests should be scheduled so as to reduce the impact of single early states and the likelihood of idiosyncratic outcomes. But the calendar should not be compressed to the point that state contests lose their distinctiveness and their relevance. At that point, a national primary might begin to look attractive, for otherwise the process could be completed prematurely in early spring. And a national primary would drastically reduce the decision-making power and organizational autonomy not only of the state parties but also of the parties in general. Trends in timing thus need particular scrutiny because the balances may be more fragile and the parties' stakes farther reaching than is at first apparent.

Additional Steps

Party rules have been only one factor among others in shaping the modern presidential nomination process. They have been a critical factor, however, and it is important to ask what additional alterations might contribute to party strength. The question is more pertinent to the Democratic party than to the GOP. Republican rules, far more deferential to state law and party practice, have shaped the presidential nomination process far less, for good or for ill, than those made by the Democrats. One might argue—and many Republicans have—that certain changes in the GOP rules, such as consistently enforcing the openness of first-stage caucuses or upgrading affirmative action efforts, might help the party broaden its base or strengthen it in other ways. But the Republican rules are generally more reflective than they are determinative of the roles and practices of state and local organizations. In them one is not likely to find either a convincing explanation for the current condition of these organizations or a very promising vehicle for change.

The Democratic case differs considerably. Democratic reform has greatly altered the environment within which both parties nominate their presidential candidates, and the Democratic rules have had a marked impact on the roles and resources of state and local Democratic organizations. It is an interesting but academic question whether those organizations would be better off under the Republican party's rules. There is no single hypothetical set of rules that would maximize a party's strength; rules take their place in a larger complex of party norms and practices and cannot be abstracted from that context. One might argue, for example, that both American parties are well-served when their members of Congress participate extensively in platform deliberation and presidential nomination. But what kind of rule would achieve that result—or whether a rule *could* achieve that result—depends on the role of national rules in the life of the party and the content of rules already in place. For the Democrats, adding a kind of "quota" for public officials, among other quotas and allocations, as the Hunt Commission did, may be the most promising course, while such a rule would be both inappropriate and unnecessary for the GOP.

Although there is thus a certain "fit" between party rules and other aspects of party life, there is no reason to assume that a given set of rules is functional in terms of the party's health. In fact, our examination of Democratic party rules has pointed up some marked dysfunctions, although we have argued that many of the Hunt Commission's changes moved in the right direction. We now ask, in conclusion, what further changes might be productive in terms of the party-building goals that this commission, more single-mindedly than earlier reform commissions, set for itself. Again, the point is not to draw up an ideal set of rules. Rather we take as given the authority that Democrats have granted their national party and the scope of the rules they have adopted. The question then becomes what sort of changes would make this regime more compatible with and supportive of party strength.

The four proposals presented below may seem modest and marginal when placed alongside the difficulties of the parties or the problems besetting the nomination process (although the Hunt Commission experience suggests that even proposals of this scope would face spirited opposition). Indeed, these proposals hold very little promise apart from party renewal on other fronts. At best, they would make the nomination process less debilitating to parties experiencing revitalization in other respects.

(1) *Consolidate the bloc of party leader and elected official delegates.* The Hunt Commission's division of this group into pledged and unpledged components, which was rooted in temporary political expediency rather than in any enduring party interest, is overly complicated and administratively unworkable. The overall number of PL/EO delegates could be reduced somewhat (say to 25 percent of each state's base delegation, or 20 percent of the convention overall), but they should all be unpledged. This would give almost every state enough flexibility to name

its key officials, including important women and minority officials, as delegates. The 20 percent number would contribute to the convention's flexibility and responsiveness, but would not be sufficient to overturn a decisive primary-caucuses verdict.

(2) *Treat women identically with other affirmative action target groups.* In all likelihood, the demographic result would be similar to that produced by the present equal division quota, but with fewer constraints on and distortions of the district-level selection process. Although states should be encouraged to give special consideration to women and minority group members in filling their party leader/elected official "add-on," specific affirmation action "representation goals" should apply only to their base delegation.

(3) *Remove the rules that have given candidates undue influence over the slating and selection of delegates.* As argued above, the requirement that candidates for national delegate declare their presidential (or uncommitted) preference is a justifiable one. But the rest of Rule 11 should be dropped. Some states would no doubt retain candidate right of approval or continue to hold candidate caucuses to choose delegates, but they should not be required to do so. Political constraints should suffice to keep delegates true to their candidate commitments unless circumstances arise that make a shift clearly defensible. It is important to discourage disingenuous declarations of preference, but the complex rules the Mikulski and Winograd commissions erected to deal with the problem have placed unacceptable, party-debilitating limits on the ability of party members to run for delegate, on the authority of party bodies to choose delegates, and on the rewards and incentives available to party organizations. The Hunt Commission took a step in the right direction in repealing the national binding rule, but it did little to redress the imbalance that has developed between candidate and party organizations in the process of slating and selecting delegates.

(4) *Inhibit front-loading.* Decisive action in this area is distasteful because it violates the presumption one should have against placing additional constraints on the states. But the state-by-state selection system, in which party organizations have a tremendous stake, cannot survive if large numbers of contests are perceived as irrelevant to the outcome. If a de facto national primary develops in March or April, the genuine article may not be long in coming. The parties' interest in preventing such a development is strong enough to justify the imposition of reasonable timing constraints on the states.

In 1984 only two primary states would have run afoul of the Hakes Amendment, discussed in the preceding chapter: Ohio and Maryland, which adopted direct-election primaries and moved them forward by four weeks and one week, respectively. California, however, adopted a direct-election system and seriously considered adopting a March or April primary date—a move that would have had profoundly destabilizing effects. Another rule that was discussed, forbidding direct-election primaries before the third Tuesday in April, would have affected only Illinois and Florida.

Either or both of these restrictions would seem a prudent safeguard against the most extreme kinds of front-loading and would offer states a reasonable option: increase your impact through either district-level winner-take-all or early scheduling, but not both. Such rules would encourage large industrial states to go late and also make it more difficult for those that do go early to lock up the outcome. This is far more important than placing further constraints on Iowa and New Hampshire. If the Hunt Commission rules do not produce at least a marginal reduction in the impact of these first contests, the best course may yet be to shut the "window" tight. But New Hampshire and Iowa must also be evaluated in relation to the timing of contests *within* the "window," for it is the latter problem that is now of far greater concern.

The parties would benefit from changes in two additional areas, but national party rules may not be the preferred vehicle for these changes. The first concerns the desirability of registration-by-party in the states. As we saw in Chapter 5, there is little difference between a "pure" open primary and one that requires only same-day "declaration" of party preference. Party registration is an important requisite of organizational integrity and strength for state parties. But surely the long Wisconsin saga is sufficient to discourage anyone from seeing national rules as a promising lever for inducing change in the 13 states that now have a same-day system. Similar considerations apply to the proliferation of primaries. There is no reason to doubt that the present mix of caucuses and primaries is debilitating to the parties, despite the encouraging return of a number of states to caucus systems in 1984. Party rules forbidding certain *kinds* of primaries bear some responsibility for this movement, but as the Hunt Commission concluded, to address the problem directly would require complex and coercive measures that taxed the party's legitimacy to its limits. Thus, while parties have a stake in registration-by-party and in the shift from primaries to caucuses, these goals can realistically be pursued only in arenas and through means beyond those provided by national rules-writing commissions.

Finally, a comment on process. It is perhaps unreasonable to expect the staff director of a party commission to think objectively about whether that commission's existence was justified. A good case could certainly be made, in terms of the intensity of interest in rules changes after 1980 and the scope of the review many groups within the party thought was unnecessary, for John White's and Charles Manatt's decision to appoint another rules commission on the model of McGovern-Fraser, Mikulski, and Winograd. The party cannot afford, however, to regard these quadrennial exercises as setting a binding precedent. Barring unforeseen developments, 1985 would seem a good time to bring rules-writing back within the national committee.

Setting up a free-standing commission every four years diverts money, time, and energy that could be better spent on other national party tasks. It reinforces the Democratic preoccupation with rules battles and an unrealistic sense of the efficacy of rules as opposed to other mechanisms of change. It gives to interest groups, candidates, and incumbent presidents a role in rules writing that, if it took place within the

DNC, would have to take fuller account of the party's broader interests. Writing party rules is properly the national committee's business and leaving the responsibility there would help ensure that party renewal remains a focal point of such efforts.

NOTES

1. Commission on Party Structure and Delegate Selection (McGovern-Fraser Commission), *Mandate for Reform* (Washington, D.C.: Democratic National Committee, 1970), 10; Delegates and Organizations Committee, *Progress Report*, pt. II, "The Delegate Selection Procedures for the Republican Party" (Washington, D.C: Republican National Committee, 1970), 2.
2. The *Congressional Quarterly Weekly Report*, December 29, 1979, 2965, lists four states—Arizona, Arkansas, Delaware, and Montana—where Republican first-stage caucuses in 1980 were limited to local party officers. The RNC's Technical Amendments Subcommittee, in its 1982 report (12-13), notes that some 18 states give ex-officio status or selection powers of some sort to precinct committee members "notwithstanding the clear existing rules proscribing automatic delegates." The committee, however, declines to recommend rules changes that would either accommodate or specifically forbid the practice. "While the committee generally conceives its task in this area as validating existing procedures, we concluded that the policy issue involved was substantial and should be deferred to other bodies."
3. McGovern-Fraser Commision, *Mandate for Reform*, 10-11.
4. Data on Democratic identifiers from the 1980 national election survey of the Center for Political Studies, University of Michigan. On the makeup of the Democratic coalition, see Robert Axelrod, "Where the Votes Came From: An Analysis of Electoral Coalitions, 1952-1968," *American Political Science Review* 66 (March 1972): 11-20, and the update through 1980 in *American Political Science Review* 76 (June 1982): 393-396.
5. See Austin Ranney, *Participation in American Presidential Nominations, 1976* (Washington, D.C.: American Enterprise Institute for Public Policy Research, 1977), 15-16; *Congressional Quarterly Weekly Report*, July 26, 1980, 2126; and *Public Opinion* 3 (April-May 1980): 36.
6. Data from *Congressional Quarterly Weekly Report*, July 5, 1980, 1874-1875; *Public Opinion* 3 (April-May 1980): 36-37 and 3 (June-July 1980): 29. Compare the analyses in Ranney, *Participation in Nominations;* Richard L. Rubin, "Presidential Primaries: Continuities, Dimensions of Change, and Political Implications," in *The Party Symbol*, ed. William Crotty (San Francisco: W. H. Freeman & Co., 1980), chap. 6; Harvey Zeidenstein, "Presidential Primaries: Reflections of 'The People's Choice'?" *Journal of Politics* 32 (November 1970): 856-874; and Steven Schier, "Turnout Choice in Presidential Nominations," *American Politics Quarterly* 10 (April 1982): 231-245.
7. See Austin Ranney, "Turnout and Representation in Presidential Primary Elections," *American Political Science Review* 66 (March 1972): 26-27; James I. Lengle, *Representation and Presidential Primaries* (Westport, Conn.: Greenwood Press, 1981), chaps. 2, 5; Commission on Presidential Nomination and Party Structure (Winograd Commission), *Openness, Participation, and Party Building: Reforms for a Stronger Democratic Party* (Washington, D.C.: Democratic National Committee, 1978), 10-17; and Barbara G. Farah, M. Kent Jennings, and Warren E. Miller, "Convention Delegates: Reform and the Representation of Party Elites, 1972-1980" (Paper delivered at the Conference on Presidential Activities, College of William and Mary, 1981), 4-6.
8. Lengle, *Representation and Primaries*, 62.
9. Herbert Kritzer, "The Representativeness of the 1972 Presidential Primaries," *Polity* 10 (Fall 1977): 121-129; Farah, Jennings, and Miller, 'Convention Delegates," 5-10. See also Ranney's earlier findings in New Hampshire and Wisconsin in "'Turnout and Representation," 29-34.
10. Thomas R. Marshall, "Turnout and Representation: Caucuses Versus Primaries," *American Journal of Political Science* 22 (February 1978): 180.
11. Warren J. Mitofsky and Martin Plissner, "The Making of the Delegates, 1968-1980," *Public Opinion* 3 (October-November 1980): 43; "Opinion Roundup," *Public Opinion* 6 (October-November 1983): 22.
12. Jeane Kirkpatrick, *The New Presidential Elite* (New York: Russell Sage Foundation, 1976), 295.
13. U.S. Bureau of the Census data and Mitofsky and Plissner, "Making of the Delegates," 41.
14. The 1980 Republican figures were 4 percent for teachers, 4 percent for union members, 2 percent for blue-collar workers, and 5 percent for farmers. The disparity between the numbers of union members and blue-collar workers at the Democratic convention is accounted for by the prominent role of white-collar unions, particularly the National Education Association. Mitofsky and Plissner, "Making of the Delegates," 38, 40-43.

15. Herbert McCloskey, Paul J. Hoffman, and Rosemary O'Hara, "Issue Conflict and Consensus Among Party Leaders and Followers," *American Political Science Review* 54 (June 1960): 410, 419, 422.
16. Kirkpatrick, *New Presidential Elite,* 297, 305-315. Kirkpatrick seemed unsure to what extent the "political unrepresentativeness" of the 1972 Democratic convention "was a result only or perhaps even mainly of the new rules"; compare pp. 43, 49, 292, 328. For a useful discussion of how three factors—the basic mass-elite differences identified by McCloskey, the group quotas, and the McGovern candidacy—reenforced one another in widening the "liberalism gap" in 1972, see Denis G. Sullivan et al., *The Politics of Representation: The Democratic Convention 1972* (New York: St. Martin's Press, 1974), chap. 2.
17. See John S. Jackson, III, Jesse C. Brown, and Barbara Z. Brown, "Recruitment, Representation, and Political Values: The 1976 Democratic National Convention Delegates," *American Politics Quarterly* 6 (April 1978): 197; and Winograd Commission, *Openness, Participation, and Party Building,* 20. Compare with the findings of Everett Carll Ladd, Jr., in *Where Have All the Voters Gone? The Fracturing of America's Political Parties* (New York: W. W. Norton & Co., 1978), 63-67.
18. Kirkpatrick, *New Presidential Elite,* 314-315; Farah, Jennings, and Miller, "Convention Delegates," 17-22. The ideological orientation scale used in Figure 7-1 is based on responses to "feeling thermometer" questions eliciting attitudes toward liberals and conservatives (7).
19. See John S. Jackson III, Barbara L. Brown, and David Bositis, "Herbert McCloskey and Friends Revisited: 1980 Democratic and Republican Party Elites Compared to the Mass Public," *American Politics Quarterly* 10 (April 1982): 158-180. See especially the comparisons of attitudes toward cutting public services, Medicare, education, and the Equal Rights Amendment.
20. Farah, Jennings, and Miller, "Convention Delegates," 22.
21. See Jackson, Brown, and Bositis, "McCloskey Revisited"; and Martin Plissner and Warren Mitofsky, "Political Elites," *Public Opinion* 4 (October-November 1981): 47-50.
22. See John G. Stewart, *One Last Chance: The Democratic Party, 1974-1976* (New York: Praeger Publishers, 1974), 58-59.
23. Kenneth A. Bode and Carol F. Casey, "Party Reform: Revisionism Revised," in *Political Parties in the Eighties,* ed. Robert A. Goldwin (Washington, D.C.: American Enterprise Institute for Public Policy Research, 1980), 19.
24. On the limited utility of polls for assessing or predicting party legitimacy, see James W. Ceaser, *Reforming the Reforms: A Critical Analysis of the Presidential Selection Process* (Cambridge, Mass.: Ballinger Publishing Co., 1982), 87-88.
25. Ibid., 51.
26. Austin Ranney, *Curing the Mischiefs of Faction: Party Reform in America* (Berkeley: University of California Press, 1975), 153.
27. The language bore the marks of tortuous compromise: "In the selection of party and elected official delegates ... priority of consideration shall be given to, among others, Democratic Governors, followed by State Party Chairs and Vice Chairs and other members of the Democratic National Committee, United States Senators and United States Representatives." Democratic National Committee, *1980 Delegate Selection Rules,* Rule 8A.
28. McGovern-Fraser Commission, *Mandate for Reform,* 46.
29. See Winograd Commission, *Transcript,* January 22, 1978, 74; and Donald M. Fraser, "Democratizing the Democratic Paraty," in *Political Parties in the Eighties,* 129.
30. John Charles Daly, moderator, *Choosing Presidential Candidates: How Good is the New Way?* (Washington, D.C.: American Enterprise Institute for Public Policy Research, 1980), 7.
31. The quote is from George Norris; see Ranney, *Curing the Mischiefs,* 125.
32. See the account in James W. Davis, *Presidential Primaries: Road to the White House* (New York: Thomas Y. Crowell Co., 1967), 24-30, 278-291.
33. See, for example, Bode and Casey, "Party Reform," 16-18.
34. Ibid., 16; Davis, *Presidential Primaries,* 30-37.
35. Accounts that treat the proliferation of primaries as a direct consequence of reform include Polsby, *Consequences of Party Reform,* 55-59, 62-64; Jeane Kirkpatrick, *Dismantling the Parties* (Washington, D.C.: American Enterprise Institute for Public Policy Research, 1978), 7-8; and Austin Ranney, *The Federalization of Presidential Primaries* (Washington, D.C.: American Enterprise Institute for Public Policy Research, 1978), 1-3. See also Winograd Commission, *Openness, Participation and Party Building,* 1-9, 24-28.
36. This paragraph draws on Ceaser, *Reforming the Reforms,* 25-26.
37. Polsby, *Consequences of Reform,* 165.
38. See Stephen J. Brams, "Approval Voting: A Practical Reform for Multicandidate Elections," in *A Danger of Democracy: The Presidential Nominating Process* by Terry Sanford (Boulder, Colo.: Westview Press, 1981), 159-160.
39. On the recent tendency of some conservative critics to "find the primary system more tolerable than the party caucus system"—and, conversely, the tendency of reformers to become more critical of primaries as they become party insiders—see Pope McCorkle, III, and Joel L. Fleishman, "Political Parties and Presidential Nominations: The Intellectual Ironies of Reform and Change in the Mass Media Age," in *The Future of American Political Parties,* ed. Joel L. Fleishman (Englewood Cliffs, N.J.: Prentice-Hall, 1982), 142-148, 153-155.

40. James I. Lengle, "Changing the Rules Changes the Game: An Assessment of the Nomination Reforms for 1984," *Commonsense*, vol. 4, no. 2 (1981): 17. "The ratio of primaries to caucuses," Lengle concludes, "is less important than the correct match of delegate selection method to state party condition" (18).

41. Paul T. David and James W. Ceaser, *Proportional Representation in Presidential Nominating Politics* (Charlottesville: University Press of Virginia, 1980), 68-84; Farah, Jennings, and Miller, "Convention Delegates," 11-21; Winograd Commission, *Openness, Participation, and Party Building*, 20-21. Caucus-primary contrasts among Republicans, although not great, tend to be larger than those among Democrats; caucus states tend to select more women, and caucus-state delegates are marginally more conservative than those sent from primary states (Farah, Jennings, and Miller, "Convention Delegates," 12, 18).

42. Michael Walzer, "Democracy vs. Elections," *The New Republic*, January 3 and 10, 1981, 18.

43. McGovern-Fraser Commission, *Mandate for Reform*, guideline C-6, 48.

44. Ibid., guidelines B-6 and C-1, 44-46.

45. Jeane J. Kirkpatrick et al., *The Presidential Nominating Process: Can It Be Improved?* (Washington, D.C.: American Enterprise Institute for Public Policy Research, 1980), 5.

46. The Forum on Presidential Nominations, *A Statement of Purpose for Political Parties* (Durham, N.C.: Duke University Institute of Policy Sciences and Public Affairs and Woodrow Wilson International Center for Scholars, 1981), 4-5. This bipartisan forum highlighted "freeing the delegates" as its most important recommendation (10). See also Sanford, *A Danger of Democracy*, chaps. 7, 14.

47. Denis G. Sullivan, "Party Unity: Appearance and Reality," *Political Science Quarterly* 92 (Winter 1977-1978): 637.

48. For a tabulation of state requirements as they stood in 1977, see Ranney, *Participation in Nominations*, 13.

49. Ceaser, *Reforming the Reforms*, 37.

50. McGovern-Fraser Commission, *Mandate for Reform*, guideline B-6, 44.

51. Ceaser, *Reforming the Reforms*, 34-35, 44-45; *Congressional Quarterly Weekly Report*, May 24, 1980, 1415-1426; David and Ceaser, *Proportional Representation*, 269-271.

52. In two states, Alabama and Pennsylvania, primary participants continued to vote for delegates directly, but with the number to be allocated to each candidate determined by the concurrent presidential preference poll. In New Hampshire, New Jersey, and Ohio, delegates were slated in rank-order in preprimary caucuses, then allocated in accordance with the preference poll. In Georgia, Louisiana, Maryland, Nebraska, and New York, delegate slots were filled at postprimary caucuses or conventions. Data collected by Herbert Hedden for the Commission on Presidential Nomination (Hunt Commission), Democratic National Committee, 1981.

53. David and Ceaser, *Proportional Representation*, 77.

54. Ibid., 83; see also Ceaser, *Reforming the Reforms*, 37-40.

55. For an examination of the extent to which divisive presidential primaries have caused alienation within both parties and have harmed their general election prospects, see Lengle, *Representation and Primaries*, 85-98.

56. Ibid., 82-85.

57. David and Ceaser, *Proportional Representation*, 43. Projections about how Gerald Ford and Ronald Reagan, the two Republican contenders in 1976, would have fared under alternative systems are not conclusive, despite Reagan's claim that he would have won had PR been in effect. Ford would have benefited, but only slightly, from a uniform winner-take-all system at the district level in primary states. These figures, and the Democratic results of 1980 as well, suggest that winner-take-all systems are more likely to eliminate also-ran candidates than to increase decisively the margin of the winner in a two-candidate contest. See Ibid., chap. 4; and Gerald Pomper, "New Rules and New Games in Presidential Nominations," *Journal of Politics* 41 (August 1979): 792-798. Compare the negative assessment of district-level winner-take-all, particularly in contrast to the increasingly unrealistic option of statewide winner-take-all, in James Lengle and Byron Shafer, "Primary Rules, Political Power, and Social Change," *American Political Science Review* 70 (March 1976): 31-40.

58. Under *pure* winner-take all, Carter's Illinois margin would have been 167-12. Voters in three congressional districts elected mixed slates of delegates, but in the remaining 19 districts the winning presidential candidate won all delegates. State-by-state calculations all assume PR at the at-large level.

59. See David and Ceaser, *Proportional Representation*, 68, 84-85; Winograd Commission, *Openness, Participation, and Party Building*, 21.

60. For comprehensive data on 1976 primaries and caucuses, see Rhodes Cook, "Media Coverage of the 1976 Nominating Process,' in *Party Symbol*, 156-175.

61. Winograd Commission, *Transcript*, January 21, 1978, pt. II, 140; Democratic National Committee, *1980 Delegate Selection Rules*, Rules 10A, 20. The contrast with the harsher treatment given open primary states (see Rule 2B) was justified by reference to the four additional years (since the 1976 rules) these states had had to come into compliance.

62. Michael J. Robinson, "Media Coverage in the Primary Campaign of 1976: Implications for Voters, Candidates, and Parties," in *Party Symbol*, 183.

63. Lengle, "Changing the Rules," 14-15.
64. See the exchange between James Lengle and John Rendon at the Harvard Conference reported in *Commonsense*, vol. 5, no. 1 (1982): 48-50.

The Parties and Political Finance 8

The transformation of the presidential nomination process, which began in the late 1960s, was followed in the mid-1970s by major changes in the American system of campaign finance. The regulation of political finance, unlike delegate selection reform, seldom took direct aim at party organizations and practices. Nonetheless, it has altered the parties' roles, their base of resources, and the campaign environment to which they must adapt. In this chapter we will examine the impact of campaign finance reform on the parties and ask what changes in this regulatory regime might make it more compatible with party strength.

Regulating Campaign Finance

Of all the problems encountered during the long history of presidential campaigns and elections, "none has become more troublesome than that of providing adequate financial support for campaigns" and of removing the taint of "shoddiness" from political finance. Thus concluded President John F. Kennedy's Commission on Campaign Costs in 1962.[1] Congressional and other studies during the 1950s and 1960s also found the costs of campaigns to be spiraling and the spending limits and disclosure requirements of the Federal Corrupt Practices Act of 1925 to be antiquated and unenforceable. The first major legislative breakthrough did not come until 1971, when Congress approved the Federal Election Campaign Act (FECA), a measure limiting media spending by presidential and congressional candidates and requiring the detailed reporting of contributions and expenditures. At the same time the Revenue Act of 1971 provided tax credits (and, until the law was revised in 1978, tax deductions) for political contributions and a one-dollar tax checkoff to subsidize presidential general election campaigns. To avoid President Richard Nixon's threatened veto, the latter provision was made inapplicable to the 1972 election.

It was the Watergate revelations, however, that provided the decisive impetus for reform. In their wake Congress passed the Federal Election Campaign Act Amendments of 1974, a far-reaching measure that set austere spending and contribution limits for the campaigns of federal candidates, strengthened disclosure requirements, established a scheme of public financing for presidential primary and general election campaigns, and created the Federal Election Commission (FEC) to enforce the law. Although the Senate also approved public funding of congressional campaigns, the House did not, and this provision was dropped from the final version of the legislation. President Gerald Ford was unenthusiastic about the public financing of presidential elections and many other provisions of the FECA Amendments of 1974, but he nonetheless signed the bill. "The times," he said, "demand this legislation." [2]

The Supreme Court in 1976 determined that major portions of the new law were unconstitutional. In *Buckley* v. *Valeo* the Court ruled that campaign spending limits, and restrictions on the amount of their own money that candidates could spend, represented unconstitutional limitations on freedom of expression, except when they were applied to candidates who voluntarily had accepted public funding. The Court also affirmed that "independent" expenditures by individuals and groups (that is, expenditures not "coordinated" with candidates or their organizations) could not be limited. On the other hand, limits on individual and group contributions to campaigns were upheld as "only a marginal restriction upon the contributor's ability to engage in free communication." [3] The Court also sustained the 1974 law's disclosure and public funding provisions.

The FECA Amendments of 1976 brought the 1971 and 1974 legislation into line with the *Buckley* opinion. They also provided detailed rules for solicitation of funds by corporate and union political action committees (PACs), which the earlier legislation had legitimated. Renewed attempts in 1977 and later years to provide public funding for congressional campaigns failed; this meant, under the terms of the Court's ruling, that limits on contributions but not on expenditures applied to these contests.

The 1976 presidential race tested the campaign finance reforms for the first time. Some $24 million in matching funds were provided to contenders in the Democratic and Republican presidential primaries. In the general election, each major candidate's organization received a grant of $21.8 million and was forbidden to raise or spend additional funds; the national parties, however, were permitted to spend an additional $3.2 million each on behalf of their presidential contenders. The combined total for general election spending reached approximately $50 million, considerably less than the $90 million spent by Nixon and George McGovern in 1972. While such reductions in overall spending were in accord with the FECA's objectives, it was widely recognized that certain types of traditional campaign activity had been inadvertently restricted. Both the stringency of campaign budgets and the necessity of accounting for the expenditures of state and local units led the presidential campaign organizations to discourage activities at those levels. Thus, Congress approved the Federal Election Campaign Act Amendments of 1979, a relatively noncontroversial measure simplifying reporting requirements and permitting state and local organizations to carry out voter registration, get-out-the-vote, and other "volunteer" activities on behalf of the national ticket without restriction.

More controversial matters, such as public financing for congressional campaigns and limitations on the amount candidates could receive from PACs, were put on the back burner in 1979, where they have remained ever since. But the continuing escalation of congressional campaign costs and the increased volume of PAC contributions and "independent" expenditures have prompted renewed interest in such measures, both in Congress and in reform-minded groups such as Common Cause. The Republican National Committee's Committee to Study Election Reform, chaired by RNC committeeman Ernest Angelo, in 1982 proposed numerous changes in the FEC's administrative and enforcement procedures and a general loosening of the restrictions applying to political parties. Additional proposals have been made by the bipartisan Campaign Finance Study Group from the Kennedy School of Government at Harvard University, which undertook major studies of the FECA's impact for the House Committee on House Administration after the 1976 election and for the Senate Rules and Administration Committee after 1980.[4]

Congress thus far has not acted on these various, often conflicting, proposals for change. Even critics of the FECA sometimes have been reluctant to amend it, lest changes be made that are even worse than the status quo. But discontent with the current system of financing campaigns is widespread enough and the existing law sufficiently flawed to make it likely that the FECA will be the object of renewed legislative battles in the near future. In this chapter we will assess the impact of the FECA on the parties and suggest changes in the law that would strengthen the parties' campaign role.

The FECA and the Parties

The major provisions of the Federal Election Campaign Act, as amended, are as follows:

- *Limits on contributions.* Individuals may give no more than $1,000 to a federal candidate for each primary, runoff, or general election in which he/she is engaged, and no more than $5,000 per year to a political committee; aggregate contributions to such candidates and committees may not exceed $25,000 annually. Political committees and most party organizations may give no more than $5,000 to a candidate per election and no more than $5,000 per year to another committee; here no aggregate limits apply.
- *Restrictions on expenditures.* Presidential candidates who accept public funding may spend no more than $10 million in the campaign for nomination and $20 million in the general election. Adjusted for inflation, these limits came to $14.7 and $29.4 million respectively in 1980. (Beyond these limits, candidates are permitted to raise and spend money to cover fund-raising expenses and the costs of complying with the law.) In addition, the national parties may each spend two cents per every member of the voting age population ($4.6 million in 1980) on behalf of their presidential nomi-

nees. State and national parties may each make expenditures based on population and consumer price index figures on behalf of House and Senate candidates. These limits ranged from $36,880 in several small states to $655,874 in California for Senate candidates in 1982. Limits were set at $18,440 for House candidates. No expenditure limits apply to the personal campaign organizations of congressional candidates.

- *Federal financing of presidential campaigns.* Candidates for nomination for president who qualify, by raising $5,000 (in contributions of no more than $250 each) in each of 20 states, may have every contribution of $250 or less matched, up to a total of one-half of the spending limit. In the general election the presidential aspirants of the major parties are funded up to the spending limit; candidates who accept such funding may not raise or spend additional funds, except to cover compliance costs. Minor party and independent candidates are eligible for funding according to a formula based on past or current votes received.

Neither Congress nor Common Cause and other groups pushing campaign finance reform intended to reduce the role of political parties in campaigns. In fact, several provisions reflect a degree of solicitude for the parties. The public financing provisions ensure a role for the national parties in presidential campaigns by giving to them alone the authority to raise and spend private money beyond the public subsidy. Parties, unlike other political committees, may make "coordinated" expenditures on behalf of congressional candidates beyond the $5,000 they may contribute to them directly. The parties also receive public funds ($4.4 million in 1980) to conduct their national conventions, and since 1978, national and state parties have been provided a bulk-mail rate that greatly facilitates voter contact and fund raising. Individuals are permitted to give $20,000 to national party committees and $5,000 to state and local parties, as opposed to the $1,000 that they may give to individual candidates. The 1979 amendments raised to $5,000 the spending threshold that triggered reporting requirements, thus relieving many local party organizations of these obligations, and they freed state and local parties to carry out grassroots organizational efforts on behalf of the national ticket without expenditure restrictions.

Despite such provisions, it is often claimed that campaign finance reforms have weakened the parties. Steven Stockmeyer, former executive director of the National Republican Congressional Committee (NRCC), contemptuously dismisses the proparty features of the FECA—"The law really only throws us a few small crumbs"—and argues that the law has, in fact, "accelerated the decline" of the parties.[5] Critics do not always agree on exactly which aspects of the law are harmful, but a number of the features of the regulatory regime established by the FECA contribute to a negative assessment.

First, most public subsidies flow to candidates rather than to parties. When Sen. Russell Long first attempted in 1966 to establish a tax checkoff for presidential campaign funding, his plan was attacked for placing inordinate power in the hands of the national party committees that would receive the funds. Subsequent versions of the proposal channeled the bulk of funds directly to the candidates. While the present law reserves a financial role in the general election for the national committees, it builds into the law the assumption that these committees are separate from and ancillary to the candidates' campaign organizations.

Second, the current system of prenomination financing has encouraged candidates to bypass party organizations and has contributed to party fragmentation. The parties have no role in certifying who is eligible for public funding. Eligibility is not difficult to establish; candidates must raise only $5,000 in small contributions in each of 20 states. In fact, the easy availability of public funds probably encourages a proliferation of hopeful candidates. But fund raising in general has become more demanding; the need for "up-front" money to make an early impact, coupled with the stringent limits on how much individuals can give, forces candidates to begin serious fund raising and organizing in many states at least a year before the first primary. Thus, the finance laws, in addition to other factors—such as the proliferation and "front-loading" of primaries, rules assuring primary/caucus losers a share of delegates, and the media's early focus on the "horse race" aspects of the nomination contest—have contributed to the system described in Chapter 7: a prolonged nomination process, characterized by a large number of candidates organizing early campaigns in a highly individualistic fashion. It is not a process that enhances the party's role.

Third, provisions for the funding of third-party and independent candidates promote electoral fragmentation. John Anderson's 1980 presidential campaign starkly pointed up many of the act's weaknesses. Since Anderson's eligibility for funds depended on his performance in the general election, he could not get the money during the campaign period when he needed it most. The act then compelled him to *stay* in the race because otherwise he could not qualify for postelection public funding with which to pay his debts. And having established his effort (too easily) as the "functional equivalent of a party" in 1980, he has assured funding and a strong incentive to run again in 1984. The act should give third-party candidates a fair chance to compete, but it should not throw up barriers to their withdrawal or provide strong incentives for them to run again, unless they are linked to a genuine, ongoing party organization. As the Campaign Finance Study Group concludes:

> We do not feel that campaign laws should lightly encourage third party and independent candidates. Public funding should not be used to fragment unduly the national consensus, by making it more likely that presidents will be elected with less than a majority of the votes.... The act leaned too far [in the 1980 campaign period] towards a "closed door" provision and, for the 1984 elections, it now leans too far toward encouraging fragmentation.[6]

Fourth, campaign finance regulation has enhanced the role of PACs at the potential expense of the parties. The Federal Election Campaign Act of 1971, Edwin Epstein argues, "is the foundation-stone of the PAC explosion of the 1970s."[7] The act permitted corporations and unions to communicate on political matters with their stockholders and members respectively; to conduct nonpartisan registration and get-out-the-vote campaigns within these constituencies; and to establish and administer a "separate segregated fund" (that is, a PAC) to be utilized for political purposes. The 1974 amendments confirmed that restrictions on contributions or expenditures by government contractors did not preclude the formation of PACs by unions and corporations, and the 1976 amendments established liberal conditions for financial solicitation by PACs and for the utilization of payroll deduction plans. As we will see, these changes in the law have been followed by a rapid proliferation of PACs, particularly in the corporate sector, and by substantial increases in both the absolute amount and relative share of campaign funds coming from PAC sources.

There is considerable debate as to the causes and consequences of PAC proliferation. PACs were being organized well before the FECA was adopted; several of the act's provisions, in fact, were pushed by organized labor as a means of legitimating existing practices. But the FECA's encouragement of PACs—coupled with restrictions on what businessmen and others could give as individuals, and concerns on the part of business and the professions to protect their interests against an increasingly active government—created a fertile field for PAC growth. Furthermore, the *Buckley* decision, in opening up the "independent expenditure" loophole, gave to certain kinds of ideological and single-issue PACs the prospect of a greatly expanded campaign role, free of the rules constraining candidates and parties.

PACs may have had little to do, directly, with the decline of party roles and resources. "At the most," Frank Sorauf argues, "PACs have only nudged the parties' downward slide." [8] Nevertheless, PACs have emerged as major competitors of the parties in financing campaigns, aggregating interests, and claiming the attention and loyalty of candidates and officeholders. Hence the widespread perception that the FECA, in unleashing PACs, has hurt the parties.

Fifth, low contribution limits, some have claimed, damage the parties by eliminating their most reliable sources of funds and ignoring their distinctive role vis-à-vis PAC and other nonparty organizations. Parties, Austin Ranney notes, have characteristically relied on "their long-term connections with wealthy donors, not on their ability to inspire and capitalize on short-term enthusiasm for issues or candidates of the moment.... The FECA has largely rendered obsolete the money-raising techniques most suitable for party organizations and put a premium on [direct-mail] techniques most suitable for nonparty—indeed, antiparty— groups dedicated to ideological causes and candidates." [9] The fund-raising successes of the Republican party since the late 1970s suggest that this indictment must be qualified. But the structure of contribution limits still fails to give parties the advantages it might. Although individuals may give $20,000 to a national party committee, they may give no more to a state party than they may give to a PAC or other nonparty committee ($5,000). Similarly, state and national party organizations can contribute only $5,000—no more than a PAC—to each of their own federal candidates.

Sixth, expenditure limits may lead candidates to eliminate those aspects of campaigns in which parties traditionally have specialized. We have already seen how the rise of television as the dominant campaign medium has reduced the role of party organizations. Austere limits on public funding and spending may compound this effect, leading candidates to emphasize television advertising as the sine qua non of a viable campaign and the most certain way of reaching the maximum number of voters. To this are added problems of control. As Gerald Ford's campaign chief testified after the 1976 election:

> One of the major results of the spending limitations has been to encourage the development of highly centralized campaign organizations with elaborate controls over spending.... The experience of the Ford campaign in 1976 showed conclusively that it was easier to discourage grass-roots activity than to try to control and report it. In previous campaigns, it was possible to tell a local campaign or party official to go ahead with a project as long as he could raise the money to finance it. Now, federal law places a premium on actively discouraging such activity because of the danger that it could well lead to a violation of contribution or spending limits in the primary. Furthermore, in the general election, because no contributions are permitted once federal funds become available, it is even more important to discourage such activity.[10]

The 1979 FECA amendments addressed this problem and helped alleviate it, but many of the incentives that candidate organizations have to short-change and constrain state and local party operations remain.

Finally, the FECA has restricted the ability of state and local parties to pursue their own campaign strategies and has created disincentives for their involvement in presidential and congressional campaigns. State and local party organizations are permitted to maintain separate federal and nonfederal accounts. This has certain advantages. It often allows them to avoid reporting requirements because they are not obligated to report until contributions or expenditures in the segregated federal account reach the relevant threshold; if the funds were combined they would reach the threshold at an earlier point. Moreover, in instances where state law is less restrictive than federal law, the separate account allows organizations to enjoy that greater latitude in their nonfederally-related activities. But the need to keep the nonfederal account "clean," and a desire to avoid a complicated prorating of expenses between accounts, also can encourage party organizations to forego involvement in federal campaigns.

Expenditure limitations sometimes have a similar effect. The limits on expenditures on behalf of congressional candidates apply to the state party and its subunits collectively. A local party that wishes to include its U.S. Senate candidate in a newspaper advertisement therefore is required to coordinate that expenditure with the state party. The situation is even more complicated with regard to the presidential candidate: here any such expenditure that does not fall within the exempted category of volunteer activity is technically subject to the overall spending limitation imposed on the *national* party committee. Such complexity invites evasion, but it also has an unmistakably chilling effect on party participation in federal campaigns.

Party Fund Raising

The FECA has posed serious problems for the parties, problems that largely offset the positive provisions Congress made for parties in the legislation. But the performance of the national and state parties since the legislation was passed has been stronger, particularly on the Republican side, than one might have expected. It is therefore important to consider, not simply the impact of this or that provision on the parties' standard operating procedures, but also the extent to which the parties have been able to adapt successfully to new circumstances that the FECA has helped create. If the law constricts the role of the parties' biggest donors, it also creates a larger potential pool of substantial donors, freeing up money that formerly was given to candidates before the law limited or forbade such gifts. And of course the law places a premium on the mobilization of large numbers of small donors. In other words, opportunities and incentives as well as constraints have been created by the FECA. The responses of the parties suggest that it is legislation they can live with, although it does not by any means do all that it might to enhance party strength.

The impact of the FECA can only be estimated in light of the role played by the parties before reform. Presidential and congressional campaigns during the fifties and sixties generally found neither party in the driver's seat. In the 1972 presidential campaign, the last before federal financing, the Democratic National Committee spent approximately $4.5 million on the presidential race while the Republican National Committee spent some $6 million.[11] This represents about the same share of presidential campaign spending that the current law allows, and suggests that the financial dominance of the candidates' personal organizations developed long before the campaign finance reforms went on the books. The national Democratic party was in a particularly weak financial position. Having assumed debts from Hubert Humphrey's and Robert Kennedy's 1968 campaigns, the DNC was more than $9 million in debt at the time the FECA was adopted. It can be argued that campaign finance reform, far from sending the national Democratic party into further eclipse, actually effected a partial financial rescue.

The argument that the parties have adapted successfully to the new campaign finance environment is strongest for the GOP. As we saw in Table 2-2, $190 million flowed into the federal accounts of the three national Republican committees in the 1981-1982 election cycle, an increase of almost 50 percent over their 1979-1980 total and more than six times as much as the Democrats raised. Over $27 million of this, almost as much as the Democrats raised altogether, came from contributions of $500 or more. The RNC's "Eagles," persons pledging $10,000 or more, numbered 865 in 1979-1980 and 1,100 in 1981-1982. But the bulk of the GOP's money comes from small gifts in response to direct-mail solicitation, which has grown enormously since its beginnings under Ray Bliss's tenure at the RNC in the 1960s. Nor has it shown any signs of leveling off: the three national Republican committees managed to almost double their donor bases between 1980 and 1982. During 1981-1982 some 1.6

million individuals gave to the RNC alone; the average contribution was $26, somewhat modifying the GOP's traditional "fat cat" image.

As we have seen, this war chest financed extensive institutional advertising, media production, polling, field organization, and candidate services. It also enabled the Republicans to give $18.6 million to their candidates in 1981-1982, up 25 percent from 1979-1980 despite the absence of a presidential candidate. The NRCC contributed at least $10,000, and in most cases considerably more, to all of its House incumbents and to some 165 challengers in 1982. For 85 House candidates and most of the party's Senate candidates the national committees "maxed out," that is, spent all that the law allowed. Under the "agency agreements" that the FEC permits and the courts have upheld (despite a Democratic challenge),[12] national committees may pick up the contribution and expenditure entitlements of state committees. Thus, for most House candidates in 1982, the NRCC could contribute $20,000 directly ($5,000 at the national and the state level, for the primary and general elections respectively) and make $36,880 (twice the national committee limit) in coordinated expenditures. For Senate candidates, the party contribution limit was $17,500 at the national and $5,000 at the state level, and far more generous coordinated-expenditure limits applied; seven Republican Senate candidates received more than $400,000 in party funds in 1982.[13]

Although the $28.4 million raised by the three national Democratic committees in 1981-1982 appears paltry when compared with GOP fund raising, it is somewhat more impressive when compared with where the party was a few years ago, particularly in its direct-mail operations. A greater proportion of Democratic contributions still comes from large givers (22 percent of 1981-1982 receipts were gifts of $500 or more, compared with 14 percent of Republican receipts), although the GOP has more such contributors. But the Democratic committees have made a long-delayed start toward expanding their donor base. Contributions to both the Democratic House and Senate campaign committees tripled between 1979-1980 and 1981-1982, and the House committee was especially successful in expanding its direct-mail operations (see Table 2-2). The Senate campaign committee, still raising most of its money from larger gifts, was able to give $2.4 million to its candidates, "maxing out" on seven. But these were mainly from small lowlimit states; only five Democratic Senate candidates received as much as $100,000 from their party. The Democratic Congressional Campaign Committee (DCCC) was able to give, or to stimulate contributions of, $1.1 million to 126 incumbents and 163 challengers but was not generally able to assume expenditure entitlements from the states. Still, the 1982 performance suggests that Democrats have "firmly accepted that drastic changes in their operations are in order and have started down the path that Republicans first walked almost a decade ago."[14]

How promising is the financial role pioneered by the GOP as a path to party renewal? It is often said that fund raising by direct mail threatens the traditional ideological breadth and moderation of the par-

ties because it requires a certain amount of oversimplification and alarm-
ism to be effective. As one Republican fund-raiser said:

> One thing that concerns moderate Republicans is that in off-election
> years, the direct mail has to go right wing.... The Democrats can go to
> the left for collecting money and the Republicans go to the right.... You
> can run campaigns in the center, but that's no way to raise money.[15]

Or as one of the DNC's direct-mail consultants put it in a speech that
gave party regulars mixed feelings:

> The approach the DNC used to take—mealy-mouthed, general letters—
> got nowhere. People give because they're angry or alarmed. The New
> Right knows this, and we're learning.[16]

Others, while not denying that extremist appeals work for some
groups and candidates, point to the GOP experience as proof that more
moderate appeals, properly targeted, also can stimulate widespread giving. "While I concede that our direct mail sometimes employs a somewhat negative tone," NRCC Director Steven Stockmeyer said at a conference in 1979, "we have not used more than two or three single-issue
appeals out of the ten or twelve mailings we have done each year for the
past five years. Our most successful mailings this year have concerned a
poll of choices for the Republican presidential nomination and a rather
bland appeal for our contributors to renew their membership." [17] But
while accepting Stockmeyer's characterization of NRCC appeals, political
scientist David Adamany refused to take any comfort in it on the Democrats' behalf. His analysis of the demographic basis of the GOP's successes led him to conclude that the Democrats could never match them:

> The party-oriented successes [of the Republicans] ought not to be
> confused with the fund-raising programs of ideological candidates and
> groups. Although mail techniques characterize both, they are not the
> same. The Republican fund-raising successes have been possible because
> the GOP was a more narrowly class-based party than was the Demo-
> cratic party, and it encompassed the nation's professional and mana-
> gerial classes. Hence, it was able to project a clearer, though moderate,
> issue posture that appealed to persons with the education, motivation,
> and means to make contributions. Moreover, the structures of corpora-
> tions and professional associations constituted preexisting networks
> through which Republican fund solicitations could be made. None of
> these conditions prevail in the Democratic party, a loosely joined coali-
> tion, which has raised its funds from unions, from businesses whose
> fortunes were particularly linked to the Democrats ... from wealthy and
> middle-class apostates from class and caste, and from patronage employ-
> ees. These groups are not susceptible to national, party-oriented appeals,
> by mail or otherwise. It is only when Democrats—such as George Mc-
> Govern or Tom Hayden—assume the role of ideological leaders of polar
> factions within the Democratic party that they can emulate Republican
> fund-raising techniques.[18]

The Democrats may be able to do better than this analysis suggests.
To compete effectively they need not reach absolute parity with the
GOP. Moreover, it is important not to oversell direct mail as the key to
party renaissance. At least for the Democrats, it seems unlikely to pro-

duce adequate resources unless generously supplemented with other fund-raising methods. It does encourage negative and oversimplified policy stances and the direction of appeals to issue-activists within the party—which may compromise the party's moderate mainstream appeal. And while the resources it produces may underwrite more aggressive campaigns and tie candidates and officeholders more closely to the party, it offers little to the party as a membership and mediating institution at the local level. Direct-mail giving is an especially remote and private sort of participation. It can furnish the parties with essential resources, but other kinds of financial and organizational mechanisms will be needed to engage the loyalty and labor of their constituents.

PACs and Independent Expenditures

The party role in campaign finance, even on the Republican side, begins to look less impressive when one considers the overall increases in campaign costs ($350 million was spent on congressional races in 1982, up 80 percent from the 1978 midterm election) and the expanded role of political action committees. The number of PACs has increased almost sixfold since 1974, with the most pronounced growth (from 89 to 1,467) in the corporate sector. Some 2,650 PACs contributed $83.1 million to congressional campaigns in 1981-1982, an increase of more than 50 percent in just two years. The National Association of Realtors headed the list with contributions totaling $2.1 million; the American Medical Association, United Auto Workers, International Association of Machinists and Aerospace Workers, National Education Association, and National Association of Home Builders each topped $1,000,000 in their giving.

The role of PACs in congressional campaign financing has increased steadily in relative as well as absolute terms during the past decade. The share of House candidates' receipts coming from PACs has increased in a step-by-step fashion, from 16 percent in 1972 to 28 percent in 1980 and 30 percent in 1982. The PAC share of Senate candidates' receipts reached a record 19 percent in 1980. National and state party contributions, by no means dominant before the FECA (estimates of the party share of House candidates' receipts in 1972 vary from 11 to 17 percent), became even less significant as overall spending rose and PAC proliferation progressed; party funds accounted for only 6 percent of House candidates' receipts in 1980 and 1982. Republican efforts brought the party share of contributions for its candidates up to 10 percent for the House and 15 percent for the Senate in 1982; comparable figures for the Democrats were 2 percent party funds for House candidates, 4 percent for Senate candidates.[19]

PAC involvement in the 1980 congressional election attracted notice, not only because of its extent (the volume of contributions was up 62 percent from 1978), but also because of certain shifts in patterns of giving. "For the most part the people who run PACs are not gamblers," observed Rep. Richard Cheney in 1979. But they became considerably more willing to support congressional challengers in 1980. This was especially true of corporate and associational PACs, each of whom easily outdistanced labor in their giving for the first time.[20] The national Republican committees developed aggressive programs to attract PAC support for their candidates. The Democratic party, by virtue of its labor support and incumbent status, traditionally has received a higher percentage of PAC contributions to congressional campaigns than the GOP has. But its 55-45 percent advantage in 1978 slipped to 52-48 in 1980. Speculation that "a turning point in group mobilization" had been reached proved premature, however. Democrats regained a 54-46 advantage over the Republicans in PAC giving in 1982. Labor giving increased substantially and was targeted more effectively, and overall PAC giving swung back toward incumbents (66 percent of contributions, compared with 61 percent in 1980). As Larry Sabato explained:

> Corporate and trade PACs lost their zest for Republican challengers for three primary reasons. First, business PACs had a major stake in the freshman Republican House class, who had first been elected in 1980 in part thanks to "challenger" PAC targeting and financing. Quite naturally, PACs sought to shelter their earlier prize investment. Secondly, the election handicappers in the PAC world and in the press saw 1982 as being at least a mildly Democratic year, which encouraged corporate PACs even more to protect vulnerable GOP incumbents and also, where possible, to swim with the Democratic tide rather than make enemies unnecessarily. Thirdly, the Democrats made adjustments in their own campaign and legislative strategy to attract corporate and trade PAC money, although their efforts met with only limited success.[21]

Another trend that attracted widespread attention in 1980 continued apace in 1982: the growth of "independent" expenditures by PACs apart from any formal collaboration with the candidate being assisted. Such spending added $12.2 million to the total spent on Ronald Reagan's behalf in 1980; of this, $10.6 million, equivalent to more than one-third of the supposedly inclusive public subsidy, was spent in the general election. (Independent spending for Carter and Anderson, by contrast, totaled only $46,000 and $199,000 respectively.) Independent expenditures also figured prominently in the campaigns *against* Democratic liberals in the Senate. The chief targets were Frank Church of Idaho ($339,000 in negative independent expenditures) and George McGovern of South Dakota ($222,000); more than $100,000 also was spent against John Culver (Iowa), Alan Cranston (California), Birch Bayh (Indiana), and Thomas Eagleton (Missouri). Of these senators, only Cranston and Eagleton were reelected.

Most of the Senate expenditures were made by the National Conservative Political Action Committee (NCPAC), which added $1 million in congressional spending to the $2.3 million it spent on Reagan's behalf. The other top spenders were Sen. Jesse Helms's National Congressional Club ($4.6 million on Reagan's behalf), the Fund for a Conservative Majority ($3.1 million for Reagan), and two groups formed explicitly to raise money for the Reagan cause, Americans for an Effective Presidency ($1.3 million) and Americans for Change ($712,000).

The amount of independent spending on congressional races increased from $2.3 million in 1980 to $5.7 million in 1982 (91 percent of it by some 70 PACs, the rest by other individuals and groups). The top spenders were again NCPAC ($3.2 million) and the Fund for a Conservative Majority ($390,000), plus the Citizens Organized to Replace Kennedy ($349,000). About 80 percent of this money was spent "negatively," against rather than for candidates. Among the 87 targets of this spending, the chief victims were Senators Edward Kennedy of Massachusetts ($1.1 million) and Paul Sarbanes of Maryland ($698,000), plus the Democrats' party leaders, Speaker Tip O'Neill ($301,000) and Minority Leader Robert Byrd ($270,000). In contrast to the 1980 pattern, however, none of the most prominent targets was defeated.[22]

Independent spending differs from other PAC financial activity in important respects. It is more ideologically motivated (overwhelmingly right-wing), more often negative than supportive, and less likely to benefit incumbents. It also is unlimited by the law, thanks to the 1976 *Buckley* decision and to *Common Cause* v. *Schmitt*, a more recent decision in which the Supreme Court (on a 4-4 division) let stand a district court ruling that the First Amendment prohibits limits on independent expenditures even for a presidential candidate who accepts public funding.[23] Although independent spending is supposedly carried out independently of the candidate or his party, those who wish to be helpful can generally obtain the information they need. As Jesse Helms, the head of 1980's top independent-spending PAC, put it when he was asked whether he had conferred with Reagan:

> Well, as you may know, we have had an independent effort going on in North Carolina. The law forbids me to consult with him, and it's been an awkward situation. I've had to sort of talk indirectly with Paul Laxalt [Reagan's campaign chairman] and hope that he would pass along, uh, and I think the messages have got through all right.[24]

The proliferation of PACs and the growth of their role in campaign financing, which was facilitated if not prompted by the FECA, is not a development that augurs well for the parties. It threatens the efforts of parties to make campaigns more party-centered, to highlight broad partisan appeals, to invest the party label with renewed meaning. The escalation of campaign costs, coupled with the availability of PAC money and the unavailability of sufficient funds from other sources, has touched off a scramble for PAC funds that accentuates the entrepreneurial, individualistic campaign styles described in Chapter 3. It also heightens the officeholder's inclination to think of "representation" as a matter of accommodating and balancing the interests of organized groups, as opposed to responding to those broader interests that parties supposedly articulate. This is not to say, of course, that members will be inclined to vote with their PAC supporters down the line. But the need to attract and retain their support can hardly strengthen the member's responsiveness to the organized party or to party leaders in government.

Although PAC giving may pull candidates to and fro and complicate the development of coordinated partisan approaches, it is channeled through mechanisms subject to candidate or party control. The same is not true of independent spending. These expenditures underwrite free-wheeling appeals to the electorate that are often misleading or confusing and generally contain no partisan reference. They can play havoc with candidate or party campaign strategies. While acknowledging that his party's candidates had thus far received most of the benefits from independent expenditures, RNC Chairman Richard Richards described the operation of these groups as the "greatest single threat [to] party responsibility. . . . They interject themselves into campaigns and work all kinds of mischief." [25] Such efforts can threaten even favored candidates by making exaggerated or otherwise counter-productive appeals on their behalf; certainly it reduces the account-ability of candidates for their own campaigns and dilutes their partisan content.

Campaign Finance and State Parties

The 1979 FECA amendments had a marked impact on levels of campaign activity and spending in 1980, although it was not always clear that the prime beneficiaries were the state and local parties the legisla-tion was supposed to invigorate. Under these amendments, which permit-ted unlimited "volunteer" activities by state and local parties to promote the national ticket, Republicans raised and spent some $15 million in 1980, an amount equivalent to half of their federal subsidy. The Demo-crats raised only $4 million for these purposes, although they benefited from registration and get-out-the-vote drives conducted by organized labor.[26]

From the reformer's perspective, these "soft money" provisions might seem to be a massive loophole, allowing private funds again to flow into presidential campaigns. Elizabeth Drew suggests that that is exactly what both parties had in mind in pushing the amendments, despite their "high-minded" talk about local "party building." It was the Republicans who developed the more aggressive program for "raising large sums of money from individuals and corporations and funnelling it into states where it would have the most impact." A single state party fund-raiser in Texas, attended by candidate Reagan, produced $3 million for newly permitted party activities. The definition of "volunteer activity" was loose enough to permit the financing of professionally managed phone banks, voter-registration drives, and election-day canvasses. Since certain portions of this activity could be funded out of nonfederal state party accounts, individuals and corporations often could contribute, subject only to the often minimal constraints of state law. "Soft money," one lobbyist told Drew, "is where rich people can play again." [27]

Critics such as Drew are too quick, however, to condemn all loop-holes in the FECA indiscriminately. The 1980 experience suggests that the law, as written and administered, may be open to abuse; certainly contributions to large voter-mobilization efforts on behalf of the national ticket should be subject to the FECA's limits and disclosure require-ments. But to regard the 1979 amendments simply as a loophole is to beg important questions: if private and party money have *any* role to play in presidential elections, then one must ask through what channels that money is best raised and spent. The 1974 law, while providing an ancil-lary role for national party committees, clearly tended to remove state and local parties and their voter-contact activities from the presidential campaign. Assuming that some "loopholes" for party initiatives are desirable, the 1979 provisions seem, on balance, to be well conceived. They open up the possibility of a significant campaign role for state and local organizations and make the presidential campaign a less centrally controlled, media-dominated affair.

This is not to say that the 1979 amendments have been an unqualified success from the standpoint of state and local party building. Republican state and local parties often found themselves to be junior partners at best in a nationally financed and directed effort. The RNC's "Commitment '80," an elaborate program to organize neighborhood meetings and to send volunteers door-to-door, did not meet its planners' expectations; it demonstrated the difficulty of implementing such activities where functioning grass-roots structures are not already in place.[28] Nevertheless, these programs gave state and local parties organizational resources and a role they would not otherwise have had in the national effort. Coupled with the RNC's other consultation and support services for state parties, "soft money" helped underwrite ongoing party programs and defray overhead expenses. In both parties, stronger and more self-sufficient state organizations were able to use the 1979 "loophole" precisely as its authors intended—to overcome the FECA's segregation of presidential races from other races and to implement voter-contact programs on behalf of the entire ticket.

Turning from the FECA, one finds extensive additional regulation of political finance at the state level—much of it, like the federal statute, dating from the 1970s. In all 50 states the disclosure of campaign contributions and expenditures is now required, and in all of these except Alabama, South Carolina, and Wyoming a report must be filed before the date of the election in question. Expenditure limitations were enacted in half the states by 1976, but *Buckley* v. *Valeo* and similar state court decisions required the abolition or alteration of almost all of these statutes. The amounts individuals can contribute to candidates is limited in 25 states; in a number of these, the limits are higher or are removed altogether for political parties. Twenty-five states ban and 11 limit direct corporate contributions, while 10 prohibit and 10 limit union contributions. The political action committee, however, is almost universally accepted as a vehicle for unions or corporations that wish to give. In addition, 16 states provide public funding of elections in one form or another, and 17 permit state tax credits or deductions for political contributions.[29]

Of these laws, public funding has the most obvious impact on the health of the parties. As Table 5-1 indicates, eight states—Idaho, Iowa, Kentucky, Maine, North Carolina, Oklahoma, Rhode Island, and Utah—channel these funds wholly or substantially through political parties. In most of these states, funds are distributed to the parties according to the preferences "checked off" by taxpayers on their returns. Some of the statutes restrict the uses to which parties may put the funds—forbidding candidate support in Rhode Island, for example, and permitting only candidate support in Idaho—but most give the parties wide discretion. The rate of taxpayer participation has been lowest (generally 4 percent or less) in those states where checking-off increases one's tax liability. In most states, where the checked-off $1 or $2 is taken from tax already paid, participation rates have averaged around 20 percent, slightly lower than those registered at the federal level. However, only in Michigan and New Jersey, both of which give funds to candidates rather than parties, have checked-off funds proved sufficient to provide anything approaching total public financing of gubernatorial elections.[30]

Public funding can increase the resources of the parties, enhance their campaign role, and foster the kind of organizational development described in Chapter 2. None of the states provides for total public funding; such a removal of the need to raise funds, in fact, would remove an important spur to party organization and outreach. But a base of public support can help the parties stabilize their operations and reduce the need for them to compete with candidates for campaign funds. North Carolina's experience is indicative of the ways such plans can strengthen state parties. Although the participation rate of North Carolina's taxpayers has been atypically low, public funds have provided both parties with about one-fourth of their revenue over the two-year budget cycle, plus a like amount to be disbursed among or spent on behalf of the parties' statewide and congressional candidates. Checkoff funds enabled the state Democratic party to purchase a computer in 1978; this in turn permitted the party to multiply its resources through direct-mail Sustaining Fund solicitations and to provide targeting and other data for registration and voter-contact programs. Checkoff funds then enabled the party to coordinate and produce data-processing backup for statewide get-out-the-vote programs in 1980 and 1982. Public funding, in other words, helped the state party reach a critical threshold of financial viability and, by placing key resources in the party's hands, gave candidates new incentives to cooperate with one another and to work through the party structure.

At the state as at the national level, campaign finance reform has affected not only the parties' campaign capacities but also their patterns of internal organization. Federal and state reporting requirements have caused local organizations to turn to the state parties as sources of advice and expertise. This kind of contact is not invariably positive, however. Although it can give the state party an important service to perform, it also can identify the state party in the minds of its local units with obligations and restrictions that they often resent. Interdependence of a more positive sort is fostered by public financing when it is channeled through the state parties. These funds support the development of voter-contact programs beyond what local resources would permit and allow the state organization to shape and monitor these programs to maximize their effectiveness.

Refining the Law

At a time when the FECA is being criticized on many fronts and numerous proposals for its revision are afloat, it is important to consider what implications various changes might have for the party system. We will briefly examine a range of major and minor proposals, all of which bear some promise for increasing party strength.

(1) *Adopt partial public financing of congressional campaigns, with funding channeled through the state parties.* There are a number of good reasons for putting this, the FECA's major missing component, on the statute books. One such reason is the way a properly designed statute could enhance the parties' role. Careful design is important, however; a public funding law that bypassed the parties could weaken them further.

Such a law probably should be applied, at least initially, at the general election stage only. The parties could be provided grants to support their nominees, matching on a 1-1 or 2-1 basis the funds privately raised by the parties and their candidates. Appropriate safeguards could be written into such the law, as Herbert Alexander suggests:

> One might be a requirement that a certain percentage of the total fund for each state party be reserved for House campaigns—varying of course with the needs to fund statewide Senate contests; further, a major share of this House campaign fund might be required to be divided equally among all of the party's certified House candidates as "floor" or base grants, thus assuring these candidates the threshold access to the voters that is a principal rationale for public funding in the first place; and there might even be a requirement that a good portion of the funds set aside for the parties' discretionary use go to activities that tend to benefit all candidates equally—for example, voter registration, issues awareness, and the like. . . . Congress would doubtless want to move with caution and due regard for equity—in order to help bring the parties more centrally into the process, without at the same time reducing the candidates' independence too much too fast.[31]

At the same time, parties would retain sufficient discretion to target key races for special attention and to invest heavily in local efforts at organization and voter mobilization.

Organizing campaign finance in this way should strengthen the partisan component in campaigning and voting; strengthen the authority, influence, and resource base of party organizations; and heighten party awareness and cohesion in government. It also would dilute the impact of the parties' institutional competitors—PACs and "independent" spenders. Reform advocates often have proposed countering those competitors more directly, for example by combining public funding with severe limits on the amount of money candidates can receive from PACs. Such additional steps should be taken with caution, however. Gary Jacobson's work shows conclusively that, while public funding has the potential for making congressional elections more competitive, tying that funding to low ceilings on candidate spending or to severe restrictions on individual or group giving would have the opposite effect. Incumbents start with tremendous advantages in name recognition and staff resources; challengers (and their parties) must raise and spend *more* if they are to compete effectively. "Any reform measure which decreases spending by the candidates will favor incumbents," [32] and socking in incumbents, even beyond their present 90 percent reelection rate, is hardly the way to strengthen the party in government or anywhere else.

There is also the question of effectiveness. Limiting the amounts candidates could receive from a given source, such as PACS, might divert rather than stem the flow of money. "Proliferation of political action committees, perfectly legal cooperation among PACs, and a rapid expansion in independent expenditures by PACs are the clearly predictable consequences," according to the Campaign Finance Study Group.[33] This is not to say that contribution or expenditure limits have no place at all in the regulation of campaign finance. But it is to suggest that legally restricting the role of the parties' institutional competitors may be less effective and more problematic than diluting their influence by other means. One such means would be public funding, channeled through the parties. By providing a solid "floor" of assured funding, public funding would lessen candidate dependence on PACs and on private sources in general. It also would strengthen the parties as counterweights to PACs, enhancing their claims on candidate loyalty and their role in shaping campaign strategy.

(2) *Increase public support of the national parties.* A portion of the Federal Election Campaign Fund (the repository for national tax checkoff monies), equivalent to what the national committees are now given every fourth year to run their conventions, could be given to the committees *each* year to give them a predictable and secure base for the maintenance of key campaign capabilities. Such support would not strain the fund unduly; its receipts have approached $40 million annually during the past several years, and it showed a balance of more than $100 million after the bills for 1980 were paid. If public funding for congressional elections were enacted (and that clearly should have priority over increased support of the national committees), the strains on the present checkoff system would be more severe, perhaps necessitating a move to a $2 checkoff and/or the tapping of additional revenue sources.

(3) *Provide free television time for party-sponsored presidential debates and other party presentations.* "I would urge Congress," Adlai Stevenson testified in 1960, "to say to the television industry: we reclaim for a few hours every four years the public airwaves." [34] While Congress has toyed with the idea of requiring the networks to furnish time to candidates, it has gone no further than to suspend the equal-time requirements of the Communications Act of 1934, thus enabling the networks to donate time for presidential debates. But such exercises should not be contingent on the whims and calculations of networks, or candidates, or sponsoring organizations. For all their flaws, candidate debates are far more effective than 30-second spots in exposing the candidates and exploring the issues, and other formats might be more effective yet in conveying the parties' messages. Public funds might be authorized to cover network or station costs, and provisions eventually might be made for debates among congressional candidates. But at a minimum, the parties should be responsible for staging presidential debates or comparable presentations, and public policy ought to compel or encourage the provision of television time for such events.

(4) *Revise the funding scheme for third-party and independent presidential candidates.* The proposal of the Campaign Finance Study

Group for a matching-fund scheme for such candidates, modeled on the existing prenomination public funding plan, is worthy of serious consideration.[35] It would give these candidates support when they most need it, while removing the prospect of funding as an inducement to stay in the race. The qualification threshold should be set high enough to discourage frivolous or narrowly based candidacies, and the terms for prospective funding in the *next* election should be heightened to ensure that only *genuine* parties qualify—that is, those that are on the ballot in a number of states and endorse candidates for a range of offices.

(5) *Selectively revise contribution limits upward.* The $1,000 limit on individual contributions to candidates, which has not even been adjusted for inflation since its enactment in 1974, has exacerbated problems as serious as those it was designed to cure. As Michael Malbin notes, the disappearance of large contributors has left candidates who are not personally wealthy with three main alternatives:

> ...tapping the Washington issue networks; spending huge blocks of time—much more than ever used to be spent at fund raising—at upper middle-class cocktail parties; or delegating work to professional fund-raising specialists, many of whom rely on direct mail techniques. Every one of these fund-raising methods has serious drawbacks. The Washington networks may not depend on campaign gifts for their power, but it seems unwise to structure the campaign laws in a way that forces candidates to go to them. Spending time with upper-middle-class voters is not in itself bad, but a candidate who spends too much time with any single class of voters is likely to end up with a distorted view of what the voters as a whole are thinking. Finally, anything that makes nationwide direct mail fund raising look tempting to a candidate must have harmful long-range effects on our politics, for it encourages those willing to play on the polarizing emotions that make direct mail work best. These effects make the evils of the old system, such as the alleged "sales" of ambassadorships, seem mild by comparison.[36]

Partial public funding would relieve some of these pressures for congressional candidates. In addition, limits for individual contributors should be raised to the $3,000-$5,000 range. This would help dilute the impact of PACs and would relieve some of the pressures for early and continual fund raising by candidates, particularly as they affect the presidential nomination process. At the same time the advantages of parties in receiving and making contributions should be increased; a good start would be to double what individuals can give to parties (although the $20,000 that applies to gifts to *national* parties is sufficient) and what parties can give to their candidates. Limits on contributions to and by PACs should *not* be changed.

(6) *Provide a tax credit for contributions to political parties separate from and equal to the credit available for candidate contributions and eliminate the credit now available for contributions to nonparty committees.* As the Campaign Finance Study Group pointed out in proposing such a measure, "the current tax code has the effect of forcing parties into competition with their own candidates over limited campaign dollars."[37] A separate credit would provide additional incentives to give

to the party, removing the trade-off against candidate contributions. At the same time, it is unclear why tax incentives should be provided for contributions to PACs and other committees which, unlike candidate and party committees, are neither accountable to the electorate nor performing a public electoral function.

(7) *Reconsider expenditure ceilings.* The courts have disallowed expenditure ceilings on candidates except at the presidential level (when the candidate has accepted public funding), and a number of critics have urged that they be raised or abolished even there. Certainly both the public subsidy/spending entitlement and allowable presidential spending by the national parties should be raised. Campaign costs have escalated more rapidly than the cost of living, the present limits have encouraged off-budget independent expenditures, and they have necessitated a complicated set of allowances whereby candidates can raise and spend money for fund-raising expenses, compliance costs, and so forth. Expenditure limits in presidential campaigns should not be entirely abolished, however. Reopening "the biggest game in town" for direct private contributions and unlimited spending would reduce the incentives that contributors have to give to the parties for other purposes and that candidate organizations have to channel money into "exempted" party activities.

The case for removing the limits on what parties can spend on behalf of individual congressional candidates at first seems much stronger, whether or not some sort of public funding is added to the mix. Assuming that spending will go on in any case, what reason is there to limit the amount that can flow through party channels? Does not such a limit on parties virtually guarantee a separate, probably dominant, role for candidates' personal campaign organizations? Certainly there is a strong case for increasing what national and state parties can spend for specific candidates, especially in House races. Paradoxically, however, to remove these limits altogether (or limits on party contributions to candidates) might weaken rather than strengthen the party's hand under certain circumstances. The effects would depend on the prior strength of the party organization and how susceptible it was to candidate control. The present party-expenditure limits in congressional races (and the limits on national committee presidential expenditures) can make the party less vulnerable to demands that it pour all its resources into the election of a specific candidate, or that its funds simply be used, no questions asked, to pay the bills for a specific campaign. Limits on expenditures for and contributions to individual candidates can protect party funds for organizational efforts, voter-contact, and other purposes. Thus the case for the complete removal of such limitations is not as simple as it is sometimes assumed to be.

(8) *Limit the use of "agency agreements."* Assuming that a system of expenditure entitlements continues, should the FECA's provision of *separate* entitlements for state and national parties also be retained? The Federal Election Commission's practice of permitting "agency agreements," whereby national committees may pick up state party contribution and spending entitlements, was challenged by the Democratic Senatorial Campaign Committee in 1980. The Supreme Court, reversing a

Court of Appeals decision, upheld the commission.[38] But this ruling threatens to undermine a major purpose of the expenditure entitlements—encouraging a campaign role for party organizations at both the state and national levels. Agency agreements, as the lower court put it, can make the state party no more than a "legal shell." Congress should raise these entitlements at both levels, but it also should make clear that one entitlement is not to be absorbed into the other. Provisions for unlimited transfers of funds between party committees would continue to give parties flexibility in targeting funds and in taking full advantage of contribution and expenditure entitlements, but without completely bypassing the state organizations.

(9) *Extend the exemptions from expenditure limitations granted by the 1979 FECA amendments to congressional elections and to a broader range of activities on behalf of the party ticket.* These amendments freed state and local organizations to organize voter-registration and get-out-the-vote drives. But there was considerable uncertainty concerning whether statewide expenditure limits permitted the inclusion of congressional candidates in such efforts. And for campaign initiatives that did not qualify as "volunteer" activities—for example, the inclusion of presidential and congressional candidates in party tabloids or in local newspaper advertisements—the law still created confusion and discouraged a unified party effort. Therefore, congressional campaigns should be included under the exemption, and the criterion for an exempted activity should be broadened to include not only "volunteer" activity but all campaign activity undertaken on behalf of a *ticket* of two or more candidates. This would remove useless constraints on state and local party activity and would encourage individual candidates to undertake cooperative campaign efforts under the party banner.

(10) *Expand state-level public funding beyond its current base of 16 states and channel all or most of these funds through state parties.* The case for partial public funding is as strong for statewide campaigns as it is for congressional races, and the two programs could be administered similarly. Funding statutes could contain safeguards for candidates and guarantees that funds would be spent for campaign purposes as opposed to mere organizational aggrandizement. They should be flexible enough, however, to enable the parties to invest in the year-round development of organizational and campaign capabilities.

(11) *Limit independent expenditures or at least dilute their impact.* The FECA Amendments of 1974 matched limits on contributions with a $1,000 limitation on a person's or a group's spending "relative to a clearly identified candidate." The Supreme Court upheld the contribution but not the expenditure limits in *Buckley* v. *Valeo*, arguing that independent-expenditure restrictions constricted freedoms of speech and association far more substantially than did limits on how much a person or group could give to a campaign organization.[39] This view has not gone unchallenged. In a dissenting opinion that agreed with the lower court decision, Justice Byron White argued that the two provisions were integrally related and that the First Amendment should stand in the way of neither. "Limiting independent expenditures is essential to prevent

transparent and widespread evasion of the contribution limits," he wrote. Moreover, White suggested, exempting independent spenders from the law was inequitable to those persons and groups who chose to work more directly with candidates and parties.[40]

As already noted, the Court in 1981 let stand a lower court decision that extended the *Buckley* reasoning to prohibit any limitations on independent expenditures on behalf of a presidential candidate who accepted public funding. Although the Court was closely divided, it seems likely that the independent expenditure loophole will remain in place for the indefinite future. The most promising means of reducing the effects of this kind of spending is not to try to limit it outright but to dilute it by encouraging contributions and spending from other sources. Many of the proposals just enumerated would give such encouragement by increasing limits for individual and party giving, providing an infusion of public funds, and expanding the opportunities and incentives for party-centered campaign activity.

Although this list of proposals is a long and varied one, it represents a coherent package that would make the FECA more conducive to party strength and would help give parties a secure role in the contemporary campaign environment. Such refinements in the law would increase the parties' resources and their control over campaign strategy. They would help give elections a partisan, as opposed to single-issue or single-candidate, focus and would strengthen the partisan ties and orientations of candidates and officeholders. By easing the prenomination scramble for funds and altering the treatment of independent and third-party candidates, these proposals could reduce in marginal ways the current system's tendency toward party and electoral fragmentation. They would give added advantages to parties vis-à-vis PACs and independent spenders and make the parties and candidates less reliant on immoderate direct-mail appeals. The trend toward party centralization would be inhibited and an active campaign role for state and local, as well as national, party organizations would be encouraged. They would place a premium on those kinds of grass-roots, voter-contact activities that personally involve people and put them to work effectively—and that make the party an effective mediating institution.

While much campaign finance law necessarily restrains and restricts, it is best seen as channeling rather than limiting campaign activity. The parties (and the country) need full and effective campaigns. The opportunities and incentives provided by campaign finance law can do a great deal to direct that activity through party channels and to strengthen party organization.

NOTES

1. President's Commission on Campaign Costs, *Financing Presidential Campaigns* (Washington, D.C.: U.S. Government Printing Office, 1962), 2.

2. Historical accounts include Alexander Heard, *The Costs of Democracy* (Garden City, N.Y.: Doubleday, 1962), chap. 9, 13: David E. Price, *Who Makes the Laws?* (Cambridge, Mass.: Schenkman Publishing Co., 1972), 155-163; Robert L. Peabody et al., *To Enact a Law: Congress and Campaign Financing* (New York: Praeger Publishers, 1972); Herbert E. Alexander, *Financing Politics: Money, Elections, and Political Reform*, 3d ed. (Washington, D.C.: CQ Press, 1984), chap. 2; Gary C. Jacobson, "Campaign-Finance Regulation: Politics and Policy in the 1970s," in *Paths to Political Reform*, ed. William Crotty (Lexington, Mass.: Lexington Books, 1980), chap. 7; and *Congress and the Nation, 1973-1976*, vol. 4 (Washington, D.C.: Congressional Quarterly, 1977), 985-1007, and *Congress and the Nation, 1977-1980*, vol. 5 (1981), 943-953.

3. *Buckley* v. *Valeo*, 424 U.S. 1 (1976), at 20.

4. For a recent article that was instrumental in prompting renewed calls for reform, see Elizabeth Drew, "Politics and Money," *The New Yorker*, December 6, 1982, 54 ff, and December 13, 1982, 57 ff. For the recommendations of the Angelo Committee, see Committee to Study Election Reform, *Report* (Washington, D.C.: Republican National Committee, 1982), 1-5. For the recommendations of the Campaign Finance Study Group, see U.S. House of Representatives, Committee on House Administration, 96th Cong., 1st sess., *An Analysis of the Impact of the Federal Election Campaign Act, 1972-78* (Washington, D.C.: U.S. Government Printing Office, 1979); and *Financing Presidential Campaigns* (Institute of Politics, J. F. Kennedy School of Government, Harvard University, 1982).

5. Steven Stockmeyer, "Commentary," in *Parties, Interest Groups, and Campaign Finance Laws*, ed. Michael J. Malbin (Washington, D.C.: American Enterprise Institute for Public Policy Research, 1980), 309-313; see also Austin Ranney's indictment in "The Political Parties: Reform and Decline," in *The New American Political System*, ed. Anthony King (Washington, D.C.: American Enterprise Institute for Public Policy Research, 1978), 241-245. For more positive assessments see Xandra Kayden, "The Nationalizing of the Party System," in *Parties, Interest Groups, and Campaign Finance Laws*, 257-282; Kayden, "Campaign Finance: The Impact on Parties and PACs," in *An Analysis of the Impact of the FECA*, 82-99; and Bill Loughrey, "Reform as Bogeyman: The Law without a Constituency" (mimeo, 1980).

6. Campaign Finance Study Group, *Financing Presidential Campaigns*, 1-36.

7. Edwin M. Epstein, "The Emergence of Political Action Committees," in *Political Finance*, ed. Herbert E. Alexander (Beverly Hills, Calif.: Sage Publications, 1979), 164. See also Epstein, "Business and Labor under the Federal Election Campaign Act of 1971," and Bernadette Budde, "Business Political Action Committees," in *Parties, Interest Groups, and Campaign Finance Laws*, 9-25, 107-151.

8. Frank J. Sorauf, "Political Parties and Political Action Committees: Two Life Cycles," *Arizona Law Review* 22 (1980): 454; in the same issue see also David Adamany, "PACs and the Democratic Financing of Politics," 593-594.

9. Ranney, "Political Parties," 243. Loughrey's data suggest, however, that few, if any, of the contributions made to national and state party committees in 1972 would have been forbidden under the 1974 FECA limits. "Reform as Bogeyman," appendix D.

10. Richard B. Cheney, "The Law's Impact on Presidential and Congressional Election Campaigns," in *Parties, Interest Groups and Campaign Finance Laws*, 240.

11. Herbert E. Alexander, *Financing the 1972 Election* (Lexington, Mass.: Lexington Books, 1976), 85-86.

12. *Federal Election Commission* v. *Democratic Senatorial Campaign Committee*, 50 LW 4001 (1981).

13. Data from Federal Election Commission releases of February 21, 1982, and April 26, 1983; the 1982 RNC "Chairman's Report," *First Monday* (January-February 1983): 20; Richard E. Cohen, "Giving Till it Hurts: 1982 Campaign Prompts New Look at Financing Races," *National Journal*, December 18, 1982, 2144-2152; and interviews with national party committee staff.

14. Larry Sabato, "Parties, PACs, and Independent Groups," in *The American Elections of 1982*, ed. Thomas Mann and Norman Ornstein (Washington, D.C.: American Enterprise Institute for Public Policy Research, 1983), 82-83.

15. Kayden, "Campaign Finance," 87; see also Drew, "Politics and Money," pt. II, 80-85.

16. Frank Tobe, address at the DNC Training Academy, Des Moines, Iowa, September 25, 1981.

17. Stockmeyer, "Commentary," 312.

18. Adamany, "Commentary," in *Parties, Interest Groups, and Campaign Finance Laws*, 317. For a later assessment, see Adamany, "Political Parties in the 1980s," in *Money and Politics in the United States: Financing Elections in the 1980s*, ed. Michael Malbin (Chatham, N.J.: American Enterprise Institute for Public Policy Research/Chatham House, 1984), 105-106.

19. Data from Federal Election Commission releases of June 29, 1979, March 7, 1982, April 29, 1983, and May 2, 1983; Gary Jacobson, "The Pattern of Campaign Contributions to Candidates for the U.S. House of Representatives, 1972-78," in *Analysis of the Impact of the FECA*, 20-42; and Roland McDevitt, "The Changing Dynamics of Fund Raising in House Campaigns," in *Political Finance*, 141-149. Calculations include coordinated party expenditures on a candidate's behalf among both contributions and candidate receipts.

20. See Cheney, "Law's Impact on Campaigns," 246; and Adamany, "Political Parties in the 1980s," 101-104.

21. Sabato, "Parties, PACs, and Independent Groups," 91. For a negative assessment of the consequences of Democratic efforts to attract PAC support, see Drew, "Politics and Money," pt. I, 78-101.
22. Data from Federal Election Commission releases, March 22, 1983, and November 29, 1981. On factors contributing to the reduced success rate of independent spending in 1982, see Sabato, "Parties, PACs, and Independent Groups," 100-102.
23. 102 Sup. Ct. Reporter 1266 (1982).
24. Drew, "Politics and Money," pt. II, 87. See also Common Cause, "Brief of Appellants," *Common Cause* v. *Harrison Schmitt*, U.S. Supreme Court, May 9, 1981, 30-32.
25. Speech to the California Committee for Party Renewal, December 1982, reported in *Party Line*, February 1983, 5.
26. Herbert E. Alexander, "Making Sense about Dollars in the 1980 Presidential Campaigns," in *Money and Politics in the United States*, 20-22.
27. Drew, "Politics and Money," pt. II, 58, 64.
28. For an assessment, see Xandra Kayden, "Parties and the 1980 Presidential Election," in *Financing Presidential Campaigns*, chap. 6, 11-14.
29. Data from Richard Smolka, "Election Legislation," in *The Book of the States, 1982-83* (Lexington, Ky.: Council of State Governments, 1982), 96-103; Karen J. Fling, "The States as Laboratories of Reform," in *Political Finance*, chap. 9; and Herbert E. Alexander and Jennifer Frutig, *Public Financing of State Elections* (Los Angeles: Citizens' Research Foundation, 1982), 15-24.
30. See Ruth S. Jones, "State Public Financing and the State Parties," in *Parties, Interest Groups, and Campaign Finance Laws*, 283-303; Jones, "State Public Campaign Finance: Implications for Partisan Politics," *American Journal of Political Science* 25 (May 1981): 342-361; Jack L. Noragon, "Political Finance and Political Reform: The Experience with State Income Tax Checkoffs," *American Political Science Review* 75 (September 1981): 667-687; and Alexander and Frutig, *Public Financing*, 5-14.
31. Herbert E. Alexander, "Public Funding of Congressional Campaigns," *Regulation* (January/February 1980): 31-32.
32. Gary Jacobson, "The Effects of Campaign Spending in Congressional Elections," *American Political Science Review* 72 (June 1978): 489.
33. Campaign Finance Study Group, "Summary of Findings and Major Recommendations," in *An Analysis of the Impact of the FECA*, 5.
34. U.S. Congress, Senate, Commerce Committee, *Hearings on S. 3171*, 86th Cong., 2d sess., May 16, 1960, 8.
35. Campaign Finance Study Group, *Financing Presidential Campaigns*, chap. 1, 36-40.
36. Michael Malbin, "Of Mountains and Molehills: PACs, Campaigns, and Public Policy," in *Parties, Interest Groups, and Campaign Finance Laws*, 180.
37. Campaign Finance Study Group, "Summary of Findings," 10. The group's 1982 report advocates a 100 percent credit for contributions of up to $50 but does not suggest separate credits for candidates and parties. *Financing Presidential Campaigns*, chap. 1, 27-29.
38. *Federal Election Commission* v. *Democratic Senatorial Campaign Committee*, 50 LW 4001 (1981).
39. *Buckley* v. *Valeo*, 424 U.S. 1, at 14-23.
40. Ibid., at 261-262. See also *Buckley* v. *Valeo*, 519 F2d 821 (1975), at 841-842, 853; and J. Skelly Wright, "Money and the Pollution of Politics: Is the First Amendment an Obstacle to Political Equality," *Columbia Law Review* 82 (May 1982): 609-645.

Parties and Policy 9

"Parties and policy. That should be a short chapter," wryly remarked one DNC official when the topic was broached. Historically, American parties have not been highly ideological or programmatic, nor has their governmental role generally involved policy initiation. A major point of contention in the modern debate on the future of the parties has been whether this could or should be changed. Responsible-party advocates believe that the parties should devote more time to debating issues; formulate, and campaign on the basis of, more sharply defined platforms; and exercise the discipline needed to enact the platform once in office. Defenders of the conventional parties argue that this is unrealistic, given the breadth of party coalitions, and undesirable, given the ways the vagueness and inclusiveness of the parties' policy positions serve political moderation and stability.

The differences between these viewpoints should not be exaggerated. The authors of the 1950 report of the American Political Science Association's Committee on Political Parties stressed that they did not wish to erect an "ideological wall" between the parties:

> Clarification of party policy will not in itself cause the parties to differ more fundamentally or more sharply than they have in the past.... There is no real ideological division in the American electorate, and hence programs of action presented by responsible parties for the voter's support could hardly be expected to reflect or strive toward such division.[1]

Nor did critics of the report completely dismiss the parties' policy role. In fact, one of their arguments was that the American parties were *already* more "responsible" than the report acknowledged. Moreover, developments since the 1950s have made it both less visionary and more important to emphasize the place of the parties in the policy process.

Why less visionary? Because the parties have become in certain respects more issue-oriented—in the motivations of their leaders and workers, in the behavior of their voters, and in the activities of their state and national organizations. And why more important? Because the fragmentation of the system through which issues are articulated and policies initiated—useful up to a point in fostering innovation and diversity—has passed the point of diminishing returns. Party members are demanding a more active policy role, and party organizations are beginning to pay closer attention to platforms and issues. As candidates and officeholders have become more isolated, more dependent on single issues and on narrowly based groups, the need for a deepening and a broadening of policy debate has become more evident. The mobilization of governmental majorities remains an important responsibility of the parties. But the need for a more creative, catalytic party role earlier in the process of policy development has become apparent as well.

Accordingly, we turn in this chapter to the role of the parties in the articulation of issues and the formulation of policy. We will survey the work of the policy councils that have been based in the national committees, the experiments of Democrats with a midterm convention, the efforts of party leaders in Congress to set the policy agenda, and the process of platform writing and implementation. The picture will be a mixed one, only partially justifying the DNC official's expectation of a "short chapter." What the parties do in the policy realm, we shall find, depends less on the laws and rules under which they operate than on how they define their role and how skillfully and energetically they pursue it.

Instruments of Policy Formulation

Early Policy Committees

Only in the past 30 years have interelection policy committees become an established component of national committee operations. The best known of these is probably the National Democratic Advisory Council (DAC), which was established at the DNC in 1956 under Paul Butler's chairmanship and was instrumental in developing the party's policy agenda for the 1960s. The DAC has served as a model for subsequent efforts, pointing up both the kind of role the national committees can play and certain pitfalls that await such efforts. But while the DAC was "new" in its "degree of formalization ... and the national committee's recognition of it as an official body for stating policy," it did not represent the first effort at interelection policy formulation by a national committee.[2] The Republicans took the lead as far back as 1920, when GOP National Chairman Will Hays appointed an Advisory Committee on Policies and Platform "to gather facts and data, to invite a full expression of opinion of leading Republicans, and to submit its recommendations ... to the Resolutions Committee of the National Convention."[3] The committee numbered 173, with some 18 subcommittees studying a broad range of topics, but its output and its influence disappointed those who had hoped to use it to shape the convention's platform.

The next comparable effort was the Republican Program Committee, formed after the crushing GOP defeat of 1936. Followers of defeated nominee Alf Landon and of former president Herbert Hoover were divided over Hoover's proposal for a midterm national convention, but they agreed that an extensive assessment of the party's philosophy and program was needed. The RNC thus authorized the Program Committee, which was chaired by Glenn Frank, former president of the University of Wisconsin. The committee eventually reached the unwieldy size of 280 members. Congressional leaders let their coolness toward the effort be known, and the committee's report, produced in early 1940, apparently had little impact.[4]

Another intraparty struggle, between the internationalist wing of the party represented by 1940 presidential nominee Wendell Wilkie and the old-guard isolationists, contributed to the formation in 1943 of the Republican Post-War Advisory Council. RNC leaders set up the committee, although it operated independently once in place. The council's 51 members were all governors and members of Congress, except for a handful of RNC representatives. Their only meeting, the "Mackinac Island Conference," produced two short statements on postwar domestic and international policy. Eight committees were appointed to consider specific issues; many were not heard from again, although Sen. Arthur Vanderberg's work on the foreign policy committee was influential in shaping the 1944 platform and in developing his own position.[5]

These early party councils shared certain common characteristics. First, they were all out-party efforts, often spurred by electoral adversity and/or an attempt to shape the outcome of factional battles within the party. The Democratic party, possessing an authoritative spokesman in the president, saw little need for such a national committee role. Second, the councils risked treading upon the turf of the party's congressional leaders. On a number of occasions these leaders themselves issued declarations of party principle and policy, sometimes in cooperation with the RNC.[6] In general, congressional leaders did not welcome the intrusion of the party councils, although they sometimes agreed to work with or serve on them. Finally, these councils had a rather ephemeral existence. Short-lived, loosely organized, sparsely funded, they had only a limited impact. Modern party councils, presented in Table 9-1, have been more institutionalized and in some cases more influential. Many of the patterns evident in these early efforts still hold, however; their infirmities have by no means been completely overcome.

Two Landmark Efforts

During President Dwight D. Eisenhower's first term, the Democratic party—assuming the out-party role for the first time in 20 years—did not organize a body to speak for the party on policy matters. That role was left to the party's members in Congress, led by Majority Leader Lyndon Johnson and Speaker Sam Rayburn. These Texans tended to see the Democratic congressional victories of 1956, in the midst of the Eisenhower landslide, as a vindication of their philosophy of moderation and "responsible" opposition. But the leaders of the presidential wing of the party, as James Sundquist notes,

Table 9-1 Policy-formulating Bodies Sponsored by National Party Committees Since 1950

Years	Designation	Chair or Presiding Officer	Membership	Working Group Structure
REPUBLICAN				
1959	Committee on Program and Progress	Businessman (later senator) Charles Percy	41—7 public officials including House and Senate minority leaders	Members distributed among 4 task forces
1965-1968	Republican Coordinating Committee	RNC Chairman Ray Bliss	36—all public officials or former nominees (plus top RNC officers); 16 members of Congress	8 task forces and 3 study groups involving about 250 people
1977-1980	RNC Advisory Councils	RNC Chairman Bill Brock	No central structure; 34 members of Congress on Advisory Councils	5 Advisory Councils, involving 36 subcommittees and 404 people
DEMOCRATIC				
1956-1961	National Democratic Advisory Council	DNC Chairman Paul Butler	27—about 40 percent current or former public officials; congressional leadership declined to serve	2 (eventually 10) advisory committees, involving 50 to 180 people
1969-1972	Democratic Policy Council	Former vice-president Hubert Humphrey	119—40 percent public officials. 22 members of Congress	6 committees; later 15 planning groups. Total membership around 425.
1973-1976	Democratic Advisory Council of Elected Officials	Businessman Arthur Krim	61—all public officials except chair; 26 members of Congress	2 task forces, involving 16 study groups and 234 people
1981-	National Strategy Council	DNC Chairman Charles Manatt	130—all public officials (plus top DNC officers); 67 members of Congress	4 advisory panels, involving about 200 people

... could see only defeat, and they ascribed it to two causes: the Democrats had not undermined the Eisenhower prestige by forcefully pointing out to the country the mistakes and folly of his policies, and they had not developed and presented to the country a distinct and liberal party program that would have given the voters a clear and attractive alternative to Eisenhower.... The "responsible" compromises which were the pride of the congressional leaders might be necessary to get bills passed but they blurred the image of the Democratic party.[7]

What sort of mechanism might be utilized to develop and promote a distinctive Democratic agenda? DNC Chairman Paul Butler and other leaders of the Adlai Stevenson wing of the party were aware of the RNC's earlier policy committees and of the proposal for a continuing party council made by the APSA Committee on Political Parties. Drawing on these precedents, Butler proposed and the DNC's Executive Committee in late 1956 established an advisory council to speak for the party and to develop policy positions between conventions.

The National Democratic Advisory Council (DAC) immediately hit a roadblock in the form of the Democratic congressional leadership. Sam Rayburn, speaking for the House leaders who had been invited to join, informed Butler that it was "the considered opinion of the four of us that it would be a mistake for the Democratic leadership of the House to join in any program with any committee outside of the House of Representatives." [8] Johnson, who had at first seemed receptive to the DAC idea, also refused, along with other Senate party leaders. While jealousy of congressional prerogatives and fear of interference were major motivating factors, so also was an apprehension, especially among southerners, that the DAC would be dominated by liberals and would press for advanced civil rights and other positions. Hubert Humphrey and Estes Kefauver (who had been invited as the 1956 vice-presidential nominee rather than as a Senate representative) were the only members of Congress who agreed to join. Gov. Luther Hodges of North Carolina and former governor John Battle of Virginia brought to 11 the number of 20 original invitees who declined to participate.

Butler and other supporters of the DAC resolved to proceed with or without the congressional leadership on board. "To be an effective opposition, the Democratic Party must have a broader base than the Democrats in Congress," declared 1956 presidential nominee Stevenson. The reconstituted council, given a "thumping endorsement" by the DNC in early 1957, consisted of 23 members, most of them from the DNC executive council; three governors were initially included, as well as senior public figures such as Stevenson, Eleanor Roosevelt, former senator Herbert Lehman, and former president Harry S Truman.[9] A number of members were added during the council's four-year life, including prominent contenders for the 1960 presidential nomination, but the group never exceeded 31. Additional people were involved through a series of specialized advisory committees, the longest-lived and most active of which were the Advisory Committee on Economic Policy, chaired by Harvard economist John Kenneth Galbraith, and the foreign policy group, headed by former secretary of state Dean Acheson.

The expressed hope of Butler and other DAC founders to assemble a broadly representative leadership group was not fulfilled. This reduced their influence on the party in Congress, but it allowed the council to go beyond bland, least-common-denominator sorts of pronouncements to develop "hard-hitting, reasonably specific criticisms of the Eisenhower administration and proposals for alternative policy." [10] During a period of more than three years, the DAC and its advisory committees turned out more than 60 pamphlets and statements. Of particular significance was the DAC's uncompromisingly liberal position on civil rights and its development of the case for an activist, growth-oriented economic policy.

The DAC was not without its congressional allies. Its activities coincided with the intensification of organizational efforts and policy initiatives among liberal Democrats in both houses, who became more numerous and more restless under Johnson's and Rayburn's leadership after the 1958 elections. House liberals formed the Democratic Study Group in 1959, and senators such as Humphrey, Paul Douglas, and Joseph Clark pushed area redevelopment, manpower training, education aid, and Medicare measures with renewed effort. In this context, the DAC served effectively as an attention-getting and legitimating device, giving the party imprimatur to proposals despite the reluctance of the congressional leadership. James Sundquist concludes:

> What emerges from a study of Democratic program development in the 1953-60 period is a picture of block-by-block building under the leadership of those making up the activist triangle in the Senate, the House, and the Democratic Advisory Council. Individual activists on Capitol Hill took responsibility, often working closely with interest groups, for molding particular blocks.... These activists developed general public support and mobilized backing within the Democratic presidential party. In sequence, although not always in the same order, the three corners of the triangle endorsed the measure.[11]

On some measures, such as area redevelopment, liberals were strong enough to establish the bill as a party measure and to obtain Senate passage. On more controversial matters such as Medicare and civil rights, where floor votes were not feasible, the DAC provided an alternative kind of party endorsement. This tripartite effort of party activists in the House, Senate, and DAC produced by 1960 a genuine *party* agenda, a more focused set of proposals with a broader national appeal than the established congressional leadership could or would have developed. The work of the DAC directly contributed to the 1960 platform, the presidential campaign of John F. Kennedy, and the eventually successful Kennedy-Johnson legislative program.

Butler's hope for a party council that would outlast the out-party status of the Democrats was never realized. After Kennedy's nomination Butler was replaced as national chairman by Sen. Henry Jackson, and elements of the DAC and its committees were absorbed into the Kennedy campaign organization. The demise of the DAC was formally confirmed by the DNC's new chairman, John Bailey, at a "harmony meeting" he held with the leaders of the House and Senate Democratic campaign committees in early 1961. The advisory council, Bailey said, had "served a function" when the party did not control the presidency. But now "policy should be made at the White House and by the leadership of Congress." [12]

The Republicans had organized a less ambitious policy group of their own, the Committee on Program and Progress. After a White House post-mortem on the party's midterm losses in 1958, President Eisenhower asked RNC Chairman Meade Alcorn to form a committee to define the goals of the Republican party. Alcorn put together a group of 41 prominent Republicans, chaired by businessman (later senator) Charles Percy of Illinois. Some party leaders feared that Percy wished to use the committee to "liberalize the party," and congressional leaders sent out unmistakable signals that infringement on their prerogatives would not be welcomed.[13] The House and Senate minority leaders, Charles Halleck and Everett Dirksen, nonetheless agreed to serve on the committee. Its final report, approved in mid-1959, raised few hackles and gained for the party a good deal of favorable publicity.

It was not until 1965 that the GOP mounted an effort comparable to the National Democratic Advisory Council. Former president Eisenhower called a well-publicized All Republican Conference at his farm in Gettysburg and aided in the formation of a National Republican Citizens Committee in 1962—prompting observations that he was showing more interest in the Republican party in retirement that he had while in office. Highly suspicious of these efforts, House and Senate leaders released their own "Declaration of Republican Principle and Policy" in mid-1962.[14] A 17-member Critical Issues Council chaired by Dr. Milton Eisenhower, a spin-off group from the National Republican Citizens Committee, produced a number of papers during the 1964 preconvention period. But such activities were not integrated within the national committee until after the landslide defeat of presidential nominee Barry Goldwater in 1964, when pressures built within the Republican Governors' Association and other groups for intraparty efforts to "restate basic principles and develop positive Republican solutions to current problems." The party's congressional leaders, Senator Dirksen and Rep. Gerald Ford, agreed that such an effort was needed and, in contrast to the stance of Rayburn and Johnson eight years earlier, took an active part in its initiation. The result was the Republican Coordinating Committee (RCC), appointed by incoming RNC Chairman Ray Bliss in early 1965.[15]

The RCC avoided many of the conflicts previous policy groups had had with elected officials, in large part because all but six of its 29 members *were* elected officials; Congress claimed a dozen of the committee's original seats, and the governors five more. But there were other reasons as well. Bliss was mindful of congressional sensibilities in appointing the committee's task forces and in clearing their reports with party leaders in Congress before sending them to the full RCC. National committee publications gave prominent coverage to the policy pronouncements of Dirksen and Ford, who were often featured spokesmen for the RCC. Moreover, the Republican party did not suffer from internal divisions as serious as those afflicting the Democrats. An all-party operation was thus more feasible for the RCC than it had been for the DAC, and the policy implications of deferring to the party's congressional leaders were less substantial. Finally, the congressional leaders themselves had less to lose. The GOP, unlike the Democratic party in the late 1950s, was in the congressional minority; its leaders had fewer prerogatives and less control over policy to protect than had been true of Johnson and Rayburn.

Bliss assigned a high priority to RCC activities and was relatively generous with staffing and funding. GOP publications frequently heralded the committee as "the first successful effort of either major political party to bring together all elements of the party in a single, continuing body devoted to the formulation of positions on the issues of public policy" and as a "front-runner in the fight against administration fiscal policies." The RCC, like the DAC, had a major impact on the party's next platform; its staff director became director for the 1968 Platform Committee, and Bliss later claimed that 90 percent of the platform had come from RCC recommendations.[16] It was instrumental in promoting the idea of revenue sharing, which became a policy centerpiece of the Nixon administration.[17] But the Republican Coordinating Committee did not survive the Republican victory. President Nixon replaced Bliss with Rogers Morton and centralized political and policy operations in the White House to an unprecedented degree.

Modern Policy Councils

Since 1969 policy councils have been routinely established by the party losing the presidency, as Table 9-1 suggests. But these efforts have not been equally ambitious or influential; only the Republicans have given policy development high priority as a national committee function.

The most active of the three Democratic groups that succeeded the DAC was the Democratic Policy Council, appointed by DNC Chairman Fred Harris in 1969 and chaired by the party's unsuccessful 1968 presidential nominee, Hubert Humphrey. Harris, himself a senator, was anxious to avoid the DNC-congressional split that had characterized the Butler effort and to use the policy council to unify a party badly divided in the wake of the 1968 convention and campaign. The council initially had a three-tier structure: an executive committee of 20 high party officers and elected officials; a full council that eventually had 119 members, including a number of prominent officeholders and senior party notables but also several Eugene McCarthy supporters and issue activists; and six policy-area committees chaired by well-known figures within the party. A fourth tier of 15 "planning groups" was later formed to lay groundwork for the 1972 platform.[18]

The full council, unwieldy in size and unpredictable because of its diversity, convened only occasionally, but the committees produced some three dozen papers and reports during the 1969-1972 period. Their main importance, suggests John Stewart, who served as the council's executive director, was not in developing striking new policy positions but in providing a forum where leaders of a conflict-ridden party could search for common ground, especially on the ongoing war in Vietnam and longer range questions of defense policy. "The Policy Council gave a lot of groups within the party an opportunity to be heard," Stewart recalls. "But it also represented an attempt to contain and channel the debate. Both its work and that of the Platform Committee were more integrated and balanced than one might assume.... The Council tended to be remembered as more controversial and left-wing and 'out of it' than it actually was, because people saw it in the shadow of the [George] McGovern defeat." [19]

When Robert Strauss became national chairman in 1973 he seemed more impressed with the dangers than with the promise of DNC policy development efforts. Like many others, he tended to link the Democratic Policy Council retrospectively to the failure of the McGovern candidacy. "He knew the DNC couldn't simply walk away from policy activity," Stewart surmises, "but he wanted a more stable, predictable structure." His solution was to form the Democratic Advisory Council of Elected Officials, a small group composed entirely of public officeholders (except for its chairman, businessman Arthur Krim). The full council received considerable notice in 1975 when it proposed an alternative to President Ford's energy program, but it otherwise accomplished little and seldom met. [20] Somewhat more active were the council's 16 "study groups," one of which included the men who later served as secretaries of state and defense and as national security adviser in the Carter administration.

Overall, the Advisory Council of Elected Officials was less active and less influential than the policy councils that had preceded it. Strauss's fear of offending Congress and his wariness of fractious policy debates led him to deemphasize the entire effort, virtually shutting down the full council and giving the study groups only limited support. Ironically, this may have worked against the policy moderation he wished to promote. As columnist David Broder noted on the eve of the 1976 campaign:

> The issues forums that are being conducted around the country this fall are not being organized by the party, but by a coalition of liberal unions and interest groups.... In the absence of any negotiated party position on policy questions—which might have been hammered out in the more representative advisory council—[the party's presidential candidates] are vying with each other for the favor of the most liberal elements in the party, taking positions of doubtful utility in the general election....
> The Democratic Party under Strauss has spelled out its rules and procedures in mind-boggling detail. But it has said virtually nothing about its goals, its policies, and its programs. It will be little short of amazing if the Democrats do not pay a price for this neglect. By keeping the party away from national policy, Strauss has left the issues to the left. [21]

As it turned out, of course, the party in 1976 nominated a candidate with whom "the left" had only limited influence. But that candidate and his presidency nonetheless suffered from the failure of Democrats to work through their policy approaches while they were out of power.

The Republican party was far less cautious and constrained in the policy development program it undertook after the 1976 election returned the Democrats to the White House. Chairman Bill Brock appointed five advisory councils on national resources, human concerns, national security and international affairs, general government, and economic affairs. The advisory councils housed 36 subcommittees and involved more than 400 people, including numerous cabinet and subcabinet officials from the Nixon and Ford administrations. As one RNC official noted, there was also "a substantial congressional presence ... but the Councils weren't dominated by the congressional leadership." Some of those working with the councils expressed disappointment that a more active collaboration between Brock and congressional leaders Howard Baker and John Rhodes in developing and presenting GOP initiatives "never worked out completely." But cooperative relationships were maintained with the House and Senate policy committees, and advisory council leaders generally were able to move ahead without fear of congressional opposition.

The RNC advisory councils had no parent body, no central structure. They and their subcommittees met periodically to critique position papers and to develop policy statements. They released about two dozen pamphlets on housing, transportation, inflation, defense, energy, and other issues, sometimes presenting them as the products of group deliberation but often as the work of an individual spokesman. The staff assigned directly to the advisory councils was quite small (Executive Secretary Roger Semerad, plus two others), but they also drew on the RNC's much larger research and publications staffs. Michael Baroody, director of research, edited their reports. Their work was complemented by a number of ongoing RNC activities—publications on the Carter record, newsletters oriented toward various constituency groups, and an issue-research operation that developed and disseminated background materials on economic and foreign policy questions. Particularly important in conveying the image of the GOP as the "party of ideas" was the publication of a high-quality quarterly, *Commonsense*.[22] The RNC advisory councils from 1977 to 1980 thus were part of a larger effort within the national committee to give priority to policy development and to the dissemination of ideas.

Personnel and ideas from the advisory councils had a marked impact on the 1980 platform. Semerad became the platform committee's executive director, and Baroody its editor-in-chief. The Advisory Council on Economic Affairs had raised the stock of the Kemp-Roth proposal for massive tax cuts, and many lesser proposals—such as tax sheltered accounts for down payments on houses, endorsed by the Housing Subcommittee—found their way into the platform as well.[23]

The advisory councils, like their predecessor groups, were disbanded after the election. For a time it appeared that research and policy operations in general would be cut back drastically. But by 1982 these RNC functions had been restored almost to their preelection level, a level far exceeding what the Democrats, now the out-party, were able to attain. There was, of course, a considerable shift in emphasis from what the RNC had done during the Carter years. No longer did advisory councils come up with policy alternatives: "Obviously," said one RNC aide, "we no longer have the latitude to present a range of options." *Commonsense* was gradually discontinued: "It would lose credibility if it was merely an apologist for the administration, but a more critical role would be a problem too," observed Baroody from his new post as director of the White House Office of Public Affairs.[24] Various publications designed mainly to criticize the Carter record were replaced with "good news" reports designed to shore up the troops.

There was still a need, however, for issue materials for candidates and party leaders and, as the 1984 campaign took shape, for "opposition" research on the Democratic contenders as well. As of mid-1983, the RNC's research staff consisted of 12 people, close to its 1980 level. It was a less senior staff and its tasks left less room for independence and innovation. The RNC no longer has a policy development operation comparable to those Ray Bliss and Brock created. But it retains an appreciable research and communication capacity and continues to influence the way the party's case is presented by its leaders, candidates, and officeholders across the country.

Recent Democratic Experience

Charles Manatt, elected Democratic national chairman in early 1981, has gone through the now-routine exercise of assembling an out-party policy council. In campaigning for the DNC post, Manatt encountered the expectation that he must "do something" about policy, must help the party develop and debate "new ideas." But he did not have any well-formed notion of how to proceed, and he quickly received an education in the perils awaiting such efforts. Manatt brought in an associate from California, Harold Kwalwasser, to put the policy operation together. One close observer describes what ensued:

Hal, not quite understanding ... the problems or the history, went charging up to see [Democratic congressional leaders] Byrd and O'Neill ... and started talking about how the chairman had this hot idea ... to create this policy council and lay out the "Democratic alternative." Well, it took him about one week, and the Democratic leadership was up in flames. They were saying what the hell is this new guy Manatt doing? Doesn't he know that Democratic policy is made by House Democrats and Senate Democrats?

It thus fell on Eugene Eidenberg, brought in as the DNC's executive director in the spring of 1981, to untangle the situation and put the policy council on a new footing.

Eidenberg and Manatt settled on an approach similar to that chosen by Strauss in 1973: appoint a policy council consisting *only* of elected officials. Eidenberg describes some of the considerations that led him to this approach:

The more I studied the Paul Butler experience, the more I concluded it was not relevant to the problems we faced.... [We've tried] to get the Strategy Council not so much to see itself as issuing pronouncements on this issue or that, which gets into a fire fight with congressional Democrats or, even worse, leads elected Democratic officials or candidates to think that these are the positions that they have to take (or defend against) when they're running. Our idea is more to give elected officials a hospitable environment in which broad discussion of public policy, unencumbered by narrow constituency or special interests, or lobbying, can occur.... The party is not the mechanism that defines the policy positions its candidates are going to take.... What we can do is provide a forum, a place where policy alternatives ... can be aired in an environment in which it is safe to experiment, to test some new ideas with peers in public office around the country ... not a place where you can hand down the papal bull and say, "Here are the five points on economic policy to which all Democrats must adhere...." [25]

Mollified, the congressional leadership agreed to support the effort. Senate Minority Leader Robert Byrd cooperated only reluctantly, however; out of deference to him, Manatt even dropped the word "policy" from the council's name, dubbing it the "National Strategy Council" (NSC) instead. Members of Congress make up more than half of the NSC's 130 members; it also includes 13 governors, 18 mayors, some 20 other state and local officials, and the top officers of the DNC. In 1982 four advisory panels were formed on economic growth and opportunity, "making government work," energy and environment, and national security. Each of these includes a sizable core of elected officials from the NSC as well as a number of outside experts and group spokesmen. The Advisory Panel on Economic Growth and Opportunity, for example, is chaired by Reps. Tim Wirth and Richard Gephardt, two leading spokesmen among House Democrats for new approaches to economic policy and active members of the House Democratic Caucus's Committee on Party Effectiveness. The panel's 61 members include Sen. Gary Hart, former secretary of commerce Juanita Kreps, economists Lester Thurow and Robert Reich, and several prominent business and labor leaders.

In general, the National Strategy Council has failed to live up to even Eidenberg's and Manatt's modest expectations. Although Manatt announced at the time of the council's first meeting in the fall of 1981 that it would meet "several times a year on a continuing basis," it had met only three times by late 1983. Little had been accomplished by the advisory panels, and one had yet to meet. The council's top staff member, DNC Director of Policy Bernard Aronson, had only two aides working with him, and their responsibilities included not only the NSC but *all* of the national committee's research and issues operations—candidate workshops, opposition research, speech preparation, the midterm party conference, responses to presidential addresses, and so forth. Although there had once been talk of hiring consultants to work with the advisory panels, such support never materialized. "We just cover them the best we can, sometimes with volunteers," Aronson said.[26] With good reason David Broder declared that the DNC had "treated the issue area as its lowest priority." He concluded:

It's no wonder the voters think Democrats are devoid of ideas. What's more worrisome is that the ideas the Democrats are developing are not being tested in serious party debate.[27]

Part of the explanation for the striking contrast with the RNC's earlier policy operations (or even with the RNC's current issue and research capacity) lies in the disparity between the two parties' financial resources. But that is only part of the story, for while DNC capacities have increased in other respects, its policy operations have *declined* from earlier levels. Manatt, like Strauss before him, simply has given the matter low priority—partly out of fear of giving offense on Capitol Hill, but also because of an apparent lack of ideas or interest. "In order to have a Strategy Council you've got to have a strategy," said one close and otherwise sympathetic observer. "And Manatt has never had one.... This is not something a staff can make work on its own, and the DNC doesn't have the power to get the party committed to anything. It simply can't work unless you have a strong chairman, deeply interested, who really wants to bulldoze it through." The explanation is perhaps a bit overdrawn, but a look at the leadership that underlay the three "success stories" from Table 9-1—Butler, Bliss, and Brock—suggests that it is not far off the mark.

This is not to say that the NSC has been without value. It has sparked useful discussions among the officials involved, particularly in sessions closed to the press. Some of its more assertive members, such as Reps. Wirth and Gephardt and Sen. Gary Hart, have used it as a forum for testing ideas. The work of the advisory panels could yet prove helpful in the writing of the 1984 platform. And in bringing elected officials into the NSC, Manatt reinforced what he was trying to do in other areas— namely, encourage the party's officeholders to attend the national convention and give an "establishment" cast to the party's midterm conference.

Midterm Party Conferences

In fact, the 1982 midterm conference and the work of party groups in Congress have made the out-party performance of the Democrats in policy development somewhat more credible than the Strategy Council experience alone would indicate. The past history of midterm conferences suggests that one must judge them as much in terms of damage control as of more positive accomplishment. From that perspective, the 1982 National Party Conference could be deemed a success. As Eidenberg remarked with only slight exaggeration, it was probably the first large party gathering since 1964 "in which the Democrats did more damage to the Republicans than to themselves." [28]

Biennial conventions, complete with adoption of a platform, have long been a favorite idea of responsible-party advocates. "Party platforms should be formulated at least every two years in order to relate to current issues and provide a closer connection with the off-year congressional campaigns," advised the APSA's Committee on Political Parties in 1950. But the committee also recommended that the party conventions be reduced in size to between 500 and 600 delegates, that some 150 of these be ex-officio delegates (national committee members, state party chairmen, congressional leaders), that a "select group" of about 25 "prominent party leaders outside the party organizations" also be included, and that a party council have broad powers to draft and then interpret the platform between conventions. [29] It thus might be argued that the operations of the policy councils established by the national committees have come as close to what the APSA committee had in mind as would biennial national conventions, given the size and shape the quadrennial conclaves have assumed.

The idea of a midterm convention has gained currency in Democratic circles, not so much because of its responsible-party credentials as because of its appeal to policy-oriented "amateurs" within the party and its congruence with the participatory/"representative structures" line of reform. The 1972 convention authorized "a conference on Democratic Party organization and policy" to be held in 1974. The document presented by the Charter Commission to that conference provided for "a National Party Conference between National Conventions," but it left the determination of whether such a conference would be held in a given year to the DNC (or national convention) and did not require that the conference adopt a platform. The national conventions of 1976 and 1980 subsequently resolved that national party conferences should be held in 1978 and 1982.

DNC Chairman Robert Strauss and other national party leaders were nervous about the 1974 midterm conference, and with good reason: the party remained deeply divided on foreign policy and other issues, and the charter debate threatened to become a last-ditch battle between the proponents and opponents of party reform.[30] The conference resembled a national convention in its size (2,038 delegates) and delegate-selection procedures, but the absence of mandated primaries and of competing candidate organizations made those procedures considerably more party-centered. Moreover, some 17 percent of the delegates were seated automatically by virtue of holding high public office or serving on the national committee. The 1974 midterm conference thus contrasted with the 1972 convention in its delegates' higher level of involvement in and loyalty to the party, a fact that made it easier for Strauss to negotiate compromise agreements on the charter and to avoid divisive battles on the floor. Among the strategies adopted by the leadership to dampen conflict was to remove *policy* debates from the floor altogether. This was reversed at the last minute to permit passage of a resolution supporting strong measures—including wage-price controls, tax reform, and public employment—to deal with the nation's economic "crisis." Otherwise, policy debate was confined to a series of "issue seminars." One of the few tangible products of the Democratic Advisory Council of Elected Officials was a booklet summarizing these discussions, generally in noncommittal terms.[31]

The 1978 midterm conference in Memphis was intended by the Carter White House "to show the administration's accomplishments, gain valuable media exposure, and launch Jimmy Carter's drive for renomination."[32] Presidential aides worked with the DNC leadership, on this as on the Winograd Commission, to ensure an outcome favorable to the administration. They only partially succeeded. The 1,633 delegates, chosen mainly by state party central committees, supported the administration by a comfortable margin on the conference's key vote on budget reductions. But the White House had hoped to avoid such plenary session showdowns altogether by limiting most policy debate to a series of carefully structured "workshops" and making it procedurally difficult to bring resolutions to the floor of the conference. As it turned out, disputes within the workshops also made the news: Carter and his policies were attacked both by delegates and by members of Congress, and Sen. Edward Kennedy used a workshop address on national health care policy to sharply question the president's budget priorities.

Despite rules of selection that were designed to give state party leaders a decisive hand in choosing delegates, issue-oriented activists from the liberal end of the ideological spectrum were well-represented in Memphis—perhaps demonstrating the extent to which they had supplanted the regulars in positions of state and local party leadership.[33] Especially prominent were the feminists, whose greatest victory came not in the conference itself but in a concurrent DNC meeting: the decision of the Winograd Commission on equal division was reversed, and a 50 percent quota for women was included in the preliminary call to the 1980 convention (see Chapter 6). Attendance by elected officials at the conference was sparce, perhaps because they did not expect anything of significance to be decided but more probably because they were wary of becoming embroiled in intraparty conflicts and being called to task by issue activists. It was, all in all, a conference that left no one—not the administration, nor the party leadership, nor the activists groups seeking leverage—feeling that they had gained very much.

Understandably, the Carter forces were not eager to have another conference midway through what they hoped would be a second term. But reform elements within the party, many of them associated with Kennedy's challenge to the president, pushed the idea, and it was adopted as a part of a compromise Rules Committee resolution at the 1980 convention. Because of President Carter's subsequent defeat, the resolution was implemented under far different circumstances than its sponsors had anticipated—a situation that encouraged the subordination of factional policy agendas and a focus on the practical requirements of winning the 1982 elections. Chairman Manatt proposed that the midterm conference be scaled down drastically, that selection procedures be devised to favor party regulars and elected officials as opposed to issue-activists ("This is a national party leadership conference and not a mini-convention," he insisted), and that it be held in June to "pull the cast together" for the campaign ahead. The DNC's executive committee approved the plan without dissent, and the conference's managers proceeded to draw up rules that minimized the chances of open conflict. "There won't be any repeat of 1978," one DNC aide accurately predicted.[34]

The 897 delegates at the 1982 Democratic midterm conference in Philadelphia (about half the number present in 1978) included all the members of the national committee; an equal number elected by state central committees; all Democratic governors, and some 54 members of Congress, mayors, county officials, and state legislators chosen by their respective party caucuses and conferences; and an additional 100 selected by the national chairman, mainly to achieve demographic balance. Issues were debated and voted on in workshops, which were furnished drafts of position papers that had been cleared with the congressional leadership and other interested parties in advance. No debate was held or votes taken on workshop statements in the plenary sessions; they were mainly devoted to speeches by the party's prospective 1984 presidential contenders.

Members of Congress and other elected officials were initially nervous about the June date; the 1974 and 1978 midterm conferences had been scheduled for December to minimize any diversionary or negative effects on the November elections. But the deemphasis of issue debate and the focus on nuts-and-bolts campaign training made the 1982 conference appear more useful and less perilous. Manatt worked with congressional leaders to encourage participation; more than three dozen senators and representatives addressed the full conference or spoke at workshop meetings, in marked contrast to the 1978 pattern.

The position papers emanating from the 1982 conference were more specific in their indictments of the Reagan administration than in their delineation of Democratic alternatives. The discussions were no doubt of some value to party leaders and officeholders in testing ideas and approaches, and certain general themes did begin to emerge. But the main successes of Philadelphia lay in the battles avoided, the image of unity projected, the elected officials involved—not in the realm of policy development. Nor does it seem likely that midterm conferences will become more viable as arenas for serious policy formulation and debate in the future. Without the unifying force of a presidential race, there are few mechanisms for linking a midterm "platform" to congressional campaigns. Most congressional candidates, moreover, have every reason to avoid such a linkage—as their preference for a December conference date suggests. When the party holds the presidency, the midterm conference may appeal to some groups as a way of holding the administration accountable. But it is a blunt instrument for this purpose, and one with a high potential for exacerbating and exposing political divisions and policy conflicts in a way that damages the party's prospects.

It is not clear, in other words, that a policy-oriented midterm conference is suited to the circumstances and interests of the American parties. These conclaves may serve other objectives—in gaining attention for the party or building party cohesion and morale—but such objectives militate *against* giving the conference a strong policy focus or taking its discussions and pronouncements beyond least-common-denominator terms. The policy councils pioneered by Butler and Bliss are much more promising as vehicles by which the national committee can make a positive contribution to policy development. Their format permits more experimentation and debate. They are less vulnerable to the pressures of single-issue partisans and offer elected officials both the occasion and incentives to take broad views. They can gain press attention when they need to but have more control than midterm conferences over how and to what extent they are covered—thus creating a relatively "safe" environment for the exploration of alternatives as opposed to the mere taking of positions.

Although the 1982 midterm conference could be judged a success in terms of damage control and the presentation of a positive party image, it did not fill the gap left by the default of the National Strategy Council. The resulting lack of structured policy deliberation within the party threatened once again to leave the national party and its candidates vulnerable to demands presented by the most intensely interested constituency groups. There were, however, some encouraging signs, attributable in part to unusual policy formulation efforts by party organs on Capitol Hill.

The Congressional Parties

The congressional parties, like the national committees, are likely to take a more active role in policy development when they are not in the majority and/or do not have a president in power. There is a distinct parallel, in fact, between the formation of party policy councils and the activation of party policy machinery on Capitol Hill: both have often been responsive to electoral adversity. The House Republican Policy Committee was formed in 1949 in reaction to the party's 1948 defeats and was reactivated in 1959 after the same midterm setbacks that led to the formation of Charles Percy's Committee on Program and Progress. But the House committee's role differed considerably before and after the subsequent change in administrations. As one member reflected:

> [During] the Eisenhower administration, we were seeking to support the administration—even though we were a minority in the House. . . . Now we are more a mill for developing alternatives—for developing more positive positions in the legislature.[35]

Between 1961 and 1968, when the GOP controlled neither Congress nor the presidency, its House leadership undertook policy initiatives to an unprecedented degree. The party's policy operations became a major point of contention between the established leadership and the younger, more assertive members who first overthrew Rep. Joseph Martin (1959) and then Rep. Charles Halleck (1965) as minority leaders. The first revolt produced a renovated House Republican Policy Committee, no longer chaired by the minority leader. The results of the second revolt were more complex: because the new leader, Gerald Ford, could not place a chairman of his own choosing on the Policy Committee, he set up a Committee on Planning and Research within the Republican Conference, which to some extent became a rival of the Policy Committee. The Planning and Research Committee, chaired by Rep. Charles Goodell of New York, established a series of task forces that held hearings, commissioned studies, critiqued administration policies, and developed proposals on subjects ranging from agriculture to East-West trade. In some instances task forces were created to cover areas where it was felt that Republicans on standing committees could not or would not develop alternatives to majority proposals. At the same time, the Policy Committee became more active, articulating party positions on pending legislation and urging the administration to deal with a range of additional problems. Ford joined with Senate Minority Leader Everett Dirksen in presenting an alternative "State of the Union" address each year. The party's specific approach continued to vary from committee to committee and from bill to bill. Sometimes the party cooperated with the majority to secure compromises and concessions; sometimes it preferred to eschew compromise and "make a record" for future reference. But House Republicans during this period, in loose cooperation with the Republican Coordinating Committee, invested unprecedented time and energy in policy formulation and made *party* organs the focal point of their efforts.[36]

As we saw in Chapter 3, the roles and resources of the Democratic party, particularly in the House, were expanded in important ways during the 1970s. But it was not until the 1980 election removed the presidency and the Senate from Democratic control that the party's policy role went appreciably beyond the mobilization of legislative majorities to the formulation of distinctive partisan proposals. The assumption of such a role, which far exceeded what the congressional party had undertaken during the Nixon and Ford administrations, was facilitated by previous institutional changes—expanded party staffs; rules that increased party control over committee assignments, bill referrals, and scheduling; and perhaps most importantly, the presence and prominence of the congressional budget process. But, as we saw in examining national committee policy operations, such rules and procedures do not guarantee an assertive role; much also depends on personal leadership.

Since 1980 the most conspicuous congressional contribution to the development of the Democratic party's policy agenda has come from the Committee on Party Effectiveness of the House Democratic Caucus. This effort grew out of an issues conference and other discussions held by (mostly junior) House Democrats early in 1981. Caucus Chairman Gillis Long and Executive Director Alvin From organized the committee, largely bypassing the leadership of the standing committees and taking special care to include members from the moderate-to-conservative wing of the party. Also appointed were ancillary task forces (in areas such as housing, small business, national security, and crime), which included leaders from the relevant standing committees as well as members from the caucus committee. The committee met weekly over a 20-month period, reviewing the task force reports in detail and producing a 135-page report on the eve of the 1982 elections. The volume's centerpiece was a paper on long-term economic policy produced by a task force of only three: Long, Wirth, and Gephardt. Wirth and Gephardt were vocal advocates of rethinking the Democratic approach to the economy in light of the need to spur investment and growth and to secure the country's competitive position in high technology "sunrise" industries. Their paper advocated governmental measures to encourage private investment, a national research and development effort, educational and worker-retraining programs, investment in the public "infrastructure," and formation of an Economic Cooperation Council to map long-term industrial strategy.[37]

At first Speaker O'Neill and his staff were somewhat "nervous" about the caucus committee, From recalled, "but they eventually saw its work as reflecting favorably on the Speaker's leadership." He added:

One of our main achievements was simply to get people talking to each other, to break down some of the barriers that had grown up. We wanted to see if we couldn't find common ground on a lot of these issues and get some policy ideas developed and distributed.... Also, it was important in providing an outlet for younger members, for new talent.

Both the ideological spread of its membership and the necessity of deferring to the views of standing committee leaders made it difficult for the caucus committee to make specific recommendations in many areas. "Much of it is still at the level of rhetoric," From acknowledged.[38] But after the 1982 election the caucus took an unusual step: it directed the Democratic caucuses of the standing committees to report within three months on their disposition with respect to proposals in the caucus report that fell under their jurisdiction.

The 1982 election returns and shifts in the political climate created a favorable situation for Democrats in the House. Their most conspicuous success in 1983 was the passage of an alternative budget resolution. During Reagan's first two years, House Democrats had great difficulty both in formulating and in passing alternatives to the president's tax and budget proposals. In 1983, however, O'Neill and Long worked with Budget Committee Chairman James Jones to produce a budget resolution that reflected a number of recommendations in the caucus committee report and attracted a broad partisan consensus. The resolution prevailed despite the fact that it fell far short of the recommendations of powerful committees such as Armed Services and Ways and Means—thus confirming that the budget process could be a powerful tool for enhancing *party* (as well as presidential) leadership.

Party policy leadership was not as easily attained in other areas, however. Democratic leaders attempted to assemble a program for economic recovery to follow up the emergency jobs assistance bill passed in early 1983. These measures included emergency relief for homeowners and farmers facing foreclosure, health insurance for the unemployed, and public works and public-service jobs bills. The authorizing committees, frustrated by years of fiscal stringency and the constraints of the budget process, proceeded to write ambitious measures, which led to charges of extravagance and malcoordination. "I'd like to see some of these weaknesses tightened up," Democratic Whip Thomas Foley complained. "But the House is run by committees." From concurred: "We [the caucus] don't really have much control." [39] Party leaders were of considerable importance in scheduling the measures, keeping them off the floor when troubles threatened, and suggesting changes to enhance their chance of passage. But it was a traditional brokering role, largely reactive to initiatives taken elsewhere. A number of the economic recovery bills passed the House, but few survived the Republican-controlled Senate.

The caucus's Committee on Party Effectiveness continued to meet throughout 1983, but it shifted the focus of its work considerably. Directing the committees to report back to the caucus on specific proposals, From noted, was "easier said than done." [40] Several caucus proposals slowly made their way through the standing committees, and caucus committee members had appreciable influence in shaping some of these bills. But as the Democratic presidential nomination contest warmed up and as it became clear that the DNC National Strategy Council was essentially defunct, Representative Long and other caucus leaders increasingly attempted, not simply to shepherd party proposals through the House, but to influence the direction of wider policy debate within the party. Therefore, Long joined with former DNC chairman Strauss in late 1983 to form a National-House Democratic Caucus that extended beyond congressional circles and began holding "forums" across the country. The caucus committee also planned an early 1984 revision of its 1982 report in which the earlier focus on industrial policy would be broadened to include tax simplification, deficit reduction, and other economic questions.

Senate Democrats organized nothing comparable to Long's caucus effort during the 97th Congress, but Minority Leader Byrd named several task forces—by late 1983, they numbered nine—to draft new policy approaches. Although the Senate's parties, unlike the House's, have policy committees established by law, they have played a less active role in policy formulation. Lyndon Johnson, while opposing the efforts of Paul Butler's DAC in the 1950s, made no effort to use the Senate's party organs to comparable ends:

> By the time Mike Mansfield took over as Senate majority leader in 1961, the Democratic Policy Committee had become a far different instrument than its framers had intended. . . . Insofar as there was any demand for partisan presence in the Senate in the 1950s, it was met personally by the dominating figure of the majority leader. As a separate institution, the Majority Policy Committee had virtually no identity. It did not make policy. It did not coordinate the work of standing committees. It functioned primarily as one of many channels through which the majority leader took soundings in preparation for scheduling floor activity.[41]

Mansfield convened both the party conference and the Democratic Policy Committee more frequently than Johnson, utilizing them less to ratify his own predetermined objectives and more to identify strategies generally acceptable to majority members. But Mansfield's reluctance to attempt to impose party discipline and the fact that he served initially under Democratic presidents militated against a more ambitious definition of the party's policy role. Occasionally, and somewhat more frequently after the Democrats lost the White House in 1968, the Democratic Policy Committee passed resolutions on matters of substance (for example, on the withdrawal of troops from Vietnam in 1971) and took them to the conference for approval. In 1975 Mansfield appointed an ad hoc committee that researched and promoted a Democratic "program" on energy, mainly relying on work already under way in the standing committees. But such efforts were rare: the conference and policy committee mainly concerned themselves with legislative scheduling and strategy, keeping their staffs small and their ventures into substantive policy development quite limited.[42]

When Robert Byrd succeeded Mansfield as majority leader in 1977, he had few incentives to change the role of party organs drastically: the party's committee chieftains valued their independence, and there was a

Democratic program emanating from the White House. He used party organs more energetically than his predecessor, and as part of a staff buildup he began to hire a few aides with substantial policy expertise. But it was not until the 1980 elections removed both the Democratic president and—for the first time since 1954—Democratic control of the Senate that the need for a new kind of policy role seriously presented itself.

Byrd did not respond quickly or dramatically, but Democratic Policy Committee operations underwent a significant change, taking on some of the character the GOP Policy Committee had assumed under Howard Baker's and John Tower's leadership during the Carter administration. By mid-1983 the combined Democratic Conference/Policy Committee staff had expanded to 35, including 15 substantive issue specialists. Staff output included not only the traditional briefings on scheduled floor action and roll-call vote analyses, but longer, more substantive pieces. Most of these were "special reports" aimed at the opposition—for example, "Reagan Recession Reviews" and analyses of interest rates and monetary policy—but some sought to lay the groundwork for Democratic initiatives in areas such as foreign arms sales, Latin American policy, and the Federal Reserve Board's control of interest rates.

In the meantime, Byrd organized the nine party task forces. Some of them (for example, Strategic Forces and Arms Control, Agriculture and Rural Development, and Crime) consisted mainly of Democratic members from a single standing committee, while others were structured to address specific problems across committee lines (Emergency Human Needs, Monetary Policy). The most noteworthy of the task forces was the one on long-term economic policy, chaired by Senator Edward Kennedy, the only one to which Byrd named himself. This group paralleled the Long-Gephardt-Wirth task force in the House; by mid-1983 the two had worked out a cooperative relationship, making a joint presentation on legislative priorities to the DNC's National Strategy Council although the Senate group did not publish its analysis until late in the year.[43]

Structures of this sort have been rare in the Senate, where traditions of committee (and member) autonomy have been stronger than in the House. But as the Democratic Policy Committee's staff director noted, the loss of committee chairmanships greatly reduced members' resistance to this kind of policy effort:

> Things are very partisan around here now. There's very little of this business of bipartisan committee leadership. [Robert] Dole *runs* the Finance Committee; [former chairman] Russell Long has very little say. They've really shut us out.... Since our people are pretty much excluded from committee work anyway, it bothers them less to have [cross-committee] task forces working in their area.[44]

As Republican unity began to crumble early in the 98th Congress and Democrats gained more leverage over policy outcomes, there were some indications that the minority might lose interest in developing comprehensive policy alternatives and find it more difficult to agree on specific formulations.[45] But the tendency of the Reagan administration to eschew compromise, widespread demands for Democratic alternatives, and the increased willingness of Democratic senators to see their committees bypassed still provided incentives and opportunities to the leadership for a new kind of party policy role.

The development of partisan machinery to formulate policy is an important component of party renewal on Capitol Hill. In this area as in others, strengthening the parties may be less a matter of restoring lost functions than of finding new ones in an altered environment. Lyndon Johnson and Sam Rayburn saw such efforts as both unnecessary and politically threatening. But stronger issue orientations among voters and party activists have placed a greater political premium on policy development, a fact reflected in the demands and expectations of members of Congress themselves. The reduced power and increasing moderation of Southern Democrats have made policy formulation less threatening to party unity. Centrifugal tendencies in congressional organization have reduced the powers of committee barons to resist and have increased the sense that leadership efforts to overcome fragmentation and promote concerted action are needed. And the budget process confronts the opposition party with the necessity (and opportunity) of asserting itself in policy formulation.

The congressional parties, however imaginative and aggressive their leaders, are not likely to be all-sufficient formulators of policy for the out party. As promising as the work of the House Democratic Caucus's Committee on Party Effectiveness may be, it displays a lack of boldness and specificity that probably owes less to the qualities of this particular group than to the constraints under which it was bound to labor—ideological divergences among members, the interests of committee leaders and constituency spokesmen, and a disinclination on the part of legislators to probe too deeply or to depart very far from conventional approaches. Modern party leaders have rightly rejected the DAC model—however useful it might have been in the 1950s—because of its tendency to perpetuate the gap between the congressional and presidential parties. It is no solution, however, to leave preplatform attempts to formulate policy solely to elected officials, in Congress or elsewhere. Fortunately, the House Democratic Caucus and Senate Democratic Policy Committee have been able to take up some of the slack left by the default of the DNC's Strategy Council. But such efforts are not enough.

Party Platforms

National committee and congressional efforts to formulate policy have a much greater impact on party platforms than one might think, given the extent to which candidates and their organizations have come to dominate the presidential nomination process. Despite conventional cynicism about the meaningfulness of platforms, the fact is that a large percentage of their promises and proposals are implemented. Party policy development is not a vain academic exercise: whether it is done imaginatively or reflexively, and which groups and actors are involved in the process, may well have a significant impact on governmental priorities and performance.

Michael Malbin's careful study of platform writing in 1980 finds the Republicans following what has become the normal out-party pattern: the platform basically was a joint product of the party in Congress and the Washington-based "issue networks" (former administration officials, Republican-oriented lawyers and policy specialists, and group spokesmen). RNC Chairman Brock appointed John Tower, chairman of the Senate Republican Policy Committee, as platform committee chairman; Trent Lott, chairman of the Research Committee of the House Republican Conference, was named vice-chairman (along with Indiana Gov. Otis Bowen). The staff members directing the RNC advisory councils, Executive Director Roger Semerad and Editor-in-Chief Michael Baroody, were given the two top platform committee jobs. Reagan was represented by Richard Allen for foreign policy and Martin Anderson for domestic policy. The initial drafts were written under Baroody's direction and then reviewed by an executive committee consisting of Tower, Lott, Bowen, seven platform subcommittee chairmen appointed by Tower (all members of Congress), and Reagan's representatives. "Although the executive committee reviewed the drafts extensively, the platform remained a party statement that Anderson and Allen cleared, as opposed to a Reagan document." [46]

Many of the ideas in the platform were developed and legitimated through the RNC's advisory councils. While members of Congress clearly had the upper hand in the platform-writing process, the national committee was not as dependent on ideas generated on the Hill as the Democrats had been in 1976 and were likely to be in 1984; one side effect of Brock's vigorous advisory council effort, Semerad noted, was that "the Hill staff had to contend with the RNC." [47]

Once the platform moved from executive committee drafting to the sessions of the platform subcommittees and full committee, other forces had to be reckoned with: single-issue activists and ideologues in Congress. After vigorous debate, the draft was amended to include support for a constitutional amendment banning abortion and to clearly assert a goal of military "superiority" over the Soviet Union. A sentence affirming the party's past support of the ERA was removed. But despite hundreds of amendments, the great bulk of the platform remained basically unchanged from the advance draft reviewed by the executive committee.[48]

The Democratic platform was essentially a White House document. The platform committee's executive director, Elaine Kamarck, worked with White House staff to produce a draft platform in the spring of 1980. The Drafting Committee, chaired by South Carolina Gov. Richard Riley and dominated by Carter forces, largely endorsed this draft. But when the full platform committee met in late June, it was clear that White House control would be seriously challenged.

To some extent these challenges were the mirror image of those mounted by Republican antiabortionists and ERA opponents. Nuclear power opponents, "pro-choice" women's groups, and advocates of gay rights won concessions that, as Malbin notes, "demonstrated the permeability of the process in the clearest possible terms." [49] But the determination of the Kennedy forces to make the platform a battleground for their challenge to the president gave numerous dissenting groups a rallying point they otherwise would have lacked and a mechanism for taking their battles to the convention floor. Kennedy went so far as to call the Platform Committee document "Democratic only in name"; "basic differences remain," said his chief issues adviser, on "such issues as inflation, unemployment, national health insurance and the MX missile." [50] Of the 23 minority reports filed to the Platform Committee report, 17 supported Kennedy proposals.

The appeal of many of the minority planks, not merely to a scattering of single-issue groups, but to major groups such as labor, the National Education Association, and women's and minority organizations, weakened Carter's position. The impact of the Winograd Commission rules giving candidates the ability to slate delegates of their own choosing was apparent in the loyalty Carter was able to command on the test vote on the rule binding delegates to their declared presidential preference. But since constituency groups had also had a hand in slating hundreds of these delegates, they were susceptible to crosspressures if sensitive platform issues were pressed to a vote. "There are Carter delegates who are labor delegates ... who are women delegates ... who are teacher delegates," said one Carter operative. "It's just not possible for a Carter whip to walk up and down the aisle and say 'thumbs up,' 'thumbs down.' " [51] Moreover, even if Carter could have prevailed on most votes, he had a tremendous stake in avoiding bitter battles on national television.

Carter thus conceded to Kennedy on a number of issues and refrained from pushing others to roll-call votes. After losing a roll-call to Kennedy and labor forces on the designation of a guarantee of work for every able-bodied citizen as the "single highest domestic priority," Carter forces negotiated an agreement accepting much of Kennedy's economic plank (but not wage and price controls). Carter also was forced to concede on two issues pushed by the National Organization of Women with considerable help from the NEA and from the Kennedy organization: one plank supporting Medicaid funding of abortions and another that instructed the party to deny campaign support to candidates who did not support the Equal Rights Amendment. On several proposals sponsored or supported by Kennedy (a "comprehensive" approach to national health insurance, repealing tax breaks for oil companies, and halting deployment of the MX missile system), Carter insisted on a roll-call vote and prevailed. But when Carter issued his written comments on the platform (an exercise required by another Kennedy-sponsored resolution), he was forced to qualify his endorsement with a number of "understandings" and "reservations." [52]

In both parties, then, there is a marked disparity between the early and late stages of platform writing. The drafting stage is dominated by the White House if the party holds the presidency, by the congressional party and committee leadership if it does not. It is also primarily at this stage (for the out party) that the impact of national committee policy councils is felt—an important complement to the congressional role in recent Republican experience but much less significant for the Democrats.

The work of the staffs and committees that first draft the platform is important, despite the prevalent impression that it is later chopped to bits by issue activists in the full platform committee and at the convention. In fact, most of their work remains in place, and the candidate is likely to place greater stress on their themes and proposals than on much that is added later. This is because many of the latter-stage amendments are accepted grudgingly by the candidates; they are relevant to intraparty nomination politics but may actually be a handicap at the general election stage. There, the broad interparty differences and the major policy initiatives stressed by the early drafters are likely to be more pertinent.[53]

They will also be pertinent as the administration puts together its legislative program. A new president's State of the Union address and leading proposals to Congress typically draw heavily on themes and promises contained in the platform. Studies of administrations since the 1940s show that almost two-thirds of the promises contained in the platforms of parties winning the presidency have been fully or substantially implemented. Parties that do not win the presidency are generally able to redeem more than one-half of their pledges, their chances being improved, of course, if they win control of Congress. While these success rates reflect the presence of similar pledges on many issues in the platforms of both parties, they generally hold up on issues where the parties' positions differ or where the platform departs from majority public opinion on behalf of a particular group in the party coalition. They also reflect party voting on platform issues in Congress: the modest levels of party polarization and intraparty cohesion reported in Chapter 3 often rise on issues where the parties' platforms are in conflict.[54]

Although such findings belie much of the conventional cynicism about platforms, they should not be exaggerated. Recent years have seen some falling off from the platform fulfillment levels of the 1950s and 1960s, particularly in the number of pledges fully redeemed. Nor can it be assumed that the platform pledge is always of independent importance in prompting action. Its presence merely may indicate that a given idea has already become ascendant in Congress or among the "issue networks." Of course, neither the specificity of platform pledges nor the rates of fulfillment measure up to "responsible-party" standards. Still, party members are not acting irrationally or futilely when they fight to influence the platform. Platforms represent a kind of "national plan" that politicians and officials often take seriously and that influences markedly what they set out to accomplish.[55]

It seems likely that fulfillment rates are lower for planks added at the platform committee and convention stages than for those that have percolated through Congress, the administration, and the issue networks. The dynamics of these latter stages led President Carter's chief adviser on domestic policy to characterize the platform as "the sum total of the maximum demands of every group."[56] The kind of platform-amending activity that went on at both conventions in 1980 bears witness to the rise of issue-oriented "amateurism" in both parties and, especially on the Democratic side, to the impact of rules that have facilitated participation by candidate and issue enthusiasts and have reduced the role of party leaders and elected officials. In both parties, spokesmen for single-issue groups find it easy enough to work their way onto the platform committee and relevant subcommittees, although the Republicans have done more than the Democrats to balance this influence with greater elected-official involvement. (Only five members of Congress served on the Democratic platform committee in 1980 compared with 20 for the GOP.)

Platform amending can provide a safety valve for dissent within the party and build enthusiasm among groups needed to fuel volunteer campaign activities. But it also can reduce the credibility of the platform—both as a campaign standard and as a "national plan"—and jeopardize the party's broad, mainstream appeal. The need to produce a responsible platform that will effectively shape congressional and executive action is one of the best reasons for restoring, in some measure, the influence of party leaders and public officeholders within the national convention and its platform committee.

Policy Development and Party Renewal

Much of the discussion following the 1980 election seemed to belie the textbook verities about the nonprogrammatic character of the American parties. The Republicans, having cultivated an image as the "party of ideas," proceeded in a disciplined fashion to propose and to enact an unusually comprehensive economic program. The response of various Democratic organizations, leaders, and potential candidates was to embark on a well-advertised search for "new ideas"—a critical component, it was argued, of a revitalized party. "I think the people felt we were getting a little stale," said Vice President Walter Mondale soon after the election. "One of the virtues of losing is that it gives you time to think again . . . to really focus on the central questions." [57]

In several respects this Democratic quest was an overreaction based on questionable assumptions about what underlay the Republican victory and how the Democratic "alternative" was likely to emerge. [58] First, the role of ideas and ideology in producing Reagan's victory was overestimated. The content and the coherence of the Republican appeal was a much less potent factor than electoral reactions to economic and foreign policy adversities linked to the Carter administration. Second, the intellectual quality and coherence of the Republican ideas themselves was overestimated. The Kemp-Roth plan for reduced taxes/increased defense spending/balanced budgets was an unstable amalgam at best, and much of the campaign consisted of evoking stock responses to big government, high taxes, and perceived national weakness. Third, in their rush to innovate, some underestimated the continuing validity and appeal of Democratic attempts at social amelioration and agreed too readily that domestic programs—many of them, after all, aimed at society's most intractable problems—had "failed." Finally, there was a tendency to overestimate both the extent to which the party could embrace wholistic "ideas" and the possibility of generating new policy approaches apart from the slow process of testing and consensus building in Congress and on the campaign trail. The American political environment still militates against programatically precise and tightly disciplined parties.

While such caveats are worth noting, they do not gainsay the role that policy formulation and debate can play in renewing the Democratic party's sense of purpose and its electoral viability. To recognize the incompatibility of classic "responsible" parties with the cultural and institutional environment should not preclude the possibility that environmental changes might encourage and facilitate new policy roles.[59] As already suggested, the parties now face a better educated, more issue-oriented electorate. And with the increasing complexity of the problems faced by governments, and the increasing acceptance of a positive role for the state (persistent bursts of laissez-faire nostalgia notwithstanding), has come a heightened sense that governing *requires* coherent planning and policy development. Richard Neustadt has shown how such expectations have transformed the presidency.[60] They also have created, not merely a tolerance for a more programmatic party role, but a widespread expectation that parties will come forward with relatively specific diagnoses and "solutions." These pressures and incentives are reinforced by the new interest in policy among activists within the parties themselves and by the concerns increasingly expressed among officeholders that centrifugal forces within government be checked and mechanisms of coordination and leadership be strengthened.

In this context, policy-germination efforts may prove critical to party strength—both in heightening the parties' electoral appeal and in increasing their capacity to induce loyalty and cohesion within the party-in-government. In the modern Congress, restoring the levels of party cohesion that Johnson and Rayburn periodically attained may require the sort of partisan policy-development efforts that they scorned. The parties' perceived legitimacy and their capacity to retain the allegiance of their diverse constituency groups require that the process of policy formulation be open and permeable. But what strengthens the parties on one front may weaken them on another: the groups that take advantage of the permeability of the process have tended, in recent experience, to take the parties' policy positions in directions that reduced their mainstream electoral appeal and their credibility as a standard around which the party-in-government might cohere. Thus it is important to balance openness with mechanisms to give party leaders and officeholders a central role in establishing the baseline for debate. Such a role surely is consistent with their "representative" status vis-à-vis the parties' broader constituencies.

The Democrats have had a harder time than the Republicans in achieving such a balance in recent years. This is partly because the party has been more divided—presidential versus congressional "wings," reformers versus regulars. Controversies linked to party reform have had a major impact—creating disputes, for example, over how the preferred policy structures of the issue activists (midterm conferences, platform committees) were to function and pressures to "open up" the advisory councils (or, alternatively, to render them inactive). It is thus of particular significance that the quest for new ideas and approaches has proceeded as vigorously as it has on so many Democratic fronts since 1980. But it is also important to ask to what extent the quest in its present form will serve the party's long-range interests and needs.

The mechanisms for policy formulation currently at work within the Democratic party—the DNC's National Strategy Council, the midterm party conference, the House Democratic Caucus and Senate Democratic Policy Committee—are dominated substantively and strategically by the party's congressional leadership. This is the normal out-party pattern but with some distinctive features: the efforts at policy germination on Capitol Hill have surpassed what Democratic party leaders have attempted in the past, and the national committee's role has fallen far short of what has become the normal Republican out-party practice. And none of these party organs has a monopoly on the shaping of the agenda. In the Democratic case it is important to take note of two additional sets of actors: the private "policy shops" linked to the party and the candidates lining up for the 1984 presidential derby.

Think-tank Proliferation

For many of those who reflected on the Republicans' electoral and policy triumphs in 1980 and on the country's perceived shift to the right, the role of periodicals and think tanks in giving currency and respectability to conservative ideas seemed of considerable importance. Washington research organizations such as the Brookings Institution and Urban Institute, although identified with relatively progressive approaches to public policy, have been less inclined than their conservative counterparts (the American Enterprise Institute for Public Policy Research, the Heritage Foundation, or the Institute for Contemporary Studies, for example) to develop and disseminate specific policy recommendations. What was needed, some argued, was a new kind of Democratically-oriented think tank to develop working relationships between scholars and policy makers, "to bring disciplined thinking to bear on major public policy issues, to help develop realistic choices for the nation's future, and to communicate these options to policy-makers and the public." [61] Thus between March 1981 and April 1982 four new institutions were launched:

● The Center for National Policy (changed from the Center for Democratic Policy to make clear that it was not an official party organ). Initially chaired by Duke University President and former governor Terry Sanford; then by former secretary of state Cyrus Vance; directed by Ted Van Dyk, former assistant to Hubert Humphrey and George McGovern.

● The National Policy Exchange. Headed by former labor secretary Ray Marshall. The vice president and chief editor, Paul Jensen, was deputy director of the 1976 Democratic platform committee and former study director of the Democratic Advisory Council of Elected Officials.

● The Democracy Project. Headed by author and former Ralph Nader associate Mark Green.

● The Roosevelt Center for American Policy Studies. Chaired by Chicago businessman and philanthropist Richard Dennis; directed by Douglas Bennet, former assistant secretary of state and staff director of the Senate Budget Committee.

There were discernible shades of difference among these institutions. The National Policy Exchange, financed primarily by organized labor, focused its attention on domestic economic and social-welfare policy. The Democracy Project was the group closest to the muckraking tradition, frequently exposing outrages and abuses. It was the Roosevelt Center that made the most of its nonpartisanship and that most closely resembled the traditional center for visiting scholars. The Center for National Policy was the group with the broadest base of support and the strongest relationship with the DNC and Democratic groups on Capitol Hill. This proliferation of policy "shops" produced a beneficial diversity of approaches, but it also set up competition for scarce dollars and talent. All of the operations were small, mainly relying on outside authors and panels rather than in-house research staffs. What kind of institutional staying power they would have, once the Democratic fervor for new ideas had faded, remained to be seen.

Only the Center for National Policy established an ongoing relationship with policy-formulating bodies within the party. Its main focus was on commissioning and assembling papers on "alternatives for the 1980s," treating such issues as wage/price policy, taxation and fiscal policy, strategic weapons policy, and conventional military programs. Usually the papers were presented at press conferences and then discussed by the authors and members of Congress at meetings arranged by the party leadership. The center also geared up a long-range project on industrial policy, naming a broadly based panel that included Sens. Edward Kennedy and Bill Bradley, AFL-CIO President Lane Kirkland, and financier Felix Rohatyn. "We plan a report similar to what a presidential commission would produce," said the center's president in mid-1983. "We'll be working especially closely with Kennedy's [Senate Democratic Conference] task force on industrial policy." [62]

The Center for National Policy has not developed as fully as some of its sponsors hoped; its staff, originally projected at 20, still numbers eight, and it fell considerably short of the $1 million budget targeted for 1982. Several anticipated research projects have been cut back. But the Center nonetheless has played a useful role as a catalyst for policy analysis and as a resource for policy makers, filling some of the gaps left by the DNC's Strategy Council. Its ties with and orientation toward Congress have heightened its influence, while perhaps rendering it less likely than some of the other groups to develop unconventional ideas.

Candidates and "New Ideas"

Candidates, especially presidential candidates, are both consumers and interpreters of the policy ideas generated within the party. While major initiatives are often linked with their names (Kennedy and the "war on poverty," Nixon and revenue sharing, Reagan and "supply-side" economics), they often represent a repackaging or a highlighting of proposals that have germinated for many years in Congress, policy councils, and party platforms. A look at the 1984 presidential candidates as they began to test the waters should shed some light on how the process of issue assimilation and interpretation works.

The addresses made by presidential hopefuls at the Democratic National Party Conference in Philadelphia in mid-1982 furnish a useful point of reference. Table 9-2 provides a rough indication of the issues that were emphasized by the six then-active contenders (Kennedy had not yet withdrawn, and former governor Reubin Askew elected not to speak). The similarities in the themes they enunciated are more striking than the differences, except for the remarks of two, quite different speakers: Sens. Ernest Hollings and Gary Hart.

Hollings differed from the others in his emphasis on fiscal responsibility and his scolding of the party for catering to "single issue interests" at the expense of the whole. His strategy (except on the issue of nuclear weapons) was apparently to distinguish himself by appearing more single-mindedly conservative than one might have expected on the basis of his overall record. Hart was distinctive in a quite different way: he presented himself as the champion of "new solutions.... A new Democratic vision for the eighties and nineties." He touched upon many areas where he and other so-called "neoliberals" had been calling on their colleagues to rethink their traditional positions: promoting economic growth and productivity, building a cost-effective and no-frills system of national defense, establishing a tax system that is "simple and just and fair," and proving that "it's possible to be fiscally responsible and morally responsible at the same time." [63]

John Glenn entered a strong caveat against the "neoliberal" emphasis on promoting "sunrise" industries: "We can no more turn our backs on our older industries than we can turn our backs on our older communities." But it was Edward Kennedy who made the most pointed jabs at those who would depart from liberal orthodoxy:

> Rethinking our ideas must never be an excuse for retreating from our ideals.... We do not seek new ideas solely for the sake of their novelty. For us the test of an idea is not whether it is new or old, but whether it is right or wrong. And for those old ideas which are right, we must continue a never-ending fight. [64]

Kennedy's speech, and those of the other contenders as well, revealed more change than one might have inferred from such rhetoric. To be sure, they all touched a number of constituency bases—with newly ascendant groups such as teachers and women receiving more scrupulous attention than labor and farmers. They sounded traditional Democratic themes on unemployment and high interest rates and attacked Reagan's tax cuts as a bonanza for the rich. But national health insurance and welfare reform, the major pieces of unfinished business from the 1970s, were hardly mentioned, even by Kennedy, health insurance's erstwhile Senate sponsor. And while Kennedy pointedly praised President Carter's record on international human rights, a longstanding interest of his, the others hardly mentioned either that theme or another Carter favorite, environmental protection. [65]

While a theme analysis of this sort cannot support definitive conclusions, the midterm conference performances suggest that a party that depends wholly on its candidates for its new ideas and policy directions

Table 9-2 Themes Emphasized by Prospective Presidential Candidates in Addresses before Democratic National Party Conference, 1982

	Cranston	Kennedy	Mondale	Glenn	Hart	Hollings
Unemployment	X	XX	XX	XX		
Interest rates	X	XX	X	X		
Tax simplicity/fairness		XX	XX	X	XX	
Special interest money in politics			XX			
Catering to single interests at expense of whole						XX
Budget deficits	X			X		XX
Increase American productivity, economic growth		X	X	X	XX	
Foster basic as well as "sunrise" industry			X	XX		
Control nuclear weapons	XX	XX	XX	XX	XX	XX
Rational, balanced defense policy		X	X	XX	XX	
International human rights		XX				
ERA, women's rights	X	XX	XX	X	X	
Voting rights, discrimination	X	X	X	X		X
Environmental protection		X				
Protect the helpless and needy	X	X	X	X	X	
Protect social security		XX	X	X		
Protect farmers		X	X	X		
Safeguard gains of labor		X	X			
Support education		X	X	X	X	
National health insurance		X				
Welfare reform				X		

XX = major theme   X = secondary theme

SOURCE: 1982 Democratic National Party Conference, *Official Proceedings*, and personal observation.

may have a rather long wait. Every indication in 1982 was that the candidates had begun to abandon themes and proposals that seemed out of phase with the current public mood but had developed very little to take their place. Every candidate, to be sure, responded to the growing concern over the perils of nuclear war. Most tipped their hat to the ideas of tax simplification and industrial development that were gaining currency among "neoliberals" in Congress and elsewhere. But these speeches mainly revealed not what the emerging themes of policy debate would be but how fluid and undeveloped they remained.[66]

The mechanisms for policy formulation examined in this chapter contribute critically to the strength and viability of the parties and to the content of their programs. As of late 1983, the Democratic party's performance on this front was more impressive than it was during the Nixon-Ford years. But there are disconcerting signs as well. Debates on industrial policy have broken some new ground, but much less imagination and energy have gone into defending old positions or defining new ones in other policy areas. The National Strategy Council, while failing to broaden the policy initiatives under way in Congress, also has left a vacuum at the DNC that various groups less oriented toward the party mainstream may successfully attempt to fill. Critical tests lie ahead: translating statements of principle into legislative programs on Capitol Hill; activating the NSC's advisory panels to develop and legitimate proposals with an eye to the platform; and integrating the new ideas being generated and the old ones that retain their force into a coherent and politically viable campaign appeal. (The televised response to the 1983 State of the Union address, which drew on the report of the caucus's Committee on Party Effectiveness and on which congressional and DNC staff collaborated, was a promising first attempt.) The Republicans had a party agenda largely in place when they won in 1980. The Democrats, looking toward 1984, cannot afford to do less. The need and the potential for the parties to contribute substantially to the nation's policy agenda have increased considerably in recent years. But it is up to the parties to generate the will and the resources to carry out this role effectively.

NOTES

1. Committee on Political Parties, American Political Science Association, "Toward a More Responsible Two-Party System," *American Political Science Review* 44 (September 1950 supplement): 20-21.
2. Hugh A. Bone, *Party Committees and National Politics* (Seattle: University of Washington Press, 1958), 226.
3. Cornelius P. Cotter and Bernard C. Hennessy, *Politics Without Power: The National Party Committees* (New York: Atherton Press, 1964), 193-194.
4. See the accounts compiled by the Republican Coordinating Committee in "The Development of National Party Policy Between Conventions" (Washington, D.C.: Republican National Committee, 1966), 3-6.
5. Ibid., 6-7, 16-23.
6. For an example from 1942, see Ibid., 7-8, 24-26.
7. James L. Sundquist, *Politics and Policy: The Eisenhower, Kennedy, and Johnson Years* (Washington, D.C.: The Brookings Institution, 1968), 406. For an account of the Democratic Advisory Council,

see 405-415; Bone, *Party Committees,* 219-233; and Cotter and Hennessy, *Politics Without Power,* 211-224.

8. Bone, *Party Committees,* 220.
9. Ibid., 223-224; *Democratic Digest* 4 (April 1957): 11.
10. Cotter and Hennessy, *Politics Without Power,* 217.
11. Sundquist, *Politics and Policy,* 415.
12. Cotter and Hennessy, *Politics Without Power,* 223.
13. See the account in Ibid., 195-204. For the committee's full report, see Republican Committee on Program and Progress, *Decisions for a Better America* (Garden City, N.Y.: Doubleday, 1960).
14. See Republican Coordinating Committee, "Development of Party Policy," 27-32; and the account in Cotter and Hennessy, *Politics Without Power,* 204-210.
15. See the account in John F. Bibby and Robert J. Huckshorn, "Out-Party Strategy: Republican National Committee Rebuilding Politics, 1964-66," in *Republican Politics,* ed. Bernard Cosman and R. Huckshorn (New York: Frederick A. Praeger, 1968), 218-223.
16. See *The Republican,* May 10, 1968, 8-10; February 7, 1969, 2, 15.
17. RCC reports are collected in Republican Coordinating Committee, *Choice for America* (Washington, D.C.: Republican National Committee, 1968); on revenue sharing, see 81-94.
18. Council publications included an early manifesto formulated by the committees and approved by the full council, *America in the 1970s* (Washington, D.C.: Democratic National Committee, 1970); and a series of reports from the planning groups addressed to the platform committee, *Alternatives '72* (Washington, D.C.: Democratic National Committee, 1972).
19. Interview with John Stewart, June 7, 1983.
20. See *New York Times,* April 6, 1975, 23. The council's only publications were *An Interim Report* (1974), which listed the study groups and the papers they had commissioned and several brief resolutions passed by the council, and *Democratic Reports* (1975), a summary account of discussions in "issue seminars" at the 1974 midterm party conference.
21. David Broder, "The Democratic Party," *Washington Post,* October 29, 1975, A27.
22. "We must not forget," wrote Chairman Brock in his introduction to the inaugural issue, "that the last great partisan coalition of American politics [i.e., the New Deal] was built on ideas. These were no less forceful and appealing, if also debatable, for their identification with a political party.... Accordingly, the Republican Party finds itself in opposition not only to a majority party that controls the machineries of government, but to the force of certain such ideas. It is our continuing obligation, therefore, to articulate our own.... The contest for votes must also be a contest of ideas." *Commonsense* 1 (Summer 1978): iv.
23. RNC Advisory Council on Economic Affairs, "The Republican Tax Cut" (1978); RNC Advisory Council on Human Concerns, "Housing Issues" (1979); Michael J. Malbin, "The Conventions, Platforms, and Issue Activists," in *The American Elections of 1980,* ed. Austin Ranney (Washington, D.C.: American Enterprise Institute for Public Policy Research, 1981), 102.
24. Interview with Michael Baroody, April 16, 1982.
25. Interview with Eugene Eidenberg, April 1, 1982.
26. Interview with Bernard Aronson, April 8, 1983.
27. *Washington Post,* March 14, 1982, D7.
28. Jack Germond and Jules Witcover, "Lack of a Leader Clouds Democrats' Picture of Unity," *Raleigh News and Observer,* July 1, 1982, 5A.
29. APSA, Committee on Political Parties, "Toward a More Responsible Two-Party System," 38, 43, 56.
30. See *Congressional Quarterly Weekly Reports,* November 30, 1974, 3209-3214; December 14, 1974, 3330-3332. On the composition of the conference and the orientation of the delegates, see Denis G. Sullivan, Jeffrey L. Pressman, and Christopher Arterton, *Explorations in Convention Decision Making* (San Francisco: W. H. Freeman, 1976), chap. 3.
31. Democratic Advisory Council of Elected Officials, *Democratic Reports.*
32. William Crotty, *Party Reform* (New York: Longman, 1983), 116. See also *Congressional Quarterly Weekly Report,* December 16, 1978, 3431-3435.
33. See Alan Ehrenhalt, "The Democratic Left Faces a Dilemma," *Congressional Quarterly Weekly Report,* December 16, 1978, 3431-3432. The 1976 convention had narrowly missed approving a resolution requiring a conference of at least 2,000 delegates, with at least two-thirds of them selected at or below the congressional district level. *Congressional Quarterly Weekly Report,* July 17, 1976, 1938-1939.
34. Dom Bonafede, "Democrats Hope their Midterm Meeting Will Send a Message of Party Unity," *National Journal,* June 19, 1982, 1098-1100. See also *Congressional Quarterly Weekly Reports,* September 26, 1981, 1857; June 19, 1982, 1467-1469; July 3, 1982, 1591-1595.
35. Charles O. Jones, *Party and Policy-Making: The House Republican Policy Committee* (New Brunswick: Rutgers University Press, 1964), 84.
36. Charles Jones in 1970 described the organizational changes in the House Republican party since 1959 as "the most important developments in the role of the minority party in policy making in this century." See *The Minority Party in Congress* (Boston: Little, Brown & Co., 1970), 160.
37. Committee on Party Effectiveness, Democratic Caucus, U.S. House of Representatives, *Rebuilding the Road to Opportunity: A Democratic Direction for the 1980s,* September 1982, 16-31. On caucus

operations under Long's tenure, see Richard E. Cohen, "Gillis Long Presses House Democrats to Establish a New Party Identity," *National Journal*, December 4, 1982, 2075-2076; and Diane Granat, "Democratic Caucus Renewed as Forum for Policy Questions," *Congressional Quarterly Weekly Report*, October 15, 1983, 2115-2119.

38. Interview with Alvin From, November 19, 1982.
39. Richard E. Cohen, "Fill in the Democratic Blanks," *National Journal*, May 14, 1983, 1020; *Congressional Quarterly Weekly Report*, April 30, 1983, 851; and interview with Alvin From, June 6, 1983.
40. Interview with Alvin From, December 15, 1983.
41. Donald A. Robinson, "If the Senate Democrats Want Leadership: An Analysis of the History and Prospects of the Senate Policy Committee," in *Policymaking Role of Leadership in the Senate* by the Commission on the Operation of the Senate (Washington, D.C.: U.S. Government Printing Office, 1976), 42. On the early operation of the Senate policy committees, see Bone, *Party Committees*, chap. 6. On the contrast between the Senate Republican Policy Committee and its more active House counterpart in the 1960s, see Jones, *Minority Party*, 160-174.
42. See Robinson, "If Senate Democrats Want Leadership," 42-47; and John G. Stewart, "Two Strategies of Leadership: Johnson and Mansfield," in *Congressional Behavior*, ed. Nelson W. Polsby (New York: Random House, 1971), chap. 5.
43. For the final report of the Kennedy Task Force, see U.S. Senate, Democratic Caucus, *Jobs for the Future: A Democratic Agenda*, November 16, 1983.
44. Interview with Robert Liberatore, May 31, 1983.
45. See Richard E. Cohen, "Minority Status Seems to Have Enhanced Byrd's Position among Fellow Democrats," *National Journal*, May 7, 1983, 958-960.
46. Malbin, "Conventions, Platforms and Issue Activists," 103. According to Michael Barnes, executive director of the Democratic platform committee in 1976 (and later representative from Maryland), the Democrats produced their platform as the out-party in a similar fashion. The document, he said, "was basically written by congressional staff. Obviously the Carter campaign was very important to us, as were the various leaders of the Democratic coalition. The Carter people pushed on maybe two or three things, but it was not basically a Carter document" (101-102).
47. Ibid., 102.
48. See Ibid., 104-116; *Congressional Quarterly Weekly Report*, July 12, 1980, 1923-1925; July 19, 1980, 2005-2008 (Republican platform text: 2030-2056).
49. Malbin, "Conventions, Platforms, and Issue Activists," 126.
50. *Congressional Quarterly Weekly Report*, June 28, 1980, 1796.
51. Ibid., August 16, 1980, 2363.
52. See Malbin, "Conventions, Platforms and Issue Activists," 126-153; *Congressional Quarterly Weekly Report*, August 16, 1980, 2360-2366 (Democratic platform text, 2390-2420; Carter statement, 2421-2422).
53. On the relation between platforms and campaign speeches, see John H. Kessel, "The Seasons of Presidential Politics," *Social Science Quarterly* 59 (December 1977): 418-435, and Malbin's insightful refinement of Kessel's analysis: "Conventions, Platforms, and Issue Activists," 136-139.
54. See Gerald M. Pomper, with Susan S. Lederman, *Elections in America: Control and Influence in Democratic Politics*, 2d ed. (New York: Longman, 1980), chap. 8; Kessel, "Seasons of Presidential Politics"; and Alan D. Monroe, "American Party Platforms and Public Opinion," *American Journal of Political Science* 27 (February 1983): 27-42.
55. Pomper, *Elections in America*, 173-176; and Paul T. David, "Party Platforms as National Plans," *Public Administration Review* 31 (May-June 1971): 303-315.
56. Stuart Eizenstat, quoted in Malbin, "Conventions, Platforms and Issue Activists," 135.
57. Tom Wicker, "Democrats in Search of Ideas," *New York Times Magazine*, Jan. 25, 1981, 34, 39-40.
58. This paragraph draws on Martin Kaplan, "Elections Aren't Won by 'New Ideas,'" *Washington Post*, November 19, 1981, C3; and Elizabeth Drew, "The Democrats," *The New Yorker*, March 22, 1982, 130-131.
59. For a balanced assessment focusing on the national committee's potential, see John G. Stewart, *One Last Chance: The Democratic Party, 1974-76* (New York: Praeger Publishers, 1974), 180-182.
60. For Richard Neustadt's account of the circumstances compelling President Eisenhower to assemble a comprehensive legislative program during his first term, see "Presidency and Legislation: Planning the President's Program," *American Political Science Review* 49 (December 1955): 980-1021.
61. Prospectus of the Roosevelt Center for American Policy Studies, April 13, 1982.
62. Interview with Ted Van Dyk, June 8, 1983.
63. 1982 Democratic National Party Conference, *Official Proceedings* (Washington, D.C.: Democratic National Committee), 80, 82-83. For contrasting assessments of the neoliberal phase of the quest for "new ideas," see Randall Rothenberg, "The Neoliberal Club," *Esquire* (February 1982): 37-46; and Sidney Blumenthal, "Carterism without Carter," *Working Papers* 8 (May-June 1981): 12-17.
64. *Official Proceedings*, 85, 201-203.
65. "I had my disagreements with the last administration," Kennedy said. "But on the vital issue of human rights, Ronald Reagan is wrong—and Jimmy Carter was right." Ibid., 204.
66. For a somewhat more optimistic assessment see Morton Kondracke, "The Democrats' New Agenda," *The New Republic*, October 18, 1982, 15-17.

Conclusion

The evidence presented in this book does not support either those who find the political parties irreversibly "in decline" or those who assert, as one student of Republican politics put it recently, that at least *one* of the American parties (that is, the GOP) is *already* "renewed." Rather, the evidence is mixed. Levels of identification with and reliance upon the parties in the electorate have declined, and independent identification and split-ticket voting have increased. Party organizations at all levels have lost much of the control they once had over the dispensing of jobs and patronage, the nomination of candidates, and the running of campaigns. Party cohesion within Congress and state legislatures has showed a long-term decline, and strong trends toward member individualism and organizational fragmentation have appeared. Even more serious has been the erosion of the parties' role in the executive branch. In short, there is ample reason for alarm about the state to which our parties have fallen.

There are, however, more signs of recovery and renewal than the burgeoning literature on party decline would lead one to expect. The decline of party voting and identification in the electorate seems to have leveled off, and the congruence between voters' policy views and partisan identifications has increased. Since the mid-1970s, party voting in Congress has become slightly more pronounced. The congressional party leadership, particularly in the House, has become more institutionalized and influential. State and national party organizations, especially within the GOP, have attained a degree of institutional permanence that they have never known before and have carved out a secure niche for themselves by virtue of their fund-raising and campaign-services capabilities. Even the Democratic party has taken tentative steps to offset the destructive aspects of modern party "reform," and both parties have increased their capacity for policy formulation.

The new-model parties that are emerging from the postwar period of transition differ in significant respects from their predecessors. They are more issue-oriented, both in the motivations of their activists and in the activities they undertake. While their local organizations display more "slack," their national committees have increased in authority and resources. Their hold on candidates and public officials has, in general, loosened, but they have begun to establish themselves as purveyors of the services required in the new campaign environment. These changes should not be exaggerated: our parties continue to blur ideological distinctions and to project an image (usually) of moderation. They are still, by most measures, decentralized organizations, with loose criteria of membership and limited means of inducing or enforcing party fidelity. But the trends toward "amateurism," "nationalization," and a redefined campaign role are pronounced and significant—indications of "qualitative" change that are imperfectly reflected in simple generalizations about resurgence or decline.

To what extent are these new-model parties likely to fill the "place" of party as defined in Chapter 4? Here it becomes necessary to distinguish between the Democratic and Republican cases because the parties differ considerably in the relative strengths and weaknesses they display. Advocates of increased participation and broadened representation within the Democratic party often have talked the language of party renewal, and their "reforms" have had certain positive effects, increasing the perceived legitimacy of party operations and the stake that previously underrepresented groups have in party affairs. But party renewal on the reformers' model has jeopardized the party's "mainstream" image and appeal and has weakened further the already eroding authority and resources of party organizations and of the party-in-government.

The experiences of the Hunt Commission, and of the Democrats' successive national party councils as well, illustrate the importance and the difficulty of striking an optimum balance in critical areas of party life—addressing policy questions in a creative way, but not so narrowly as to alienate critical elements in the party coalition; strengthening the "web" of party within the bounds of the American tradition of inclusive, coalitionist politics; ensuring fairness and broad participation, but not in ways that deny party organizations critical powers and resources. The breadth of the Democratic party's base and the permeability of its organizational structures represent substantial assets, at least up to a point, and some of the "corrective" trends of recent years hold considerable promise as well—increased staying power and attention to organizational work on the part of party activists and concerted attempts by party leaders to rebuild the party's organizational resources and campaign role. The Democratic party's capacities as an instrument of electoral accountability and responsiveness, as a mediating institution between citizens and the broader political community, and as an integrative mechanism within government thus look more hopeful than they did a decade ago. But how successfully the new-model party can recapture these roles is still very much an open question.

Republican efforts at party building have been, in some respects, more successful. The national Republican party and, to a lesser extent, the GOP's state organizations have developed ambitious programs of candidate recruitment, fund raising, campaign services, policy development and communications. The party-in-government seems to have been strengthened as a result, not so much through the overt exercise of party discipline as through an enhanced sense of dependence on and identification with the party on the part of elected officeholders. The national Republican party's organizational renaissance under the leadership of

RNC chairmen Ray Bliss and Bill Brock partially refutes the prophesies of inexorable party decline. But while the GOP case illustrates the *possibility* of "renewal," it also suggests what *kind* of renewal is adapted to the modern electoral environment. It is a pattern that the Democrats have felt constrained to replicate. "We're doing our best to copy them," states the director of the Democratic Congressional Campaign Committee, "because it doesn't make any sense to try to re-invent the wheel."[1]

This sense that the GOP model of party renewal is one the Democrats must emulate if they are to adapt successfully to modern circumstances is probably accurate. The Republican model, however, is not all-sufficient with regard either to the role of parties in general or to the Democrats' own potential. The GOP pattern is essentially one of party renewal from the top down. Mainly initiated by the party's national leaders, it requires a measure of subordination of state and local units and prompts a predominately financial and often impersonal mode of participation. The party almost becomes, in Christopher Arterton's phrase, a "super PAC."[2] This model has some promise for strengthening the role of parties in electoral choice, as candidates and issues become more strongly identified with the parties and are presented in partisan terms. But the model does not speak to the *quality* of partisan participation or to the role of the party as a mediating institution.

Strengthening the party as a local organization, however, is intrinsically important, both in providing a channel for the effective pursuit of group and community interests and in tempering "particularity" in light of more inclusive concerns. Moreover, such a strengthening is necessary for the long-range sustenance of party renewal at other levels. The party loyalties of voters and officeholders are likely to prove fleeting and opportunistic unless they are mediated by enduring organizational ties. Face-to-face contact motivates voters in ways that television and direct-mail cannot, and the GOP's disappointing experience in 1980 with the "Commitment '80" grass-roots mobilization effort suggests that it is difficult to engineer such contacts in the absence of enduring local organizations. Renewal of the party as a mediating structure is a process in which the Democrats have some natural advantages. It is an aspect of renewal that the top-down strategies pioneered by the GOP and subsequently emulated by the Democrats do not effectively address—but without which the "place" of party will not be adequately filled.

We have concentrated throughout this book on practical means of bringing the parties back. This is not to deny that complex sociological and economic factors have contributed to the parties' difficulties, nor is it to imply that the parties can or should be restored to their former state. It is to argue, however, for a certain indeterminancy in the way political institutions work; their fate is not beyond human control. Governmental enactments and the policies of the parties themselves have played an important part in bringing the parties to their current state, and they will be an important determinant of whether (and in what form) they re-emerge. Moreover, as Robert Harmel and Kenneth Janda have stressed, environmental forces may be less constraining than has sometimes been thought. Enduring features of the American political landscape—"twopartyism," plurality elections (as opposed to proportional representation), the "moderation" of public opinion, crosscutting patterns of political cleavage, federalism, the separation of powers—continue to foster ideological and organizational slack in the party system and to inhibit moves in the responsible-party direction. But other developments, such as reduced sectional differences within the parties' popular bases, heightened issue awareness and consistency among party adherents, and "nationalizing" trends in communications and government, suggest the possibility of reduced party fragmentation and a new leadership role for national party organizations.[3] The parties' future depends not on emerging social and political conditions alone, but also on the extent to which public officials and party leaders exploit the opportunities they have for strengthening the parties' role at the national, state, and local levels.

We have offered a number of specific suggestions for changes in law and procedure, particularly in the areas of state election law (Chapter 5), presidential nomination (Chapter 7), and the regulation of campaign finance (Chapter 8). The measures that are needed to strengthen the parties affect every level of government and of party organization. They include the restoration of partisan elections at the municipal level, the adoption of registration-by-party and the "closed" primary, a heightened role for caucuses and conventions in endorsing candidates and allocating national delegates, a reduction in the slate-making powers of presidential candidates, the channeling of public funding through state and national party organizations, and the modification of recent Supreme Court rulings on patronage and independent expenditures. It is a varied list of measures which, taken together, would remove substantial barriers to party strength and could help the parties reclaim a prominent and productive role in American political life.

The revitalization of America's parties will depend, however, not only on laws and rules and court decisions, but also on the choices that are made and the initiatives that are taken day by day by thousands of voters, politicians, and party leaders. Recent efforts of the House Democratic Caucus to strengthen the party role in policy formulation, for example, have depended on the willingness of individual members to give party activity precedence over other roles and responsibilities. As the norms and incentives that formerly ordered member behavior have declined in force, the functioning of the parties and of other instruments of collective responsibility in Congress has become increasingly dependent on members' own values and concerns.[4] Legislators have a great deal of leeway in deciding how to vote, how to spend their time and energy. How the parties fare will depend in large part on the choices they make.

A comparable range of choices is open to governors and other executive officeholders: What role will be given party networks in working with the legislature and in making appointments? Will public officials espouse a responsible partisanship or succumb to the temptation to place themselves "above" party, to work only through their personal organizations and networks? Candidates at various levels may feel that the direct primary system forces them to cultivate a personal organization apart from the party. But to integrate that following with the party organization has much to recommend it as a strategy of both general election campaigning and governance. The point is not that candidates and officeholders should sacrifice their political interests and values for the sake of the party but rather that a *range* of viable strategies of campaigning and governance are available, some of which tend to reinforce and others to undermine party strength. It is important to bring to light the implications of these strategies and practices for the welfare of the parties, and for politicians to give these implications greater weight in the choices that they make.

Finally, the current state of the parties offers great challenges and opportunities to party leaders themselves. We have seen how important the vision and the skill of national chairmen have been in shaping the renaissance of the GOP. There are encouraging signs in both parties that leaders are prepared to press for a strengthened party role in presidential nomination, to take on major responsibilities in general election campaigns, and to build the financial and organizational bases that credibility with candidates and officeholders will require. Certainly the times require such leadership. Regardless of other measures taken to bring the parties back, their renewal will critically depend upon the determination and ingenuity with which the parties help themselves.

NOTES

1. David Burnham, "Have Computer, Will Travel the Campaign Trail," *New York Times*, September 22, 1983.
2. F. Christopher Arterton, "Political Money and Party Strength," in *The Future of American Political Parties*, ed. Joel L. Fleishman (Englewood Cliffs, N.J.: Prentice-Hall, 1982), 135.
3. See Robert Harmel and Kenneth Janda, *Parties and Their Environments: Limits to Reform?* (New York: Longman Publishing Co., 1982), chaps. 7-8. These authors are perhaps too quick, however, to define the *strengthening* of the parties in terms of their centralization and nationalization; see 116-117.
4. See David E. Price, "Legislative Ethics in the New Congress" (Paper delivered at the annual meeting of the American Political Science Association, Chicago, Illinois, 1983).

Index